MW01196356

GEORGE WASHINGTON'S REVENGE

Also by Arthur S. Lefkowitz

Colonel Hamilton and Colonel Burr

Eyewitness Images from the American Revolution

Benedict Arnold in the Company of Heroes

Benedict Arnold's Army

George Washington's Indispensable Men

Bushnell's Submarine

(originally published as *The American Turtle Submarine*)

The Long Retreat

GEORGE WASHINGTON'S REVENGE

*The 1777 New Jersey Campaign and How General
Washington Turned Defeat into the Strategy That Won the
Revolution*

ARTHUR S. LEFKOWITZ

STACKPOLE
BOOKS

*Essex, Connecticut
Blue Ridge Summit, Pennsylvania*

STACKPOLE BOOKS

An imprint of Globe Pequot, the trade division of The Rowman & Littlefield Publishing Group, Inc.
4501 Forbes Blvd., Ste. 200
Lanham, MD 20706
www.rowman.com

Distributed by NATIONAL BOOK NETWORK

British Library Cataloguing in Publication Information available

Library of Congress Cataloging-in-Publication Data Is Available

ISBN: 978-0-8117-7041-5 (cloth : alk. paper)
ISBN: 978-0-8117-7042-2 (electronic)

♾™The paper used in this publication meets the minimum requirements of American National Standard for Information Sciences—Permanence of Paper for Printed Library Materials, ANSI/NISO Z39.48-1992.

Dedication

This book is dedicated to my friend, the late Samuel Steele Smith. Sam owned a successful printing business, which gave him experience in book production. When Sam retired he combined his knowledge of printing with his interest in history to pursue a second career as the publisher of the Philip Freneau Press. He was particularly interested in the American Revolution and published fourteen books on the subject, some of which he wrote or edited. The Philip Freneau Press closed following Sam's death in 1989. However, his titles continue to be cited in authoritative books about the Revolutionary War. Sam Smith made a valuable contribution to our understanding of the American Revolution, and I am grateful to have this opportunity to acknowledge his work.

Sam was working on a book about the 1777 Middlebrook Encampment prior to his death. He introduced me to the subject, and I accompanied him on several outings to survey the sites occupied by the Continental Army during the encampment. The narrative you are about to read is based on my field trips with Sam Smith.

George Washington was not a revengeful person. But he was a fast learner who barely survived 1776, the first full year of the American Revolution. Washington learned from his mistakes and returned in 1777 with new strategy and tactics that forced the British to acknowledge him as a wily and elusive opponent.

—*Dave R. Palmer, U.S. Army Lieutenant General (Ret.), former superintendent of the United States Military Academy at West Point, and historian whose books include* The Way of the Fox: American Strategy in the War for America, 1775–1783

Contents

Acknowledgments

This book deals primarily with events that took place in New Jersey during 1777. As a result, the majority of the people that I turned to for assistance are knowledgeable about New Jersey's role in the American Revolution. Some of their names may not be familiar, but they are all experts in New Jersey history. This unique group of historians who generously shared their knowledge with me are Eric Olsen, Park Ranger/Historian at Morristown National Historical Park; William B. Brahams, Chief Librarian of the Camden County (New Jersey) Library System; Ken Kaufman, Librarian, New Jersey Room, Somerset County Library System of New Jersey; Asher Lurie, Chief of Historical Interpretation at the Old Barracks Museum in Trenton; and (the late) Kels Swan, the historian of the Washington Campground Association.

I also turned to a group of people with expertise in other aspects of the Revolutionary War. They are Eric H. Schnitzer, Park Ranger/Military Historian, Saratoga National Historical Park; Don N. Hagist, whose special interest is the role of the British Army in the American Revolution; Raymond Andrews, an authority on the organization of the various armies that participated in the American Revolution; Edward Richi, Curator of Printed Materials at the Delaware Historical Society, who made the wartime letters of British Captain William Dansey available to me; Dave Richard Palmer, U.S. Army Lieutenant General (retired) and former superintendent of the U.S. Military Academy at West Point. General Palmer is also a distinguished historian and author whose books include *The Way of the Fox: American Strategy in the War for America, 1775–1783.*

I also wish to acknowledge Katie Blizzard, research editor at the Center for Digital Editing at the Papers of George Washington; Robbie MacNiven, author whose authoritative books about the American Revolution include *British Light Infantry in the American Revolution*; Tom Dempsey, retired engineer and fellow Revolutionary War enthusiast who read drafts of my chapters and made many helpful suggestions; Mike Kochan, whose area of interest is Revolutionary War and Civil War mines and explosives, and who joined me early in this book project to survey the crest of the Watchung Mountains; Randolph G. Flood, who is knowledgeable on many aspects of the American Revolution; and Stephen Case, author and fellow Revolutionary War enthusiast. Mr. Case is particularly proud of his ancestor Daniel Bray, who was an officer in the Hunterdon County, New Jersey, militia. Lieutenant Bray's exploits during the American Revolution included helping the Pennsylvania Navy gather boats along the Delaware River and bring them to Trenton in early December 1776. This episode in the war is described in this book.

I am also pleased to acknowledge the help of Robert Dunkelberger, Bloomsburg University Archivist and Coordinator of Special Collections. Located in Bloomsburg, Pennsylvania, the university's library includes the papers of U.S. Army Major Joseph P. Tustin (1897–1986). Many Revolutionary War enthusiasts may not recognize Joseph Tustin's name, but they owe him their gratitude for publishing the diary of Hessian Captain Johann Ewald. Titled *Diary of the American War: A Hessian Journal*, it was published by Yale University Press in 1979. Ewald's diary is one of the most important eyewitness accounts of the American Revolution. His entries include detailed descriptions of many of the important campaigns of the war, beginning with his participation in the attack on Fort Washington in 1776 to the siege of Yorktown in 1781.

Major Tustin's connection to the Ewald diary began in Germany in 1948. Tustin, who was fluent in German, served as a U.S. Army intelligence officer during the Second World War. He continued to serve on active duty in Germany after the war as the European historian for the newly established (1947) U.S. Air Force. His work on behalf of the Air

Force included an authoritative eyewitness account of the 1948–1949 Berlin Airlift.

Major Tustin first learned about the Ewald diary in 1948 from Lieutenant Colonel Eberhard von Pfister, a former World War II German Army officer. In need of money in war-ravaged Germany, von Pfister approached Tustin, asking if he was interested in buying a handwritten diary from the American Revolution. Von Pfister told Tustin that the diarist was Captain Johann Ewald, a Hessian officer who commanded a company of elite riflemen during the war. Ewald's diary was a family heirloom, but von Pfister was destitute and willing to sell it. Major Tustin was interested and met von Pfister in the German's threadbare apartment in Wiesbaden. Tustin inspected Ewald's diary and immediately recognized its significance. It consisted of three volumes labelled I, II, and IV, written in "an excellent eighteenth-century hand on handmade paper." Tustin purchased the diary after getting approval from the Allied Armies Monuments, Fine Arts and Archives program. Volume III of the diary was missing, but hopeful of its existence, Tustin spent the next eight years searching for the missing manuscript. His efforts were rewarded when he found volume III in 1957 in a library in Glücksburg, Germany. Tustin paid for the missing section to be copied, after which he translated the complete diary into English. He then edited and footnoted the diary and arranged for it to be published. In his introduction to the published work Major Tustin said, "His [Ewald's] accuracy and reliability are clear not only from corroborating evidence but from the commendations and praise he received, the esteem in which he was held, and the innate honesty of the man himself."

Tustin was born and raised in Bloomsburg, Pennsylvania. Following his death in 1986, his family donated his papers, including the original Ewald diary and maps, to the Bloomsburg University Library. I visited the Special Collections at the university library at the invitation of archivist Robert Dunkelberger to view the original diary and maps. It includes accounts of Ewald fighting alongside the British Army in New Jersey during 1776 and 1777. My readers will find material from the diary in my book, along with a biography of Ewald and a copy of his hand-drawn map showing the area around the village of Hillsborough, New Jersey. The village was at the center of several events described in these pages.

Among the other eyewitness accounts that I used in writing this book is the diary of Captain John Peebles. His diary was published in 1998 with the title *John Peebles' American War: The Diary of a Scottish Grenadier, 1776–1782*. The Peebles diary was published by Stackpole Books, a press with a long and impressive history of publishing important books about the American Revolution. Examples of other Stackpole volumes pertaining to the Revolutionary War include *The Book of the Continental Soldier* by Harold Peterson (1968); *The Philadelphia Campaign* by Thomas J. McGuire (2007), and *Campaign to Saratoga—1777* by Eric Schnitzer and Don Troiani (2019). This is my third book published by Stackpole and I am flattered to be associated with them. David Reisch, my editor at Stackpole, has been especially supportive and encouraging throughout the process of crafting this book. I also had the good fortune of having a team of talented people at Stackpole assisting me. Outstanding among them were Stephanie Otto and Hannah Fisher in the editorial department and Melissa Baker who produced the original maps for the book.

Researching this book led me to some new people who shared their knowledge of history with me. I was also grateful to be able to turn to historians who helped me in the past. I am indebted to them all for their help in writing this first-ever narrative of George Washington's defense of New Jersey during 1777.

Introduction

"Nothing under Heaven can save us but the enemy's [British General Sir William Howe] going to the southward."[1] This comment by Connecticut Governor Jonathan Trumbull in June 1777 introduces a series of events that ended with the surrender of British General John Burgoyne's army on October 17, 1777, in the village of Saratoga [modern-day Schuylerville] in upstate New York. General Burgoyne launched his campaign from Canada in June of that year with the intention of capturing the important Hudson River town of Albany, New York. Burgoyne fought his way to within twenty-six miles of Albany when he was surrounded by a Patriot army commanded by General Horatio Gates and forced to surrender. Gates's victory at Saratoga proved to be one of the turning points of the Revolutionary War as it convinced the French to enter the conflict as America's ally.

The year 1777 was also the scene of significant military activity in the mid-Atlantic states of New Jersey and Pennsylvania. The fighting in this region centered on a campaign by British General Sir William Howe to capture the rebel-held city of Philadelphia. Opposing Howe's 18,000 British and Hessian troops was an army led by George Washington that eventually numbered 12,000 Continentals and 3,000 militia.[2] Sir William's offensive culminated in the September 11 Battle of Brandywine, Pennsylvania, fought thirty-two miles south of Philadelphia. Howe defeated Washington's army at Brandywine and

1

seized Philadelphia two weeks later. These two campaigns—Burgoyne's offensive to capture Albany and Howe's to seize Philadelphia—dominate accounts of 1777 in the American Revolution.

But other significant events took place that year, which are only briefly mentioned in the histories of the war. The most important of these episodes to the outcome of the Revolution took place in New Jersey during the first half of 1777. But this six-month-long phase of the war receives little attention due to the perception that the period consisted of small-scale fighting in New Jersey between British troops foraging for food and the Americans who opposed them. Adding to the lack of interest in this segment is the visualization of George Washington cloistered in his headquarters in Morristown, New Jersey, involved in the routine business of recruiting and organizing the Continental Army. However, my research into the period reveals a much different story. What I discovered was that Washington was actively involved in deploying his understrength army during the first half of 1777 to keep the big British garrisons in New Brunswick and Perth Amboy (New Jersey) on the defensive. This was accomplished despite the fact that the Americans were sometimes outnumbered three to one. Washington also organized his troops to make the enemy believe that the Patriot forces in New Jersey were far more numerous than they actually were. I also learned that when Washington correctly decided that the British wanted to cross New Jersey to capture Philadelphia, he assembled his army at a "ridge of strong and connecting heights" in New Jersey's Watchung Mountains overlooking British-held New Brunswick. Washington's position was "on ground so advantageous as it would be dangerous to attack him."[3] Howe dared not cross New Jersey with Washington's army in his rear. Sir William knew from experience that Washington would cut his supply line, ambush whole regiments, and engage in unrelenting skirmishing. As the story unfolds, Howe spent weeks maneuvering his army, trying to entice or force Washington to come down from his mountain stronghold to fight him in a decisive battle. Washington responded by sending his newly organized Provincial Rifle Corps commanded by Daniel Morgan to harass the enemy. Unable to bring on a decisive battle, Howe gave up the idea of reaching Philadelphia by crossing New Jersey. Instead he transported his army south on ships to avoid New Jersey and eventually launched his campaign to capture Philadelphia from Chesapeake Bay. It was Washington's successful defense of New Jersey that put Howe out of reach to cooperate with Burgoyne. Isolated and with no hope of help from General Howe's distant army, Burgoyne surrendered.

Besides introducing my narrative, this introductory chapter is an opportunity for me to share some information with my readers that I believe will contribute to their understanding of the people and events described in this book. It also gives me a safe haven to include some background information that evades deletion by my editors as being "off the subject." Among the topics that I believe warrant an explanation at the outset of my book are the presence of French Army officers in the Continental Army in 1776 and 1777. The events described in these pages took place during these years prior to France's entry into the war as America's ally. To be exact, France signed a treaty of alliance with the United States in February 1778, and the first French troops arrived in America in July of that year. One French Army officer who is included in my book is Jean Louis de Vernejout, who was commissioned as a captain in the Continental Army on September 19, 1776.[4] His story is representative of the French Army officers who joined the Continental Army early in the war. Vernejout was a former captain in the French Army who was discharged during a major reorganization of the French Army and Navy in the late 1760s. He was living on the French Caribbean island of Martinique at the start of the American Revolution. In an effort to resume his military career, Vernejout travelled to Philadelphia at his own expense in September 1776, where he presented his credentials to the Continental Congress. The delegates were ready to commission anyone with military experience and appointed Vernejout a captain in the Continental Army. Following his appointment, Vernejout was instructed to report to General Washington with three other recently commissioned former French Army officers for assignments. Washington was confounded by what to do with the four Frenchmen, as they spoke little or no English. Washington wrote to Congress on October 7, 1776, about Vernejout and the other former French Army officers sent to him: "I am under no small difficulties on account of the French Gentlemen that are here in consequence of the commissions they have received.... Their want of our language is an objection to their being joined to any of the regiments here at this time."[5] Captain Vernejout was appointed later in 1776 as an aide-de-camp to General Charles Lee, who spoke fluent French.

It is difficult to determine how many French Army volunteers served in the Continental Army during the Revolution. The problem is that Americans—unfamiliar with foreign languages—were spelling the names of the Frenchmen in various ways, making it seem that each spelling represented a different person. The above-mentioned Frenchman Vernejout, for example, was also spelled in the correspondence and records of the war as Vernejous or Vernejoux. In another example, George Washington spelled the Polish national, French-trained engineer Thaddeus Kościuszko's name eleven different ways, including Cosciusko.[6]

Another more imposing former French Army officer serving in the Continental Army in 1777 was Philippe Hubert, Chevalier de Preudhomme de Borre. He was a sixty-year-old former lieutenant colonel in a French Army infantry regiment. Borre arrived in Boston on April 20, 1777, with a contract signed by Silas Deane (one of the American commissioners in Paris at the time) dated November 30, 1776, appointing Borre a brigadier general in the Continental Army. Congress honored the contract and appointed Borre a general. Besides being barely able to speak English, Borre was unpopular with the Maryland troops he commanded and "ignorant of his duty."[7] He resigned in a huff in September 1777, expecting Congress to beg him to stay. Instead Congress accepted his resignation and paid his expenses to return to France.

Washington expressed his overall impression of the French and other European volunteers who joined the Continental Army during the first years of the Revolution in a letter to Congress written from Morristown, New Jersey, on February 11, 1777. Washington wrote, "You cannot conceive what a weight these kind of people are upon the service and upon me in particular; few of them have any knowledge of the branches which they profess to understand and those that have, are entirely useless as officers from their ignorance of the English language."[8] There is more information and stories about the former French Army officers who joined the Continental Army in the pages of this book.

Also included in my book are quotes from some of the earliest histories of the American Revolution. The authors of these books include Mercy Otis Warren, David Ramsay, William Gordon, John Marshall, and Thomas Jones. Admittedly these authors did not have access to documents available to later historians, but they had one huge advantage over today's authors: they lived through the war and knew many of the people they wrote about. I like to quote these early eyewitness chroniclers of the American Revolution. David Ramsay, for example, published a two-volume history of the Revolution in 1789. He was an army surgeon during the Revolution and was captured when Charleston, South Carolina, surrendered to the British in 1780 following a long siege. Ramsay was considered one of the leaders of the Revolutionary movement in South Carolina and was imprisoned in St. Augustine, Florida, for a year before he was exchanged. He next served as a South Carolina delegate to the Continental Congress in 1782, 1783, 1785, and 1786. Ramsay was bored with the routine business of Congress and spent much of his time interviewing the Continental Army officers and politicians living or passing through New York City, where Congress was meeting at the time.[9] His personal experiences during the war and interviews were the basis of his history of the Revolution and his other works that included a biography of George Washington. Ramsay was a staunch revolutionary who "minimized the complexities of the experience of revolution, preferring instead to recount the crimes conducted by the British Amy and its loyalist allies."[10]

But despite his bias, Ramsay's descriptions are enlightening. For example, here is Ramsay's account of the raids carried out by Provincial (Loyalist) units operating from British-held New York City late in the war: "the depredations they committed in their several excursions would fill a volume, and would answer little purpose but to excite compassion and horror."[11] Mercy Otis Warren wrote another early history of the war, and her descriptions rival Ramsay's for their emotional content. Regarding the British invasion of New Jersey in late 1776, Mrs. Warren wrote: "The footsteps of the British Army in their route through New Jersey, were everywhere marked with the most wanton instances of rapine and bloodshed." She then accused the British officers leading the troops to condone the rampage: "the licentiousness of their officers spread rape, misery and despair, indiscriminately through every village."[12]

My narrative also includes passages from another of my favorite historians who wrote about the war. He is Washington Irving (1783–1859), who published a four-volume biography of George Washington. Entitled *Life of George Washington*, it was published between 1856 and 1859. Washington Irving is one of America's foremost authors, and his Washington biography includes elegant and descriptive prose as well as being historically accurate. Irving has the distinction of allegedly being kissed by George Washington. According to the eminent historian James Thomas Flexner, "George Washington was aloof and by nature shy. He didn't invite people into his personality. He never kissed a baby, I'm sure."[13] But Washington Irving said that as a child, he was kissed on the forehead by George Washington. The incident allegedly took place in 1789 when Washington was president and living in New York City, the nation's capital at the time. Irving was in a Manhattan store with his nursemaid when President Washington walked into the shop. Irving's nursemaid held the child forward and said, "Please your Honor, here's a child named after you." Washington bent down and kissed little Irving on the forehead. Irving claimed that he remembered the incident and spoke of it throughout his life.

Here is some additional information that will help the reader navigate these chapters. The basic administrative organization of the British Army and Continental Army during the American Revolution was the regiment. Each British regiment during the Revolutionary War consisted of ten companies. However, the American regiments varied according to the dictates of the individual states. The 1st New York Regiment, for example, in 1777 had eight companies. In comparison, the 2nd Canadian Regiment in 1777 had twenty companies. The term "battalion" was sometimes used to describe an American regiment, especially early in the war. Two or more regiments operating together was called a brigade. Two or more brigades was called a division.

Generals in the Continental Army held one of two ranks. The lower-ranking generals were called brigadier generals and the senior rank were major generals. George Washington held the rank of Commander-in-Chief of the Continental Army during the war. The British Army had three ranks of generals. They were from the lowest to the highest rank: brigadier general, major general, and lieutenant general. A fine point of history is that Ulysses S. Grant is often cited as the first lieutenant general in the United States Army. However, President John Adams appointed George Washington a lieutenant general during the short-lived preparations for a war with France in 1798.

Both the British and the Continental Armies had the rank of colonel. British colonels were responsible for the recruiting, clothing, and feeding of their regiment. However, they typically did not serve in the field with their regiment. Winston Churchill, for example (who, I hope my readers know, did not fight in the American Revolution), was the colonel of the 4th Queens Own Hussars. British regiments were typically commanded by lieutenant colonels. Colonels in the Continental Army, however, actively commanded their regiments.

Note that I will sometimes refer to the American Revolution as the American War. The term "American War" is historically correct. The American colonist's rebellion was referred to at the time as the American War, the War for Independence, or the War with Britain. For example, Charles Stedman titled his 1794 history of the conflict *The History of the American War*. American Major General William Heath published his account of the war in 1798 with the title *Memoirs of Major-General Heath Containing Anecdotes, Details of Skirmishes, Battles, and Other Military Events during the American War*. The earliest known printed use of the term American Revolution is a history of the conflict titled *History of the Rise, Progress and Termination of the American Revolution* by Mercy Otis Warren, published in 1805.

"Founding Fathers" is another interesting term associated with the American Revolution. The problem is that its origin dates back only to 1916, when then U.S. Senator from Ohio Warren G. Harding coined the term. I therefore refrain from using the term.

The British, German, and American armies had men armed with rifles during the American War. A rifle has spiral grooves cut inside the barrel that spun the ball (a lead sphere propelled by gunpowder) accurately over a long distance.[14] The best-known rifles from the Revolutionary War were used by the Patriots. They were expensive, handcrafted weapons that were the property of the person who carried them. The correct name for a colonial-made rifle from the Revolutionary War is the American long rifle, and the person firing it was called a marksman. The terms "sniper" (named after the snipe, an elusive bird found in India) and "sharpshooter" came later. The distance that a ball from an American long rifle could hit a target depended on the expertise of the gunsmith who made the weapon, the consistency of the black powder (gunpowder), and the skill of the marksman. A reasonable estimate is that an expert rifleman armed with an American long rifle could hit a target at 250 yards. In comparison, the smoothbore musket, which had no grooves (rifling) had an effective range of 100 yards. Claims that American long rifles had a range of up to 400 yards may be based on firing modern reproduction weapons using high-quality black powder.

I hope that I am not ruining your enjoyment of my book by revealing the ending, which is that the British lost the war. There are numerous assessments explaining why the British lost the American Revolution. Among the critiques explaining the loss is an article by Major John A. Tokar that appeared in a U.S. Army military journal published in 1999. Here is an excerpt from Major Tokar's articulate and concise explanation: "Ultimately, the lack of sufficient reserve supplies, combined with cautious generalship, insufficient transportation, widespread corruption, and the lack of a coherent strategy to maximize the potential support of British loyalists in the colonies, ensured British failure."[15]

Note that Major Tokar did not include tactics in his list of British shortcomings in the war. The word "tactics" was defined in British Army Captain George Smith's 1779 *Military Dictionary* as "the art of disciplining armies and ranging them into forms for fighting and maneuvering."[16] A modern definition of the term is "the art of handling units in combat, the planning and carrying out of ordered movements and maneuvers both before and during combat for the most efficient use of the combat power of a command."[17] The commonly held vision of Revolutionary War tactics are British Redcoats standing in a line and firing volleys of musket fire indiscriminately at Americans hiding behind trees and rocks. The reality is far different, as the British used tactics adapted for the war in America.

The conventional line formation was practical and based on the success of a line of troops with bayonets attached to their muskets charging an enemy position. Called linear tactics, American militia in particular could not withstand this frightening attack. However, the British modified their line formation from three to two men deep and increased the space between each man in line for the Revolutionary War. This change allowed the same number of men to extend across a greater distance and move quickly across rugged terrain. The British also trained their soldiers to aim their muskets. After arriving in America, the British 71st Regiment, for example, was trained so that "every man shall take the most direct aim possible at the most favorable object in his front" and "If the troops are ordered to move in any direction they are to spring from tree, stump, log & etc with the utmost agility and continue to fire, load and spring as they advance upon or retreat from the enemy."[18]

Cavalry, meaning mounted troops who fought on horseback, saw limited use during the war. Historian René Chartrand explained that "unlike Europe, in North America distances between settlements were immense; nature was overwhelming, with endless forests and mighty rivers... and cavalry was useless."[19] However, both the British and American armies found lightly armed soldiers on small, fast horses useful. Both sides called them light dragoons, and they proved to be valuable in conducting reconnaissance forays behind enemy lines, raiding, skirmishing, and attacking enemy supply lines. The British also actively employed specially chosen, equipped, and trained units during the American War. They included light infantry composed of young men: "extremely fit... and possessed of initiative and the ability to act independently."[20] Their uniforms were cut down and the accoutrements (equipment) they carried were reduced for fast-paced irregular warfare. Another type of specialized troops among the British troops who fought in the American War were grenadiers. They were the tallest and most powerful men in the army, used as shock troops to unnerve and overwhelm the rebels. The British also had ranger units trained in the tactics of operating behind enemy lines in small companies.[21] The British also had German soldiers called jägers, trained in irregular warfare and armed with rifles that could hit a target at long range. The jägers will be introduced in greater detail later in this book. Historian Dave Palmer summed up the situation perfectly when he wrote that "the British were searching diligently for means to break out of the linear stranglehold."[22] The Americans also had some of these specialized units, including light infantry and rangers.

And now we proceed to open our narrative. It begins with an account of the events of the Revolution from the first shots fired at Lexington in April 1775 to the Battle of Princeton in January 1777. This first chapter is meant to provide essential background information to appreciate Washington's astute occupation of the Watchung Mountains in 1777 that upset General William Howe's plan to quickly occupy Pennsylvania and capture Philadelphia by crossing New Jersey in a bid to end the war.

A Variety of Difficulties and Perplexities*

The American Revolution lasted for eight years, and the closest the British came to winning the war occurred on December 1, 1776. On that date, George Washington's Grand Army consisted of 3,000 exhausted and demoralized men. Facing them was a superbly equipped British force of over 10,000. The Americans were in New Brunswick, New Jersey, on December 1 with the British less than a mile away. Only the narrow Raritan River separated the opposing armies, with just four American cannons at New Brunswick to discourage the British from crossing the river. The defeat of Washington's Grand Army at New Brunswick, on top of the string of British military successes earlier in 1776, could have convinced the Continental Congress to negotiate an end to the war.

Just five months earlier, in August 1776, Washington had an army of over 21,000 men and 162 cannons defending New York City.[1] The events that reduced Washington's Grand Army from 21,000 to a few thousand threadbare men is one of the great stories of the American Revolution. In this chapter we will follow the events of 1776, which are

---

* Chapter title from a personal letter from George Washington to John Parke Custis, dated "Morris Town Jany 22d 1777." Washington wrote, "I believe I may with truth add, that I do not think that any officer since the creation ever had such a variety of difficulties and perplexities to encounter as I have." W. W. Abbot et al., eds., *The Papers of George Washington, Revolutionary War Series*, 28 vols. to date (Charlottesville: University of Virginia Press, 1985–2020), vol. 8:123.

important in order to appreciate the changes that Washington implemented beginning in the winter of 1777. The story begins in Boston where the Revolutionary War began. But an explanation of the term Grand Army seems appropriate before we proceed. The term was used during the American Revolution to identify the troops under George Washington's immediate command. It included Continental troops, state troops, and militia. Examples of the use of the term include the July 28, 1778, General Orders of the Army: "The Commander in Chief [George Washington] desires that officers who did not compose part of the Grand Army last winter and spring and who may be unacquainted with the General Orders relative to the duties of the Officers of the day."[2] Another reference appears in the *Journals of the Continental Congress*. The entry for June 16, 1775, includes: "That there be one chief engineer at [*sic*] the grand army and that his pay be sixty dollars per month."[3]

Boston was the center of colonial opposition to the British Parliament for taxing their flourishing thirteen American colonies. Beginning in 1765 with the Stamp Act, Parliament's bungling efforts to enforce its will escalated when British troops were sent to Boston in 1768 to force submission. Their presence only increased preparations by the colonial militia, a self-defense system present in all the colonies. The mounting enmity exploded into warfare on the morning of April 19, 1775, when 700 British troops commanded by Lieutenant Colonel Francis Smith sallied out of Boston. They were headed to the village of Concord, where spies had reported that the militia had gathered gunpowder and weapons. Colonel Smith seemed like a poor choice to lead this daring mission. He was a middle-aged, overweight, and indolent officer. But Smith was an experienced soldier who could be counted on to remain calm in a firefight with the militia.

Warned of Colonel Smith's approach, local militia companies hid their military equipment while additional militiamen from the surrounding Massachusetts towns converged on Concord. Recognizing trouble early on, Colonel Smith sent a courier back to Boston to get reinforcements. Meanwhile, after spending a few futile hours in Concord, Smith's detachment began the eighteen-mile march back to Boston. A fierce running battle ensued, with the militia gathering strength with each passing mile. Smith ordered his troops to burn every building along their route and sent flanking parties with fixed bayonets to drive the militia out of musket range.

Reinforcements led by British General Hugh Percy finally arrived from Boston with two field pieces (mobile artillery) as the number of hostile militiamen continued to grow at an alarming rate. According to Percy, "with perseverance and resolution" the redcoats staggered back to Boston, pursued by thousands of militiamen who surrounded the city. Percy wrote a fellow officer in England the following day with a portentous appraisal of the Patriot militia he fought on the Concord road: "Whoever looks upon them as an irregular mob, will find himself much mistaken. They have men amongst them who know very well what they are about."[4]

Within two months the spontaneous fighting on the Concord road escalated into a revolution. The transformation began when the rebellious Massachusetts Provincial Congress organized the militia surrounding Boston into a Provincial Army of Observation centered in Cambridge, which was just outside of Boston.

The hostilities quickly spread from the Boston area into the neighboring province of New York. It occurred on May 10, 1775, when a makeshift force led by Benedict Arnold and Ethan Allen captured Fort Ticonderoga. The fort's importance was that it controlled the portage that connected Lake George to Lake Champlain. Whoever occupied Fort Ticonderoga controlled this major inland water route that allowed travelers, trade goods, and armies to move quickly and safely between points as widely separated as New York City, Montreal, and the British trading post of La Baie Verte (present-day Green Bay, Wisconsin).

Meanwhile, back in Massachusetts, the colony's Provisional Congress was running out of gunpowder and money, and appealed to the Second Continental Congress to assume command of the army blockading Boston. The letter requesting help from Massachusetts's patriots was read aloud in Congress on June 2, 1775. The pertinent section reads, "As the Army [Provincial Army of Observation] now collecting from different colonies [New England colonies] is for the general defense of the rights of America, we would beg leave to suggest to your consideration the propriety of your taking the regulation and general direction of it [the army blockading Boston]."[5]

The appeal from Massachusetts followed an alarming report from Colonel Benedict Arnold. Writing from Crown Point, New York (a derelict British fort north of Fort Ticonderoga), Arnold reported that "there were four hundred Regulars [British troops] at St. John's [a British fort at the northern end of Lake Champlain] making all possible preparation to cross the lake and expected to be joined by a number of Indians."[6] According to Colonel Arnold, their objective was to retake Fort Ticonderoga. The news that the British were planning to enlist their Indian allies against the colonists raised fears in Congress of vicious Indian attacks on frontier villages and isolated farms. Arnold's report helped convince Congress to take charge of the insurrection and raise a national army to defend America.

There is no known record of the date on which Congress created an army composed of men from every colony, which they called the Continental Army. The most commonly mentioned date for the establishment of a national army is June 14, 1775, when the delegates to Congress authorized recruiting "six companies of expert riflemen." The delegates included an enlistment form for the riflemen to sign, which read in part, "voluntarily enlisted myself, as a soldier, in the American Continental Army."[7] However, there is an earlier reference to Congress using the term "Continental Army." The expression was used on June 3, 1775, when Congress resolved to borrow money "to the purchase of gunpowder for the use of the Continental Army."[8]

A significant reference to Congress establishing a national army occurred on June 15, 1775, when the delegates to Congress resolved that "a general be appointed to command all the continental forces." John Adams wrote years later that he recommended his fellow delegate George Washington that same day for the position, calling him "a gentleman, whose skill and experience as an officer, whose independent fortune, great talents and excellent universal character would command the approbation of all America."[9] There was no point in dragging out the debate in Congress as there was agreement among the delegates that Colonel Washington from Virginia was the best candidate to lead their army. The delegates reasoned that while Washington had not seen active military service for the last sixteen years, he was a wealthy, conservative fellow delegate who they could trust not to use the army to overthrow the government and establish a military dictatorship. Their prime historical example was General Oliver Cromwell, who used the army to forcibly disband the British Parliament in April 1653 and proclaim himself the Lord Protector (dictator). Thomas Johnson, a delegate from Maryland, formally nominated Washington as commander-in-chief of the Continental Army later that day. A vote was taken straightaway, and Colonel Washington was unanimously elected.[10] John Adams wrote his wife Abigail two days later (June 17, 1775) with the news of the Virginia colonel's appointment, "The Congress have made Choice of the modest and virtuous, the amiable, generous and brave George Washington Esqr., to be the General of the American Army, and that he is to repair as soon as possible to the Camp before Boston."[11]

Washington left Philadelphia on June 23 to take command of the Patriot army surrounding Boston. He was traveling across New Jersey the following day when he heard rumors of fighting that had taken place at Boston. He was in New York City two days later (June 26) where he received definitive news that a big battle had been fought near Boston on June 17, at a place called Breed's Hill. However, the battle was named for nearby Bunker Hill. It was reported that the colonial forces were defeated at the Battle of Bunker Hill, but they had inflicted heavy casualties among the British troops that were driven back twice before overwhelming the rebel's earthworks. One British officer who fought at Bunker Hill wrote home afterward, blaming "the great man among us" (General Thomas Gage, who commanded the British troops in Boston) because of his "absurd and destructive confidence, carelessness or ignorance, we have lost a thousand of our best men and officers."[12] Gage was held responsible for the pyrrhic British victory by Lord George Germain, the secretary of state for the colonies. Germain sacked Gage, saying that he was "in a situation of too great importance for his talents."[13] Gage was replaced by General William Howe (1729–1814), a much admired officer with considerable combat experience.[14] An American officer who knew Howe said that he "is all fire and activity brave and cool as Julius Caesar."[15]

The fighting near Boston had quieted down by June 30, when Washington was met at Springfield, Massachusetts, by a committee from the Massachusetts Provincial Congress. Following some speeches and ceremonies, Washington arrived in Cambridge on Sunday afternoon, July 2. It was raining when he arrived, and he waited until the following morning to formally take command of the Patriot army. It consisted of about 14,000 men from Massachusetts, New Hampshire, Rhode Island, and Connecticut. The British greeted Washington's appointment as commander of the rebel army with a poem published in the Loyalist newspapers:

When Congress sent great Washington
All clothed in power and breeches,
To meet old Britain's warlike sons
And make some rebel speeches

T'was then he took his gloomy way
Astride his dapple donkeys,
And travelled well, both night and day,
Until he reached the Yankees.

Full many a child went into camp,
All dressed in homespun kersey, ["kersey" refers to
    work clothes made of coarse woolen cloth]
To see the greatest rebel scamp
That ever crossed o'er Jersey.[16]

The New England army soon took to addressing their new dignified Virginian commander as "His Excellency." Washington purposely adopted a stately behavior to command respect and maintain discipline from his army. He was always "on stage," making sure to dress and act the part of an inspirational leader. He learned these traits during the French and Indian War (1754–1763) as a young volunteer aide-de-camp to British Army General Edward Braddock and as a Provincial (Virginia) officer serving under British General John Forbes. Washington was not unique in his military service during the French and Indian War. A number of other British and American officers and enlisted men who fought in the American Revolution were veterans of the earlier conflict. The French and Indian War was the North American segment of a global conflict fought primarily between Britain and France that became known in Europe as the Seven Years' War.

Washington made an extensive tour of the rebel works surrounding Boston in the days that followed his arrival at Cambridge. While inspecting the defenses, he met a twenty-five-year-old officer named Henry Knox. Washington had a knack for identifying talented people and encouraging them. Knox was one of the Virginian's first protégés. Others included a young Rhode Island Quaker named Nathanael Greene, and Benedict Arnold, who began the war as an impetuous Connecticut militia officer.

Washington soon realized that he had a large army surrounding Boston, but few cannons. His opponent, General William Howe, was entrenched in the city with plenty of artillery, but too few men to attack the rebels. Washington also discovered that he could not starve Howe's army into surrendering or withdrawing, because Boston was a seaport and the Royal Navy and merchant ships were keeping the beleaguered garrison supplied with victuals (from the Latin word *victualia* meaning provisions) and munitions.

Washington finally broke the standoff when Henry Knox transported fifty-nine cannons overland from Fort Ticonderoga to Boston. The artillery arrived in the American camp outside Boston in March 1776. His Excellency used Knox's artillery to threaten to bombard the city if General Howe's ministerial army did not evacuate the place. But Howe had decided to abandon Boston long before Knox's artillery arrived. Howe's predecessor at Boston, Thomas Gage, described the city's deficiencies in a letter dated June 26, 1775: "I wish this cursed place was burned.... The only use is its harbor... but in all other respects it's the worst place either to act offensively from, or defensively."[17] Colonel Knox's ordnance expedited their departure. Howe packed up his army onto a flotilla of ships, burned or smashed all the equipment he could not take with him, and sailed from Boston Harbor and out to sea.

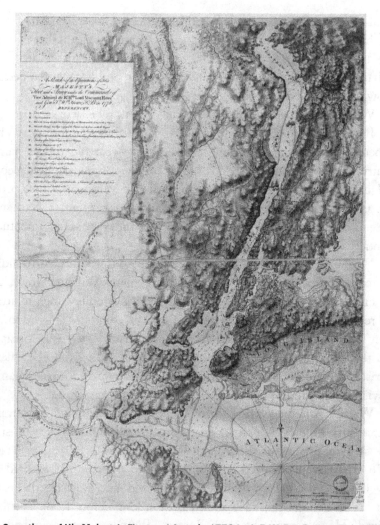

The Operations of His Majesty's Fleet and Army in 1776 by J. F. W. Des Barres. This printed map of New York City and its harbor is the work of Swiss-born cartographer Joseph Frederick Wallet Des Barres. The city of New York had a population of 25,000 in 1776 and occupied approximately a square mile on the southern tip of Manhattan Island. Des Barres (1729–1824) was one of the great cartographers of the eighteenth century. He created charts (presentations of an area consisting chiefly of water and used for navigation) of the North American coast that were unrivaled for their accuracy and beauty. Note that his map of New York includes the narrow ship channel to reach the city from the Atlantic Ocean. *Author's collection.*

There was almost unanimous agreement among the Patriots that General Howe would await reinforcements, then return in force to seize rebel-held New York City. Seizing the city made sense. The British had successfully used New York as their base of operations during the French and Indian War. Favoring the city was its central location in the colonies, with a deep water harbor sheltered from severe weather. The British wanted New York's protected harbor and extensive dock facilities to handle the critical shiploads of troops, war materials, and provisions that would be arriving from Britain to supply their army and crush the rebellion. In addition, unlike rebellious Boston, New York's estimated population of 25,000 was believed to be pro-British Loyalists except for a few deluded agitators.[18]

The delegates to the Continental Congress were as interested in retaining New York as the British were in capturing it. Even before Howe evacuated Boston, the members of Congress were insisting that the "utmost diligence" be taken to defend New York and "that by works [fortifications] thrown up in proper places, the enemy may be prevented from gaining possession of it."[19]

General Washington agreed with Congress's assessment that "the Ministry will make an effort to gain possession of New York."[20] One example we have of Washington's conviction that the British wanted to capture New York are notes of his comments at a council of his senior officers in Cambridge. The pertinent text reads, "The intelligence he [Washington] had received from sundry persons who had escaped from Boston, and from frequent observations... that in all probability they [the British] were destined for New York and would attempt to possess themselves of that City."[21]

Washington's first priority was to have an experienced officer sent from Boston to survey the city and recommend a plan for defending it. The assignment should have been given to an experienced military engineer, but the Patriots had none at this point in the war. Nor was the British Army likely to loan the rebels one of their engineers, who were graduates of the British Army's Engineering and Artillery Academy at Woolwich, England. As an alternate, Washington gave the job to General Charles Lee.

Charles Lee was an important Continental Army general during the first years of the Revolutionary War. He was also the main character in an event that historian Thomas Fleming called "the luckiest Friday the 13th in American history." The story about Lee appears later in this narrative. Although an obscure figure in our nation's history, there are a number of places in America named in his honor—Fort Lee, New Jersey; Lee, Massachusetts; Leetown, West Virginia; and Lee, New Hampshire.

Charles Lee was a former British Army officer who adopted the patriot cause. Thomas Jones (1731–1792) was a prewar Royal judge and stalwart Loyalist who wrote a history of the American Revolution. In his account of the war, Jones said that Lee was "bred to the profession of arms."[22] Lee's military service prior to the Revolutionary War included fighting the French and their Indian allies in America as a young British Army lieutenant; he was promoted to major, then lieutenant colonel commanding cavalry in Portugal against the Spanish Army, and was a general in the Polish Army. But, by 1773 he was a restless, out-of-work professional soldier looking for a war to enhance his resume and earn some money. According to Judge Jones, "as soon as Lee heard of the commotions in America, he embarked for that country [Lee arrived in New York on October 8, 1773] traveling through all the revolted colonies, harangued mobs, published treasonable pamphlets, cursed the King, the Ministry, and Parliament."[23]

Lee was beyond a doubt the most bizarre officer in the Continental Army. His eccentricities included his appearance and behavior. He was tall and thin, and a slovenly dresser. Mercy Otis Warren knew Lee and she described him as "plain in his person even to ugliness, and careless in his manners to a degree of rudeness... his garb ordinary, his voice rough, his deportment rather morose." But Mrs. Warren also said that Lee "possessed a bold genius... and cherished the American cause."[24] Lee's strange behavior included several dogs who were his constant companions. But Lee was the most experienced officer the Patriots had at the start of the war. John Adams summed up the opinion of most of the leaders of the Revolution when he said, "He [Lee] is a queer creature—But you must love his dogs if you love him and forgive a thousand whims for the sake of the soldier and the scholar."[25] Mrs. Warren offered another conclusion about Lee: "he emulated the heroes of antiquity in the field [battlefield], while in private life he sunk into the vulgarity of the clown."[26]

George Washington was a soldier at heart and welcomed the distinguished half-pay (reserve officer) British colonel to Mount Vernon before the war. Lee visited Washington's estate twice, staying for five days during one trip. Washington was mesmerized by Lee's military knowledge and battlefield exploits. Washington's military experience prior to the American Revolution was impressive, but limited to leading often impertinent colonial troops on the frontier or serving as a Provincial officer under condescending British Army officers. Washington's most impressive command was the rank of Provincial colonel commanding the 700-man 1st Virginia Regiment assigned to protect the frontier during the French and Indian War. He retired from the regiment in December 1758, sixteen years prior to the start of the Revolutionary War.

After lengthy and stimulating conversations with Lee, Washington became one of his foremost admirers and believers in Lee's assertion that the colonists could stand up to the British Army.

In Congress, there was some talk early on about appointing Charles Lee the commander-in-chief of the Continental Army. But Lee's foreign birth (the congressmen wanted an American to lead their army) and his eccentric behavior prevented him from being seriously considered. But Congress agreed with Washington's opinion that the Patriots needed Lee's military acumen. As a result, Lee was commissioned as one of the four Continental Army major generals authorized by Congress at the start of the war. Lee was commissioned based on his military experience, whereas the other three major generals (Philip Schuyler, Israel Putnam, and Artemas Ward) were selected for their political affiliations as much as for their military experience. Schuyler was from New York, Putnam from Connecticut, and Ward from Massachusetts.

Lee joined Washington in Cambridge at the start of the war where he proved to be a capable officer and close advisor to Washington. His Excellency did not want to lose Lee's expertise at Cambridge, but planning New York City's defenses was important and Lee was given the assignment. Lee's orders were dated January 8, 1776, instructing him to go to New York "to put that city in the best posture of defense."[27] Lee set out in the middle of winter but his arrival in New York was delayed by snowstorms and a debilitating attack of gout. He finally arrived in New York carried on a litter, on February 4, 1776.

Lee was given a difficult assignment that is best understood by describing the topography of the New York City region. Using the example of a ship approaching the city, it would first sail into what was called the outer harbor or Lower New York Bay. It was a treacherous section of the Atlantic Ocean due to shifting sand bars that constantly altered the narrow deep-water channel leading to the city. A harbor pilot came aboard to safely steer the ship through the channel. As the ship drew closer to land, Staten Island was visible to the west and Long Island to the east. A narrow deep-water passage between Staten Island and Long Island was called the Narrows. Today crossed by the Verrazano Narrows Bridge, the Narrows was like a gate that opened onto New York City's spectacular inner harbor. The inner harbor, also known as the Upper Bay, was nearly landlocked and appeared to be a lake. Looking north, Manhattan Island loomed in the distance. The compact City of New York occupied the southern tip of Manhattan with the balance of the island's twelve-and-a-half mile length dotted with coves, elegant country homes, farms, forests, and the villages of Greenwich and Harlem. The city's old gun batteries faced the harbor, which accounted for New York City's southern tip being called the Battery.

The Hudson River bordered the west side of Manhattan Island, its mouth opening into the inner harbor. The Hudson, or North River as it was also called at the time, was navigable for ocean-going ships of the period for 150 miles north to Albany, New York. The eastern shoreline of Manhattan Island is created by a complex system of waterways. The East River bordered about two-thirds of the eastern side of Manhattan beginning at the inner harbor. The East River was not a river, despite its name, but a brackish (containing saltwater) estuary of the inner harbor. Also classified as a tidal strait, the East River flowed into Long Island Sound. The brackish water of the East River kept it from freezing during the winter. This was why all of the colonial city's docks and warehouses were located along the East River. North of where the East River met

Long Island Sound, a narrow waterway called Harlem Creek formed the balance of the eastern shore of Manhattan Island. Harlem Creek turned west, creating the northern end of Manhattan Island, and emptied in the Hudson River at a place called the Spuyten Duyvil (Dutch for the Spewing Devil or the Devil's Whirlpool). The site was aptly named because of the treacherous currents created where the two waterways met. Author Washington Irving gave the Spuyten Duyvil its popular but fictitious translation from Dutch, which is "in spite of the devil."[28]

After arriving in New York in early February 1776, General Lee was joined by Captain William Smith, an officer described as an engineer.[29] During their survey of the New York area, the pair were attracted to an area of high ground on the Long Island side of the East River, close to the river's mouth. The site is the modern Brooklyn Heights section of Brooklyn. Brooklyn Heights (also known as Columbia Heights at the time) was directly across the East River from colonial New York City. Lee recognized the strategic importance of Brooklyn Heights. Artillery placed there could easily fire into the city and docks if necessary, as well as block any attempt by the Royal Navy to navigate the East River.

Realizing its significance, Lee made Brooklyn Heights the key to his defense plan for New York City. On February 19 he wrote a report to Washington in which he called fortifying Brooklyn Heights his "capital subject" and recommended "a post [a fort or gun battery] or retrenched encampment [a military compound surrounded by ditches and anything else to stop an enemy] on Long Island opposite to the City [Brooklyn Heights] for three thousand men." Continuing his report, Lee wrote, "Should the enemy take possession of New York, when Long Island is in our hands, they will find it almost impossible to subsist."

Lee also warned Washington of a serious problem in his February 19 report. The danger Lee expressed was that New York was surrounded by waterways and the British had a fleet of warships, while the Patriots had a few gunboats [small boats armed with a cannon or two] to oppose them. Lee alerted Washington to the problem in a key sentence: "What to do with the city, I own, puzzles me; it is so encircled with deep navigable water, that whoever commands the sea must command the town."[30] Lee's assessment was good advice, but any thoughts Washington had of evacuating and burning the city was inconceivable, as the armchair generals in Congress were adamant that Washington must defend New York. They reasoned that giving up the city without a fight would be a major psychological blow to the Patriot cause.

Lee was in the midst of fortifying New York City when he received orders from the Continental Congress to go to Charleston, South Carolina, which was in immediate danger of being attacked. Lee left New York for his new assignment on March 7, 1776. Judge Jones tells the story that Lee lodged at Mrs. De La Montaine's public house while he was in New York.[31] According to Jones, General Lee and his "friends, his suite, and his principal officers were all entertained and feasted; and the whole was at the poor woman's expense." When Mrs. De La Montaine presented Lee with her bill, "he damned her for a tory, cursed her for a bitch, and left the house without paying her a sixpence."[32]

Following Lee's departure, the first Patriot contingent left Boston for New York on March 15, with other troops following close behind. Five regiments left under the command of General Nathanael Greene on April 1, 1776, and an addition five regiments left a few days later. Washington left Cambridge on April 4, and arrived in New York on April 13. He established his headquarters in a house on Pearl Street in the heart of the city. He moved his headquarters in June to the Mortier House, on what is today the corner of Varick Street and Charlton Streets at the southern edge of Greenwich Village.[33] The name of the estate was changed to Richmond Hill and purchased by Aaron Burr after the war.

Convinced that the British would attack New York, Washington implemented Charles Lee's complicated and expensive defense plan upon his arrival. Washington said that he "never spared the spade and pickax," preparing earthworks and gun batteries during the summer of 1776.[34] His efforts included building a string of forts connected by earthworks to safeguard the artillery on Brooklyn Heights from being attacked from the rear. Washington also took advantage of some high ground in eastern Long Island called the Gowanus Heights (also called the Guan Heights). Gowanus Heights dominated the surrounding area and was a natural defense line that the rebels fortified as further protection for the artillery on Brooklyn Heights. The crest of Gowanus

Heights is present-day Eastern Parkway in Brooklyn. By mid-July 1776, Washington was confident that the Patriot fortifications on Long Island rivaled those on Bunker Hill. The British, he reasoned, might overrun the American defenses on the Gowanus Heights but "they would have to wade through much blood and slaughter before they could carry any other part of our works." "At best," Washington declared, they would be in possession "of a Melancholy and Mournful Victory."[35] The Patriot army was zealously constructing their forts, earthworks, and gun batteries when—as anticipated—enemy warships heading toward New York were spotted by lookouts stationed on Staten Island. The date was June 29, 1776.

General Howe was aboard one of the first ships to cross the Narrows and anchor in the inner harbor. The rebels took a few long-range artillery shots at the enemy ships, but had no navy to oppose them. Howe decided to use sparsely settled Staten Island to assemble his army. An advance detachment of British troops landed there unopposed on July 2 and "lay near the landing place all night." These first troops ashore probably headed straightaway to secure an important freshwater spring on the island, near the harbor, known as the Watering Place. The spring was located in modern Stapleton, Staten Island. Ironically, the Continental Congress declared the independence of the colonies from Britain on the same day (July 2, 1776) that the first British troops landed on Staten Island. General Howe came ashore at 6:00 am on the following morning (July 3) with 2,300 troops and some compact cannons called grasshoppers.[36] They fired a three-pound cannon ball and were commonly used to support infantry. The general's older brother, Admiral Lord Richard Howe, joined his brother on Staten Island on July 14 aboard the sixty-four-gun frigate HMS *Eagle*.[37] Sixty-four-gun frigates such as the *Eagle* were the largest ships that could safely enter colonial New York because of the narrow, shifting channel through the outer harbor. It was said that Lord Howe arrived with a sword in one hand and an olive branch in the other hand, for not only was he appointed "Commander-in-Chief of His Majesty's Ships and Vessels employed and to be employed in North America," but was also empowered, with his brother, to negotiate a peaceful end to the rebellion. William and Richard Howe worked well together to methodically organize their joint responsibilities as warriors and peace commissioners.

As the summer wore on, additional convoys arrived with troops who converted Staten Island into a vast British military camp. Despite his impressive army, Howe delayed attacking New York, awaiting the arrival of his final promised troops. They were 1,000 volunteers from the elite British Army Brigade of Guards and the first contingent of hired auxiliaries. The Landgrave (the German equivalent of a count in control of a large territory) of Hesse-Cassel (called Hesse today and one of the sixteen federal states of Germany) supplied the bulk of the auxiliary troops. The Landgrave's army was known for its discipline and martial prowess. Since the Landgrave was providing a complete army, including infantry, artillery, and a professional officers corps, they were legally classified—even in colonial times—as auxiliaries. They were not mercenaries, who are individual combatants who sell their services for money.[38] The British hired 12,000 troops from the Landgrave including infantry, artillery, and two companies of elite troops armed with rifles called jägers. In summary, the Landgrave sold the British a complete army. The Brigade of Guards and first detachment of Hessians finally landed on Staten Island on August 13.[39] By mid-August, a Hessian officer camped on Staten Island counted 38 British warships and 439 transports anchored off the shore of the island.[40]

As Howe was busy building up his army on Staten Island, Washington was across the harbor strengthening his defenses in Manhattan and Long Island. Washington also built additional fortifications designed to defend the lower Hudson River. The danger was that Royal Navy warships could sail north of Manhattan to encourage and arm the Loyalists and disrupt provisions and reinforcement from reaching New York City. Two fortifications were constructed on the lower Hudson River. Fort Washington was built on Mount Washington, the highest natural point on Manhattan Island. The rebels constructed another fortification almost directly across the Hudson River in New Jersey, which they named Fort Lee in honor of General Charles Lee. The idea was that the cannons at both forts could sink an enemy ship that dared to run the gauntlet. But the Howe brothers had more ambitious plans than sailing ships up and down the Hudson River to show Mr. Washington and his civilian bosses the futility of their rebellion.

The arrival of the elite British Brigade of Guards and Hessian troops completed the army General Howe planned for his campaign to capture New York. Now that every detail had been arranged, the Howe brothers were ready to launch their attack.

The sullen Continentals and militia defending New York City could only speculate where Howe would strike first. As a result, the rebels were spread out and dug in throughout Manhattan Island and nearby western Long Island. But regardless of Howe's intentions, Washington and his senior officers knew that they were about to face a formidable opponent. Here is what the rebel commanders most likely knew about General Howe as they waited for him to unleash his army against them. They knew that Howe was a wealthy member of the British aristocracy and a member of Parliament. Stories of his exploits against the French during the French and Indian War and his leadership at Bunker Hill proved his courage. They knew that besides his older brother, Admiral Lord Richard Howe, he had another older brother named George Augustus who was killed leading troops against French-held Fort Carillon (later renamed Fort Ticonderoga) during the French and Indian War. Howe's experience fighting the French and their Indian allies made him an early advocate of light infantry; as previously noted, light infantry were detachments of active, agile soldiers trained to take initiative in combat. They were outfitted with distinctive and less bulky uniforms and accoutrements (equipment) than other infantrymen. The lighter gear allowed light infantrymen to maneuver quickly in the rough terrain and dense forests of North America. Howe also adopted organizing infantry assaults using a looser, more open arrangement than the traditional tight formation of three rows of troops. The troops also were encouraged to protect themselves whenever possible by positioning themselves behind trees. An example of General Howe's reforms is a comment by British Captain Sir James Murray, whose company sustained few casualties by "favor of some pretty large trees, which by a good deal of practice we have learnt to make a proper use of."[41] But despite his innovative reforms, General Howe was a conservative textbook general who thought in terms of defeating an enemy by seizing their cities and fighting general engagements. The term general engagement meant a battle (engagement) large enough such that the number of troops involved were commanded by a general.

Washington was aware that William and his older brother, Admiral Lord Howe, were authorized to negotiate an end to the war with the rebels by offering generous concessions and pardons. Washington also knew from his own experience as a Provincial Virginia officer attached to the British Army during the French and Indian War that Howe's noble rank, influence, and money could only go so far in advancing his career in the British Army. In order to obtain high rank, British Army officers, including Howe, had to take their profession seriously and demonstrate personal courage in combat. Cowards and fops were quickly weeded out of the British Army—an army of professionals that could be seen stirring on Staten Island on the morning of August 22, 1776.

General William Howe paid rebel General Charles Lee a compliment when he recognized the need to secure Brooklyn Heights before he could safely occupy New York City. Also, as Lee had predicted, Howe's attack to seize Brooklyn Heights would come from the rear. In anticipation of the attack, the Continental Army spent the summer protecting the land approach to Brooklyn Heights with a formidable chain of forts and earthworks that extended the length of Gowanus Heights.

General Howe launched his attack with the cooperation of his brother, the Admiral, on the rebel's defenses aimed at the western end of Long Island (today's Borough of Brooklyn). It began on the afternoon of August 22 with a perfectly executed amphibious assault originating on Staten Island, crossing the harbor, and alighting on the beach at Brooklyn's Gravesend Bay. After securing a beachhead, the Crown forces quickly moved inland less than a mile to the village of New Utrecht (today's Bath Beach section of Brooklyn) where General Howe made his headquarters at the Cortelyou Mansion (demolished in 1850). Stephen Kemble, an officer in Howe's army, was on the scene and he described the landing in his journal: "Thursday, August 22nd, Embarked in Flat Boats; were towed over to Long Island [Brooklyn] and landed about 9 in the Morning, at New Utrecht, without the smallest opposition... the whole [army] on Shore by 12 o'clock making Fourteen Thousand Seven Hundred Men." They included 120 horsemen from the 17th Light Dragoons.[42] Additional boatloads of British and Hessian troops arrived, bringing Howe's total field-strength army to 20,000. Opposing them were an estimated equal number of Patriot troops. However, the rebel army was spread out all over the region in an effort to defend every approach to New York City; 9,000 on Long Island, 7,000 on Manhattan Island, and 4,000 along the New Jersey coast. Of the 9,000 rebels on Long Island, it was estimated that 4,270 of them were entrenched along the length of Gowanus Heights.[43] The British and Hessian detachments quickly spread out from New Utrecht and took up advance positions along the passes through the rebel defenses. Stephen Kemble said these advance posts skirmished with the rebels for the next few days, "but of no consequence." Meanwhile, General Howe implemented a plan with the help of several veteran British officers and local Loyalists familiar with Long Island. Howe's idea was to outflank Gowanus Heights and attack the rebels from behind. He organized constant patrols by the 17th Light Dragoons to prevent the rebels from reconnoitering to determine the size and locations of his army. This led to Washington believing that Howe had only 8,000 troops on Long Island when the actual number was 20,000.[44] Howe kept the substantial portion of the army that he was going to use for his flanking attack hidden from view near New Utrecht until the night of August 26.[45] At 11:00 pm on August 26 an estimated force of 10,000 men with horse-drawn field artillery broke camp and began silently marching below the rebel defenses on Gowanus Heights. Leading the way were British light infantry commanded by General Henry Clinton. General Howe was with the main column, which included the Brigade of Guards. Three local Loyalists led the column to the weakly guarded Jamaica Pass located at the far eastern end of Gowanus Heights. Once through the pass, they followed a country lane called the Rockaway Path for three miles to the village of Bedford (today's Bedford-Stuyvesant neighborhood of Brooklyn), where they arrived at 9:00 am. A section of Rockaway Path still exists in the Evergreen Cemetery in Brooklyn. Howe had superbly outflanked the Americans on Gowanus Heights and his army was now behind them. Two cannon blasts from Howe's column was the signal for the other Crown forces detachments to end their feints (diversions) and begin their frontal assaults aimed at the other passes along Gowanus Heights. A flanking attack, particularly against inexperienced combatants, is frightening. As American Major General William Heath observed, "A few shots on the flank or rear of an army, serves to disconcert them more than heavy fire from the front."[46] The coordinated British attack broke the American defense line along Gowanus Heights and the dazed rebels incurred heavy losses as they fought their way to their fortifications on Brooklyn Heights. According to Stephen Kemble, the rebels lost "upwards of 3,000 men" in the Battle of Long Island including 1,100 men taken prisoner. Their captives included three Continental Army generals (John Sullivan, Lord Stirling, and Nathaniel Woodhull), three colonels, four lieutenant-colonels, three majors, eighteen captains, and forty-three lieutenants.[47] In comparison, Kemble said that total British casualties were 313 killed, wounded, or missing.[48]

The Battle of Long Island was over by the late afternoon of August 27 and the victorious Crown forces were within a few hundred yards of the rebel fortifications on Brooklyn Heights. Historian Washington Irving said that only the intervention of General Howe prevented the British troops, "flushed with success" from storming the works.[49] Howe decided it was too risky to attack the strong rebel fortifications and decided instead to take the rebel defenses by regular approaches (a siege).[50] Euphoric with his triumph, Howe sent a fast ship to England with an account of the battle. The news reached London on October 10. King George III, who had insisted on aggressively pursuing the war, was ecstatic with the news and awarded Howe the prestigious Order of the Bath.[51] With the title came the right to call himself Sir William Howe, the name by which he is best known in history. Howe's victory was also celebrated by his army on Long Island. General Earl Percy, who fought in the Battle of Long Island, wrote to his father in England, "I think I may venture to assert, that they will never again stand before us in the Field. Everything seems to be over with them and I flatter myself now that this campaign will put a total end to the war."[52]

But despite their humiliating defeat on Long Island, the rebels continued to man their formidable ramparts on Brooklyn Heights. Their defenses consisted of forts and earthworks protecting an area two miles long and one mile deep. The East River was within the rebels' lines, including the main ferry operating between New York City and Brooklyn. Washington rushed boatloads of troops from Manhattan to reinforce the exhausted survivors of the Battle of Long Island. Including his reinforcements, Washington had 9,000 men on Brooklyn Heights in the days following the Battle of Long Island. At the same time, a few hundred yards away, the British were methodically digging their parallels (trenches dug parallel to the defense of the place being besieged) and saps (trenches approaching the enemy's defenses) while Royal Navy warships were ready to sail into the East River as soon as a favorable wind prevailed to cut off communications between Brooklyn and New York. By August 29 (two full days following the Battle of Long Island), Washington realized his army's precarious position. He called a council of war with his senior officers that afternoon, and they agreed to evacuate the army from Brooklyn while there was still time. The orders were given and boats were hastily gathered and dispersed near the New York City side of the East River ferry dock. The boats began crossing the river during the night and evacuating the troops on Brooklyn Heights. The withdrawal was a masterpiece of organization, apparently executed without arousing curiosity from the nearby enemy siege lines. Tents were left standing, campfires were burning, and sentries methodically withdrawn from the posts. The boats carrying the troops, artillery, and horses across the mile-wide East River extinguished their running lights. "The troops," wrote nineteenth-century historian Henry Johnston, "were pushed across as fast as possible in every variety of craft—row boats, flat-boats, whale-boats, pettiaugers [a small boat with a mast], sloops and sail boats—some of which were loaded to within three inches of the water."[53] The evacuation continued through the dark moonless night. Historian William Gordon described how a strong unfavorable wind had the Patriot flotilla struggling to cross the river during the early evening. But at about 11:00 pm, Gordon said, "a favorable southwest wind blew fresh... [and] made the passage from the island to the city, direct, easy and expeditious." Gordon, a pro-American clergyman, published the first history of the Revolutionary War in 1788. He attributed fortuitous events, like the sudden change of wind during the evacuation of Long Island, to the righteousness of the Patriot cause. Gordon also accurately stated that a fog developed during the night of the evacuation, which he attributed to divine intervention: "Providence further interposed in favor of the retreat army, by sending a thick fog about two o'clock in the morning, which hung over Long Island, while on New York side it was clear."[54]

Whether it was divine intervention or luck, 9,000 American combatants were ferried to New York in nine hours. Every Continental soldier and militiaman got away, including George Washington, who was the last man to leave. At dawn, a British patrol noticed that the American pickets were missing. After entering the deserted rebel fortifications, they alerted the British camp that the rebels were gone. A detachment of Hessians ran down to the waterfront to see the last of the rebel boats in the distance approaching the safety of Manhattan Island. The American evacuation of Brooklyn Heights ended the fighting on Long Island, but the battle for Manhattan Island was about to begin.

Trying to defend New York against the firepower and mobility of the Royal Navy was hopeless from the start. Historian David Palmer summed up the situation when he said, "New York was a trap. The unopposed British fleet could have placed troops ashore anywhere."[55] Washington was too inexperienced at this point in the war to grasp the folly of risking his army to defend New York.

Critiquing George Washington's mistakes in the New York campaign sometimes includes his having banished a detachment of Connecticut horsemen soon after they arrived on Long Island. Historian Washington Irving, for example, believed that the Connecticut horsemen could have been patrolling the Jamaica Pass. Irving said that the "fatal scheme of the enemy might have been thwarted [Howe's flanking movement] had the army been provided with a few troops of light-horse, to serve as videttes [a mounted sentinel stationed in advance of the outposts of an army]."[56] But the memoirs of Continental Army Captain Alexander Graydon (1752–1818) tells a different story that helps vindicate Washington's decision to send the Connecticut horsemen home:

Among the military phenomena of this campaign," Graydon recalled, "the Connecticut light horse ought not to be forgotten. These consisted of a considerable number of old fashioned men, probably farmers and heads of families, as they were generally middle aged, and many of them apparently beyond the meridian of life. They were truly irregulars; and whether their clothing, their equipment or caparisons [a cloth laid over a horse for protection and decoration] were regarded, it would have been difficult to have discovered any circumstance of uniformity.... Instead of carbines and sabers, they generally carried fowling pieces; some of them very long, and such as in Pennsylvania, are used for shooting ducks. Here and there, one, his youthful garments, well saved, appeared in a dingy regimental [military uniform coat] of scarlet, with a triangular, tarnished laced hat." Graydon said that one of these horsemen was captured by the British and, "on being asked what had been his duty in the rebel army, he answered, that it was to flank a little and carry tidings."[57]

The Patriot army was dazed following their ill-fated defense of Long Island. Although Washington's forces were now united on Manhattan Island, they had to defend the twelve-and-a-half-mile-long island (on both sides) with numerous inlets and beaches along its length suitable for the Royal Navy's precision amphibious landings. In addition there were New York City's streets to defend. A prompt attack following the Battle of Long Island anywhere along the Manhattan coastline would probably have dealt the demoralized rebels a second devastating blow. But the Howe brothers waited two weeks before resuming the offensive. Their reasoning was their decisive victory in the Battle of Long Island should persuade the rebels of the futility of their insurrection and bring them to their senses. It will be recalled that Admiral Lord Howe and his brother were authorized to negotiate a peace treaty with the rebels. The brothers wanted to return to England as heroes by ending the war after one brilliant campaign. A genial meeting now with a delegation from the Continental Congress, they reasoned, should lead to a negotiated peace. They had plenty of captured high-level army officers to send to Congress with their offer to meet. General John Sullivan, a prewar lawyer from New Hampshire, was selected from among the prisoners for the assignment. The members of Congress were interested in listening to their terms and selected a blue-ribbon delegation consisting of John Adams, Benjamin Franklin, and Edward Rutledge to meet with a British delegation headed by Lord Howe. The two sides met for three hours on September 11, 1776, at the Staten Island home of Loyalist Colonel Christopher Billop. The house was used because it was close to the rebel-held town of Amboy (also called Perth Amboy), New Jersey.[58] The meeting, or peace conference as it was called, was cordial but futile. Lord Howe delivered his message too late. By the time of the peace conference, Congress was insisting that Britain recognize American independence, while the Howes were only authorized to offer pardons to the leaders of what they considered to be an unlawful rebellion.

The Americans used the two-week-long hiatus wisely. General Washington had the time to call a council of war during which it was decided that it was not feasible to continue to try to defend all of Manhattan Island. It was decided to concentrate the army on the rugged northern tip of the island, called Harlem Heights, where the army had built Fort Washington atop lofty Mount Washington. The area occupied by the Americans includes the present-day neighborhoods of Washington Heights, Morningside Heights, and Sugar Hill. The Patriots were busy moving everything their limited number of wagons would allow from lower Manhattan to Harlem Heights while the Howe brothers were absorbed in their peace efforts.

Having failed in their bid to end the war through negotiation, the Howe brothers decided that it was time to teach Mr. Washington another lesson in military science along with occupying New York before the rebels could torch the city. This time Lord Admiral Howe, an expert on amphibious operations, selected a lightly defended cove on the East River side of Manhattan Island for their latest operation. Called Kips Bay, the cove was situated at present-day 34th Street in Manhattan. In 1776, the cove opened onto a large, flat meadow within range of the cannons of Royal frigates moored on the East River. Even better, Kips Bay was defended by some inexperienced New England militia whose only emplacements were the shallow ditches they had dug in the meadow. The militiamen had no artillery—just muskets to repeal an attack.

Sixteen-year-old Joseph Plumb Martin was a private in a Connecticut militia regiment defending Kips Bay. He wrote an account of what happened on September 15, 1776, the day of the British attack. Martin said that he awoke at daybreak to see five enemy frigates anchored in the East River with their broadsides facing Kips Bay.[59] Aboard one of the ships, the frigate HMS *Phoenix*, was Commodore William Hotham, in command of the naval operation. The *Phoenix* flew Hotham's broad red commodore's pennant from its mainmast to identify the frigate as the squadron's flagship. As the sun came up, the five ships ran out their big guns on Hotham's signal and opened fire on the crude rebel earthworks with rolling volleys of cannon fire. Martin wrote, "I made a frog's leap for a ditch and lay as still as I possibly could and began to consider which part of my carcass was to go first." Martin claimed that his regiment was "entirely exposed to the rake of their guns," which pounded the rebel positions nonstop for two hours. There were prearranged signals from Commodore Hotham aboard the *Phoenix* that could be seen by the British troops waiting in boats across the East River. A red flag flown from the *Phoenix*'s mainmast was the signal that it was safe for the troops to commence their amphibious landing; a blue flag meant to delay the crossing, and a yellow flag a warning to abort the mission.[60] At noon, Commodore Hotham ordered a red flag to be flown by the *Phoenix*. It was not long afterward that the militiamen defending Kips Bay saw rowboats loaded with soldiers emerging from the opposite side of the river. Joseph Plumb Martin said that he watched the boats spread out as they started across the river "until they appeared like a large clover field in full bloom." The first wave of disciplined Redcoats and Hessians, numbering 4,000 men, came ashore with fixed bayonets and charged across the cannon fire–scarred meadow toward the militiamen. By now some experienced Continental troops were being rushed to the cove, but terror had already spread among the poorly armed militiamen by the time the reinforcements arrived. Martin recalled that "the demons of fear and disorder seemed to take full possession of all and everything on that day."[61] The Continentals joined the rout and even General Washington, who arrived on the scene, could not stop them. Nineteenth-century historian Henry Johnston summed up the so-called Battle of Kips Bay as "an ungovernable panic."[62] By mid-afternoon, the Royal Navy had landed 14,000 troops at Kips Bay. They could have easily dashed across to the west side of Manhattan and cut off the 3,500 rebels still in New York City.[63] But General Howe, who accompanied them, did not take advantage of this golden opportunity. Instead, the story goes, he stopped for afternoon tea at the home of Mrs. Robert Murray while the rebels in the city got away and joined the rest of the army camped in Harlem Heights.

Meanwhile, British troops raced south from Kips Bay to occupy New York City that afternoon (September 15). The Loyalist Reverend Ewald Gustav Shewkirk was in the city at the time. He described how the rebels left to defend the city had retreated to Harlem Heights when they heard that "the king's troops had landed on York Island [Manhattan] about three miles from the city [a reference to Kips Bay]." The city fell silent after the rebels left until "some of the king's officers from the ships came on shore, and were joyfully received.... And thus," Reverend Shewkirk said, "the city was now delivered from those Usurpers who had oppressed it so long."[64] The British had captured New York City completely intact without firing a shot.

The Grand Army was now concentrated in northern Manhattan around Fort Washington. It now numbered 18,730 officers and common soldiers fit for duty.[65] They were in a strong position but their only safe escape route was across Harlem Creek into lower Westchester County (today the Bronx borough of New York City). There was only one bridge across Harlem Creek, a wooden span called the Kings Bridge, which was heavily defended by the rebels.[66] The Kings Bridge was also important because it was the only practical way for provisions and reinforcements to reach Washington's army from New England. General Howe realized that the way to defeat the well-entrenched rebels in northern Manhattan Island was to seize Kings Bridge, which would isolate them. Howe could then pry the Americans from their stronghold by starving them into surrendering.

The expeditious approach to seize Kings Bridge was to land troops on the eastern side of the Bronx and threaten the bridge from the rear. It made sense, as it was only nine miles through open country from several excellent amphibious landing places in Pelham Bay (the eastern shoreline of the Bronx) to threaten Kings Bridge. General Howe began outflanking Harlem Heights on October 12 when 4,000 Crown troops came ashore at Frog's Point (today's Throg's Neck) in Pelham Bay. Washington rushed troops to the scene. The British vacillated, mainly because Frog's Point was "a kind of island" with only a narrow approach to the mainland at low tide.[67] Alerted to the landing, Washington realized that it was only a matter of time before the British would put troops ashore elsewhere in Pelham Bay as the first step to seizing Kings Bridge. Realizing his perilous situation, His Excellency held a council of war on October 16 with his senior officers. They included Charles Lee, who had just returned from successfully defending Charleston, South Carolina. The decision was made to abandon Harlem Heights because "the enemy's whole force is now in our rear." At the same meeting the officers, including Charles Lee, "agreed that Fort Washington be retained as long as possible."[68] But when the situation changed, Lee would claim to influential members of Congress that he was in favor of abandoning Fort Washington.

The Main Army began retreating from Harlem Heights on October 18 and took up positions on the hills surrounding the Westchester County village of White Plains. Washington left behind 2,000 men to man Fort Washington which, for the moment, seemed secure and could continue to discourage Royal Navy ships from navigating the Hudson River. It turned out that Washington exited northern Manhattan just in time because, as his troops started across Kings Bridge, the British executed a second amphibious landing in Pelham Bay. This time 4,000 troops successfully came ashore at Pell's Point. The site was three miles north of their futile landing at Frog's Point.

After putting additional troops ashore at Pell's Point, the British and Hessians pursued the rebels inland to White Plains where an indecisive battle was fought on October 28. Washington retreated again, this time to a strong defensive position about a mile and a half north of White Plains called North Castle.[69]

Washington's Grand Army now consisted of 16,969 officers and common soldiers fit for duty.[70] General Howe followed Washington north, but on November 5 he abruptly turned his army west to the village of Dobbs Ferry on the Hudson River, where a Royal Navy frigate and two civilian transports had provisions and military supplies waiting.

Stephen Kemble was shocked by the amount of plundering being done by the British and Hessian troops during their march to Dobbs Ferry. Kemble's diary entry for November 6, 1776, expressed his concern: "Marched early in the morning to Dobbs Ferry; found a frigate and two victuaiers [ships with food] who had come up the day before. The march marked by the licentiousness of the troops who committed every species of rapine and plunder."[71] Pilfering civilian property was officially discouraged, and perpetrators occasionally suffered capital punishment for their actions. But British and Hessian officers often turned a blind eye to the practice as a means for their men to augment their diet. Kemble's comment that British ships met Howe's army at Dobbs Ferry is interesting, as this river town was north of the heavily fortified Fort Washington–Fort Lee defense line that was intended to prevent any enemy ships from navigating the Hudson River.

The safe arrival of the three ships to Dobbs Ferry was in fact just the latest example of British warships and transports sailing past the Fort Washington–Fort Lee rebel gauntlet with little damage. Washington was alarmed by the inability of the forts to control river traffic and wrote to General Greene on November 8 expressing his concern. Greene was in command of the two forts. Washington wrote Greene: "The late passage of the 3 vessels up the North [Hudson] River is so plain a proof of the inefficacy of all the obstructions we have thrown into it... what valuable purpose can it answer to attempt to hold a post [Fort Washington] from which the expected benefit cannot be had?" But, His Excellency added, that since Greene was "on the spot" he would leave it up him to decide if and when the fort should be abandoned.[72]

Gathering intelligence from interrogating deserters and prisoners of war, and reading intercepted letters and orders at Washington's headquarters, indicated that Sir William was planning to cross the Hudson River into northern New Jersey to seize the rich farmland of the Hackensack River Valley. Known as the "garden of America" at the time, the region could provide fresh food and provender for the Crown forces.[73] But unknown to Washington at the time, Sir William wanted to capture Fort Washington to complete his conquest of Manhattan Island before crossing the Hudson to seize the Hackensack River Valley farms.

Acting on his intelligence sources, Washington held a council of war on November 6 during which it was decided to "throw a body of troops into the Jerseys immediately."[74] But still unsure of Howe's intentions, Washington decided to cover every contingency by splitting the Grand Army into three independent commands. He would personally lead 5,000 troops into New Jersey. In addition, he put 3,000 men under the command of William Heath, a reliable, unpretentious general, to garrison the town of Peekskill, New York, on the eastern shore of the Hudson River. Washington left the third and largest part of the army with General Lee in North Castle. Lee's mission was to deter any British thrust aimed at New England and to stand by until the enemy's intentions became clearer. Washington gave Lee lengthy written instructions on November 10 prior to departing for New Jersey. The key passage in Washington's missive read: "If the enemy should remove the whole, or the greatest part of their force to the west side of Hudsons [sic] River [New Jersey], I have no doubt of your following with all possible dispatch."[75]

Washington assumed that he would also be reinforced by the troops at Fort Washington and Fort Lee once he reached New Jersey. Additional numbers would come from the so-called Flying Camp that had been defending New Jersey in addition to mobilizing the New Jersey militia.

Washington's 5,000 men began crossing the Hudson on November 8, 1776. The senior officer assigned to lead the troops into New Jersey was Major General Israel Putnam, an aged Connecticut brawler past his prime. But "Old Put" was popular with the men and could be counted on to follow orders. Washington himself crossed the Hudson on the morning of November 12 and reached General Greene's headquarters at Fort Lee on the following afternoon. After meeting with Greene, who reassured him that Fort Washington was secure, Washington rode six miles west to the village of Hackensack, where he established his headquarters at the home of Peter Zabriskie.[76] Events now moved fast. On the afternoon of November 14, Greene sent Washington an urgent message that the situation at Mount Washington had deteriorated; Sir William had the fort surrounded. His Excellency believed that about 1,800 troops were defending Mount Washington. But unknown to Washington at the time, General Greene sent reinforcements from Fort Lee across the river to Fort Washington. The total garrison on Mount Washington was actually 2,800 officers and common soldiers when the Crown forces brought up artillery and surrounded the hilltop fortress.

The commander of Fort Washington was Colonel Robert Magaw, an ardent Patriot but with limited military experience. Magaw was a graduate of the Pennsylvania Academy (today's University of Pennsylvania) and was practicing law in Carlisle, Pennsylvania, at the start of the war. He joined the Continental Army early in the war and quickly rose through the ranks and was appointed a colonel and commander of the 5th Pennsylvania Regiment. His regiment helped to construct Fort Washington in the months leading up to the Battle of Long Island. Magaw's regiment was pressed into service briefly to reinforce the troops trapped on Brooklyn Heights following the Battle of Long Island before returning to Fort Washington. Colonel Magaw was later named the fort's commander. With his 2,800 troops, he was expected to hold a two-and-a-half-mile-long fortified area of rough terrain jutting up from the Hudson River. The area's steep hills, heavy underbrush, and ravines favored defense. Colonel Rufus Putnam, the Continental Army's chief engineer, had planned the fortifications on Mount Washington. Putnam designed three defense lines encircling an earthen fort. Putnam's plan was that if attacked, the troops manning the outermost line, which was embedded in rough landscape, would hold out as long as possible before falling back to a second line of entrenchments surrounding the fort. The fort itself was the third defense line. The problem was that it was estimated that 10,000 men were needed to properly man the sprawling defenses. Captain Alexander Graydon, who was there, said that "the line of entrenchment was too extensive to be manned without leaving intervals."[77]

On the morning of November 14, General Howe ordered Field Jäger Corps Captain Johann Ewald to reconnoiter Fort Washington. The jägers were the elite Hessian soldiers who fought in the American War. "Jäger" means hunter, and the jägers were aptly named: they were all agile marksmen armed with rifles. Jäger Captain Ewald said that he carried out his dangerous mission with Georg Henrich Pauli, a captain in the Hessian artillery corps, and "two of my bravest jägers [enlisted men]." Ewald described how they crept along the heavy underbrush along the bank of the Hudson River before scaling the face of a cliff. They hid at the crest of the precipice from where they could stealthily observe the rebel fort in the distance. Ewald reported that the fort was situated on a hilltop surrounded by woods, boulders and deep ravines. The space around the fort however had been leveled "for the distance of rifle or grapeshot shell range." Grapeshot was a bag or canister filled with small metal pellets fired from a cannon. The maximum range of an American long rifle or cannon grapeshot was about 300 yards.

Ewald also observed that there was a single road apparently leading from the river bed to the fort. The part of the road that he could see "has been made completely impassable by many abatis." An abatis, according to the *Military Dictionary* published in London in 1779, "is formed by cutting down many entire trees, the branches of which are turned towards the enemy, and as much as possible entangled one into another." Ewald also observed that "small works lie in the wood on the steepest height in front of the fort, one behind the other, which can fire upon the entire road."[78]

General Howe had a good idea of the rebel fortifications on Mount Washington based on Ewald's reconnaissance and a map provided by a deserter from the garrison. On November 15, Colonel James Patterson, Howe's adjutant general (senior administration officer), approached the fort carrying a white flag and accompanied by a drummer beating the parley (from French, "to speak"). Colonel Magaw came out of the fort to parley. Patterson was blunt and delivered an ultimatum for Magaw to surrender the fort or suffer death by the sword. Magaw answered with a stirring reply, "I am determined to defend this post to the last extremity." Sir William had his answer, but he waited a full day before launching his attack. The plausible reason for the delay was that Howe wanted to give the rebels a chance to evacuate the fort that night by crossing the Hudson River to Fort Lee rather than have his Redcoats suffer heavy casualties assaulting the rebels' well-entrenched lines. But even if Magaw wanted to evacuate, there were few boats available to get his troops across the river.

Several Continental Army generals were across the Hudson at Fort Lee at the time, which raises the issue of why a colonel was left to command 2,800 men in an important outpost. Commenting on the subject, retired Lieutenant General Dave Palmer said, "Despite having a force of 2,800 defenders at Fort Washington, it was customary for a colonel to be the commanding officer of fortifications during the American Revolution."[79]

General Greene sent an urgent message to Washington's headquarters in Hackensack as the crisis unfolded. Washington immediately rode back to Fort Lee. He arrived there at dusk on November 15 and was being rowed across to Mount Washington when he met Greene and Putnam returning from the fortress. The three generals conferred in the middle of the river. Greene told Washington that "the troops were in high spirits and would make a good defense." They returned to Fort Lee to await the inevitable attack.

A total of 8,000 British and Hessian auxiliaries began their assault on Fort Washington on November 16. There are several good eyewitness descriptions of the attack, including a letter that Captain William Leslie, an officer in the 17th British Regiment, wrote to his father: "Everything was ready for the important event at daybreak; about 9 o'clock the signal was given and the attack began from all quarters; the rebels kept a constant fire with grape and musquetry from behind rocks and trees in spite of which our troops gained the top of the hill and drove all the rebels into the fort."[80] The garrison's situation became hopeless when the British brought up mortars that could lob shells into the crowded earthen fortress (a shell was a hollow iron ball filled with gunpowder, with a fuse

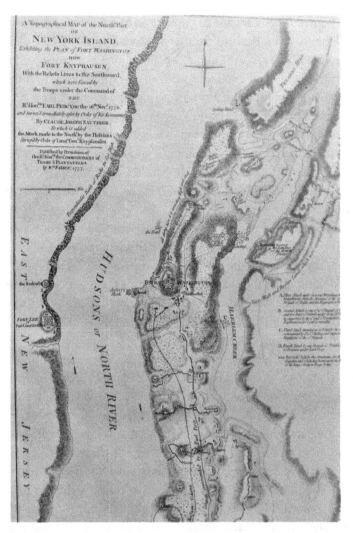

A Plan of the Attack of Fort Washington, by Claude Joseph Sauthier. This printed map shows the British and Hessian attack on American-held Fort Washington on November 16, 1776. Note that a Royal Navy frigate, HMS *Pearl*, is shown on the Hudson River above Fort Washington. The *Pearl* gave supporting fire to the Hessian assault against Fort Washington's northern defenses. Fort Lee, New Jersey, is located almost directly across the Hudson River from Fort Washington. The Fort Washington–Fort Lee defense line was constructed at great expense by the Patriots during 1776 to prevent Royal Navy warships from navigating the Hudson River. The defenses included obstructions planted in the river. *Author's collection.*

inserted in it that was meant to explode in the air over an enemy position). Captain John Peebles from the 42nd Regiment described what happened next in his diary: "about 3 o clock in the afternoon all the different attacks had succeeded and we were in possession of all the High Grounds in the environs of Fort Washington, having taken & killed a good number between 300 & 400 of the Enemy & driven the rest into the Fort." Peebles said that the fort was surrounded on all sides and the garrison surrendered "to the Number of about 2,600."[81] Colonel Magaw was among the prisoners of war. He had boasted that Fort Washington could withstand an attack for weeks, but the fort surrendered after just four hours.[82]

Washington, Greene, and several other senior officers watched the action through their glasses (telescopes) from Fort Lee. Their view was shrouded in gun smoke during the fighting and they could not tell what was happening until they saw the rebel stripes being lowered from Fort Washington's flagpole and the Union Jack raised. Fort Washington was an enormous defeat for the Patriots. It was only surpassed by the surrender of Charleston, South Carolina, in 1780.

Following the loss of Fort Washington, Washington and Greene realized that Fort Lee was in imminent danger of being overrun. Fort Lee was situated on the crest of the Palisades—a line of steep cliffs along the west side of the Hudson River.[83] General Greene had lookouts posted along its length, watching for an enemy attack while provisions and equipment at Fort Lee were being hurriedly moved inland. But time ran out when boats concealed in the Spuyten Duyvil emerged at 11:00 pm on the night of November 19 and began crossing the Hudson River. Aboard the flotilla were the first contingent of troops assigned to the mission. The invasion force totaled 5,000 troops under the command of Major General Lord Charles Cornwallis, Sixth Earl of Eyre and a member of the House of Lords. They were guided by local Loyalists who showed Cornwallis an unguarded path five miles north of Fort Lee that led to the top of the Palisades. The Redcoats and Hessians climbed the steep path, dragging their artillery to the top with ropes. It was hard work and took until mid-day on November 20 to assemble the entire invasion force with their artillery on the crest of the Palisades.

The presence of British troops on the summit of the Palisades marked the start of New Jersey's role in the American Revolution. The enemy's presence was observed by Patriot lookouts who sent couriers racing to Fort Lee with the news. Defending Fort Lee was not an option. The post's 2,000 men were mostly poorly disciplined members of the Flying Camp. They were no match for Cornwallis's well-armed and trained brigades.

As General Cornwallis led the British invasion of New Jersey, knowing more about him is important as this narrative continues. Cornwallis was an ambitious and experienced officer; a man of immense personal courage who was admired by the officers and men who served under him. He wanted to be a soldier from childhood. Just prior to his eighteenth birthday, his rich and indulgent father brought him an ensign's (junior officer, equivalent to a second lieutenant) commission in the prestigious First Regiment of Foot Guards. But instead of joining his regiment, Cornwallis toured Europe with a Prussian officer and attended a military academy in Italy. He returned home to participate in the Seven Years' War in Europe where he proved to be a bold and enterprising young officer whose battlefield experience, money, and influence advanced his career. But money and political clout were not enough to achieve high rank in the British Army. A candidate had to be a person of impressive bravery and superb leadership skills as well as being well-versed in military science. Cornwallis was such a man. He was also sympathetic to the Americans' prewar petitions. But as a British officer, he arrived in Boston in 1775 determined to crush the colonists' insurrection. Cornwallis fought throughout the New York campaign, where he distinguished himself as a fighting general whose aggressiveness was constrained by General William Howe, his commanding officer. Howe picked the right officer when he ordered Cornwallis to lead the hazardous invasion of New Jersey.

Fort Lee was abandoned by the time Cornwallis's column descended on the place at dusk on November 20. All the rebels had fled by then to Hackensack and, according to one account, "they left some poor pork, a few greasy proclamations and some of that scoundrel Common Sense man's letters [Thomas Paine] which we can read at our leisure."[84] That night, Cornwallis's men feasted on the tons of provisions that the rebels abandoned in their haste to evacuate Fort Lee. At the same time, the American troops were nearby and crammed into houses and barns in and around Hackensack.

By the time the Crown forces entered Hackensack on the following morning (November 21), Washington was gone. He led his army southwest along back roads to the town of Newark on the Passaic River. His exhausted and demoralized army included just one artillery company, a New York State unit assigned to the Continental Army. Its commander was a young Kings College (today's Columbia University) student named Alexander Hamilton.

The vanguard of Washington's army arrived in Newark on November 22. Newark was not really a town but a scattering of hundreds of houses along two miles facing the Passaic River. Some of Newark's 3,000 inhabitants were fisherman who earned their living from the brackish Passaic River's clam and mussel beds.[85] Newark was important because it was on the main road that connected New York City with Philadelphia. The rutted dirt road connecting the two cities was known by different names including the Assunpink Trail, the Kings Highway, the Old Dutch Road, and the Upper Road. But by the time of the Revolutionary War the route was often called the High Road. It was the busiest road in colonial America, with a steady flow of freight wagons and crude stage wagons.[86] The route from New York City to Philadelphia was a ferry across the Hudson River from New York City to Paulus Hook (today's Jersey City), then to Newark, Elizabethtown (present day Elizabeth), Rahway, Woodbridge, New Brunswick, Princeton, and Trenton. There were two ferries at Trenton to take traffic across the Delaware River to Pennsylvania where the road continued through the town of Bristol and on to Philadelphia. The route following the High Road from Paulus Hook to Philadelphia, including several ferries, was ninety-five miles.

Cornwallis was eager to pursue the demoralized remnants of Washington's Grand Army, but his orders from General Howe were to go no further than Hackensack. Sir William insisted on sending additional troops to Cornwallis from New York, including the 16th Light Dragoons, before allowing him to penetrate deeper into New Jersey. The dragoons gave Cornwallis the advantage of having cavalry. Howe wanted Cornwallis to have a large force as the British did not know the where-abouts of General Charles Lee, who was reported to be in command of a sizeable portion of the rebel army. The British considered Washington an amateur, as evidenced by their string of victories against him since they arrived on Staten Island in July. Lee was the serious threat, and Cornwallis finally advanced cautiously on November 26 toward Newark, keeping his dragoons patrolling for Lee's brigades.

His Excellency stayed in Newark for just over five days, keeping a watchful eye on Cornwallis's movements. Washington's extended stay in Newark was meant to give the New Jersey militia a rallying point to join his little army. But the militia never arrived, and the few hundred that responded to the urgent call had mustered in the village of Morristown, twenty miles west of Newark. Morristown was located on a fertile plateau sheltered by the Watchung Mountains. There were only a few roads through the mountains to Morristown and each could be easily defended. In addition, the local population of small farmers supported the rebellion. Retreating into the Watchung Mountains was tempting, especially since Washington could see them in the distance from Newark. In fact, several of his officers wanted him to take the army to Morristown where they would be relatively safe shielded by the mountains. Once there, they could help rally the New Jersey militia and wait for General Lee to arrive with reinforcements.[87] But Washington demurred and insisted on keeping his army on the High Road to oppose any attempt by Cornwallis to seize Philadelphia.

The Grand Army left Newark early on the morning of November 28 when lookouts reported that Cornwallis was less than a day's march away. The Grand Army's ranks numbered 5,300 officers and enlisted men at the time.[88] The enlistment of 2,000 of them would expire on December 1, and they were determined to leave. Many of them had been fighting for months. They were exhausted and sick, and they said that it was time for other Patriots to take their place.

The rebels were able to move much faster than the Crown forces who were slowed down by wagonloads of provisions, equipment, artillery, and baggage. The looting of homes along their line of march continued to be a problem. Stephen Kemble said that their plundering was "carried to a most unjustifiable length."[89] Historian Leonard Lundin summed up the situation when he wrote, "the invaders found themselves in a promised land, where everything they could desire was theirs for the taking."[90]

There is a story that Cornwallis's army entered Newark from the north as Washington's army was leaving the town from the south. This is technically correct, except that Newark was spread out over two miles and it refers to the vanguard of Cornwallis's army cautiously entering Newark from the north while a tenacious American rear guard was exiting the town from the south. In fact, Washington was able to keep his army a day or two ahead of the pursuing Crown forces as evidenced by the journal of a British Army officer with Cornwallis's corps: "'tis almost impossible to catch them. They will neither fight, nor totally run away. But they keep at which a distance that we are always above a day's march from them. We seem to be playing at Bo peep."[91]

The Grand Army followed the High Road southwest toward New Brunswick. A small but important Patriot unit joined the rebels on the road near Elizabethtown. It was Captain Daniel Neil's Eastern Company of New Jersey Artillery. Neil was a merchant living in Acquackanonk (modern Passaic, New Jersey) at the start of the war. He commanded one of the two artillery companies raised by the New Jersey Provincial Congress in February 1776. His company was stationed along the New Jersey coast throughout the New York City campaign. As a result, Neil's artillerists had no combat experience when they joined Washington's retreating army.[92] Neil's two cannons, along with the two guns of Captain Hamilton's company, were critical in helping to sustain the rebellion as the Grand Army continued to retreat across New Jersey.

Following the High Road, the vanguard of Washington's army crossed the farming region of Piscataway, New Jersey, where they crossed the Raritan River and entered New Brunswick early on the morning of November 29. There was no bridge across the Raritan at New Brunswick, and the Inman Ferry was the only means of crossing the river between Piscataway and New Brunswick.[93] However, there was a bridge across the Raritan one mile upstream from New Brunswick in the village of

Raritan Landing (no longer existing). It was a wooden structure named Landing Lane Bridge.[94]

While a river like the Raritan seemed to have endless places to cross by boat, that was not the case. With the exception of a few men traversing a river in a boat, an army—with its horses, wagons, and artillery—had to cross the Raritan where there was a bridge, ferry, or ford. Ferries were usually located at narrow places along a river where there was deep water and a dock or a firm, gradual slope (no marshes, swamps, or soft footing) on the opposite riverbanks to allow horses, wagons, and artillery to be boarded on and off boats. A ford was a shallow place in a river or stream where people, horses, and wagons could cross on a solid bottom with water up to a person's midsection. Despite its length, the shallow Raritan River upstream from New Brunswick could only be safely crossed at fords. The closest ford on the Raritan from New Brunswick was six miles upstream from Landing Lane Bridge.

The majority of what remained of the Main Army, led by Washington, crossed the Raritan at Inman Ferry and arrived in New Brunswick during the afternoon of November 29. They had marched twenty-five miles through continuous rain on the previous day. They were moving fast, as Cornwallis was now in hot pursuit. His army, estimated at 10,000, passed through Newark on the morning of November 29, the same day that Washington's army reached New Brunswick. Cornwallis's legion camped that night in Elizabethtown and Rahway where his troops and the women camp followers spent the night plundering the two villages and surrounding countryside. The next day, Saturday, November 30, Cornwallis's army moved out early and resumed their march along the High Road toward New Brunswick. The weather that day was miserable; heavy rain and wind had turned the unpaved dirt road to a sea of mud. Despite the harsh weather, by the afternoon of November 30 Cornwallis was about five miles away from New Brunswick and moving fast to reach the Raritan.

Back in New Brunswick, Washington was in a desperate situation. His headquarters were at Cochrane's Tavern (at the corner of Albany and Neilson Streets in New Brunswick, no longer existing) where he was up early on November 30 to confront several crucial problems. The only reinforcements waiting for him at New Brunswick were some stragglers from the Flying Camp. In addition, Washington had given up hope that Lee's corps would meet him at New Brunswick. This painful conclusion was based on a dispatch Washington received from Lee a few days earlier, saying that he was still in North Castle, New York, waiting for New England militia to arrive to take over the defense of Westchester County. Lee also complained that he could not march because he had no shoes or blankets for his men.[95] Adding to Washington's problems was the enlistments of half of his army would expire the next day, and they were determined to leave. Also, the enlistments of some of his others troops ended on January 1, and they were already sneaking off as Cornwallis's army was approaching the Raritan River. He summed up his situation in a dispatch to Congress that day (November 30), writing, "the situation of our affairs is truly alarming." He asked Congress to call out the Philadelphia militia, whose official name was the Associators of the City & Liberties of Philadelphia, and have them meet him at Trenton.[96]

The next day, December 1, 1776, was the darkest day of the American Revolution. It was the day that the British came the closest to a military victory in the American War. Despite Washington's ardent appeals, 2,000 of his remaining troops marched off early that morning toward Philadelphia, leaving him with just 3,000 men. Cornwallis's legion of 10,000 troops with artillery reached the Raritan that afternoon and was firing artillery shells across the river into the town. At the same time, some Hessian troops rushed Landing Lane Bridge but fell back when they discovered that some of the span's wooden planks were removed. The Hessians also faced a detachment of American riflemen who were shooting at them at long range from across the river. One marksman shot and mortally wounded a mounted Hessian officer named Captain Von Weitershausen from across the bridge. The "unfortunate shot" discouraged the Hessians from attempting to cross the span.[97] Meanwhile, one mile downstream, Hamilton and Neil's cannon fire was discouraging Cornwallis from attempting to cross the Raritan at Inman Ferry or trying to navigate the river in some commandeered boats.

Cornwallis had the numbers to defeat Washington's army that day if he could have made it across the Raritan River. Defeating Washington at New Brunswick, on top of the string of British successes throughout 1776, may have convinced Congress to end their seemingly hopeless rebellion. Lord Admiral Howe and his brother were nearby and eager to negotiate an end to the war. It is staggering to realize that the 3,000 Patriots who stood with Washington at New Brunswick were sustaining the American Revolution.

Washington realized that he had to retreat with his remaining troops toward the Delaware River while there was still time. In anticipation of crossing the Delaware into Pennsylvania, Washington gave a written order to Colonel Richard Humpton to "proceed to the two ferry's [sic] near Trentown and see all the boats there put in the best Order."[98] Humpton, one of the army's most reliable and experienced officers, was also instructed to collect all the other boats along the Delaware River and bring them to Trenton. Washington also sent a dispatch to New Jersey Governor William Livingston, asking him to call upon the militia to help Humpton secure all the boats along the Delaware River and bring them to Trenton or to the Pennsylvania side of the river. Washington did not repeat the mistake of not having boats available to evacuate the Fort Washington garrison. In addition, he wanted to make sure that there were no boats left at Trenton that Cornwallis could use to follow him across the river.

Washington then waited until dark that night (December 1) when he had huge bonfires lit along the New Brunswick waterfront with a detachment of troops marching back and forth in front of the fires and making noise as if they were digging trenches. Then he quietly slipped away with his little army toward Princeton. The troops marching around the campfires in New Brunswick left later that night and caught up with the main column. General Greene, recalling the desperate nighttime march, wrote, "When we left Brunswick we had not 3000 men, a very pitiful army to trust the liberties of America upon."[99]

The 3,000 soldiers who remained with Washington that night were the dedicated Patriots of the American Revolution. They camped for a few hours about six miles south of New Brunswick and filed through Princeton sometime between 8:00 and 9:00 am on the morning of December 2. The village was abandoned, its residents having fled into the countryside with their most valuable possessions when they learned that the British were swarming through New Jersey like locusts, plundering and burning everything in their path.

Nassau Hall was the largest building in Princeton and the home of the College of New Jersey (today's Princeton University). Captain Alexander Hamilton was among the stalwarts who were retreating with Washington. Hamilton had applied to the college before the war but decided to attend Kings College instead. He must have glanced at the deserted college building as he passed through the village on the morning of December 2, 1776, perhaps thinking of earlier times when he was a carefree student.

Princeton was twelve miles from Trenton, and the army pushed on past the college town and arrived at Trenton in the late afternoon. They found the two ferries there were overrun with frightened civilians and sick and wounded soldiers. According to one account, the scene at the riverfront was akin to the Day of Judgement.[100] Washington reached the waterfront at Trenton to find that Colonel Humpton had performed admirably. Humpton not only had boats waiting and guarded for the army's use, but the colonel had cleared the Delaware River of anything that could float for a forty-mile distance. The feat was accomplished with the help of the galleys of the Pennsylvania Navy and the Hunterdon County (New Jersey) militia.[101] Also raising Washington's spirits was that detachments from the Philadelphia militia were waiting for him at Trenton. They were the first reinforcements that Washington received since crossing the Hudson River on November 12. Among the first units to arrive from Philadelphia were twenty-six dragoons from the 1st Troop of Philadelphia City Cavalry. They included Private Benjamin Randolph, in whose house Martha Washington had been living during the New York campaign.[102]

Unknown to Washington at the time, there was no need for him to rush to Trenton. To explain, Cornwallis occupied New Brunswick on the morning of December 2 when he realized that the rebels had run off during the previous night. He wanted to go after them, but his orders from General Howe were not to go beyond New Brunswick. Sir William's concern was that Cornwallis's supply and communications lines already stretched all the way back to New York City and could be severed by Lee's column or militia. In addition, the British were straining to find enough wagons and teams of horses to keep Cornwallis's army supplied with victuals. Besides, Howe reasoned, his army had already conquered far more of New Jersey than he anticipated when Cornwallis invaded the state. Sir William decided to meet with Cornwallis in New Brunswick to assess the situation for himself and decide if the army should advance any further.

General Howe took his time getting to New Brunswick. He sailed from New York City on December 5 to Perth Amboy on the New Jersey coast where he spent the night. The following morning he began riding through central New Jersey to New Brunswick. He was travelling across country under British control, but he still risked being ambushed by roving militia or rebel riflemen. Howe was an easy target to identify, as he was probably dressed for the field in a scarlet, gold-laced uniform coat. A falling collar (wide collar turned down over the shoulder) of dark blue velvet and buttonholes set in threes would have indicated his rank of lieutenant general.[103] Taking no chances, Howe was accompanied by a substantial bodyguard. They included Hessian grenadiers whom Howe admired and in whom he had great confidence. Riding close by would have been Howe's aides-de-camp. Their duty was to assist him in his innumerable military and personal duties. His aides were also responsible for delivering important dispatches and other privileged information. During a battle, his aides would be used to deliver verbal orders.

One of Howe's aides during the war was Captain Levin Friedrich Ernst von Muenchhausen. He was a young German aristocrat and an officer in the Hesse-Kassel Lieb regiment. He signed his name Friedrich and was fluent in German, French, and English. Friedrich served as an aide to Howe from November 1776 to May 1778, when Howe resigned his command and returned to England. Friedrich's presence as an aide to Howe was essential, as Sir William spoke only English and General Leopold Philipp, Freiherr von Heister, commander of the Hesse Kassel forces in America, spoke only German and French. Captain Muenchhausen translated Howe's orders into German. The young captain also kept a diary during the time he served as Howe's aide. Friedrich's diary is a valuable eyewitness account from the war, especially since General Howe's wartime letters and other documents were destroyed in a fire after Howe returned to Britain. For example, in writing about Howe's overland trip from Perth Amboy to New Brunswick, Friedrich said that he was responsible for twenty dragoons, "and deployed them all around the General about a quarter of an hour's march from him, to search out any harm that might befall him."[104] Friedrich's diary is an important source of accurate information about the war, and I will refer to it as this narrative continues.

Accompanied by his suite including his aide Friedrich, Sir William was ambling through New Jersey while Lord Cornwallis was vegetating in New Brunswick. He was sitting there with 10,000 men, learning from spies and Loyalist sympathizers that Washington's army was just a hard day's march away in Trenton, transporting their baggage across the Delaware River to Pennsylvania.

Howe arrived in New Brunswick in the late afternoon of December 6 and dined with Cornwallis that evening. Howe was reluctant to allow Cornwallis to go further, but he changed his mind when he was briefed on the destitute condition of Washington's army. It was conceivable that the Crown forces could defeat Washington's Grand Army and march all the way to Philadelphia by Christmas.

General Howe agreed to allow Cornwallis to resume his offensive and joined Cornwallis's army as it advanced toward Trenton. The Crown forces left New Brunswick on December 7 and spent the night in Princeton. The looting there included pilfering the books from the college library. The soldiers used the volumes to keep their campfires glowing or carried them off to sell later. The Loyalist Thomas Jones, who was imprisoned by the Patriots during the war, said that he saw "books publicly hawked about the town [New York City] for sale by private soldiers, their trulls [prostitutes], and doxeys [mistresses]. I saw an Annual Register [a yearly summary of current events] neatly bound and lettered, sold for a dram [one gulp of whiskey, technically 1/8 ounce of a liquid] and Freeman's Reports [an English law book] for a shilling."[105]

As the Crown forces were advancing cautiously toward Trenton, Patriot spies and army skirmishers were keeping Washington informed of their location. Washington moved his troops, artillery, and remaining baggage across the Delaware River on the night of December 7, while the British were camped in Princeton. The Patriot operation went on throughout the night and into the following morning. Among the militiamen who arrived from Philadelphia to reinforce Washington's army was a lieutenant named Charles Willson Peale. Peale was an unusual soldier: he was one of the first Americans to earn his living as an artist. His clientele was exclusive and included George Washington, whose portrait he painted in 1772. Peale's militia company was posted on the Pennsylvania side of the Delaware during the night of December 7. Peale witnessed the threadbare soldiers of the Grand Army crossing the river. He described the scene as a "grand but dreadful appearance" with enormous fires on both shores illuminating the boats jammed with men, equipment, weapons, and horses crossing the river. Peale thought he saw a familiar face as he watched "the sick and half-naked veterans of the long retreat streaming past." He looked closely at a ragged and feeble man wrapped only in an old, dirty blanket. Shocked, Peale realized that it was his younger brother James, who had been with Washington from the start of the New York campaign.[106]

Generals Howe and Cornwallis finally reached Trenton in the late afternoon of December 8. Historian Henry Carrington calculated that the Crown forces spent seventeen hours in Princeton during their so-called overnight stay and took almost the entire day to march the twelve miles between Princeton and Trenton.[107] Sir William and Lord Cornwallis arrived to find Trenton deserted. Washington welcomed them to the town with a volley of cannon fire from across the river.

Howe stayed in Trenton until December 14 when he started back to New York City. Before leaving Trenton, Sir William issued the following orders: "The approach of winter putting a stop to any further progress, the troops will immediately march into quarters and hold themselves in readiness to assembly on the shortest notice."[108] Howe's assessment was that Lord Cornwallis had advanced much further into New Jersey than originally planned. Sir William believed that he could defeat what was left of Washington's ragtag army in the spring, seize Philadelphia, and end the upstart rebellion.

But before returning to the comforts of New York City, Sir William had to decide how to maintain control of the New Jersey territory Cornwallis had seized. His solution was to establish garrisons through-out the conquered region for the winter and let them buy or forage for their provisions and feed for their horses from the local farmers. His most distant and isolated garrison from New York was at Trenton. Its location, closest to the enemy, made it the post of honor, and Sir William gave the coveted command to Hessian Colonel Johann Gottlieb Rall as a reward for his courage during the assault on Fort Washington. Rall was a good combat officer, but never should have been given command of the 1,586 troops assigned to winter in Trenton.[109] The problem was that Rall spoke no English and had no respect for the rebel army. When it was suggested that he erect redoubts [a stand-alone enclosed fortifica-tion] to defend the town, Rall bellowed, "Lasst sie nur kommen! Keine Schanzen! Mit dem bajonet wollen wir an sie!" (Let them come! We want no trenches! We'll at them with the bayonet!).[110] British General Clinton said that he questioned Howe's decision to establish a chain of isolated posts across New Jersey for the winter. Clinton claimed that he cautioned Howe "against the possibility of its being broken in upon in the winter, as he knew the Americans... knew every trick of that country of chicane [deception] and would quickly catch any opening that might offer in that way."[111] Events would prove Clinton right. Washington began planning a surprise attack on Trenton shortly after Rall's brigade occupied the town.

Across the Delaware River from Trenton, Washington was safe for the moment, but he knew that the war was going badly and that he had to do something soon to restore his reputation and prevent what Thomas Paine called "slavery without hope—our homes turned into barracks and bawdy houses for Hessians."[112] Adding to his distress was that the Continental Army's most experienced officer, General Charles Lee, was captured by British dragoons on December 13. What happened was that after numerous delays, Lee finally crossed the Hudson River into New Jersey on December 2, with only 3,500 men. Lee had to leave the rest of his force at North Castle because they were too sick or had no shoes or warm clothing to make the long winter trek. His army was bivouacked in Vealtown (today's Bernardsville), New Jersey, a few miles south of Morristown on the night of December 12 when Lee decided to leave the protection of his camp to spend the night at the nearby Widow White's Tavern in Basking Ridge.[113] Thirty British dragoons were led to the tavern by local Loyalists. The dragoons surrounded the place early in the morning of December 13. After scattering Lee's guards, they forced the British turncoat to surrender. A popular legend is that Lee was wearing his nightshirt when he was captured. But an eyewitness report said that Lee, who was a notoriously slovenly dresser, was wearing "an old blue coat... an old cocked hat, and greasy leather breeches" when he was apprehended.[114] General John Sullivan, Lee's second-in-command, tried to rescue Lee but the British had too much of a head start. Fearing attack, Sullivan broke camp at Vealtown and marched rapidly to the Delaware River which he crossed to Easton, Pennsylvania, and continued south to Washington's camp.

Besides Lee's brigade, other Continental Army troops and militia reinforced Washington until he had assembled 10,000 men by late December. Despite their numbers, despair prevailed, and Washington desperately needed a major victory over the British to restore Patriot morale and his own reputation. Washington had been eyeing Colonel Rall's isolated garrison of just over 1,500 men as a target for a badly needed coup. Favoring a Patriot attack was the fact that Rall had done little to fortify the town. In addition, Rall had a relatively weak force at Trenton consisting of three Hessian regiments and a detachment of twenty British dragoons. Detailed instructions from Washington to his senior officers during December show that raiding Trenton was not a spur-of-the-moment idea but one he had been considering for some time.

Rall must have realized that his isolated garrison was in trouble when rebel skirmishers ambushed two of his dragoons on the road to Princeton. The two horsemen were carrying dispatches to General Alexander Leslie at Princeton when they were attacked. One of the dragoons was killed and the other rider's horse was shot. The surviving dragoon jumped on his dead comrade's horse and rode back to Trenton. Rall had to send 100 men armed with a field artillery piece to get his dispatches through to

Princeton. His letters included a request to General Leslie to send him reinforcements. His request was answered by General James Grant, who was in overall command of the British occupation of New Jersey. Grant wrote Rall from New Brunswick on December 21, telling him that the rebels were "strolling about... in small parties" and not to worry. "You may be assured," wrote Grant, "that the rebel army in Pennsylvania... have neither shoes nor stocking, are in fact almost naked, dying of cold, without blankets and very ill supplied with provisions."[115]

Washington launched his carefully planned attack against Trenton on the night of December 25, just four days after Grant penned his note to Rall. Washington crossed the Delaware that night with 2,400 men and sixteen cannons.[116] They crossed the Delaware at McConkey's Ferry located nine miles north of Trenton. Additional troops were supposed to cross the river further south, but the current had piled up the river ice into impenetrable mounds, forcing them to abort their part of the mission. Despite freezing rain and piercing wind, Washington's corps reached Trenton on the morning of December 26. Their raid was a success due in part to Colonel Knox's insistence on including a large number of cannons, which were massed on high ground facing into the town. The fighting lasted for about 45 minutes and when it ended, the Americans counted 22 Hessians killed, 83 wounded, and 896 captured (including the wounded). American losses were two deaths during the march to Trenton and five wounded, including James Monroe, a future president of the United States.

The Americans gathered up their prisoners and booty from their successful attack and marched back over the same route to McConkey's Ferry. Their swag included 1,000 muskets, four standards [flags] and six brass cannons.[117]

Washington's victory invigorated militia resistance and encouraged him to return to Trenton on December 29 to support the uprising. Back in New York, General Howe's aide Friedrich was preparing to send a letter home when he reopened it to added the following postscript:

I have reopened this letter to report an unhappy affair. Colonel Rall, who was at Trenton with the Knyphausen, Lossberg and Rall regiments and 50 jägers, was compelled to surrender at dawn on the 26th, after a fight of one hour, owing partly to the suddenness of the enemy surprise, and partly to their superior power. We know no further details at the moment.[118]

General Howe was settling down for a winter of high-stakes gambling, concerts, and dinner parties with his gorgeous young mistress, Elizabeth Loring, when he learned about Washington's surprise attack at Trenton. He promptly ordered Lord Cornwallis to retake Trenton with 9,000 troops and rout Washington's army, which had returned to Trenton. Cornwallis promptly took action and started back toward Trenton. After skirmishing with rebel detachments as he approached Trenton, Cornwallis's army reached the town on the afternoon of January 2 where they fought the rebels to a stalemate. The fighting ended at dusk with Trenton's Assunpink Creek separating the opposing armies. Believing that he had Washington cornered, Cornwallis camped for the night while Washington silently slipped away with his army and after marching sixteen miles on back roads during the night, emerged the next morning at Princeton.[119] Washington had spies and scouts reporting on the number of British troops at Princeton and their positions for days. The nighttime march of his 6,000-man army and thirty to forty horse-drawn field guns to Princeton was no last-minute gamble, but a plan based on effective intelligence gathering.[120] The Americans arrived three miles outside of Princeton at sunrise on the morning of January 3, 1777, to surprise 392 British troops on the road to Trenton. They comprised the 17th and 55th British Army Regiments and a troop of dragoons under the command of Lieutenant Colonel Charles Mawhood. The British detachment under Mawhood's command departed Princeton before dawn to escort a convoy of supply wagons and invalids to Trenton. A third British regiment (the 40th) totaling 450 men was left behind to guard Princeton.[121]

Led by General Hugh Mercer, the Americans came charging across the farm of William Clark toward Mawhood's column. The British colonel was not intimated easily and ordered his men and artillery off the road and into a skirmish line on the Clark farm facing the rebels.

Fierce fighting ensued. The casualties included General Mercer, who was mistaken for Washington and repeatedly bayoneted and clubbed by the Redcoats. Other American losses during the battle included Captain Neil, who was killed leading his artillery company. The dramatic moment of the fighting occurred when Washington rallied his troops and led them in a charge against the British. Heavily outnumbered, Mawhood eventually ordered his men to "run away as fast as they could."[122] Some, including Mawhood, sprinted down the road toward Trenton while others ran back toward Princeton. Mawhood was on horseback and managed to escape into the woods. The Redcoats who managed to reach Princeton from the Clark farm joined their comrades from the 40th Regiment and barricaded themselves in Nassau Hall, the solid stone building that housed the college. Once inside, they shattered the building's windows and exchanged shots with the rebels who surrounded the place. The Americans brought up artillery, which began pounding away at the building. It was said that one cannon ball decapitated a portrait of King George II hanging in the prayer hall of the college. The omen of hitting the painting, in addition to the intense rebel musket and cannon fire, persuaded the 200 men inside the building to surrender. The victorious Americans immediately began to gather the provisions and supplies they found in Princeton. Barrels of flour were loaded into wagons and the flour that they could not carry off was destroyed by smashing the kegs and spilling the contents on the ground. Other rebels traded their dirty old blankets and worn shoes for new British ones. The rebels burned the hay that they could not carry off and "destroyed such other things, as the shortness of the time would allow." Two valuable brass cannons were captured but, as Washington later reported, "for want of horses, could not bring them away."[123] His soldiers threw the two cannon barrels down a well and burned the wooden gun carriages. The ransacking lasted for an hour when a drum roll signaled the men to form up and march off.

The sound of cannon fire coming from Princeton on the morning of January 3 alerted Cornwallis that he had been duped. He came racing back from Trenton to Princeton to find the rebels were gone. Commenting on the campaign, Colonel John R. Elting, a historian and World War II combat veteran, said that "Trenton had been an unexpected American victory. Princeton proved that Trenton had been no lucky accident. British generals suddenly became reluctant to take chances against him [Washington]."[124]

Washington's aggressive ten-day Trenton-Princeton campaign is often depicted as a brilliant but isolated example of his generalship. But there was an obscure occurrence during the retreat across New Jersey, prior to the Trenton-Princeton campaign, that showed that behind Washington's reserved, stoic facade was a warrior ready to risk bold, aggressive moves. The incident occurred on December 2, 1776, during one of the perilous days of the New Jersey retreat. It will be recalled that Washington abandoned New Brunswick on the night of December 1 and dashed through Princeton on the morning of December 2. Down to just 3,000 men, he faced the possibility that Cornwallis's 10,000-man army was just behind him. Yet despite his dangerous situation, Washington ordered half of his little army to remain in Princeton.[125] It was an audacious move, and Washington made his intentions clear in a December 5 letter to Congress from Trenton saying that he planned to get his baggage and stores across the Delaware River and then "face about with such troops as are here fit for service and march back to Princeton and there govern myself by circumstances."[126] In other words, despite his small numbers, Washington was looking for a fight, hopefully with a detached brigade of Cornwallis's army. Washington further explained his intentions in his same letter to Congress, stating, "I conceive it to be my duty, and it corresponds with my inclination, to make head against them, as soon as there shall be the least probability of doing it with propriety."[127] Washington left General Lord Stirling in command of the troops in Princeton. Stirling was joined at Princeton by General Greene on December 6 to assess the situation and report back on the enemy's movements. "Country people" (civilian Patriot sympathizers) were spying on Cornwallis's army, which was still in New Brunswick.

Apparently tired of waiting, Washington started out for Princeton with his available troops on the morning of December 7. While en route he received an urgent dispatch from Greene warning him that Cornwallis "was making a disposition to advance" from New Brunswick on several different roads toward Princeton.[128] Realizing that he could be outflanked and surrounded at Princeton, Washington immediately turned around and ordered Stirling and Greene to abandon Princeton and follow him back to Trenton. Once back, the troops, horses, and artillery began to be ferried across the Delaware to Pennsylvania.

Looking back, Washington's depleted army snuck off during the night of December 1, 1776, from New Brunswick and passed through Princeton on the following morning. When Washington returned to Princeton a month later, on January 3, 1777, he was the aggressor who surprised and defeated the British troops defending the town. Writing to his wife Catharine with news of the fighting in New Jersey, General Nathanael Greene said, "This is an important period to America, big with great events. God only knows what will be the issue of this campaign, but everything wears a much better prospect than they have for some weeks past."[129]

2

Providence Has Heretofore Saved Us*

There is a crossroads near Princeton, New Jersey, where one of the most dramatic events of the American Revolution took place. Currently a car approaching the intersection from downtown Princeton drives on modern New Jersey Route 27. About four miles from Princeton, the highway crosses a concrete bridge that spans the narrow Millstone River. Just beyond the bridge the road ascends a steep hill. The historic crossroads is at the top of the hill. A left turn at the crossroads leads to Laurel Avenue, a paved road that borders the meandering Millstone River. At the time of the American Revolution Laurel Avenue was a nameless, narrow, rutted country lane. The colonial forerunner of Route 27 was not in much better shape, but at least it had a name—the High Road. Despite its poor condition, the High Road was the busiest road in colonial America because it was the most direct way to travel overland between New York and Philadelphia. The High Road's route included a sixteen-mile section between Princeton and New Brunswick. Washington knew this portion of the High Road, although he had last travelled it in the dark after abandoning New Brunswick with his last 3,000 men on the night of December 1, 1776.

---

* Chapter title from a personal letter from George Washington to John Parke Custis, dated "Morris Town, Jany 22d 1777": "Providence has heretofore saved us in a remarkable manner." See W. W. Abbot et al., eds., *The Papers of George Washington, Revolutionary War Series*, 28 vols. to date (Charlottesville: University of Virginia Press, 1985–2020), vol. 8:123.

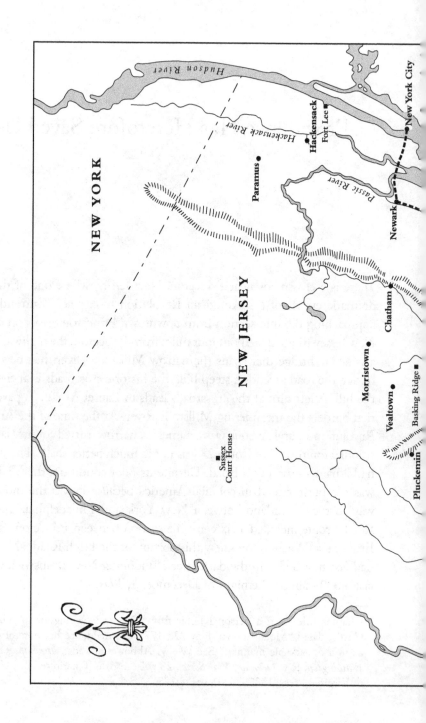

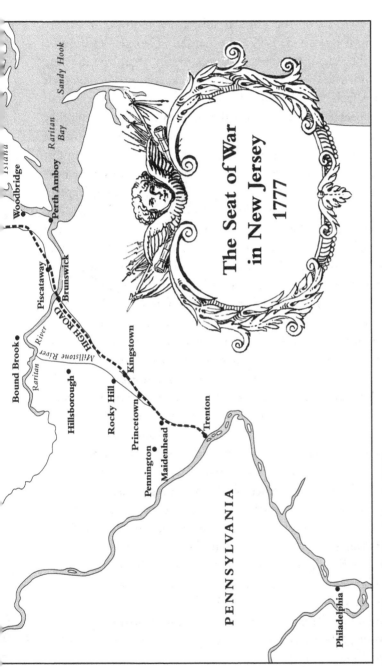

The seat of the war in New Jersey in 1777.

The little crossroads on the High Road had its moment in history on the afternoon of January 3, 1777. On that date George Washington was huddled at the side of the crossroads in a hastily organized meeting with his senior officers. They were all on horseback, accompanied by their aides-de-camp. Washington's generals were both ecstatic and exhausted following their spectacular victory over the three British regiments they surprised that morning at Princeton after marching through the night from Trenton. They also must have felt fortunate to be alive, having lost some of their fellow officers who were wounded or killed during the brutal fighting earlier that day. They included Colonel John Hazlet, Captain John Fleming, Marine Captain William Shippen, and Daniel Neil, all killed; Colonel James Potter, who was wounded and captured; and General Hugh Mercer, who was mortally wounded when he was surrounded and refused to surrender. Mercer was clubbed and stabbed with bayonets in seven places. He succumbed to his wounds on January 12.

Looking back from the crossroads, Washington and his generals could see the smoke rising from the fires that were destroying the provisions, animal fodder, and military stores that they could not carry off. The Patriot army was also just behind them, trying to move fast but impaired by wagons loaded with booty, along with horse-drawn artillery and over 200 captured enemy troops. Speed was critical, as lookouts warned them that Cornwallis was leading his 9,000 men toward them. Lord Cornwallis started racing back to Princeton upon waking on the morning of January 3 to find that the Americans were gone. The sound of "very brisk fire of small arms and smart cannonading" coming from the direction of Princeton that morning made him realize that Washington's army was attacking the three British regiments left there in his rush to reach Trenton.[1] Henry Knox later wrote to his wife that Cornwallis was leading his army from Trenton "in a most infernal sweat, running puffing and blowing & swearing at being so outwitted."[2] Cornwallis came barreling into Princeton about an hour after Washington evacuated the place.[3] After hearing how Lord Cornwallis had been hoodwinked, British General Henry Clinton said it was, referring to Cornwallis, "the most consummate ignorance I ever heard of in any officer above a corporal."[4]

Washington's troops were exuberant but physically exhausted when they left Princeton. Many of them were wearing dirty, threadbare clothing and worn-out shoes. The fortunate ones had on good shoes or wrapped themselves in the clean British Army blankets they had commandeered in Princeton. But none of them had slept for over forty-eight hours, with almost nothing to eat.

In the midst of this intense activity Washington sat motionless at the little crossroads on the High Road, absorbed in animated dialog with his officers. Just twelve miles down the High Road was New Brunswick where Washington's intelligence network reported the British had a small garrison guarding stockpiles of provisions and military equipment. Washington's aggressive character wanted to exploit this golden opportunity. In fact, he claimed that his plans were to continue on to New Brunswick after overwhelming the British troops at Princeton. But following a hasty conference with his officers, Washington decided that his men were too exhausted to go on. Washington wrote Congress that he would have gone on to New Brunswick if he had a brigade of rested troops:

My original plan, when I set out from Trenton was to have pushed on to Brunswick [from Princeton], but the harassed state of our own troops (many of them having had no rest for two nights and a day) and the danger of losing the advantage we had gained by aiming at too much [Cornwallis's army was approaching Princeton] induced me by the advice of my officers to relinquish the attempt, but in my judgement six or eight hundred fresh troops upon a forced march would have destroyed all their stores and magazines—taken as we have since learnt their military chest containing 70,000£ [British pounds], and put an end to the war.[5]

If Washington's intelligence was correct, £70,000 was a huge amount of money. Historian John Elting defined a military chest as "the funds of an army, particularly available cash."[6] In comparison, the 340 chests of tea destroyed during the 1773 Boston Tea Party were valued at £9,659.

Having made his decision, Washington ordered his Continentals to wheel to the left at the crossroads and follow the country lane that would lead them to the village of Hillsborough and then on to Morristown. Taking his army to Morristown was not a sudden decision. Washington planned to take his army there even while he was organizing his Christmas Day attack on the Hessians at Trenton. More about Washington's attraction to Morristown follows a description of the army's march there and the mystery surrounding the burial of a British officer along the way.

The by-road that Washington's army took following their victory at Princeton took them through the farmland bordering the Millstone River. They marched along the east side of the river to a wooden bridge at Griggstown, where they crossed the Millstone River and continued along a road on the west side of the stream for five miles to the village of Hillsborough. The men were in high spirits because of their recent victories, but worn out as a result of cold and hunger.[7] They moved slowly and reached Hillsborough at sunset on January 3 where they finally camped for the night. The hamlet was also the county seat of Somerset County at the time, which accounts for Hillsborough also being called Somerset Court House. The modern name of the village is Millstone Borough.

A detachment of British light dragoons arrived in Princeton in advance of Cornwallis's army and chased after the Americans for a few miles on the opposite (west side) of the Millstone as far as the village of Rocky Hill where the road ended at a wooden bridge across the river. Seeing the enemy horsemen, Washington rode forward to the vanguard of his army and ordered Delaware Militia Captain Thomas Rodney to break up the bridge with his forty-five-man company with the help of some carpenters.[8] Rodney said that the destruction of the bridge obliged the enemy to abandon pursuit of the rebels.[9] Unaware at the time of Washington's strength or plans, Cornwallis feared that the rebel army was going to attack New Brunswick using back roads. As a result, Cornwallis did not attempt to pursue the Americans, but halted in Princeton briefly until his entire army arrived from Trenton, including the rear guard. Cornwallis's army was fully assembled in Princeton at 4:30 in the afternoon and began a forced march to New Brunswick.

According to British Army engineer Archibald Robertson, who was there, "after a most fatiguing forced march all night long in frost and ice we reached Brunswick about 6 in the morning of the [January] 4th." Thinking back on recent events, Robertson said, he hoped "it would serve as a lesson in future never to despise any enemy too much."[10]

Lord Cornwallis arrived to find Brigadier General Edward Mathew, the commanding officer at New Brunswick, to be exceedingly agitated. The reason was that during the previous night an exhausted captain, who had managed to avoid being captured at Princeton, arrived in New Brunswick with the news of the successful American surprise attack on Colonel Mawhood's brigade. Other British survivors stumbled into New Brunswick later that night with exaggerated accounts of the fighting. Upon hearing these stories, General Mathew was preparing "to escape with the army treasure [money chest]" when Cornwallis's army arrived.[11]

Cornwallis had his army take up defensive positions on the perimeter of New Brunswick in anticipation of an assault by Washington's army. The Crown forces also began constructing log redoubts (small defensive emplacements) on the outskirts of the town to help secure it against an attack.

The situation on the morning of January 4 was much different at the American camp at Hillsborough. The previous night was cold, but the exhausted men found shelter in the village's houses and barns as well as its two taverns, two churches, and courthouse. The county jail was used to house the 200 Redcoats captured at Princeton.[12] Washington ordered commissaries to precede the troops to Hillsborough to notify the inhabitants of the army's approach and urged them to bring provisions to feed the troops. The local population cooperated and a large amount of food was waiting for the troops when they arrived.[13] Christian Foering was the pastor of the village's Dutch Church and a devoted patriot. He converted his church into a military hospital and helped to procure food for the army.[14] Washington established his headquarters at the Van Dorn family farmhouse (still standing) at the edge of town, where he spent the night.

The Grand Army continued its march to Morristown the following morning. The order of march leaving the village was organized in anticipation of any enemy attack and to guard the British soldiers captured at Princeton. The army left Hillsborough led by an advance guard that

The Hillsborough Dutch Reformed Church in present-day Millstone, New Jersey. Washington's army arrived at the village of Hillsborough (modern Millstone) on the night of January 3, 1777, following their victory at the Battle of Princeton. The army camped overnight in the village. The Dutch Reformed Church, located in the center of the village, was converted into a military hospital during the night. The original building was badly damaged during the brief British occupation of Hillsborough in June 1777 but was rebuilt after the war. The present church building dates from 1828. *Author's photo.*

The Van Dorn House, Hillsborough (modern Millstone), New Jersey. Washington spent the night of January 3, 1777, in this house following his victory at the Battle of Princeton. The house is privately owned. *Author's photo.*

was followed by the thirteen British officers captured at Princeton.[15] The Philadelphia Light Infantry was next in line, trailed by 194 captured common soldiers. They were guarded by the 190 riflemen of Colonel Edward Hand's regiment.[16] The enlisted prisoners were separated from their officers to help discourage an organized attempt to overpower their guards and escape. The prisoners were followed by the horse-drawn field artillery. Next in line were what was described as "the main column" of the army. These were the Continentals who had fought at Trenton and Princeton. The wagons loaded with equipment and provisions seized at Princeton were behind the main column. Bringing up the rear were "about one hundred cattle" captured from the British at Princeton. Typically the army's own baggage wagons carrying tents, blankets, ammunition, and provisions would have been in the line of march. But, these wagons with the army's baggage were sent to Burlington, New Jersey, on the night of January 2 when the army slipped away from Trenton and made a rapid overnight march to Princeton.[17]

The Grand Army with its prisoners and wagons followed the road north from Hillsborough and crossed the south branch of the meandering Raritan River at Van Veghten's bridge (located in modern Finderne). Washington halted his army at the bridge, where he held another council with his generals. At this point they were only ten miles west of New Brunswick. Adding to the temptation to march there was that there was a good road from Van Veghten's bridge to the crossroads village of Bound Brook, where there was a road leading to New Brunswick. But Washington and his generals agreed that it was too dangerous to attack New Brunswick, as spies had informed them that Cornwallis's army was there and on high alert. Instead, the army crossed Van Veghten's bridge and turned west, following the river as far as Tunison's Tavern (now the site of the Somerset Hotel in Somerville) where they turned north again and followed a road (today's Grove Street in Somerville) to Foothills Road that gradually climbed into the Watchung Mountains. The army marched ten miles that day before reaching the village of Pluckemin on the afternoon of January 4 and spent two days there camped in and around the village. Washington decided to remain in Pluckemin for two days to give the estimated 1,000 men who had fallen behind from fatigue and hunger to rejoin the main column.

The army was received with kindness by the people of the area. Farmers' wagons laden with provisions hurried to the relief of the men.[18] Several soldiers who camped in Pluckemin wrote accounts of their experience. Among them was the artist and militia lieutenant, Charles Willson Peale, who noted in his diary that "many of the men, in their hard march to Pluckemin on an icy road, were entirely barefooted."[19] Captain Thomas Rodney described how many of the troops "were obliged to encamp on the bleak mountains whose tops were covered with snow, without even blankets to cover them." Rodney said that at least they were, "well supplied with provisions."[20] After being well fed, the troops made copious campfires to warm themselves. Nineteenth-century historian Andrew Mellick described the first night of the army's encampment:

When night closed around Pluckemin's mountains, the ruddy glow of camp fires shone among the trees near the foot of its northern slopes.

The flames flashing up, illumined groups of soldiers, stacks of arms, and tethered horses; nearby, wagons, caissons and cannon were parked in military lines, while here and there the shadowy forms of sentinels could be distinguished. It was not long before the tired men were full-length at the foot of the trees, forgetting the travail of a soldier's life in needful sleep.[21]

Washington established his headquarters in Pluckemin at the home of John Fenner. The first full day that the army spent at Pluckemin was Sunday, January 5. It was the first opportunity that Washington had to write Congress with an account of everything that had transpired since he led his army from Trenton to Princeton. Writing from the Fenner house, Washington described how he marched "by a roundabout road to Princeton, where I knew they could not have much force left [*sic*] and might have stores [provisions and equipment]." Washington closed his letter with "I am just moving to Morristown" [to find shelter for the army] and "hitherto we have been without any and many of our poor soldier's quite bare foot and ill clad in other respects."[22] Having completed his dispatch, His Excellency instructed Captain James Henry to ride at once to Philadelphia and deliver it to John Hancock, the president of the Continental Congress.[23]

Later that Sunday, Washington participated in the funeral of British Army Captain William Leslie. Captain Leslie was buried "with the honors of war" in the graveyard of the old St. Paul's Lutheran Church in Pluckemin where his tombstone can be seen today.[24] An honor guard of forty American soldiers participated in the ceremony, which was also attended by generals Mifflin, Sullivan, and Knox as well as His Excellency General Washington.

After over 200 years, the circumstances of Captain Leslie's death continues to produce a multiplicity of stories. To appreciate the diversity of the accounts, here is what is known about Leslie. He was born in 1751 in Scotland, the second son of David Leslie, the Earl of Leven. According to the prevailing right of primogeniture, the earl's whole estate, including his property, passed to his eldest son upon his death. This left young William with no inheritance and few gentlemanly career options. One was to join

The gravestone of British Captain William Leslie in the graveyard of the present-day Pluckemin, New Jersey, Presbyterian Church. Leslie was either killed or mortally wounded during the January 3, 1777, Battle of Princeton and buried with military honors two days later in the village of Pluckemin as Washington's army retreated toward Morristown. *Author's photo.*

the army, using the advantage of his father's wealth and influence to arrange a commission for his son as an officer in a prestigious regiment. Thus, in 1771, William joined the 42nd Highland Regiment as an ensign. He transferred to the 17th Regiment in 1773 with the rank of lieutenant and was promoted to captain in February 1776. His regiment arrived in Boston from England on New Year's Day 1776. The regiment was later transferred to Staten Island where it joined General Howe's army. Once Howe's New York campaign began, Captain Leslie fought in the 1776 Battle of Long Island, the Battle of White Plains, and the attack on Fort Washington. His regiment was escorting supply wagons just outside of Princeton on the morning of January 3, 1777, when it was attacked by the American army. Leslie was badly wounded in the ensuing battle.

The great raconteur George Washington Parke Custis included an account of Leslie's capture at Princeton in his 1860 book, *Recollections and Private Memories of Washington*. His story begins with Washington riding through the fields where the Battle of Princeton took place and seeing some captured British soldiers gathered around a wounded officer. Custis wrote that Washington

> *reined up his horse when he saw the British soldiers supporting an officer and upon inquiring his name and rank, was answered, Captain Leslie. Doctor Benjamin Rush, who formed a part of the general's suite, earnestly asked, "A son of the Earl of Leven" to which the soldiers replied in the affirmative. The doctor then addressed the general-in-chief: "I beg your excellency to permit this wounded officer to be placed under my especial care, that I may return, in however small degree, a part of the obligations I owe to his worthy father the many kindnesses received at his hands while I was a student in Edinburgh." The request was immediately granted; but alas! poor Leslie was soon past all surgery. He died the same evening [in Hillsborough], after receiving every possible kindness and attention and was buried the next day in Pluckemin with the honors of war.[25]*

George Washington Parke Custis is correct; Dr. Benjamin Rush, a Pennsylvania member of the Continental Congress and signer of the Declaration of Independence, knew Captain William Leslie. Rush met William when Rush attended medical school at the University of Edinburgh from 1766 to 1768. While studying in Edinburgh he befriended the 7th Earl of Leven. Rush was a frequent guest of the Earl's estate called Melville in nearby Fife, where he befriended the earl's second oldest son, William.

But Benjamin Rush tells his own version of what happened to Captain Leslie. According to Rush, Princeton was occupied by the British Army in the days following the Battle of Princeton. Rush said that he went to Princeton on the day after the battle to attend to the badly wounded General Mercer. While in Princeton, Rush treated some of the British troops wounded during the fighting, including a British Army captain named James McPherson.[26] The officer asked, "are you Doctor Rush, Leslie's friend." Captain McPherson told Rush that Leslie was killed in the battle. Rush said that he was told that Leslie's body was thrown into a wagon and carried off when the American army retreated from Princeton. Leslie's corpse was found when the army arrived in Pluckemin. Rush described what happened next in his autobiography:

In his [Leslie's] pocket was found a letter from me, in which I had requested if the fortune of war should throw him into the hands of the American army, to show that letter to General Washington or General Lee, either of whom would, I expected indulge him in a parole to visit Philadelphia, where I begged he would make my house his home. This letter was carried to General Mifflin who obtained an order in consequence of it to bury him with the honors of war, in the church yard at Pluckemin. In the summer of 1777, I visited his grave and plucked a blade of grass from it, and at the end of the war placed a stone over it with an inscription designating his age, family, rank in the army and the time and manner of his death. I informed his sister, Lady Jane Belsches of this act in a letter several years afterwards. In her answer to this letter she says, "Why did you not send me that blade of grass? I would have preserved its verdure [freshness] forever with my tears."[27]

The tombstone that Rush wrote and paid for reads,

In memory of the Hon. Captain William Leslie of the 17th British Regiment, son of the Earl of Leven in Scotland. He fell January 3d, 1777, aged 26 years, at the battle of Princeton. His friend Benjamin Rush M.D. of Philadelphia, caused this stone to be erected as a mark of his esteem for his worth, and respect for his noble family.

The accounts of Captain Leslie's death by George Washington Parke Custis and Dr. Benjamin Rush are examples of how different stories of the young officer's death have been reported over the years. A sampling of some other accounts of Leslie's death are from historian Samuel Steele Smith, who claimed that Leslie died as the Grand Army was approaching Pluckemin on the afternoon of January 4 and was buried the next day. Another was published by James P. Snell in 1881. Mr. Snell said that Leslie died on the porch of an inn after the army arrived in Pluckemin.[28]

British General Alexander Leslie was Lord Leven's half-brother. General Leslie wrote several letters to the Leven family describing young William's death. According to General Leslie, William died in the arms of his servant Peter McDonald during the Battle of Princeton. Sparse on details, General Leslie wrote that "a General Mifflin found the cart the body was in... his body was carried to Pluckemin and there interred with all military honors by order of General Washington."[29] Captain Leslie is also depicted in John Trumbull's painting, *The Death of General Mercer at the Battle of Princeton.* Trumbull shows Captain Leslie lying dead on the ground on the lower right side of the painting.

But that is not the end of Captain Leslie's story. The tombstone that Benjamin Rush had made stood for nearly sixty years before it weathered to a point where the inscription was difficult to read. In 1835, Professor John D. Ogilby of Rutgers College (now Rutgers University) visited Scotland where he met David Leslie-Melville, the 8th Earl of Leven. The Earl inquired about his ancestor's grave. Upon his return to New Jersey, Professor Ogilby found the burial site and wrote the Earl describing the tombstone's poor condition. The Earl paid for a new tombstone to be made with Dr. Rush's original inscription.[30]

The old graveyard next to what is now the Pluckemin Presbyterian Church includes a number of men who fought in the American Revolution. But Leslie's tombstone stands out from the rest, not because it is bigger than the others, but it is the only soldier's grave marked with both a British and an American flag.

The Grand Army's stay in Pluckemin ended on Monday morning, January 6. Peale's entry for January 6 said that the army left Pluckemin that day and marched "through a very mountainous country, about twelve miles to Morristown."[31]

Washington spent almost five months in Morristown. The Grand Army wintered in Morristown from January 6 to May 28, 1777. Morristown was described as "a very clever little village situated in a most beautiful valley."[32] The valley (today's Washington Valley) where the village was located was encircled by mountains with few roads into the region. Morristown was described as a natural fortification—easy to defend and difficult to attack. An additional incentive for the Grand Army to winter at Morristown was that many of the region's people were of Scottish descent who supported the rebellion. Later known as the "Scotch-Irish," they came to America from Scotland and Ireland during the half-century preceding the American Revolution, seeking religious freedom and land. They included a large number of persecuted and exploited tenant farmers from Ulster Province in Ireland. By the time they arrived in New Jersey, the desirable level farmland bordering the colony's rivers was owned by earlier Dutch and English immigrants. It forced the so-called Scotch-Irish to settle in the less attractive mountainous northern region of New Jersey surrounding Morristown. Although their farms were smaller than those of New Jersey's fertile river valleys, the area surrounding Morristown was a farming region that could at least partially supply the Grand Army with food while denying victuals to the enemy. The supply of farm produce and livestock near Morristown was in stark contrast to the farms of central New Jersey, which had been picked clean by both armies in 1776.[33]

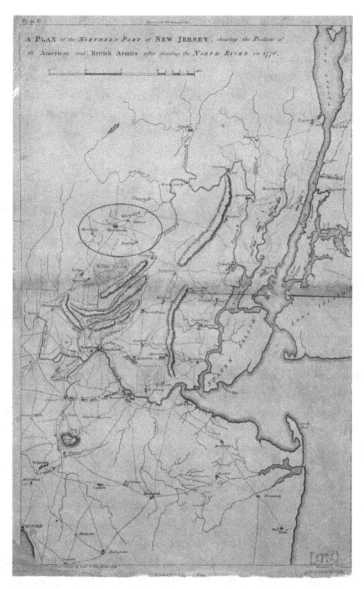

A Plan of the Northern Part of New Jersey. This map of northern New Jersey appears in the atlas that accompanies the American edition of John Marshall's *Life of George Washington*. Marshall, a staunch Federalist, published his five-volume Washington biography from 1805 to 1807. The atlas was published in 1807. The area around Morristown has been circled to show its location. *Author's collection.*

Morristown had about fifty buildings and a population of 250 people surrounding a spacious village green when the Grand Army arrived there. The adjacent forests provided abundant firewood for the army, and the Whippany River supplied the area with fresh water. Morristown was the largest town in Morris County and its county seat. Prominent buildings in the town in 1777 included the courthouse with a jail, two taverns, and two churches located around a village green. One of the largest houses in the area was owned by Jacob Ford. Jacob's house, which was situated on his 200-acre estate, was known locally as "the Great White House at the far side of town."[34] However, it is best known as the Ford Mansion. Colonel Ford owned local iron forges and gristmills, and his stature in the community and support of the Revolution resulted in his appointment as the colonel and commander of the Eastern Battalion of the Morris County militia. Captain Thomas Rodney's Delaware Company stayed at the house after they arrived in Morristown. They probably got this coveted invitation because their commander, Thomas Rodney, was the younger brother of Caesar Rodney, who was a member of the Continental Congress. Colonel Ford was ill when Rodney's company arrived at his house. While Colonel Ford was suffering in an upstairs bedroom, his son Gabriel recalled that some of Rodney's officers "were gentlemen by birth, but rowdies in practice. They damaged a downstairs room very much by their nightly carousals."[35] Ford, who was thirty-six years old at the time, died of pneumonia at his home on January 10. His death was a devastating loss to his wife and five children. Washington ordered Rodney to provide Colonel Ford with a military funeral. Rodney had a subordinate perform the funeral since Ford was only a militia officer. Rodney's company continued to live in the house until their enlistments were up and they went home.[36]

Perhaps the largest public building in the village was Jacob Arnold's Tavern (moved in 1918, used as a hospital and later burned down), located on the northwest corner of the village green. It was a three-story building where Washington established his headquarters. He occupied the second floor, which was reserved for army business and his private quarters. Washington was security minded and would not have conducted official business in any public area of the tavern.

Martha Washington joined her husband in Morristown in the middle of March. General Greene wrote to his wife following Martha's arrival at headquarters, "Mrs. Washington is excessive fond of the general and he of her. They are happy in each other." Officers and aides welcomed Martha's presence in camp. Her husband's mood softened and his spirits improved when she was with him.[37] Martha stayed in Morristown until May 12, 1777, when she departed for Philadelphia accompanied by Washington's aide, Colonel Tench Tilghman.[38]

Because of its small size, the village could only provide housing for the army's senior officers. While their specific lodgings are not known, officers were mentioned living in the homes owned by the Ely, Smith, Beach, and Thompson families. General Greene said that he billeted at the home of a "Mr Hoffman—a very good natured-man."

Most of the small army that wintered in Morristown occupied houses and barns throughout the region. This actually helped hide how few soldiers Washington had with him in Morristown. A detachment of troops were quartered four miles east of Morristown at a place called Bottle Hill (now Madison) to guard the road leading to Morristown from Newark and Elizabeth. Approaching Morristown from the east was particularly difficult due to swamps surrounding Bottle Hill and the Watchung Mountains that stretched for thirty miles from the Raritan River to the south to the northern border of New Jersey. The mountains continued north into New York State where they were called the Ramapos. There was one pass through the mountains near the border between New Jersey and New York, called Sidman's Cove or the Clove (from the Dutch word kloove, meaning a cut or gash in the earth). The Clove was a narrow road in the Ramapo River valley that ran south from Suffern, New York, to the village of Pompton (present-day Pompton Lakes) in northern New Jersey.[39] The French Army commanded by the Comte de Rochambeau travelled through the Clove in 1781 en route to Yorktown. You can travel through the Clove today on New Jersey Route 202.

Washington's decision to take his army to Morristown after the Battle of Princeton was not a desperate gamble or last-minute idea. He had probably been planning to go there even as he was organizing his Christmas Day attack on Trenton.

The first known indication that Washington was thinking about eventually taking his army to Morristown appeared in a lengthy letter he wrote to Congress from Pennsylvania on December 20, 1776. Washington began his letter explaining that he believes that "the design of General Howe is to possess himself of Philadelphia this winter, if possible, and in truth, I do not see what is to prevent him, as ten days more will put an end to the existence of our army." Washington continued describing his desperate situation and listed the troops that were on their way to reinforce him. The general told Congress that he needed every soldier to join him, but at the same time he noted that he had ordered "the three regiments from Ticonderoga to halt at Morristown." Washington added that he understood that about 800 New Jersey militia were already in Morristown.[40] The three regiments, totaling 550 officers and enlisted men, were Continental Army units from Massachusetts.[41] Their commander was Colonel Joseph Vose who was in Peekskill, New York, when he received the order to go to Morristown.[42] A further indication that Washington was contemplating taking the Grand Army to Morristown after they entered New Jersey was his order to Brigadier General William Maxwell on December 21 to "repair immediately" to Morristown to take command of Vose's 550 troops and the New Jersey militiamen assembled there.[43] Maxwell was a hard-living New Jersey bachelor who was born in County Tyrone in Ulster Province, Ireland. He was called "Scotch Willie" during the Revolution because of his family's Scottish origins and his strong Scottish accent. Maxwell was an experienced and resourceful combat officer whose military career began as a provincial officer during the French and Indian war. He joined the Continental Army early in the revolution and led New Jersey troops in the failed 1775–1776 Canadian campaign. Ordering an officer of Maxwell's experience to Morristown shows the importance that Washington placed on securing the village as an American military base. Maxwell was also a good choice for the assignment, as it was hoped that he would be able to rally his fellow northern New Jersey Scotch-Irish neighbors to join him at Morristown.

Just when Washington first recognized the military advantages of Morristown is open to speculation. He first visited Morristown in 1773, two years before the start of the Revolution, when he passed through the village en route to visit with William Alexander, Lord Stirling, in nearby Basking Ridge.[44] It is possible that Washington first understood the military advantages of Morristown when his army was camped in Newark for five days during the Long Retreat in late November 1776. He could not only see the mountains sheltering Morristown from Newark but, according to historian Washington Irving, some of his officers urged him to take the army there.[45] Another possibility was that General Charles Lee stopped in Morristown on his way to reinforce Washington in Pennsylvania. Lee wrote to Washington describing the advantage of operating from Morristown. Historian Dave Palmer attributes Washington's interest in Morristown to Lee: "Charles Lee, in his march through the hills of northern New Jersey [the area surrounding Morristown], had pointed out the value of holding a position there."[46] Henry Knox is also cited as recommending Morristown to General Washington as a favorable site for winter quarters. Knox reconnoitered the village in early December 1776 while travelling through northern New Jersey en route to join the Grand Army in Pennsylvania.[47] General James Grant, the senior British Army officer in New Jersey, also saw the advantages of Morristown as a military base. From his headquarters in New Brunswick, Grant recommended stationing two infantry regiments at Morristown. Grant made the request on December 22, 1776, to General Howe in New York, who approved the "expedition to Morristown" on December 24. But the operation was scrapped in the crisis that followed Washington's December 26 attack on Trenton.[48] Grant later joined Cornwallis's army when it marched to retake Trenton, leaving British General Edward Mathew to defend New Brunswick with 700 troops.[49]

Regardless of the source, Washington taking his army to Morristown following the Battle of Princeton was an intelligent move. British General James Grant wrote a letter to a friend in England on January 15, 1777, which included his summary of the status of the war in America: "Washington has taken post at Morris Town where we cannot get at him."[50]

Washington arrived at Morristown in January 1777 following his impressive Trenton-Princeton campaign that restored his reputation and saved the rebellion. But it was a miracle that he had managed to survive the fighting during 1776. Some Patriots attributed Washington's survival to providential intervention, but others were more realistic and realized that his opponent, General Sir William Howe, had failed to finish off Washington's army when he had it trapped.

General Howe arrived in America in May 1775 with impressive military experience. His older brother, Admiral Lord Richard Howe, was an equally skillful officer. Besides their experience, they had the advantage of cooperation between the British Army and the Royal Navy throughout 1776. This was not the case at other times during the war when the army and navy commanders were at odds with each other. What saved Washington during 1776 was not a miracle, luck, or divine intervention, but rather that his opponents, General Sir William Howe and Admiral Lord Richard Howe, were cautious and meticulous planners. They were reluctant to take any risks, which allowed Washington to slip away when they had him cornered.

Some people at the time went further in their criticism of the Howe brothers. They believed that General Howe in particular was inept and lazy. One fellow British officer, for example, said that Howe's "behavior at Bunker Hill evinced much personal gallantry, but he had no military genius, and he loved his ease."[51] General Charles Lee, who claimed he knew Howe before the American War, called him "indolent [lazy], badly educated and a poor thinker." Lee summed up his assessment of Howe in stinging words: "He shut his eyes, fought his battles, drank his bottle, had his little whore, advised with his counsellors, received his orders from North and Germain, (one more absurd than the other), took Galloway's opinion, shut his eyes, fought again."[52] Lee's mention of Howe's "little whore" is a reference to twenty-five-year-old Elizabeth Loring, described as a "blue eyed flashing blonde" who was Howe's mistress. "Galloway's opinion" is an allusion to Joseph Galloway. He was a prominent Philadelphia lawyer, Pennsylvania delegate to the First Continental Congress (1774), and a confidant of Benjamin Franklin. Galloway was opposed to American independence and he defected to the British in late 1776. He became an important advisor to General Howe, but later turned against him and became one of Sir William's severest critics for failing to aggressively pursue the war. The Patriots mocked his running off to join the enemy by calling him "Joseph Gallop-away." More details will follow about Elizabeth Loring and Joseph Galloway, two minor but fascinating characters from the Revolutionary War.

The Howe brothers' first missed opportunity to rout Washington's army in 1776 began on the afternoon of August 27. It will be recalled that on that date Howe stealthily maneuvered 10,000 troops behind the rebel defenses on Gowanus Heights as the opening phase of what became known as the Battle of Long Island. Howe's outflanking movement reflected the military thinking of the time, which was to avoid a general engagement with its inevitable high casualties and instead to try to outmaneuver an opponent into retreating or surrendering. Washington is faulted for allowing the British to outflank his defenses on Long Island. Commenting on Washington's reconnaissance failure on Long Island, historian Edward Lengel said, "The possibility of a British movement there should have been obvious, yet he had only the haziest conception of Long Island's terrain."[53]

In the ensuing Battle of Long Island, the surviving American troops on Long Island fled in terror to their forts and redoubts on Brooklyn Heights. Washington then made the mistake of sending reinforcement from Manhattan to Brooklyn Heights instead of evacuating the position. There were 9,000 Patriot troops on Brooklyn Heights by the afternoon of August 29, representing half of Washington's army. The Crown forces facing the rebel defenses on Brooklyn Heights wanted to attack, but General Howe demurred. At the same time, Admiral Howe failed to blockade the East River to prevent the rebels from escaping across the river to American-held New York City. Had Admiral Howe been more aggressive, he could have ordered a few boats to the mouth of the East River on the night of August 29 to watch for any attempt by the rebels to retreat across the river. The admiral had several small maneuverable ships in his fleet anchored in New York's Upper Bay, including the brig HMS *Halifax* mounting six guns, or the sloop HMS *Swan* with fourteen guns.[54] He could have towed one of these small ships into position to stop the rebel retreat even if the wind and currents were not favorable. The rebel gun batteries on Brooklyn Heights would not have fired on the British ships with their own boats ferrying troops across the river. Besides, the rebels' artillerists were particularly poorly trained for hitting a small target. The point is that Admiral Howe should have done something to blockade the East River. As a result of the Howes' laxity, Washington managed to evacuate all of his 9,000 men from Brooklyn Heights to Manhattan on the night of August 29.

Allowing half of Washington's army to escape from Brooklyn Heights resulted in Admiral Lord Howe being harshly censured. Among his enraged critics was Israel Mauduit. He was a wealthy London draper [a dealer in cloth] who published pamphlets criticizing British management of the American War. Mauduit published a pamphlet during the war titled "Three Letters to Lord Viscount Howe" [Admiral Lord Richard Howe]. Mauduit wrote,

> *After the defeat at Long Island, when Washington and his army lay at your mercy, and you might have them all prisoners; you seem to have been as little disposed to intercept them at sea, as the General [Howe] was at land. He [General Howe] gave them three days leisure to prepare for their flight over to New York; and you for nine tides kept your fleet out of sight of the [East River] Ferry, as if you intended they should not be intercepted in their passage.*[55]

The Loyalist Thomas Jones, whose elegant Long Island home was ransacked by the Patriots during the war, had a different explanation for the Howes' inaction. Jones, who was forced to leave America during the war, claimed that Howe purposely allowed the rebels to escape to keep the war going so he could continue to embezzle money for himself and his sycophants from the British Treasury:

> *the almighty powers and patronage of the Commander-in-Chief [General Howe] to be continued, that Quartermasters, Barracks-masters, Commissaries, &c. might enrich themselves by amassing large fortunes out of the public. They became nabobs [Europeans who made a fortune in India] of the West, and became equally rich with those of the East. Had half the pains been taken to suppress the*

American rebellion, as there was to drain the British Treasury of its cash... it would have crushed [the] rebellion.[56]

Next, in September 1776, General Howe failed to move quickly to cut off 4,000 rebels from escaping from New York City to Harlem Heights during the Battle of Kips Bay.

Another example of Howe bungling a golden opportunity to rout Washington's army was when Howe ordered Cornwallis not to pursue Washington beyond New Brunswick during the November 1776 Long Retreat. Jäger Corps Captain Johann Ewald was with Cornwallis in New Jersey and wrote in his diary, "why did we not pursue the enemy at once, instead of lingering here [New Brunswick] for five days?" Ewald said that Joseph Galloway was so enraged by the delay in New Brunswick that he heard Galloway say in a loud voice, "I see, they don't want to finish the war!"[57]

Next, after arriving in Trenton, Howe could have built boats, rafts, or a pontoon bridge to pursue Washington's army across the Delaware. The British engineers with Howe knew how to build pontoon bridges using boats covered with wooden planks to create a roadbed. Building a pontoon bridge across the Delaware was not a silly idea. Pontoon bridges date from ancient times, and their use includes a pontoon bridge built by an English army across France's Oise River in 1441. In fact, the British Army built several pontoon bridges during the American Revolution, including one across the Arthur Kill between Staten Island and Elizabeth Point. The technique included sending a detachment of troops across a river to establish a beachhead in enemy territory and then building the bridge behind them. British Army engineers were trained on building pontoon bridges. In fact, Joseph Galloway said that Captain John Montresor, the chief British Army engineer with Howe's army, asked him to report on the materials available in Trenton to build boats, rafts, or pontoon bridges. Galloway said that he told Montresor that he found 48,000 feet of boards in the village.[58] There were also John Rickey's hardware store and two blacksmith shops in Trenton from which the British could have acquired all the nails, wire, and iron necessary to build a pontoon bridge. Thomas Jones said that he was told "by a gentleman of the first character" that there

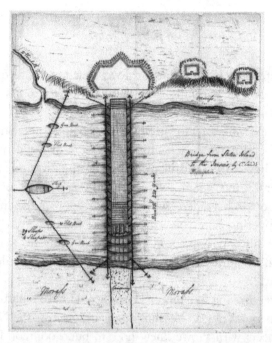

This illustration shows a pontoon bridge that British Army engineers constructed in 1780 across the Arthur Kill between Staten Island and New Jersey. On the left side of the illustration, the engineers constructed a barrier to prevent enemy fire ships or fire rafts from reaching the bridge. The British had the know-how and materials to build a pontoon bridge across the Delaware River in late 1776 after they arrived in Trenton, New Jersey. But there is no known evidence that General Howe attempted to follow Washington's beleaguered army into Pennsylvania by constructing a pontoon bridge across the Delaware. *Published with the permission of the William L. Clements Library, University of Michigan.*

was a yard filled with boards directly behind the house that General Howe was using as his headquarters in Trenton.[59] Failing all else, the invaders could have torn down some of Trenton's one hundred wooden houses for lumber. In addition, there were boats on the Raritan River that could have been transported to Trenton. But Howe did nothing except stare across the Delaware River for a few days and ride back to New York City.

Some chroniclers of the American Revolution have a different explanation for General Sir William Howe's lack of initiative when he reached Trenton: that winter was approaching, and the general wanted to return to the pleasant social life of New York City.

After returning to New York, Sir William established a ninety-mile-long chain of winter cantonments extending from New York City to Trenton. In a blistering criticism of the arrangement, Joseph Galloway said Howe "discovered no more military judgement than he had shown vigor in pursuing his enemy." Galloway said that Sir William divided the troops wintering in New Jersey "into small distant parties, liable to be cut off by the enemy, one after another." Focusing on Trenton, he called the town a "frontier post... nearest to the enemy." Putting Colonel Rall in command at Trenton was another mistake. Galloway called Rall a foreigner "who could not understand the language of the country." He was "brave but totally unfit for his situation. He was obstinate, passionate and incessantly intoxicated."[60]

But all of these examples of the Howe brothers' lost opportunity pale in comparison with the opportunity the Howe brothers had to cut off the retreat of Washington's Grand Army as it crossed New Jersey in late 1776. The story of this golden opportunity begins with Admiral Lord Howe's interest in seizing Aquidneck Island in Rhode Island. The seaport town of Newport was located on the island, and Lord Howe wanted to use it as a Royal Navy base. After conferring with his younger brother, they agreed that besides its excellent harbor, Newport would be useful for launching a campaign into New England as well as patrolling the nearby waters, which were infested with rebel privateers sailing out of New England ports. These privateers were attacking British merchant ships heading for New York City with cargoes of provisions and military stores. Also influencing their decision was their belief that they could spare the ships and troops to seize Newport following their successful campaign to occupy New York City.

Admiral Howe gave the order to Commodore Sir Peter Parker on November 23 to organize the Newport mission "while the season may still permit."[61] By December 1, 1776, Parker had assembled a fleet of one hundred transports, fourteen warships, and 6,000 troops in New York City. The troops were aboard the transports and the fleet was ready to sail. On that same date, Washington's army was in New Brunswick and retreating across New Jersey toward the Delaware River. General Henry Clinton was in command of the British troops bound for Newport. Clinton saw the opportunity to divert the Newport fleet to trap Washington's army in New Jersey. Clinton's reasoning was that it took only one day to sail from New York City to Perth Amboy, New Jersey, which was situated at the mouth of the Raritan River. British troops could be landed there and march overland ten miles on a good road to New Brunswick. Or, smaller ocean-going warships and transports could navigate the Raritan River to New Brunswick. An even more ambitious and plausible plan was to redirect the Newport invasion fleet to sail up the Delaware River, capture weakly defended Philadelphia, and encircle Washington's army between the Delaware and Raritan Rivers. Clinton proposed diverting the Rhode Island ships and troops to General Howe; "I should be landed at Amboy, and endeavor to intercept Washington in his retreat to the Delaware."[62] Other British officers besides Clinton saw the opportunity to trap the Grand Army in New Jersey, including Captain Frederick Mackenzie. His diary entry for November 15, 1776, read that once Fort Washington and Fort Lee were taken, General Howe could trap Washington by "penetrating into that Province [New Jersey] toward Philadelphia. If at the same time, a force was landed at Amboy, and a fleet with troops could be sent into the Delaware."[63] Thomas Jones also recognized the golden opportunity, writing, "Had the army, consisting of 6,000 effective men, instead of being sent upon the Don Quixote expedition to Rhode Island, penetrated the Jerseys by way of Amboy, and formed a junction with Lord Cornwallis at Brunswick, Washington's army must have been ruined, the conquest of New Jersey and Pennsylvania insured."[64]

Even Thomas Paine mentioned the opportunity Sir William had to trap Washington's army when it was retreating across New Jersey. In the *American Crisis Number One*, published on December 23, 1776, Paine wrote, "General Howe, in my opinion, committed a great error in generalship, in not throwing a body of forces off from Staten Island through Amboy, by which means he might have... seized all our stores in Brunswick and intercepted our march into Pennsylvania."

But the Howe brothers were not interested in such a daring move and ordered Clinton to sail for Newport. The town surrendered to

Clinton's awesome force on December 8, 1776, without firing a gun. The British occupied Newport for three years. It served no purpose other than eventually tying up 4,000 British troops and the capture of its commanding officer, Brigadier General Richard Prescott, by the rebels on the night of July 9, 1777. They carried off Prescott dressed only in his nightshirt and traded him for General Charles Lee.

There are other explanations for General Howe's restraint during 1776. They include the theory that Howe purposely avoided badly beating Washington's Grand Army so that they would continue fighting, seeking revenge instead of negotiating a treaty to end the war. Another idea was that the Howe brothers were empowered as peacemakers and thrashed the Americans just enough to show them the futility of their rebellion and end the war as heroes in a negotiated peace. There was also the plausible explanation that General Howe was leery of attacking entrenched rebels based on his experience at Bunker Hill earlier in the war. Commenting on this subject, Continental Army officer Henry (Light Horse Harry) Lee wrote in his memoirs of the war that at Bunker Hill, "the sad and impressive experience of this murderous day sunk deep into the mind of Sir William Howe, and it seems to have its influence, on all his subsequent operations, with decisive control."[65] The thinking was that Howe avoided any situation where his army could suffer high casualties. Writing almost 200 years after Light Horse Harry Lee's observation, British historian Sir George Otto Trevelyan gave a similar but more straightforward explanation for Howe's conduct: "he was destined to lose more than one opportunity of decisive victory by an unwillingness to risk his men's lives, and his own fame against an entrenchment with American riflemen behind it."[66]

General Howe mentioned his reluctance to attack the rebels trapped in Brooklyn Heights when questioned in 1779 by members of the House of Commons. Calling American-held Brooklyn Heights "dangerous ground," Sir William said, "to have permitted the attack in question, would have been inconsiderate, and even criminal. The loss of 1,000, or perhaps 1,500 British troops, in carrying those lines, would have been but ill repaid by double that number of the enemy."[67]

Staunch Loyalist Thomas Jones, who claimed he was never protected by the British Army during the war, elaborated on his belief that Howe let the rebels escape from Brooklyn Heights to keep the war going as a money-making scam. According to Jones, "The General's favorites were not yet sufficiently enriched; the rebellion was to be nursed, the General to continue in command, and his friends, flatterers, mistresses and sycophants to be provided for."[68]

But of all the explanations for Howe's indolence during 1776, none is as interesting as the idea that Howe was preoccupied by his sultana, Elizabeth Loring. Elizabeth Lloyd Loring was born on October 15, 1752, on Long Island, New York. Her parents, Nathaniel and Elizabeth Lloyd, died when Elizabeth was a child and she was raised by her kinsman Dr. James Lloyd. Elizabeth married Joshua Loring, Jr. on October 19, 1769 in Boston. The couple established their home in Dorchester, Massachusetts, where Loring served as the royal governor's appointed county sheriff. Loring was a zealous Loyalist, and he fled to the protection of the British Army in Boston in 1774 with his wife and two children. Elizabeth was twenty-four years old when General William Howe arrived in Boston in 1775. She was described as a flirtatious "flashing beauty" who got the attention of the forty-five-year-old general. Joshua Loring and his family left Boston with the British Army in March 1776 for the Royal Navy base in Halifax, Nova Scotia. After spending several months in Halifax, Howe sailed for New York City, which he seized from the rebels in September 1776. The Lorings came to New York following the British occupation of the city where Howe was soon socializing with Joshua Loring and his beautiful young wife. Howe became infatuated with Elizabeth, who shared his love of high-stakes gambling, drinking, theater performances, and elaborate dinner parties. Joshua Loring was interested in money, and Howe was smitten with his beautiful wife. Howe's scheme was to appoint Joshua as Commissary of Prisoners for New York to bribe him to be circumspect in his torrid affair with his spirited wife. The big enticement for Joshua was that the commissary of prisoners had a discretionary budget to feed the thousands of captured American soldiers imprisoned in New York. Howe and his army cronies let Loring steal money from the prisoner's fund for his complicity in his wife's affair. As a result, Loring was starving the American prisoners and according to one observer, "The consummate cruelties practiced on the American prisoners... exceed the ordinary powers of human invention."[69] Thomas Jones summed up the unsavory situation saying, "Joshua [Loring] made no objections... he fingered the cash and the General enjoyed madam."[70] Completing the depraved arrangement was that Frances Connolly, Howe's wife, was 3,000 miles away in England.

Thomas Jones was among those who wondered if Howe was more interested in carousing with Elizabeth Loring then he was in defeating George Washington. Jones said, "Mrs. Loring, who, as Cleopatra of old lost Mark Antony the world, so did this illustrious courtesan lose Sir William Howe the honor, the laurels, and the glory of putting an end to one of the most obstinate rebellions that ever existed."[71]

Loyalist Nicholas Cresswell also thought that Howe was too preoccupied with his mistress to fight the rebels. Cresswell mentioned his anxiety in his diary, asking when "Howe shall think proper to leave Mrs. Lorain [sic] and face them."[72] It was even speculated that Howe was purposely holding back on defeating the rebels so he could continue the war and his affair with his playful, blue-eyed, blonde mistress.

The gossip of Howe's preoccupation with Elizabeth Loring became common knowledge, especially when she accompanied Sir William during the 1777 Philadelphia campaign. Their liaison was even publicized in satirical poems. Here is an example, titled "Addressed to Sir William Howe in the Spring" that is reproduced in its entirety. It was anonymously published during the war:

Awake, arouse, Sir Billy,
There's Forage in the plain,
Ah! Leave your little filly
And open the campaign.
Heed not a woman's prattle,
Which tickles in the ear,
But give the word for battle,
And grasp the warlike spear,
Behold each soldier panting
For glory, and renown,

To them no spur is wanting,
March, and the day's your own.
Such troops had Alexander,
Two worlds, he would subdue,
For with a bold Commander
They'd conquer old and new.[73]

Another reference to General Howe's affair appeared in a poem by Francis Hopkinson in 1778 titled "The Battle of the Kegs."

Sir William, he snug as a flea,
Lay all this time a snoring
Nor dreamed of harm, as he lay warm
In bed with Mrs. Loring.[74]

The May 14, 1777, issue of the *Pennsylvania Gazette* printed a poem that included an allusion to Howe's liaison with Elizabeth Loring. The poem is about the British raid on the American supply depot at Danbury, Connecticut. Here is the passage from the poem's first stanza:

Without wit, without wisdom, half stupid and drunk,
And rolling along arm in arm with his punk,
The gallant Sir William, who fights all by proxy,
Thus spoke to his soldiers, held up by his doxy.[75]

Elizabeth Loring's affair with Sir William continued for two years. It abruptly ended when the general resigned his command in the spring of 1778 and returned to England. Elizabeth emigrated to England soon after, but apparently had no further contact with Howe. Meanwhile, Joshua Loring remained in New York where he continued to embezzle money as the commissary of prisoners until 1782 when he was finally discharged from his position for corruption. He then went to England where he was reunited with his wife and settled down on an estate with the fortune he made during the war. However, Joshua was soon tried and convicted of embezzlement. He died penniless in 1789. Elizabeth applied for a pension from the British government, which was granted. She died in 1831.

Looking back, Washington's survival in 1776 was not a matter of divine providence or good luck, but the cautious pursuit of the war by Admiral Lord Howe and his brother General Sir William Howe. Both men were competent commanders in a war that required brilliant and aggressive leaders.

As for Washington, he enjoyed one piece of good luck during 1776. It was the capture of General Charles Lee by the British. It happened on Friday, December 13, 1776, which historian Thomas Fleming called the luckiest Friday the 13th in American history. Lee was a dangerous man, and his activities in late 1776 and his fortunate capture for the Americans is told in the next chapter of this narrative.

The measured pace of the fighting in 1776 saved Washington. He was given the opportunity by his opponents to learn from his experiences and correct his mistakes. In 1776 Washington was the bewildered fox that managed to slip away from his indolent pursuers, but starting in 1777, he was the elusive fox who hunted from his lair in the mountains of New Jersey with cunning and speed. As we shall see, the culmination came when Washington advanced south from Morristown in late May 1777 to the crest of the Watchung Mountains, goading Howe to waste weeks of good campaigning weather trying to entice Washington into a battle so he could attack Philadelphia by crossing New Jersey.

3

Castled Among the Heights*

It seemed that everyone was desperately searching for General Charles Lee in late November 1776. They included His Excellency George Washington, Lord Charles Cornwallis, General Sir William Howe, and the members of the Continental Congress. In fact, a compelling reason for Cornwallis's cautious pursuit of Washington's army as it retreated across New Jersey in late 1776 was Cornwallis's fear that Lee's corps, reported to be 7,500 men, would attack his column or cut off his supply line that stretched all the way back to New York City.

To understand the difficulty in finding Lee in late November 1776, it is advantageous to go back to the council of war that Washington convened at White Plains, New York, on November 6, 1776. Washington called the meeting with his generals in response to the unexpected movement of General Howe's army toward the Hudson River town of Dobbs Ferry in Westchester County, New York. Washington told his officers during their meeting that he believed that Howe's move was in preparation to cross the Hudson River and invade Patriot-held New Jersey. The Virginian based his conclusion on the interrogation of prisoners and deserters by his headquarters staff. The officers attending the council agreed with Washington's assessment, and His Excellency

---

* Chapter title from Washington Irving, *Life of George Washington*, 5 vols. (New York: Charles T. Evans, 1856–1859), vol. 3:2.

decided to personally lead part of his army across the Hudson River to help defend New Jersey. Washington decided to take all the troops who came from states south of the Hudson River with him to New Jersey. The total accompanying Washington was 3,566 officers and private soldiers present and fit for duty, based on a November 3, 1776, strength report.[1] It was a relatively small number of men but Washington anticipated being reinforced when he reached New Jersey by the troops stationed at Fort Washington and Fort Lee, the balance of the Flying Camp, and the deployment of the New Jersey militia. At the same council it was agreed that Major General William Heath would be assigned 3,000 troops from the Grand Army to guard the strategic mid-section of the Hudson River Valley known as the Hudson Highlands. The largest town in the region was Peekskill, New York. Heath's job was to safeguard the Continental Army supply depots in the area and man the three Patriot forts in the Highlands that defended the Hudson River.[2] Washington subsequently decided to leave the largest portion of the Grand Army, amounting to 7,500 troops, at North Castle under the command of Major General Charles Lee. Lee's corps were left at North Castle to guard against a possible attack by Howe aimed at Connecticut and Massachusetts as well as being ready to move to join Washington or Heath once the enemy's intentions became clear. Washington's decision to split his army in the face of a superior enemy force was not sound military judgement, but the rationale was that Lee was just one day's march from reinforcing Heath at Peekskill and two days from reaching northern New Jersey.

Washington made his intention clear in a November 10 missive to Lee titled "Instructions to Major General Charles Lee," which included the following critical passage, "If the enemy should remove the whole or the greatest part of their force, to the west side of Hudson's River [New Jersey], I have no doubt of your following with all possible dispatch, leaving the militia and invalids to cover the frontiers of Connecticut."[3]

Note that Washington gave Lee instructions and not an order to reinforce him if necessary. The reason for Washington's ambiguity was his high regard for Lee's military prowess. Washington admired Lee and, though he was Lee's superior, the Virginian treated Lee with deference to the point of being reluctant to give him a direct order.

Howe finally revealed his plans when he moved south from Dobbs Ferry to attack Fort Washington which he did on November 16. His foreseen invasion of New Jersey under the command of Lord Cornwallis followed on the night of November 19. Washington was in serious trouble by the afternoon of November 20 as he was helping to guide the panic-stricken garrison of Fort Lee to safety before the British overran the place. Fortunately, Washington had prepared for a British invasion of New Jersey by instructing General Lee to be ready to cross the Hudson with his 7,500 men to meet the threat. Washington promptly implemented his plan by instructing his aide, William Grayson, to write an urgent note to General Lee to vacate North Castle and head for New Jersey with his corps. Grayson knew of Washington's reverence for Lee and composed his note accordingly. After describing the British landing north of Fort Lee, Grayson concluded his message by saying, "His Excellency thinks it would be advisable in you to remove the troops under your command on this side of the North River and there wait for further orders."[4] A dispatch rider raced off with Grayson's message, which Lee received the following day. Upon receipt of Grayson's urgent message, Lee took immediate action—but not as expected. Instead of heading for New Jersey, he penned a letter to James Bowdoin, president of the Massachusetts Provincial Congress's executive council. In his letter Lee created two armies for Bowdoin, saying that his corps was separate and independent of Washington's. Lee's exact words were, "it was my opinion that the two armies—that on the east and that on the west side of North River—must rest each on its own bottom; that the idea of detaching and reinforcing from one side to the other, on every motion of the enemy was chimerical." Lee played on Bowdoin's fear of a British invasion of New England by suggesting that the enemy may "alter the present direction of their operations" and their main attack was aimed at New England.[5] With this letter, Lee was laying the groundwork for pressure from the Massachusetts Provincial Congress to retain his corps in North Castle to defend New England. Lee's game was that he led the largest independent command in the Patriot army, and he was not going to give it up by joining Washington in New Jersey.

But Lee still had to act on Washington's urgent dispatch. What he did was write to General Heath in Peekskill stating that he "had just received a recommendation, not a positive order from the General to move the corps under my command to the other side of the river." Lee told Heath that it would be faster if Heath sent 2,000 troops from Peekskill across the Hudson "to apprize the General and wait his further orders." Lee promised that he would replace the 2,000 men "as soon as we have finished a necessary job."[6]

William Heath (1737–1814) was a prewar Massachusetts farmer and militia officer. It is worth knowing more about Heath as he became entangled in Lee's plot to avoid joining Washington in New Jersey. Heath described himself as a "New Englander of old stock." He mentioned having no notable formal education and boasted that he lived his entire life on his Roxbury (present-day Jamaica Plains section of Boston), Massachusetts, farm which was settled by his ancestors in 1636. Heath said that he took an early interest in the local militia and rose through its ranks to being appointed, in 1770, as the colonel and commanding officer of the Suffolk County, Massachusetts militia regiment.[7] His commission as a brigadier general (later promoted to major general) in the Continental Army was politically motivated to give Massachusetts a satisfactory number of high-ranking officers in the Patriot army. Heath turned out to be a competent but not a particularly adroit general. This accounts for Washington putting him in charge of the mundane assignment of protecting the supply depots and manning the forts in the Hudson Highlands.

In comparison to Heath, Charles Lee was an educated, professional soldier who joined the Continental Army with impressive credentials. Lee's background is worth presenting at this point as he bullied Heath to send part of his Hudson Highlands command to New Jersey. Charles Lee was born in 1732 in Cheshire, England. He was the son of Major General John Lee, who encouraged young Charles to pursue a career in the British Army. After attending prestigious local schools, Charles continued his formal education at a private military academy in Switzerland. He subsequently joined his father's 55th Regiment in the British Army as an ensign in 1747. Lee's military service included combat in America during the French and Indian War and subsequently commanding British troops in Europe. He later became a mercenary soldier in Poland and Turkey in addition to travelling in France and Italy. Lee was an intellectual and always travelled with an extensive and diverse collection of books including volumes on philosophy, law, science, poetry, and military science. Besides his native English, Lee spoke French, Latin, ancient Greek, Spanish, Italian, German, and the Native American Iroquois language.

It would seem that Willian Heath, the unpretentious Massachusetts farmer, would succumb to Lee's November 21 directive and send 2,000 of his Highlands garrison to New Jersey. Lee had an advantage in the situation; while Heath and Lee were both major-generals, Lee was appointed to the rank first, making him the senior officer.[8] Adding to Lee's authority was that following the resignation of Artemas Ward in May 1776 as the Continental Army's senior major general, Lee became second-in-command of the Continental Army.[9] But Heath's original order came from Washington, the commander-in-chief, which accounts for Heath's speedy and pithy response to Lee's request. Dated "Peek's Kill, Nov 21st, 1776 at 10 o'clock at night," Heath said that he could not comply with Lee's request. Heath's exact words were, "upon having recourse to my instructions, I find they are such as not to admit of moving part of the troops from the post assigned to me, unless it be by express orders from his Excellency, or to support you, in case you are attacked."[10]

Lee later visited Heath in Peekskill to pursue his request. According to Heath, after arriving Lee asked if he could have a cup of tea, to which Heath answered, "that he should have a good one." Lee next asked Heath for 2,000 troops "to march with me." Heath replied that he could not spare that number. Lee reduced his request to 1,000 men, to which Heath responded, "that the business might be as well brought to a point at once—that not a single man should march from the post by his order." After some blustering words, Lee left Peekskill empty-handed, ending his attempts to get Heath to send troops to reinforce Washington's beleaguered army.[11]

Meanwhile, Lee wrote Washington stalling for time while he was trying to pry troops from Heath. Lee wrote to His Excellency on

November 24, while Washington was in Newark during the Long Retreat. Lee told the commander-in-chief that he was all set to march to New Jersey when he received intelligence that an enemy brigade "lye in so exposed situation [Tarrytown, New York] as to present us the fairest opportunity of carrying them off." Lee said that he was going to attack them: "if we succeed, it will have a great effect, and amply compensate for two days delay."[12] There was a British foraging party near Tarrytown, but they retreated back to Manhattan before Lee could catch them.

Just how dangerous Lee was is best revealed in a confidential letter he wrote to Dr. Benjamin Rush, one of his admirers in the Continental Congress. In his missive to Rush, dated November 20, 1776, Lee distanced himself from the American defeat at Fort Washington while promoting the advancement of his own career. Lee wrote,

> *I must entreat that you will keep what I say to yourself; but I foresaw, predicted, all that has happened [attack on Fort Washington]; and urged the necessity of abandoning it; for could we have kept it, it was of little or no use. Let these few lines be thrown into the fire, and in your conversations only acquit me of any share of the misfortune.*

Lee concluded the letter with an offer to lead the army: "let me talk vainly—had I the power I could do you much good."[13]

Luck had given Lee an independent command, the most powerful division left to the Patriots, and he was going to do everything possible to maintain his independence. He apparently believed that if he could bring off an impressive victory, it would convince Congress to sack Washington and give him command of the Continental Army. Any appraisal of Washington's seemingly muddled retreat across New Jersey in late 1776 must take into account Lee's malicious scheming.

Encouraging Lee was the loss of Fort Washington, which had damaged the Virginian's prestige. The members of Congress were alarmed by the calamity and having second thoughts about Washington's competency. Delegate Samuel Chase from Maryland, for example, sent a report to his state government dated Philadelphia, November 21, 1776. In his report

Chase stated that a Continental Army officer arrived in Philadelphia that afternoon with an account of the surrender of Fort Washington. Chase told his state's officials "that Fort Washington could not hold anything near the number of our troops ordered for its defense.... 2,200 of our troops are prisoners. If this account is true, we have again blundered."[14] North Carolina delegate William Hooper wrote to his fellow delegate Joseph Hewes from Philadelphia on November 30, 1776. After giving an account of the fall of Fort Washington, Hooper said, "Oh, how I feel for Washington that best of men. The difficulties which he has encountered are beyond the power of language to describe but to be unfortunate is to be wrong and there are men, you know who, who are villains enough to brand him." Continuing, Hooper said that British General Cornwallis was marching across New Jersey at the head of a formidable army toward Philadelphia. "From whence I shall write you next I know not. Perhaps from this [Philadelphia]—perhaps Lancaster—perhaps Baltimore—perhaps Heaven."[15]

But Lee's duplicity, bordering on treason, was unknown to Washington, who wrote him from New Brunswick on December 1: "I must entreat you to hasten our march as much as possible, or your arrival may be too late to answer any valuable purpose."[16]

Washington felt compelled to downplay his anger at the sensitive Lee to preserve harmony and keep Congress from finding new reasons to meddle in army affairs. But the delegates to Congress got involved when they realized that no one seemed to know where Lee was with his strong division. The delegates took action on December 2 by ordering New Jersey militia Colonel Charles Stewart to "express to General Lee to know where and in what situation he and the army with him are."[17] On December 5, Washington sent his own emissary, the staunch Colonel Richard Humpton, to find Lee. Humpton's orders were to locate Lee and report back detailing his strength, condition, and route of march to Pennsylvania. Two days later, Washington sent Major Robert Hoops after Lee to inform him that boats would be waiting to take his division across the Delaware River at the village of Tinicum (also spelled Tohegan or Tohickon in correspondence during the war), Pennsylvania. The village is two miles south of present-day Frenchtown, New Jersey.[18]

Meanwhile, across the Hudson River in North Castle, Lee recognized that he had to bring his army to New Jersey. But he was only able to take 2,500 men with him across the Hudson. Lee's numbers were depleted while he was in North Castle when the enlistment of three Massachusetts militia regiments, totaling 2,000 men, expired and the men went home. Desertions and sickness had further reduced his strength. Still others had to be left behind because they had no shoes or warm clothing to survive the long march that lay ahead. Out of excuses and options, Lee cunningly took two days (December 2 and 3) to slowly cross the Hudson River.

Once in New Jersey, Lee moved at a snail's pace to join Washington. His slow line of march was through Ringwood and Pompton in northern New Jersey. Lee reached Morristown on December 8 where Washington's emissary, Colonel Humpton, found him. Lee gave Humpton a disheartening letter addressed to "His Excellency General Washington." Despite Humpton's entreaties, Lee said that he was "assured you are very strong" and planned to remain in the Morristown area where he could "make a better impression by hanging on their rear."[19] Humpton was a former British Army captain and a formidable individual. But he was a colonel and could not demand that Major General Lee, the second-in-command of the Continental Army, decamp from Morristown and join Washington in Pennsylvania.

Lee stubbornly remained at Morristown during mid-December where he was able to get intelligence from the local militiamen who were skirmishing with the enemy. As a result of his interviews, Lee was able to determine the locations and approximate troop strengths of the Crown forces' winter garrisons in northern and central New Jersey. Based on his intelligence gathering, Lee had a new scheme. What he planned to do was attack one of the British outposts in New Jersey as he marched toward the Delaware River. Having made his decision, Lee wrote an innocent-looking letter to Washington from Morristown on December 11, outlining his plan. Lee said that "without great risk [he could] cross the great Brunswick post road [the High Road] and by a forced night's march make his way to the ferry below Burlington [a town on the Delaware River south of Trenton]."[20] In other words, Lee was planning to launch a surprise attack probably aimed at the British garrisons at New Brunswick or Princeton, score an impressive victory, and then join Washington's army in Pennsylvania. If Lee's plan succeeded, it would be a spectacular demonstration of his generalship at a time when Washington's reputation was at or near a wartime low. Keep in mind that Lee intended to attack one of the Crown forces outposts in New Jersey two weeks before Washington launched his assault on Colonel Rall's garrison at Trenton.

Lee's army left Morristown on the morning of December 12 led by Brigadier General John Sullivan, Lee's second-in-command. They marched south to Vealtown (present-day Bernardsville, New Jersey) where they camped in the nearby woods for the night. What happened next was Lee's capture by a detachment of British light dragoons. An account of Lee's capture is one of the great stories of the American Revolution and worth telling in detail. The story begins when Lee left the safety of his camp at Vealtown on the morning of December 12 accompanied only by his aide William Bradford, two French Army officers, and twelve guards.[21] The two French officers were Monsieur Gayault de Boisbertrand René Etienne-Henri de Vic and Jean Louis de Vernejout. Monsieur Boisbertrand was a lieutenant colonel in the French Army on a special assignment. He was carrying confidential letters from France to Benjamin Franklin with information about the secret aid that the French were giving to the Americans.[22] As previously mentioned, Vernejout was a former French officer who was commissioned as a captain in the Continental Army and serving as an aide-de-camp to General Lee. With his entourage in tow, Lee's destination was the Widow White's Tavern in Basking Ridge where he arrived at noon on December 12.[23] Polite society has avoided any further details about the Widow White's Tavern, but it may have been a brothel. Lee's interest in visiting the place was best explained by author James Thomas Flexner who noted that "Lee had a propensity for sleeping in strange places and with strange women."[24] Historian Phillip Papas gave additional insight into Lee's visit to the Widow White's Tavern, which was that Lee was periodically obsessed with sex. According to Papas, "Lee experienced phases of hyper sexuality during which he obsessively talked or thought about sex or engaged in numerous sexual encounters with different female partners."[25] There are a few other details that point to the Widow White's being a brothel. One was that there was a commodious tavern in Vealtown where Lee could have lodged for the night.[26] Another was the Widow White's Tavern's secluded location a hundred yards down a lane from the main road. Also, there was the mention of "women of the house" at the Widow White's.[27] Finally, taverns in colonial America were sometimes frequented by prostitutes.

Lee believed he was safe at the tavern, which was twenty miles from the nearest British outpost and four miles from Vealtown.[28] Lee spent the night of December 12 at the Widow White's. Captain James Wilkinson arrived there late that evening and stayed the night. He was on a mission from General Horatio Gates, who was leading 600 troops from Fort Ticonderoga to reinforce Washington. Gates sent Wilkinson ahead to find out where it was safe to cross the Delaware River. When Wilkinson reached the northern New Jersey town of Sussex Courthouse, he was told that the British had a strong force in Trenton and were fanning out along the Jersey side of the Delaware River. He also learned that General Lee's division was in the Morristown area. After hearing the news, Wilkinson decided to go to Lee for information. He counted on a warm reception, as Lee and Gates were both former British Army officers and prewar neighbors who purchased plantations near present-day Martinsburg, West Virginia.[29]

Lee was busy the next morning, which was Friday, December 13, 1776. He attended to some routine army business and writing a letter for Wilkinson to deliver to Gates. His letter was another opportunity for Lee to confidentially criticize Washington. Lee told his friend Gates, "The ingenious maneuver of Fort Washington has unhinged the goodly fabric we had been building. There never was so dammed a stroke. Entre nous [between us], a certain great man is most damnably deficient. He has thrown me into a situation where I have my choice of difficulties."[30]

Lee was not the only person who was displeased with the military situation in mid-December 1776. Twenty miles to the south, Lord Cornwallis was alarmed that Charles Lee was on the loose with thousands of troops. Cornwallis was eight miles north of Trenton at the time in the village of Penny Town (today's Pennington, New Jersey). He was there with a strong detachment scouting for places to cross the Delaware River. Cornwallis knew that Lee was somewhere in the vicinity of rebel-held Morristown, but he needed to know Lee's exact location and the strength of his corps. The British light dragoons were the ideal soldiers for this dangerous reconnaissance mission. A small number of light dragoons, riding fast in enemy-held territory with local guides, had the best chance of success. He ordered Colonel William Harcourt, commander of the 16th Light Dragoons, who was at Penny Town, to take a detachment from his mounted regiment and find Lee.

Harcourt left on his hazardous assignment on the morning of December 12 with four officers and twenty-five troopers.[31] Richard Witham Stockton, a resident of Princeton and a captain in the New Jersey Volunteers (a Loyalist regiment), is identified as Harcourt's guide. Led by Stockton, the dragoons rode as far as the village of Hillsborough where they spent the night. It is thought that a second Loyalist guide, William Robbins, led Harcourt's detachment on the following morning (December 13) into the Watchung Mountains toward Morristown. They were now deep into enemy territory where they could be ambushed at any moment by Patriot militia. But Harcourt's luck held, especially when his troopers captured an American dragoon who had just come from Lee's lodging. Harcourt coerced from his prisoner the location and the number of men with Lee. Excited at the prospect of capturing Lee, Harcourt rode fast with his men while General Lee sat down for a late breakfast at the Widow White's Tavern. What happened next was documented by two well-known eyewitness accounts. One was penned by James Wilkinson and the other by Banastre Tarleton, a twenty-two-year-old cornet (junior officer) who rode with Harcourt.[32] Tarleton eventually was appointed commander of the British Provincial (Loyalist) British Legion whose green uniforms and ruthless tactics resulted in the Americans calling him the Green Dragoon, Bloody Ban, and the Butcher.

But there was a third witness to the capture of General Lee: his aide-de-camp, William Bradford. Captain Bradford set the scene in his account by explaining that the Widow White's Tavern "was surrounded on one side with a wood, on the other an orchard." According to Bradford, there were only twelve men guarding Lee.[33] Lee ordered his horse to be saddled and ready as he planned to rejoin his division immediately after breakfast. Wilkinson filled in some details in his account, saying that he joined Lee for breakfast and after finishing his meal he got up from the table and was casually looking out of a window. Peering through the glass he suddenly yelled, "Here, Sir, are the British cavalry." A moment later the horsemen had the building surrounded as Lee yelled, "Where is the guard—damm the guard, why don't they fire."[34] Lee's sentries tried to resist but were overwhelmed by Harcourt's dragoons, who charged at them at "full speed" and slashed at them with their deadly sabers. The surviving guards panicked and ran off as the handful of men inside the house with Lee began firing their weapons out of the windows. The dragoons, who outnumbered them, surrounded the house and fired back.[35] When Harcourt threatened to set the building on fire and "put every man in it to the sword," General Lee came out and surrendered.[36] According to one account, after Lee handed his sword to Colonel Harcourt, he fell to his knees begging the colonel to spare his life.[37] Tarleton said that following Lee's "cowardly manner, frantic with terror and disappointment," the dragoons placed "their noble prisoner upon a horse and led him off by a different road from that which we had come with all possible expedition" and delivered General Lee to Lord Cornwallis at Penny Town.[38] The dragoons also took French Colonel Boisbertrand captive.[39]

Following his capture, General Lee was brought to New York where he was confined to a second-story room in City Hall and guarded by an officer and fifty soldiers.[40] Washington called his capture "a strange kind of fatality."[41] Perhaps Washington would have been more circumspect in his reaction to Lee's capture if he was aware of what Lee's biographer Phillip Papas concluded, which was that Lee suffered from poor judgement and "delusions of power."[42] Historian Thomas Fleming's observation was that Lee's capture on Friday, December 13, 1776, was "the luckiest Friday the Thirteenth in American history."

Lee remained a prisoner of war in New York for sixteen months. He was finally exchanged in April 1778 for Richard Prescott, a British general whom the Americans captured in July 1777. Lee fought in the 1778 Battle of Monmouth, where he claimed the disorderly retreat of his division was "instigated by some of those dirty earwigs [an insect reputed to crawl into people's ears] who will forever insinuate themselves near persons in high office."[43] Lee was court-martialed and died in 1782 a bitter and forgotten man.

Lee's capture and imprisonment came at a propitious time in the American Revolution. A short-term benefit of Lee's confinement was that Washington received full credit for the successful Trenton-Princeton campaign that was launched within two weeks of Lee's capture. Washington's brilliantly executed offensive, including his astutely planned flight to Morristown, demonstrated his military skill and restored confidence in his leadership.

There was also an important long-term benefit to Lee's capture; with Lee locked up in New York, Washington was free to pursue creating a European-style disciplined army composed of long-term professional soldiers. Lee was opposed to the idea and believed that the war could be won by properly led short-term militia. Washington saw the shortcomings of relying on militia serving on active duty for three or six months early in the war. Referring to the militia, Washington said, "who come in [*sic*], you cannot tell how—go, you cannot tell when—and act, you cannot tell where—consume your provisions—exhaust your stores, and leave you at last at a critical moment."[44] But Washington's most compelling remarks about the shortcomings of militia appear in a letter he wrote to Congress in September 1776 following the panic by the militia at Kips Bay. Washington told Congress,

> To place any dependence upon militia, is, assuredly, resting upon a broken staff. Men just dragged from the tender scenes of domestic life—unaccustomed to the din of arms—totally unacquainted with every kind of military skill... when opposed to troops regularly trained—disciplined and appointed—superior in knowledge and superior in arms, makes them timid, and ready to fly from their own shadows.[45]

Prior to his capture, Lee openly disagreed with Washington. He insisted that the war could be won by militia. He saw the war as a popular movement and believed that the proper use of militia could win the war. Lee's trust in the citizen soldier was also war on the cheap and gained him many influential followers, including Massachusetts Congressman Samuel Adams, who was opposed to a standing [professional] army. Writing to James Warren, the president of the Massachusetts Provincial Congress at the time, Adams said, "A standing Army... is always dangerous to the Liberties of the people. They have their arms always in their hands. They soon become attached to their officers and disposed to yield implicit obedience to their commands." In the same letter Adams continued to focus on the perils of a professional army: "The militia, is composed of free citizens. There is therefore no danger of their making use of their power to the destruction of their own rights."[46] Even when Congress gave Washington the authority of raising a professional army, Lee continued to voice his opposition to the decision. For example, on November 30, 1776, when half of Washington's army went home from New Brunswick when their enlistment expired, Lee wrote to his admirer James Bowdoin:

for when the soldiers of a community are composed of volunteers [professional soldiers], war becomes quite a distinct profession. The arms of a republic get into the hands of its worst members. Volunteers being composed in general of the most idle, vicious, and dissolute part of every society, the usual catastrophe is, that they become the tools of some general more artful than the rest and finally turn the arms put into their hands for the defense of their country, against their country's bosom. This has and must be the fate of every people who have not wisdom enough to make and virtue enough to submit to, laws which oblige every citizen to serve in his turn as a soldier.[47]

Despite Lee's warnings, Congress gave Washington the authority to recruit eighty-eight regiments "as soon as possible to serve during the present war." The delegates to Congress offered a bounty to attract men to enlist in what they called the "new establishment" for the duration of the war or, "unless sooner discharged by Congress."[48] They later amended the terms of enlistment to three years or the duration of the war. With Lee out of the way, Washington was able to create what he called a "respectable army" during the Morristown encampment.[49] He also called his long-desired professional army the "new establishment" or the "new army." Active recruitment for the new army began in earnest soon after the army arrived in Morristown. The need for replacements was urgent, as the enlistments of many of the men who joined the army in 1776 were over. Many of the men who agreed to extend their enlistments and fought at the Battles of Trenton and Princeton left shortly after the army arrived at Morristown. By mid-January Washington described the army as "a handful of men" and "scare [frightened at not] having any army at all."[50] Among the units that he mentioned going home from Morristown during January 1777 were the Philadelphia militia, most of the men from five Virginia regiments, Colonel Edward Hand's Pennsylvania Rifle Regiment, Colonel Smallwood's Maryland brigade, a New Jersey militia brigade, and over 300 men from Colonel Nicholas Haussegger's German battalion. Haussegger's battalion was composed of ethnic Germans who shouted out in German for the Hessians to surrender during the Battle of Trenton. Desperate for speedy replacements, Washington asked Congress to call on the states to send militia "for a month or limited time." Based on his experience with militia during the New York campaign, Washington specified that the militia's active service should start when they arrived at Morristown and not when they left their homes.

Washington tended to be circumspect in his official correspondence, as he knew from experience that antagonizing his civilian bosses was counterproductive. Instead, he inundated them with gloomy reports to spur them to act. A good example of his technique of terrifying his recipients into action appears in a letter Washington wrote to Congress later in the war after arriving at Valley Forge: "I am now convinced beyond a doubt... [that] this army must inevitably be reduced to one or other of these three things, starve—dissolve—or disperse."[51] But Washington was able to vent his anger and frustration in his personal correspondence. We get a good idea of Washington's real feelings during the winter at Morristown in a personal letter he wrote to his stepson, John Parke Custis. His letter included the following: "The misfortunes of short enlistments, and an unhappy dependence upon militia, have shown their baneful influence at every period, and almost upon every occasion, throughout the whole course of this war, at no time, nor upon no occasion were they ever more exemplified than since Christmas [a reference to the Morristown encampment]." Washington then told Custis that the army was reduced to

inferior numbers and with a mixed, motley crew; who were here today, gone tomorrow, without assignment a reason, or even apprising you of it. In a word, I believe I may with truth add, that I do not think that any officer since the creation ever had such a variety of difficulties and perplexities to encounter as I have. How we shall be able to rub along till the new army is raised I know not.[52]

By mid-January, the army at Morristown was down to 2,000 men. It consisted of 800 Continentals, 700 Massachusetts militia (who only agreed to stay until March 15), and the remnants of a few other regiments. Facing him were 10,000 Crown forces troops wintering in nearby New Brunswick and Perth Amboy. The British had abandoned all of their other posts in New Jersey following the Trenton-Princeton campaign. Nathanael Greene confirmed this point in a January 10 letter he wrote to Nicholas Cooke, the Governor of Rhode Island: "We are now in possession again of Fort Lee, Hackensack, Newark, Elizabeth Town and Princeton. The enemy has nothing but Brunswick and Amboy."[53] Washington stationed a few hundred men under General Israel Putnam at Princeton with orders to send out mounted patrols to watch for any movements of the enemy from their winter garrisons toward Morristown. He believed that the British might have attacked him if they knew that his situation was "scarce having any army at all." But Washington took another, more aggressive step to protect Morristown and demoralize the Crown forces wintering in New Jersey. He used Morristown as a base for what was called *petit guerre* (French for small war) or partisan warfare. The modern term is "guerilla warfare." The *Universal Military Dictionary* published in London in 1779 defines "petit-guerre" as "a detachment of troops commanded by an experienced officer... separated from the army... to reconnoiter the enemy or the country; to seize their posts, convoys, and escorts; to plant ambuscades, and to put in practice every stratagem [defined as a scheme for deceiving an adversary] for surprising or disturbing the enemy."[54]

Washington had personal experience with irregular warfare from his days as a young provincial officer in the French and Indian War. During that conflict the French and their Indian allies were especially skillful at ambushing British and provincial troops.[55] Partisan warfare actually began on a small scale at Morristown even before the army arrived there. Small detachments of New Jersey militia were already using the village as a base to ambush British patrols and attack isolated guard posts and supply convoys. Nathanael Greene summed up the New Jersey militia's motivation to fight in a letter he wrote to the Governor of Rhode Island shortly after he arrived in Morristown: "The enemy's ravages in the Jerseys exceeds all description.... The country are in high spirits and breathe nothing but revenge."[56] Washington not only encouraged the militia's attacks but increased their size, boldness, and frequency by reinforcing them with experienced troops from his small garrison.

The targets of the rebels' ambushes and hit-and-run attacks were the Crown forces troops wintering in Perth Amboy and New Brunswick. Consistently short of food and fodder, and living on salted provisions imported from England, the hungry British and Hessians sent foraging parties into the surrounding farmland like swarming locusts, grabbing hay, oats, Indian corn, cattle, and horses that was "often attended with fatal consequences."[57] The "fatal consequences" were that the foragers were the favorite targets of the rebel partisans. Washington explained the emphasis on attacking foraging parties in a January 18, 1777, letter to his friend and fellow officer Philip Schuyler:

The enemy... have been obliged to abandon every part of Jersey except New Brunswick and Perth Amboy and the small tract of country between them, which is so entirely exhausted of supplies of every kind, that I hope, by preventing them from sending their foraging parties to any great distance, to reduce them to the utmost distress in the course of this winter.[58]

The militia attacks on British foraging parties increased soon after Washington arrived in Morristown. The British responded by increasing the size of their foraging parties to include troops to protect the foragers. A good example of the escalation of what historian David Hackett Fisher called "the forage war" occurred on January 15, 1777, just over a week after Washington arrived in Morristown. On that date 300 New Jersey militiamen commanded by Continental Army officer Colonel Oliver Spencer attacked a foraging party of one hundred Hessians near Connecticut Farms (modern Union, New Jersey). Spencer's men killed one of the foragers and captured seventy.[59] Another example where there is more detailed information: on January 20, New Jersey militiamen fought a pitched battle against 500 British and Hessian troops nine miles from New Brunswick. Lieutenant Colonel Robert Abercromby, an experienced British Army officer, commanded the foraging expedition, which brought along two horse-drawn pieces of field artillery. The large size of Colonel Abercromby's detachment was an indication that he was expecting trouble. It came soon enough when his foragers were attacked by 450 rebels commanded by New Jersey militia General Philemon Dickinson. General Dickinson's force consisted largely of New Jersey militia supported by fifty Pennsylvania riflemen and two companies of Continental infantry.[60] General Dickinson's men attacked the British near Van Nest's Mill (also spelled as Van Ests Mill; present-day Weston, New Jersey). The British believed that there was a large quantity of flour stored at the mill which was located on the north side of the Millstone River, two miles from the village of Hillsborough. The shallow Millstone River was covered by a thin sheet of ice at the time. There was a bridge across the river at the site (Van Nest Mill's Bridge). Abercromby's troops were across the bridge, on the north side of the river, when they were surprised by the militiamen who attacked them from the nearby woods. Abercromby had placed his two cannons on high ground on the south side of the river, about fifty yards from the bridge, to keep the span under his control. Dickinson outflanked the enemy-held bridge by sending men across the river upstream. The militiamen had to break through the ice and cross the Millstone in waist-high freezing water.[61] The flanking action put them on the south side of the river, threatening Abercromby's rear guard and control of the bridge. Facing being cut off by the determined enemy, the British raced back across the bridge through enemy gunfire, quickly hitched up their field artillery, and staged a hasty retreat back to New Brunswick. Besides inflicting casualties and taking forty-nine prisoners, General Dickinson reported that the enemy left behind 107 horses and 49 wagons in addition to 115 cattle and 70 sheep. A militia officer on the scene said that in their haste to retreat, the British left behind "a great number of newly filled sacks of wheat, flour and several other articles, which we found scattered everywhere along the road and through the woods."[62]

After returning to New Brunswick, a British officer on the foraging expedition was "absolutely certain the attackers were not militia. He was sure that no militia would fight in that way."[63] The militia's bravery at what was called the Battle of Millstone contrasted with the low estimation most British officers had of the Americans' martial spirit. British General John Forbes, for example, called their officers "a bunch of broken innkeepers and horse jockeys" (horse dealers) and their men "more infamous cowards than any other race of mankind."[64]

The militia raids continued during January, encouraged and supported by Washington. On January 30, a detachment of 300 New Jersey militia and Continental infantry commanded by Lieutenant Colonel Josiah Parker (a Virginia Continental Army officer), attacked a British foraging party near Quibbletown (also called New Market at the time: a present-day section of Piscataway, New Jersey). Colonel Parker reported "inflicting casualties" among the enemy, who retreated back to New Brunswick.[65]

By the end of January, Washington was able to write Rhode Island Governor Nicholas Cooke from Morristown, "Our affairs here are in a very prosperous train, within a month past [January 1777] in several engagements with the enemy, we have killed, wounded, and taken prisoner between two and three thousand."[66]

The 1777 winter encampment at Morristown was not a quiet break in the war in other ways besides recruiting a new army on a "regular footing" and escalating partisan warfare. Washington also devoted his time that winter to creating what he called a "respectable train." The term "train" at the time was an acronym for "train of artillery," defined as "pieces of ordnance belonging to an army in the field."[67] Washington wrote Congress on the "necessity of increasing our field artillery" in a November 14, 1776, letter to Congress. Using his technique of frightening Congress to take action, the Virginian said that without more lightweight, mobile artillery "we must carry on the war... without the smallest probability of success."[68] Washington's recommendation, which amounted to a change in the way the army used artillery, was based on his experience during the 1776 New York campaign and the influence of Colonel Henry Knox, his brilliant young artillery officer. To explain, during 1776 the Americans constructed forts, redoubts, entrenchments, and other defensive positions in an effort to defend New York City, Long Island, upper Manhattan Island, and the lower Hudson River. These fixed fortifications were defended with large-caliber heavy artillery called garrison guns that could not be easily moved. Toward the end of 1776, after the rebel fortifications around New York City were overrun or outflanked, Washington realized that he had to abandon fixed positions and operate in the countryside where he could maneuver his army to his advantage. This change meant that artillery had to be lighter and mobile (horse-drawn) to support the Continental Army's infantry brigades. Knox's contribution was to increase the number of cannons in the army assigned to each infantry brigade. Then, when advantageous, as at the Battle of Trenton, Knox would consolidate his large number of cannons to create massive firepower to overwhelm the enemy.

With the approval of Congress, Washington began to reorganize the army's artillery in late 1776. To start, Congress promoted Knox on December 27, 1776, to the rank of brigadier general and chief of the Continental Army artillery. Then, after arriving in Morristown, Washington instructed Knox to go to Massachusetts to supervise the manufacturing of brass cannon barrels. Brass was lighter and stronger than iron, making brass the preferred material for field artillery. Knox established an arsenal (manufacturing facility) at Springfield, Massachusetts, and recruited men to be trained as artillerists instead of indiscriminately assigning infantrymen to work the army's cannons. Knox rejoined the army at Morristown in mid-March, his mission a success.[69]

Another challenge that Washington confronted during the winter at Morristown was to protect the army against smallpox. Washington had good reason to be concerned. Smallpox had already decimated the American army that invaded Canada earlier in the war, and some civilians already had the disease when Washington arrived in Morristown.

Smallpox is caused by a virus called variola major. The virus is highly contagious and can easily pass from one person to another. A person can be infected for example, just by inhaling droplets of the virus from the breath of an infected person.[70]

From 1775 to 1782, smallpox ravaged the greater part of North America, killing more than a 100,000 people.[71] The epidemic in North America coincided with the American Revolution and killed more Americans during the Revolution than died fighting the British.[72] The pestilence began to spread among the troops wintering in Morristown shortly after the army arrived there. Alarmed by the outbreak, Washington wrote Congress on January 6, just days after arriving in Morristown, "We should have more to dread from it, than from the sword of the enemy." Washington had good reason to be alarmed, as it was estimated that smallpox killed one out of every three people who contracted the disease.

Smallpox has a thirty- or thirty-two-day cycle. The first noticeable symptoms are a fever, backache, and nausea, which begin within six to eleven days after being exposed to the virus. Smallpox is most contagious between sixteen and twenty days. A critical period followed during which the infected person either died or recovered with a lifetime immunity to the disease. Washington had contracted smallpox as a teenager while visiting the island of Barbados in 1751 and survived. However, his face was pockmarked from the disease, a common aftereffect.

There was a controversial medical procedure at the time that gave a person lifetime immunity to smallpox by inoculating them with a mild form of the virus. The procedure was called variolation, named after the variola major virus. The technique, believed to have originated in China in the sixteenth century, was to scratch a tiny amount of the live virus into the skin of a healthy person. Although the treatment was known to be successful, it was not without its risks. There was the possibility that even a small amount of the virus could result in a deadly case of smallpox. Also, a person who underwent variolation had to be quarantined until they were fully recovered, or they could trigger a smallpox epidemic. They could also contract typhus, typhoid fever, and dysentery in their weakened condition. These diseases were transmitted by lice in unwashed clothing, stale bed straw, and water contaminated by sewage.[73] Variolation was also an expensive procedure, requiring a patient to pay a doctor to perform the procedure plus the cost of food, lodging, and nursing during the lengthy quarantine period. Superstition and fear also convinced some people that the smallpox inoculation would result in bizarre behavioral transformations or deformity. The dangers, both real and imaginary, of purposely infecting people with smallpox was serious enough to either prohibit or restrict the procedure throughout colonial America. Variolation, for example, was outlawed in Virginia, and Thomas Jefferson went to Philadelphia to receive the treatment.[74]

Variolation is different from vaccination. Variolation refers to inoculation with the smallpox virus. Vaccination came later, in the year 1800 to be exact. The original meaning of vaccination was to inoculate a person with cowpox, a milder form of smallpox found in animals. Edward Jenner is credited with developing the cowpox vaccine, which is still used today to prevent smallpox.

Washington decided that he had to take the risk of having smallpox-inoculated soldiers unfit for duty for at least a month. But the threat of a smallpox epidemic outweighed all other considerations, and Washington ordered the mass variolation of all the troops at Morristown. Dr. Nathaniel Bond was in charge of the program. He divided the soldiers into groups called "divisions" and inoculated each division at intervals of five or six days. After being treated, the soldiers were isolated in buildings in and around Morristown, guarded by men who had survived the disease. The civilian population of Morristown and the surrounding region also underwent variolation and were quarantined. Washington also ordered all new recruits for the army to undergo variolation before coming to Morristown. Dr. William Shippen, Jr., for example, was ordered by Washington to treat "without delay" all the troops in Philadelphia and new recruits "that shall come in, as fast as they arrive."

The Americans kept their variolation program a secret. The British might have decided to attack Morristown if they knew that a good part of the rebel troops there were quarantined and unable to fight. Smallpox was not a problem for the British Army at the time, as all enlistees were inoculated against the disease. This meant that the number of British troops being quarantined was small at any given time.

The smallpox vaccination program that Washington started at Morristown saved many American lives. Historians are quick to evaluate Washington's generalship in the Revolution based on how many battles he won or lost. But they tend to overlook his other victories during the war, including his large-scale program during the winter of 1777 to inoculate his army against smallpox.

One area where Washington failed to make the improvements he wanted during the Morristown encampment was the establishment of a Continental Army Corps of Engineers. He formally proposed the ambitious idea to Congress in October 1776. The term "engineer" at the time meant an officer whose fundamental responsibility was to design and supervise the construction of fortifications. Engineers were also expected to be able to "attack such places [fortifications]... to bring the besieged to capitulate." Both the British and French armies had military academies to train engineers. The British Army had established an engineering school at Woolwich, England (today a section of London) in 1741, and the French counterpart was the "Ecole royale du genie [sic] (Royal Engineers School)" in Mézières, France in 1771.[75] Education at both the British and French engineering schools focused on mathematics, hydraulics (conducting water), design and construction of fortifications, principles of gunnery, bridge building, and drawing. The latter was important for engineers to be able to illustrate their recommendations. Washington was familiar with the work of British Army engineers during the French and Indian War and he wanted similarly educated men for the Continental Army. His desire to appoint graduates of the European engineering academies as engineers in the Continental Army was a fantasy. There were no men in the Patriot ranks at the start of the war who were graduates of the European schools. Nor was there any individual or school in America teaching even the rudiments of military engineering.

Washington eventually appointed Rufus Putnam, a Massachusetts mill-wright (mechanical engineer), as the chief engineer of the Continental Army.[76] Putnam's military experience for the job was scant, consisting of "employed on some fortifications" by British Army engineers during the French and Indian War. Despite Putnam's pleas that he had "never read a work on the subject," Putnam supervised the design and construction of New York City's defenses in 1776. In his memoirs, he stated: "I was charged as chief engineer with laying out and overseeing the works... at New York, Long Island, Fort Washington, Fort Lee and Kingsbridge." Just how unqualified Putnam was for the job is highlighted by a story he related in his memoirs. Putnam said that after being appointed an engineer he was walking past the quarters of General Heath. He decided to pay his respects to the general, who invited him into his lodgings. Putnam said that while there, "I cast my eye on a book which lay on the table, lettered "Mullers Field Engineer."[77] I immediately requested the general to lend it to me. He denied me... and told me that he never lent his books. I confessed I never had read a word about engineering and that he must let me have the book." Heath finally agreed, and Putnam got to read an engineering textbook.[78]

Putnam's lack of training as an engineer was most evident in his design of "impregnable" Fort Washington, which capitulated after four hours. The fort looked formidable, sitting on the highest point in Manhattan and surrounded by redoubts. Nathanael Greene, who was in overall command of the Fort Washington–Fort Lee defense line, had little knowledge of fortifications. Lacking a trained engineer to advise him led to Greene's mistaken belief that Fort Washington could withstand a long siege. Among the fort's shortcomings was that it was constructed of earth and wood piled up on the solid granite mountain. British Army Captain Frederick Mackenzie inspected the fort after it surrendered and commented on its poor construction: "The whole is of earth, without any fraize (sharpened wooden stakes facing outward) or palisade (large wooden upright stakes; a fence). As it is situated on very rocky ground, there is hardly any ditch (trench), as they have not blown any part of the rock to form one."[79] The absence of trenches was because there was no spare gunpowder to create them from the rock. The short supply of gunpowder also resulted in the fort not having created an underground magazine in the rock to protect its ammunition from enemy artillery fire. Another problem was that the fort was too small to hold its entire garrison when the men manning the outer works retreated into the main structure. One of the fort's defenders described the consequences: "Fort Washington was so crowded that it was difficult to pass through it, and as the enemy were in possession of the little redoubts around it, they could have poured in such a shower of shells and ricochet-balls, as would have killed hundreds in a little time."[80] Adding to its inability to withstand a siege, Fort Washington had no well, and water had to be carried up 230 feet from the Hudson River.

Colonel Putnam resigned as the Continental Army's chief engineer on December 8, 1776, soon after the catastrophic loss of Fort Washington. He had done his best as an engineer and was appointed the commanding officer of the 5th Massachusetts infantry regiment. In a letter to Congress dated December 20, 1776, Washington admitted that he could not find a qualified person to replace Putnam, including several French officers who claimed to be proficient engineers. Washington's exact words were, "I know of no other man tolerably well qualified for the conducting of that business. None of the French gentlemen whom I have seen with appointments in that way, appear to me, to know anything of the matter." Interestingly, in the same letter Washington wrote, "There is one in Philadelphia whom I am told is clever, but him I have never seen."[81] The person that Washington heard about was Thaddeus Kościuszko, a Polish national who was educated in military academies in France. Kościuszko was occupied in 1776 with constructing forts to defend the lower Delaware River.[82] There was another French-trained engineer in America at the time: Lieutenant Colonel Gilles Jean Marie Barazer de Kermorvan, Chevalier de Kermorvan. He was appointed as an engineer and lieutenant colonel in the Continental Army by Congress on July 15, 1776. Kermorvan was initially involved with constructing defenses at Perth Amboy, and subsequently joined Kościuszko to construct forts on the Delaware River to defend Philadelphia. Congress appointed another French Army officer, claiming to be an engineer, to join Washington's staff. His name was Matthias-Alexis, Chevalier de

La Rochefermoy. Like all the other French Army officers who came to America during the first years of the Revolution, Rochefermoy came at his own expense, claiming that he was inspired to join the Patriot cause. Rochefermoy joined Washington's Grand Army in time to participate in the Christmas Day attack on Trenton. He wintered with the army at Morristown until late March 1777 when Washington shipped him off to the Northern Army at Fort Ticonderoga. Rochefermoy turned out to be a fraud. He never ranked higher than a captain in the French Army, and he had no training or experience as an engineer. What motivated Rochefermoy to come to America was to make money and enhance his resume with a high rank in the Continental Army.

Washington summarized his experience with Rochefermoy and other Frenchmen: "Men who in the first instance tell you, that they wish for nothing more than the honor of serving in so glorious a cause as volunteers—the next day solicit rank without pay—the day following want money advanced them—and in the course of a week want further promotion, and are not satisfied with anything you can do for them."[83] The French government eventually covertly sent four skilled French Army engineers to America in late 1777. Their leader was a thirty-four-year-old French nobleman named Antoine-Jean-Louis LeBègue de Presle Duportial. These four men became the nucleus of Washington's vision of a Continental Army corps of engineers.

Washington also used that winter to increase his headquarters staff. From his headquarters at Morristown, Washington wrote his military secretary, Robert Hanson Harrison, on January 20, 1777, asking him to "Be so good as to forward the enclosed to Captain Hamilton." Both Harrison and Hamilton were in Philadelphia at the time. The letter that General Washington entrusted to Harrison to deliver was believed to be an invitation for the young New York State artillery captain to join the general's military family. Not knowing where Hamilton was residing in Philadelphia, Harrison placed an advertisement in the January 25 issue of the *Pennsylvania Evening Post*: "Captain Alexander Hamilton of the New York Company of Artillery, by applying to the printer of this paper, may hear of something to his advantage."[84] The chain of events that followed led to the twenty-two-year-old captain being included in the March 1, 1777, General Orders of the Army: "Alexander Hamilton is appointed aide-de-camp to the commander-in-chief and is to be respected and obeyed as such."[85]

The appointment was the start of the relationship between Washington and Hamilton, one of the most important and creative associations in American history. A decade later, Washington, as the first president of the United States and Hamilton, as secretary of the Treasury, worked together to establish the fiscal policies under which the United States still functions.

Contrary to the assertions of some historians and playwrights, Hamilton was not Washington's Revolutionary War principal advisor, right-hand man, or chief of staff. He was one of the thirty-two aides-de-camp who served as personal assistants to Washington during the war. Washington referred to them as his military family or "penmen" because their major function was to draft the estimated 12,000 letters and orders that Washington's headquarters wrote during the war. All of the head-quarters' correspondence was written under Washington's close supervision. Philander D. Chase, the retired editor-in-chief of the *Papers of George Washington*, concluded after studying Washington's correspondence: "I don't believe," Mr. Chase said, "that Washington ever signed any significant letter or other document without having considerable input and checking it to see that it accorded with both his intentions and style."[86] In fact, Washington's letters all read the same even though they were drafted by thirty-two different men. The letters are all respectful, clear in their thoughts, concise, and state what action—if any—is required.

Aides-de-camp to the commander-in-chief were given the breveted rank of lieutenant colonel. The term "breveted" means temporary: they held the rank so long as they were Washington's aides. His aides were also appointed as staff officers, which meant that they were not allowed to command troops in combat. At the start of the war Washington was authorized by Congress to personally select three aides-de-camp and a military secretary. However, as the war continued, the civilian government repeatedly relinquished the management of the army to Washington, who proved to be an expert administrator. As a result, Washington was permitted by Congress to add additional aides to assist him. His

Excellency also enlisted unpaid volunteer aides and the officers from his guard detachment (called the Commander-in-Chief's Guard) to work at headquarters. Thus, by March 1777, Washington's military family at Morristown consisted of what historian John C. Fitzpatrick called "the most remarkable group of young men to be found in the history of the United States."[87] The senior member of Washington's staff was his military secretary, Robert Hanson Harrison, whom historian Washington Irving described as "one in whom every man had confidence, and by whom no man was deceived."[88] Harrison was one of Washington's prewar lawyers with no military experience. Next to Harrison, the most important person at Washington's headquarters was Tench Tilghman. Tilghman was a Philadelphia businessman before the war and served at headquarters as an unpaid volunteer aide. Washington said of him, "No man enjoyed a greater share of my esteem, affection and confidence than Colonel Tilghman."[89] Besides Tilghman, Washington's aides during the 1777 Morristown encampment were Alexander Hamilton, John Walker, John Fitzgerald (one of Washington's prewar business associates), and George Johnson (a Virginia plantation owner and Robert Hanson Harrison's brother-in-law). In addition, Caleb Gibbs, the officer commanding the Commander-in-Chief's Guard, worked at headquarters when the workload became overwhelming.

Washington recognized Hamilton as a brilliant young man, but their association was formal and businesslike. His Excellency tended to use Hamilton to act as his personal emissary for assignments that required a sharp mind and good judgement. However, Washington's immediate concern was that experienced soldiers were leaving for home, and new recruits were arriving slowly. Washington's response to this dangerous situation was to hasten the recruitment of men for the army while he spread his existing troops throughout Patriot-held towns in central New Jersey to give the illusion that he commanded a large army. But the most important measure that Washington took from Morristown was to encourage the New Jersey militia to intensify their ambushes, skirmishes, and raids by supporting them with Continentals to keep the 10,000 British and Hessian troops wintering in New Brunswick and Perth Amboy on the defensive.

4

Shabby, Ill Managed Occasions*

By late January 1777, General Sir William Howe had withdrawn all of his troops in New Jersey to a narrow corridor along the Raritan River valley between Perth Amboy and New Brunswick. Packed into this small area were 10,000 British and Hessian troops. Every building in the two river towns was converted into barracks and filled to overflowing. One British officer described living conditions in New Brunswick in a letter home, saying he was "miserably ill lodged; my whole company, which consists of fifty-three men, are obliged to live in one small room, and I am in a pigeon hole, with eleven officers, where we eat, drink and sleep."[1] Living conditions in Perth Amboy were no better. A whole regiment was quartered in a church, and open sheds were turned into barracks by boarding up their exposed sides. Even after cramming men into every available space, some troops had to spend the winter at Perth Amboy living aboard cold and filthy transport ships anchored in the harbor.[2]

Sir William was determined to hold on to New Brunswick and Perth Amboy during the winter of 1777. He wanted New Brunswick as a base for launching his spring campaign to seize Philadelphia. Perth Amboy's attraction was its location at the deep water entrance to the Raritan River where ships could safely offload men and equipment from New York City

---

* Chapter title from a diary entry for February 24, 1777, in Ira D. Gruber, ed., *John Peebles' American War* (Mechanicsburg, PA: Stackpole Books, 1998), 98.

or Britain for Sir William's planned Philadelphia campaign. Starting his attack against Philadelphia from New Brunswick made sense. The town was only sixty miles from the rebel capital via the well-trodden High Road across New Jersey to Trenton. Once there, ferries, or a pontoon bridge built by British Army engineers, would take Howe's army across the Delaware River to Pennsylvania within thirty miles of the rebel capital. Armies at the time could march over twenty miles in a day, making Philadelphia about a three-day march from New Brunswick.

Howe assigned General Lord Cornwallis to command the troops wintering in New Brunswick and Perth Amboy. Cornwallis established his headquarters in New Brunswick at the home of John Neilson (no longer standing), described as a large brick building located in the center of the town. Neilson was a wealthy New Brunswick merchant. He was also a colonel in the New Jersey militia, which accounts for his house being confiscated by the British. Lord Cornwallis's remote assignment from the lively social life of British-held New York City was not punishment by Howe for allowing Washington to slip away from Trenton to attack Princeton. In fact, Sir William was sympathetic toward his subordinate's debacle. He told Cornwallis, "You have nothing to accuse yourself of.... Had one deserter given you intelligence of the night march from Trenton, you would have finished the war.... Better luck next time."[3]

The British troops wintering in New Jersey were adequately supplied with preserved food that was transported at great expense from England. In his authoritative study of the British Army's logistical problems (the planning and carrying out the movement, supply, and maintenance of military forces) in fighting the American War, R. Arthur Bowler explained that the British government could turn to a number of London merchants who were experienced in organizing large-scale shipments of various commodities. Britain also had a surplus of victuals and a crude but adequate knowledge of how to preserve them for long-distance shipment. Beef and pork, for example, if properly prepared, well salted, packed in sound barrels, and stored in reasonably cool surroundings, could remain edible for up to two years. But finding enough civilian merchant ships to bring the provisions and military stores such as tents and ammunition to America was a serious problem. Historian

Bowler estimated that the British Army consumed thirty tons of food and sixteen tons of grain for its horses each day during the war. But each of the available merchant ships to transport this food, grain, and military stores to America could carry only about 220 tons of cargo and were "slow under the best conditions, and almost helpless in the face of contrary winds."[4] A ship could make two trips to America and back in a year. The result was long delays in delivering the victuals and equipment that the army needed, even after every merchant ship was pressed into service. The provisions coming from England provided the daily diet of the troops; salted beef or pork, flour, oatmeal, dried peas, biscuits (from French for twice baked; later called hardtack), butter, cabbage prepared as sauerkraut, oil, and cheese.[5] But the long shipping times and spoilage from seawater, rats, or insects in transit resulted in some of the food being rotten or contaminated when it finally reached the troops.

A particular problem for Cornwallis was that provisions destined for New Brunswick were either offloaded and sent overland ten miles from Perth Amboy in wagon convoys, or shipped up the Raritan River in boats. These wagon trains and boats were being relentlessly harassed by rebel marksmen and hit-and-run attacks.

It is surprising that General Howe did not order a campaign against rebel-held Morristown during the winter. Only thirty-three miles separated the opposing armies. The argument is made that Howe did not know how weak Washington was at Morristown. Perhaps Howe would have ordered the assault if he had good intelligence about the actual number of American troops wintering there. Commenting on this subject, historian Thomas J. McGuire notes, "The failure of the British intelligence network during this six-month period [the winter and spring of 1777] was part of the reason why so little significant activity took place. Estimates of Washington's strength, as noted in British and Hessian sources, were consistently and significantly overinflated."[6] The actual difference in troop strength between the opposing armies in New Jersey is staggering. Opposing Sir William's 10,000 troops wintering in New Jersey were just 2,900 Americans. The number of Americans was less than the 3,000 troops Washington had at New Brunswick during the 1776 Long Retreat.

Among the people who wondered why General Howe did not attack Morristown during the winter was the Philadelphia Loyalist Charles Stedman, who asked why the British commander-in-chief "suffered such an enemy, so greatly inferior to his own... to remain for six months within twenty-five miles [*sic*] of his headquarters without molestation, and without taking any means to revenge the insults that were offered daily to the army under his command."[7] Loyalist Thomas Jones claimed that Howe was too preoccupied with his social life in New York to give much thought to the troops wintering in New Jersey. Jones said, "Nothing could be done without the direction of the commander-in-chief who was diverting himself in New York, in feasting, gunning, banqueting, and in the arms of Mrs. Loring. Not a stick of wood, a spear of grass, or a kernel of corn, could the troops in New Jersey procure without fighting for it."[8]

Washington recognized that he commanded a precariously small army during the first months of 1777. Although Morristown was only approachable from a few roads, his undermanned garrison would have been hard pressed to stop a British attack. As a result, Washington made every effort to keep his actual numbers a secret until a substantial number of three-year enlistees arrived. Among the steps taken by Washington in the face of overwhelming odds was to deploy his available troops to observe every road leading to Morristown. His plan was to quickly assemble men to intercept any enemy reconnaissance aimed at probing his position and keep the British preoccupied by harassing their foraging (food-gathering) detachments. Washington implemented his plan soon after arriving in Morristown by ordering Major General Israel Putnam to occupy Princeton. Putnam arrived at the college town on January 19 with 400 troops and orders from Washington to dispatch "a number of horsemen in the dress of the Country [wearing civilian clothing]... to watch for any enemy movement."[9] Bound Brook was occupied by Patriot troops even earlier, on January 13.[10] American occupation of the village was important, as it controlled one of the few passes into the Watchung Mountains.[11] Additional outposts were added, and by mid-March Washington had deployed almost his entire army, which consisted at the time of 2,543 Continentals and 976 militia in a semi-circle surrounding British-held New Brunswick and Perth Amboy.[12] Besides detachments of Continentals and militia in Princeton and Bound Brook, Colonel Eneas McKay was stationed at Quibbletown with over 300 troops from the 8th Pennsylvania Regiment.[13] Additional Patriot detachments were at Basking Ridge with General Greene and at Elizabeth with General Lord Stirling, in addition to small numbers of troops occupying the central New Jersey villages of Raritan, Chatham, Westfield, and Hillsborough. According to the "Return of the American Forces in New Jersey" dated March 15, 1777, after deploying his small army, Washington had only forty-six Continentals stationed at Morristown.[14] The information in his March 15 return was so sensitive that a copy was given to General Greene to carry to Philadelphia and hand-deliver to John Hancock, the president of the Continental Congress.

Besides getting reports from his troops in the field, Washington was also receiving intelligence from the local population regarding British activities in New Brunswick and Perth Amboy. Cornwallis should have been getting similar information about the Americans from the New Jersey Loyalists. Large numbers of New Jersey's residents had rallied to the British during their brief occupation of New Jersey during December 1776. The civilians came into the British-held towns to sign oaths of allegiance to the King. But their allegiance to the Crown was short-lived once the British and their Hessian hirelings began plundering friend and foe alike. The Hessians in particular went on a looting spree in this land of plenty. Charles Stedman observed that General Howe was unable to provide the protection he promised the people who signed the oaths; "their families were insulted, stripped of their beds, with other furniture—nay, even of their very wearing apparel; they then determined to try the other side."[15] Besides looting indiscriminately, when the British Army withdrew their troops to a small section along the Raritan River, they left the Loyalists defenseless from the revenge of their Patriot neighbors. Greene observed that British protection to the Loyalists was "like a ship plowing the ocean, they have no sooner past that the scene closes and the people rise anew to oppose them."[16] Greene made another astute observation of the inability of the British to protect their Loyalist allies when he said, "The limits of the British government in America are their out-sentinels [perimeter guards]."[17]

The failure of General Howe to authorize an attack on Morristown becomes even more difficult to comprehend as British casualties swelled as a result of foraging expeditions that were operating far from their bases. Washington ordered the removal early in the winter of any wagons and horses that the British could use as "the best mode of distressing the enemy and rendering their situation still more disagreeable."[18] But the British were still able to ransack farms for food to supplement their insipid diet. The foragers seized turnips, onions, cabbages, carrots, and parsnips that the farmers had stored and were eatable for months after harvesting. The farmers also had dried fruits, pickled vegetables, pies, hard cider made from applies or peaches, and cured hams. In addition, the farms had cattle, sheep, chickens, and pigs that could be slaughtered for fresh meat. These provisions were welcomed additions for British troops living on preserved victuals shipped from England. However, food for the army's horses was essential. Food for horses was as critical to Revolutionary War period armies as gasoline is to modern armies. Cornwallis's need for animal feed during the winter of 1777 was critical, as he needed hundreds of healthy draft horses available at New Brunswick in the spring to pull wagons for the army's planned attack on Philadelphia. Horse-drawn wagons transported everything that an army needed to function in the field including ammunition, provisions, tents, and medical supplies. Additional horses were required to mount cavalry and pull field artillery. Senior officers wanted horses for their personal use including transporting their wagonloads of clothing, food, tents, and portable furniture. In fact, Revolutionary War armies were so dependent on their wagon trains that virtually every major battle of the American Revolution was fought along a road. Examples are the battles of Saratoga, Brandywine, Germantown, Monmouth, Cowpens, and Guilford Courthouse. The hundreds of horses at New Brunswick and Perth Amboy had to be kept healthy and strong during the winter of 1777 to give the British Army the mobility it needed for its spring offensive.

Feeding horses in warm weather was not a problem as they thrived on grass which grew in abundance in pastures and uncultivated fields. This naturally available horse food is called provender or forage. But between autumn and early spring, horses and other domestic livestock had to live on crops that were specially grown and stockpiled as animal feed. This winter feed is called fodder and includes alfalfa, hay, rye, straw, and buckwheat. Based on the average body weight of 1,000 pounds, a horse consumes between fifteen and twenty pounds of provender or fodder every day. Cornwallis could have remained secure behind his defenses in New Brunswick and Perth Amboy and waited out the winter if it was not for his urgent need for tons of fodder to feed his horses. The British encampments on Staten Island and Manhattan Island could not help him; they were hard-pressed to find food for their own horses.

General Howe's original plan was to disperse his army in towns across New Jersey to maintain control, protect the Loyalists, and purchase or confiscate locally accessible food and fodder. But following the American victories at Trenton and Princeton, Howe saw that his remaining isolated garrisons including Elizabeth, Rahway, and Woodbridge were targets for rebel attacks. This accounts for his consolidation of troops in New Jersey at New Brunswick and Perth Amboy. But the new arrangement meant that Cornwallis had to send out foraging parties longer distances in search of fodder during the winter of 1777. These British foraging expeditions became the favorite prey of Americans who could refer to partisan warfare manuals to help them plan their attacks.

A fascinating aspect of guerilla warfare in the American Revolution was that there were manuals explaining how to carry out successful ambushes and hit-and-run raids. The story of these seventeenth-century books begins with the fact that British and American line officers had no formal training. They learned their duties from on-the-job training and by reading treatises. A treatise is a detailed discourse on one subject. Colonial-period Americans were avid readers of military treatises. A Hessian officer, for example, was surprised, upon examining the contents of the knapsacks of captured rebel officers, to find them "filled up with military books."[19] On finding the books he was impressed by the American officers who "only two years before were hunters, lawyers, physicians, clergymen, tradesman, innkeepers, shoemakers, and tailors."[20]

There were several good treatises on the subject of guerilla warfare that were in print at the time of the American Revolution. The most popular one was titled *Instructions for Officers Detached in the Field* by Roger Stevenson (identified only as an "officer"). First published in London in 1770, the book was reprinted in Philadelphia in 1775. The Philadelphia edition has the distinction of being the first book dedicated to George Washington. His Excellency owned a copy of *Officers Detached in the Field* and it was one of the books he recommended to a recently appointed officer who asked him what treatises to read.[21] Here is a sampling of the information in Roger Stevenson's *Instructions for Officers Detached in the Field*:

> *If the ambuscade [ambush] is placed in a wood, an intelligent non-commissioned officer should be chosen to get upon a high tree from whence he can see the march of the enemy and give notice of its most essential circumstances.*
>
> *The best season for secret marches, is the cold time of winter where neither peasants nor their dogs stir abroad, and the enemy are quiet, only thinking how to preserve themselves from the cold.*
>
> *When you place an ambush, if there is some water nearby, it may suggest to them [the partisans] to wet their clothes and cover them with dust, to give them the color of the ground.*

Included in the advice given by Stevenson was that officers leading troops behind enemy lines "should not be prone to keeping female company, to greediness, or to drinking."[22]

There were two other guerilla warfare treatises in print at the time of the American Revolution. One is entitled *The Partisan: Or the Art of Making War in Detachment Translated from the French of* [*sic*] *Mr. De Jeney*. Here are samples of the Frenchman's advice:

> *You are never to form a ambuscade with a design to cut off the enemy's retreat; for that will reduce them to despair, and inspire them with resolution to rally.*
>
> *When you are sent out with a design to reconnoiter the enemy's camp, their numbers and position, the dawn of the day is by no means the best time for this business, as you will then infallibly fall in*

*with some of their patrols or reconnoitering parties. You must there-
fore advance towards them in the night. Their position and extent
may be easily discovered by the fires of their quarter guards [a small
detachment of soldiers on active duty] and advanced piquets [soldiers
guarding the perimeter of an army camp]. There are also many other
particulars that may be observed in the night, as you have it in your
power to advance close to their camp, without the least danger.*[23]

The other influential partisan warfare treatise being read at the time
was *Manoeuvers, or Practical Observations on the Art of War* by Major
William Young. Published in London in 1771, Major Young's book
included how a partisan corps should prepare to defend themselves in a
deserted village. He began by explaining that the partisans should try to
fortify four stone houses "so situated that they flank one another." This
means that the men in one fortified house can fire on enemy troops trying
to break into one of the other occupied houses. The modern term for this
technique is crossfire. Giving further advice about protecting the fortified
houses, Major Young said, "Roofs should be taken off if covered with
straw, and the houses cleared of all combustibles, loop-holes [small open-
ings to accommodate guns] must be made in the walls, the stairs taken
away [in a two-story building], and ladders only used, as the under story
must be abandoned during the attack, the avenues to these houses must be
filled with wagons and carts, from which one wheel is removed."[24]

Supplementing the advice in the partisan warfare treatises was
the experience of colonists who had fought in the French and Indian
War. These veterans, who included George Washington and William
Maxwell, had firsthand knowledge of Indian warfare, which the French
adopted in North America to put their stronger enemy on the defensive.[25] The Indians attacked swiftly, relying on the element of surprise
to overwhelm a superior enemy force. Another Indian technique was to
identify and kill their opponent's officers to create disorganization and
confusion. Whether General Washington condoned this practice during
the Revolutionary War is unclear.

As the forage war intensified, the Americans benefited from their
superior knowledge of the terrain. Charles Stedman described the land in

which the foragers were moving as "containing numberless inaccessible posts, and strong natural barriers, formed by the various combinations of woods, mountains, rivers, lakes and marshes."[26] This rough terrain offered numerous sites for organizing ambushes and harassing the British from cover and then disappearing into the countryside. The New Jersey militia, who lacked the training, experience, and weapons to fight pitched battles, proved to be effective in knowing where to stage their ambushes and hit-and-run attacks. The British contemptuously styled their duplicitous methods as "skulking."[27] The New Jersey militia's resolve can also be attributed to the fact that they were defending their homes and farms from being ransacked. Patriot newspapers helped to rally the militia. Typical was a story in the January 29, 1777, issue of the *Pennsylvania Journal*, which described the "misery and desolation" inflicted by the British and Hessians in New Jersey: "Their rage and lust, their avarice and cruelty, know no bounds; and murder, ravishment, plunder, and the most brutal treatment of every sex and age... signalized their conquest."[28] Another factor that added to the success of the New Jersey militia was that by 1777 their ranks included some combat veterans who had served in the Continental Army earlier in the war.

By mid-February it seemed to Cornwallis that the Americans were contesting every foraging expedition. He responded by increasing the size of his foraging parties and including field artillery to protect them. The Americans countered by increasing the number of men who challenged their plundering. As a result, what started as small actions at the start of the winter in New Jersey escalated into fighting involving thousands of men.

The forage war encompassed much of central New Jersey including the present-day towns of Rahway, Metuchen, Edison, South Plainfield, and Piscataway. This area became a no man's land controlled by neither the British nor the Americans. Cornwallis was sending foraging expeditions into this contested area, and Washington's responses to their pillaging included sending General William Maxwell into the contested area.

Of all the senior American officers wintering at Morristown, William "Scotch Willie" Maxwell (1733–1796) turned out to be the most adept at partisan warfare. This style of fighting required courageous officers who could lead by example and had the experience to know when to press an attack or order a retreat. Scotch Willie had both courage and experience, which he first demonstrated as a young officer in the French and Indian War. Probably his most daunting experience during that conflict was as a lieutenant in a distinguished New Jersey Provincial regiment known as the Jersey Blues. His regiment participated in the 1758 British attack on French-held Fort Carillon (later renamed Fort Ticonderoga). Attacking the French without artillery support, the British regulars and Provincials suffered over 2,000 casualties in their valiant but failed attack. Scotch Willie's combat experience, courage under fire, and leadership skills were valued by Washington, who put him in the front line of the escalating forage war.

Maxwell's first confrontation with a sizable British foraging expedition took place near Woodbridge, New Jersey, on February 23, 1777. The foragers were commanded by Colonel Charles Mawhood, one of Lord Cornwallis's best officers. It will be recalled that Mawhood commanded the British troops at the Battle of Princeton where he organized a stubborn resistance to the American surprise attack. The weather on Sunday morning, February 23, was "a fine clear frosty morning, not so cold." At 6:00 that morning, Colonel Mawhood marched out of the fortified perimeter of Perth Amboy with 3,000 regulars and artillery on a foraging mission. His command consisted of the 3rd British Brigade, six companies of grenadiers, six companies of light infantry, and three pieces of horse-drawn field artillery. They were not carrying any provisions or knapsacks because they expected to be out foraging for a few hours.[29] Their destination was the farms in the area between Woodbridge and Rahway. The distance from Perth Amboy to Rahway was nine miles following a good road through the region. The area through which they were marauding was a precarious no man's land controlled by neither the British nor the Americans. By mid-morning, Mawhood's column was pillaging farms north of Woodbridge. General Maxwell was alerted to their presence and he ordered Edward Hand's 1st Pennsylvania Regiment and George Stricker's Maryland German Regiment into action. Both regiments were posted in Spanktown, a village two miles west of Rahway.[30] Their presence near Rahway was due to the village's proximity to British-held Perth Amboy and Staten Island. Maxwell also sent a courier to Colonel Eneas McKay to join the fight. McKay's 8th Pennsylvania Regiment was stationed in Samptown (present day South Plainfield), which was eight miles west of Rahway.[31]

Everything was quiet and the foraging ran smoothly during the early morning hours. But Colonel Mawhood was taking no chances of his column being ambushed or subjected to partisan raids. As a precaution, he ordered Lieutenant Colonel Mungo Campbell to take his 52nd Regiment and four companies of grenadiers and make a sweep of the surrounding countryside. British Grenadier Lieutenant John Peebles and twenty grenadiers composed the advanced guard of Campbell's detachment.[32] At 11:00 am, about a mile and a half west of Woodbridge, the British had their first encounter with Maxwell's Continentals and militia. It began when Lieutenant Peebles saw a group of rebels in the distance and sent a corporal off to inform Colonel Campbell. The corporal returned saying that Campbell was advancing to engage the rebels but wanted Peebles to get a closer look at their position. Peebles moved forward with his twenty men, believing that he would be quickly reinforced. But Campbell was slow in arriving as Peebles's grenadiers began exchanging musket fire with the rebels. Peebles was seriously outnumbered, and two of his men were wounded before reinforcements arrived. But, it seemed like an instant later when the Americans were gone. Campbell, now on high alert, formed his regiment in a field in battle formation and cautiously resumed his sweep when he saw a small detachment of rebels running from the edge of a swamp and "making straight for a wood." Campbell ordered Peebles to move up to a fence at the edge of the woods with his detachment and the grenadier companies from the 42nd and 28th regiments. After reaching the fence, the grenadiers were fired on by the rebels, who were shooting at them from behind the trees in the wooded area. The Americans shrouded by the trees turned out to be decoys meant for the British to charge at them while a larger rebel detachment suddenly "galled" Peebles's grenadiers on his right flank. The British had blundered into an ambush and, according to Peebles, "the men are dropping down fast." He did not hear Campbell's order to retreat and "remained at my post till I had not one man left near me. I fired all my cartridges [a ball and powder wrapped in paper], when seeing the rascals coming pretty close up I took to my heels and ran back, under heavy fire which thank God I escaped."[33] After an intensive firefight, the British finally chased off the rebels. The lull allowed the regulars to carry out their dead and wounded to the road and put them into some of the wagons that were meant to haul commandeered victuals and fodder to Perth Amboy. By late afternoon, Maxwell had mustered 900 Continentals and militia to oppose Mawhood's 3,000 troops and artillery. But despite being heavily outnumbered and outgunned, Maxwell inflicted a heavy toll on Mawhood's column by waylaying the British flanks and rear. The regulars pursued the attackers all afternoon, forcing them "from their lurking places."[34] By sundown the British were "much fatigued and harassed" from the constant fighting. Mawhood had enough, and ordered his column to turn around and start back to Perth Amboy. During their retreat the foragers were opposed by a large body of rebels "posted opposite us in a wood"; Mawhood ordered his cannons to fire at them which "set them a scampering."[35] British engineer Archibald Robertson described the scene in his diary: "the rebels hung upon the column's rear all the way home. We had four officers and about sixty men killed and wounded by the time the foragers got back to Perth Amboy at 7:30 in the evening."[36] In comparison, the Americans lost three men killed and eight wounded.[37] These comparative casualty figures appear to be accurate and prompted one frustrated British officer to exclaim, "we have been tossed and kicked about most amazingly."[38]

A Philadelphia newspaper published an account of the day's fighting, noting that the British forages were accompanied by fifteen to twenty wagons which they intended to use to carry off their plunder. But instead, "a considerable number of the wagons were employed in carrying off their dead and wounded; some of the wagons were so piled, that the dead fell off, and were left in the road." The same tabloid reported that a British officer, infuriated by the day-long rebel attacks, saw a poor countryman standing at his door watching Mawhood's column retreating toward Perth Amboy. The newspaper reported that the officer "laid hold of him," upon which the man showed the officer his protection signed by General Howe's secretary. The officer snarled "'damned him and his protection' and said those who had taken protections, were all damned rebels as those who had not, and immediately sent a ball through his body, which not providing instant death, his men stabbed the innocent countryman with their bayonets."[39]

Lieutenant Peebles visited the wounded men in the hospital the next day. Among the wounded, Peebles said, "several of them in a very dangerous way, poor fellows, what pity it is to throw away such men as these on such shabby, ill managed occasions."[40]

Why did General Howe insist on occupying a small section of New Jersey during the winter of 1777 with 10,000 men who were in constant danger of being killed or wounded? It seemed logical for Howe to have withdrawn his troops from New Jersey for the balance of the winter to British-held Staten Island and Manhattan Island. The problem was that British supply lines were already being stretched thin to provide food and fodder for the troops and horses in Howe's more secure New York bases. Importing tons of fodder from England tied up valuable cargo space on transports, besides being expensive. New Jersey had abundant farms, and foraging in the state—despite the dangers—continued out of necessity. Encouraging the practice was that some New Jersey foraging expeditions were successful. Lieutenant Peebles, for example, described going foraging from Perth Amboy on February 28, just days after Mawhood's calamitous mission. Peebles wrote in his diary that a convoy of wagons left Perth Amboy and "went about three miles into the country on the Bonam Town [modern Bonhamtown section of Edison, New Jersey] road, where they loaded the wagons with hay and straw whilst the troops were posted all around to defend them... when we marched into Town [Perth Amboy] again without seeing any of the enemy."

Daily life for the Crown forces wintering in New Brunswick was even more hazardous than what the troops garrisoned in Perth Amboy were experiencing. Virtually everything that the troops at New Brunswick needed had to be transported from Perth Amboy. The Raritan River was too shallow to accommodate large ships and, as a result, provisions, imported fodder, and military supplies had to be conveyed ten miles upriver from Perth Amboy. The ten miles between the two posts was what one British officer called a "nest of American hornets."[41] British convoys travelling by road over the ten miles were waylaid by American partisans. Even boats plying between the two fortified towns were targeted. The Raritan was deep enough at high tide to allow small ships to sail up the river to New Brunswick. An eyewitness described the ships arriving at New Brunswick as "schooners and sloops of good burden."[42] A schooner sailing in American waters in the seventeenth century was typically a small merchant ship with two masts. A sloop has a single mast. "Burden" is the nautical term for how much cargo a ship could carry expressed in tons.

In one incident along the river, a detachment of Pennsylvania militiamen armed with rifles ambushed a sloop on February 3. The riflemen were "advantageously placed" in the tall weeds and brush along the southern shoreline of the river. They reported attacking a sloop that was coming down from New Brunswick with twelve men visible on the deck "and gave them a how do you do with about twenty five rifles and two muskets." They believed that they killed or wounded at least three of the crew.[43]

Among the Crown forces wintering in New Brunswick were two companies of the elite Hesse-Kassel Field Jäger Corps. Jäger is the German word for hunter or forester, a clue to their special functions which included scouting and surprise attacks on enemy outposts. The predominant color of their uniforms was green, which was the preferred color of European huntsmen and foresters dating from the Middle Ages.[44] The Hesse-Kassel jägers wore green coats faced (exposed lining, cuffs and collar) in crimson, white or buff breeches, and a green cockade (a decorative rosette or knot of ribbon) in their hats. They exchanged their green cockade with a stylish green plume (an arrangement of feathers) in their hats when they were on parade. Their weapons were unique, consisting of a short, heavy rifle and a hunting sword.[45] A knife was carried on the same scabbard as the sword. Captain Johann Ewald commanded one of the jäger companies at New Brunswick. He was described as being of medium height, slender, and very intelligent. He lost his left eye in a prewar duel with a fellow officer and wore a glass eye and an eye patch to cover the deformity. Ewald was briefly introduced earlier in this

Portrait of a Revolutionary War–period German jäger by artist George C. Woodbridge.
Author's collection.

narrative as the officer who reconnoitered Fort Washington for General Howe during the 1776 campaign. Knowing more about Ewald and his exploits as a jäger officer is important to this narrative, as he kept a diary of his service in the American War, including detailed accounts of his fighting alongside the British Army in New Jersey in 1777.

Johann Ewald was born in the small central German principality of Hesse-Cassel (present-day Kassel) in 1744. The small nation was ruled by a hereditary nobleman called the Landgrave. Ewald's father was a bookkeeper who worked at the local post office. His mother's family were middle-class merchants. Ewald had no noteworthy education as a youth and decided at the age of sixteen to make the army his career. It was a practical decision, as Hesse-Cassel was a poor country whose major source of income came from renting out its army. It was a common practice for the smaller German principalities like Hesse-Cassel to

A page from the diary of German jäger Captain Johann Ewald. The diary is in the Special Collections of the Harvey Andruss Library at Bloomsburg University, Pennsylvania. *Author's photo.*

raise money by leasing their armies to whoever needed one, but Hesse-Cassel carried the idea to the extreme. To explain, the principality had a population of 300,000 at the time of the American War.[46] It is estimated that between 5 and 7 percent of its population was in the army. In fact, the kingdom was so heavily militarized that it was described as an army with a country instead of a country with an army. With few attractive career opportunities, the Landgrave was able to recruit an all-volunteer force whose officers in particular were well paid and held in high esteem. Besides the attraction of steady pay, decent food, medical care, and status in a militant society, there was the possibility of sharing in wartime plunder. The army was also less dangerous than some civilian occupations, as well as being much more exciting.

Ewald joined the army in 1760 as a cadet (a young gentleman studying military subjects) in the hopes of becoming an officer. It was a challenging goal, as the majority of the kingdom's officers were members of the nobility. Much of Europe was at war in 1760 in what became known as the Seven Years' War (1756–1763). As previously mentioned, the American segment of the Seven Years' War was called the French and Indian War. As a cadet, Ewald fought in several European battles during the Seven Year's War where he proved to be a courageous soldier. His bravery was rewarded with an advancement to the rank of ensign and enrollment in the technical school in the city of Kassel called the Collegium Carolinum. Ewald's course of study at the institute was concentrated on military science, and he proved to be an outstanding student. His battlefield experience, intelligence, and loyalty were rewarded by Landgrave Frederick II with a promotion to lieutenant. Ewald was further promoted to captain in 1774 in the Liebjäger, better known as the Jäger Corps. The Jäger Corps was an elite branch of the Landgrave's army. In his authoritative history of the American Revolution, Don Higgenbotham said that the Jäger Corps "compared favorably with the best in the British Army."[47] The Jägers were recruited from among spirited young men who were adept at stalking game in the forest. They were also expert marksmen who were issued expensive and accurate rifles by the Landgrave to make them even more valuable soldiers.

On January 15, 1776, Landgrave Frederick sold the British government a package deal of a 12,500-man, fully equipped army consisting of fifteen infantry regiments, four grenadier battalions, "some artillery" and two companies of elite jägers.[48] Each jäger company had 125 men. Captain Ewald commanded one of the jäger companies sent to America in 1776. Ewald's company arrived in British-held New York on October 19, 1776, and was promptly sent into action. They fought in the Battle of White Plains, the storming of Fort Washington, chased Washington's army across New Jersey in late 1776, and clashed with the rebels across Assunpink Creek during the Second Battle of Trenton.

Mid-January 1777 found Ewald's jäger company occupying a forward observation post in New Jersey facing American-controlled Bound Brook. While the entire countryside surrounding British-held New Brunswick was a dangerous no man's land the nine miles between New Brunswick and Bound Brook were particularly unsafe. One reason was that ground between the two posts was riddled with ravines, woodlands, and creek beds that were ideal for rebel ambushes. Ewald's mission was to keep the area under surveillance, especially the roads from Bound Brook and Samptown, and warn the British camp of any rebel incursions.

Ewald's dangerous assignment was considered a post of honor, one which only the most courageous men would be selected to man. He established his observation post about four miles northeast of New Brunswick. His position was along what was called at the time the Great Road Up Raritan (present-day River Road in Piscataway), which was the main road between New Brunswick and Bound Brook. Ewald's only reference to his exact location was that he occupied a "very small" house named "White's plantation." It may have been a two-room farmhouse (still standing) originally built in 1743 by John Field. The house sits on high ground overlooking the Great Road Up Raritan.

Ewald described his time at the little farmhouse as "hard duty" with skirmishing occurring on a daily basis: "when they [the rebels] did not visit us, we rendered the honors to the Americans." Ewald's arsenal included at least one amusette (a large-caliber portable weapon shaped like a gun), which Ewald mentioned using to "drive the Americans out of a barn. Not only did the men have to stay dressed day and night, but they had to stay together, with horses [probably for use by couriers] constantly saddled, and everything packed." Adding to their discomfort was that it snowed "very severely" for several days in mid-January with the accumulation "over half-man deep."[49]

Ewald and fifty of his jägers took part in a foraging expedition on February 8 under the personal command of Lord Cornwallis. Their objective was to collect fodder from the abandoned farms in the Quibbletown area. Ewald said that to protect the foragers and their wagons, his jägers provided an advance guard "supported by four hundred British light infantry men. Behind them were four hundred Scots [42nd Royal Highland Regiment], one hundred light dragoons, a number of 6-pounders [field artillery], four hundred English grenadiers, two Hessian grenadier battalions and four hundred British infantrymen." The size of the expedition is an indication of the intensity of rebel activity in the region.

Ewald's diary described how the expedition ran into a detachment of enemy marksmen whom Ewald's jägers chased into the hamlet of Quibbletown. The village's houses, surrounded by stone walls that once had vegetable gardens, had long since been abandoned and the buildings stripped bare of anything of value. Ewald walked into a trap set by a large number of rebels who were hiding behind the stone walls. They waited until the jägers were within musket range when they suddenly rose up and started firing at the Germans. The jägers took cover and artillery was brought up, which drove the rebel ambushers into the woods. But the skirmishing continued "steadily" while the foraging continued. The shooting intensified on the road back to New Brunswick. "The enemy hung on our rear," according to Ewald, "until we reached our outposts."[50] Captain Ewald survived the expedition, and we will meet him again later in this narrative.

The relentless fighting continued throughout March 1777 driven by the British Army's need for food and fodder. Their foraging expeditions, now involving thousands of men, were contested by Continentals and militia, while New Brunswick and Perth Amboy were practically besieged by periodic American attacks on the town's outposts. The British tried to use their large forays into the countryside as bait, but the rebel's superior knowledge of the topography, and their growing experience and resourceful leadership, often left the British second best. On March 22, for example, a large British foraging expedition was attacked by Patriot troops commanded by Major Joseph Bloomfield near Woodbridge, New Jersey. Bloomfield reported killing or wounding 120 enemy troops with American casualties of five dead and five wounded.[51]

The forage war in New Jersey helped account for the British taking the Americans seriously as soldiers. Prior to the Revolutionary War, British officers had a low opinion of the fighting abilities of the American colonists. Typical was the opinion of British General James Wolfe: "The Americans are in general the dirtiest, most contemptible cowardly dogs that you can conceive. There is no depending on them in action. They fall down dead in their own dirt and desert by battalions, officers and all."[52] But, by mid-1777, experienced British officers wintering in New Jersey had changed their opinion and acknowledged the

Americans as dangerous adversaries. Among the British officers who had firsthand experience with the Americans in New Jersey was Lieutenant Colonel William Harcourt, the daring dragoon officer who led the raid that captured Charles Lee. Colonel Harcourt admitted, "it was once the fashion of this army to treat them in the most contemptible light, they are now become a formidable enemy... they possess some of the requisites for making good troops, such as extreme cunning, great industry in moving ground and felling of wood [sic], activity and a spirit of enterprise upon any advantage."[53]

One measure of American success was that British losses in New Jersey during the winter of 1777 were estimated at over 1,000 killed, wounded, or captured. If their losses during the Trenton-Princeton campaign were added to this number, the total amounted to 3,000.[54] Much of the credit belongs to Washington. His management of his small force in New Jersey during the winter of 1777 is as impressive as his earlier victories at Trenton and Princeton. His policy of removing horses and wagons were among his initial moves after arriving in Morristown. He next quickly organized and encouraged the New Jersey militia to fight, and supported them with detachments of Continental troops and outstanding commanders. In addition, he positioned his available troops at forward outposts to the east and south of Morristown to protect his headquarters, serve as launching points for raids, and help create the illusion that he had a large army.

To a certain degree, General Howe had let it happen. Although Sir William's actions were handicapped by a pressing need for food and fodder, some individuals on the scene believed he lacked the self-assurance to risk his army in a full-scale attack on Morristown. Among Sir William's detractors at the time was British Army Colonel Allan Maclean. Maclean's opinion mattered, based on his record as a resourceful combat officer. A good example of Maclean's assertive character was his taking charge of defending Quebec when it was threatened by an American army commanded by then Colonel Benedict Arnold early in the war. Quebec had only a handful of troops at the time, and its befuddled civilian government was ready to surrender the city when Maclean arrived with just eighty Loyalist troops. He immediately quashed any talk of surrendering and organized Quebec's male population into militia companies. He also ordered anyone who refused to serve to pack up and leave. When Arnold's corps arrived, Maclean responded to his surrender demand with a defiant cannon blast. An officer of Maclean's daring and pluck probably would have mustered the 10,000 Crown forces troops wintering in New Jersey and attacked Morristown from all directions. But Maclean was not in charge, and was reduced to expressing his grievances in a confidential letter that he wrote while languishing in New York City during the winter of 1777. Maclean said, "General William Howe would make a very good executive officer under another's command, but he is not by any means equal to a commander-in-chief. He has, moreover, got none but very silly fellows about him—a great parcel of old women—most of them improper for American service; I could be very ludicrous on this occasion, but it is truly too serious a matter that brave men's lives should be sacrificed to be commanded by such generals."[55]

5

Much Gratified by the Mischief
They Had Done*

Eighteenth-century armies typically spent wartime winter months in cantonments (military encampments) and eagerly resumed campaigning the following spring. General Sir William Howe was different and much slower in taking the field. In 1776, for example, after wintering in Halifax, Nova Scotia, Sir William finally began his campaign to capture the city of New York in late August. His delay is attributed to his meticulous planning and caution. Howe repeated the same pattern in 1777, during which he wasted months of good weather methodically preparing for his campaign to capture Philadelphia.

But Sir William organized two well-planned and bold operations during the early spring of 1777. Both are worth studying, as they demonstrate Howe's impressive generalship when he finally acted. His two springtime campaigns were aimed at destroying American supply centers. While both were successful, Howe's critics felt that he should have been focusing on crushing Washington's army in New Jersey instead of destroying American supply depots. Among Howe's critics was Nicholas Cresswell, who was passing through New York City during May 1777. Cresswell wrote in his journal that the soldiers in the city "long to be

---

* Chapter title from George F. Scheer, ed., *Private Yankee Doodle, Being a Narrative of Some of the Adventures, Dangers and Sufferings of a Revolutionary Soldier by Joseph Plumb Martin* (New York: Little, Brown and Company, 1962), 62

in action. I am very certain," Cresswell penned, "if General Howe does nothing, the rebels will avail themselves of his inactivity by collecting a very numerous army to oppose him, whenever he shall think proper to leave Mrs. Loring and face them."[1] Loyalist Thomas Jones was furious with Howe's failure to assault Morristown, which he attributed to Sir William's desire to purposely prolong the war. According to Jones, "the suppression of a dangerous rebellion was but a secondary consideration." The slow pace of the war, Jones said, "was based on Howe and his friends methodically swindling the treasury of Great Britain... while plunder, robberies, peculation [misappropriations of public funds], whoring, gaming, and all kinds of dissipation [debauchery] were cherished, nursed, encouraged and openly countenanced."[2]

Some background information about the differences between the British and American supply system during the American War will explain why the usually cautious Howe organized daring raids in early 1777 aimed at the Patriot supply depots in Peekskill, New York, and Danbury, Connecticut. Looking first at the British supply system, there were times during the American War when British troops were reduced to eating salted provisions and wearing threadbare clothing. However, they were generally adequately fed and clothed by procedures and departments already in place as a result of three-quarters of a century of Britain at war with their European rivals.[3] This was not true of the American colonists, who began the conflict with little experience in supplying their troops with food, clothing, and the numerous other articles required to field an army.

At the start of the war, Congress adopted the British arrangement which was based on establishing autonomous departments that purchased, transported, and distributed everything that an army needed to function. Congress took responsibility for the American supply system with limited success. Historian E. Wayne Carp explained that Congress's failure was due in part to the fact that only one of the sixty-five Congressmen in attendance during the first two years of the war had any knowledge of supply matters. He was Roger Sherman, a Connecticut delegate, who was the commissary (the person responsible for furnishing provisions and fodder) for Connecticut troops stationed at Albany during the French and Indian War.[4] One result of Congress's efforts was that, unlike the British who established a secure central supply base in New York City during the war, the rebels established regional supply depots based on access to victuals and transportation but with little regard for defending their storehouses. The assumption was that American troops would be nearby to discourage the enemy from attacking their supply depots. Washington, for example, spent the winter of 1777–1778 at Valley Forge in part to protect the American supply depots in York and Reading, Pennsylvania. Several of the isolated American supply bases were tempting targets for the British in early 1777, and even the ever-cautious General Howe could not resist attacking them.

This is a good point in this narrative to elaborate on the military definition of "logistics," which was previously mentioned as the science of planning and carrying out the movement, supply, and maintenance of military forces.[5] The word "logistics" did not exist at the time of the American Revolution. The first known use of the word in the English language appeared in 1861. For the sake of brevity and clarity, I will use the word logistics going forward with the understanding that George Washington would not have been able to tell you what the word meant.

The first British attack of 1777 aimed at destroying a major Patriot storage depot occurred in mid-March. The target was the American supply base at Peekskill, New York. The village was located on the eastern shore of the Hudson River, thirty-seven miles north from British-held Manhattan Island. The supply depot was located in Peekskill because of the village's favorable logistical location: there were tolerable roads leading to the village from the New England farming regions, and Peekskill's proximity to an important rebel-held ferry that operated on the Hudson River between Verplanck's Point and Stony Point. Called the Kings Ferry, its eastern terminus was three and a half miles south of Peekskill with a road from the village to the ferry. The ferry was a vital link for reinforcements and supplies to reach Washington's Grand Army in New Jersey from American-held New England. It was also dangerously close to British-held Manhattan Island.

The depot at Peekskill consisted of a number of buildings in and around the village. The complex included a powder magazine (a place where weapons and gunpowder are stored), barracks, workshops, and warehouses "containing an immense quantity of military stores." There was also a forage yard where hay, straw, and corn was stockpiled.[6] A small fort (Fort Independence) was located on Tethard's Hill, an eminence just north of the village. The little fort had three cannons, including one twelve-pounder (a cannon that fired a twelve-pound, solid iron ball called solid shot) aimed in the direction of the nearby Hudson River. The fort, village, storage depot, Kings Ferry, and a nearby grain mill were garrisoned by only 250 militiamen commanded by Brigadier General Alexander McDougall. Adding to Peekskill's vulnerability, the Americans had no warships to help defend the place.

Locating a major American supply depot on the shoreline of the lower Hudson River was incongruous and an invitation for the Royal Navy to raid the place. General Washington had learned from experience during the 1776 campaign to keep his distance from anywhere the powerful Royal Navy could operate.

British intelligence in New York City was aware of the situation at Peekskill, as evidenced by a comment from Captain Muenchhausen, who worked at headquarters as an aide-de-camp to General Howe. The captain described Peekskill in his journal prior to the raid as "a very large but not well protected enemy magazine."[7]

The British planned a surprise attack on Peekskill to commence on March 20. Their plan was to sail north from New York City in a fast-moving flotilla of ships and come ashore on the morning of March 22 in landing barges at a secluded cove one mile south of the village. Captain Muenchhausen mentioned the composition of the British expedition in his March 19 diary entry: "A detachment of 500 men and 50 artillerist with four 3 pounders (field artillery that fired a three pound ball) under the command of [Lieutenant] Colonel [John] Bird embarked on the Hudson River today escorted by a frigate of 32 guns and two sloops of 10 guns each."[8] The frigate was the HMS *Brune*, captured from the French during the Seven Years' War. Besides the *Brune* and the two sloops, the expedition consisted of four transports to carry the troops, three armed galleys, and eight landing barges towed by the transports. Galleys were small but heavily armed and very maneuverable. Historian John W.

Jackson called them "the wasps of the navy that were often effective out of proportion to their size."[9] Two of the armed galleys on the Peekskill expedition were captured from the rebels during the 1776 New York campaign. They were probably the Connecticut Navy galleys *Whiting* and *Shark*.[10] The size of the galleys' crew and their ordnance varied, but generally consisted of fifty men and at least one large-caliber cannon.[11] The galleys usually had a single mast and sail, allowing them to cruise in a favorable wind, or they could be rowed by their crews manning large oars. Their maneuverability and shallow draft (draft meaning the minimum amount of water required to float a boat) allowed the galleys to provide Colonel Bird's landing party artillery support close to the shoreline. The three armed galleys were thus ideally suited for the planned attack.

At first the British flotilla made good progress as it proceeded up the Hudson River and was hopeful that it would reach Peekskill quickly to surprise its defenders. But the ships were delayed by contrary winds and "the incompetent pilot of the frigate," which was leading the flotilla. The pilot's error caused the frigate and two of the transports to run aground on March 21 by sailing too close to the shoreline during low tide. The ships were freed on the high tide early on Sunday morning, March 23, and reached Peekskill later that day. The first British troops finally came ashore in the flatboats at 1:00 pm. They landed at a cove a mile and a half below Peekskill. They brought ashore four cannons that were manned by sailors from the *Brune*. According to Captain Muenchhausen, the landing party "proceeded in spite of being afraid that, because of their delays, their presence had been detected and they could expect strong resistance."[12] But there was no one to oppose them. The flotilla's delay had warned the militia defending Peekskill of the pending attack. Aware that they were heavily outnumbered, the Patriots devoted their time to hurriedly moving all of their ammunition in horse-drawn wagons and their two smaller caliber cannons to safety. According to General McDougall, they "blew-up" their twelve-pounder "to prevent their using it against us."[13] Upon reaching Peekskill, the British found that the departing militia had also smashed part of the stored barrels of rum and molasses and set fire to several of the warehouses. However, there was not enough time to destroy everything, and the British confiscated

100 hogsheads of rum and molasses, 60 boxes of soap and candles, and 600 barrels of flour and sundry small stores. But with the exception of saving one prize, they burned every building and destroyed every boat along the waterfront. The prize they hauled back to New York, according to Captain Muenchhausen, was General Washington's personal barge, which was docked at Kings Ferry.[14]

American militia Colonel Ann Hawkes Hay, who lived in Haverstraw across the Hudson River from Peekskill, watched the fire spread "till at last the conflagration became general and destroyed a considerable part, if not the whole town of Peekskill."[15] McDougall and his men watched Peekskill burn from a hilltop (present-day Fort Hill) near the town. Upon seeing the rebels, the British advanced toward them "within good musket range" of the hill. McDougall fell back again with his two cannons, this time two miles north to another summit called Bald Hill. The British broke off their attack but left a picket guard (sentries located at a distance from an army to give notice of an approaching enemy) of one hundred men "posted on strong ground" to observe McDougall's position and warn the main body of a rebel counterattack. The picket guard remained in position overnight and into Monday, March 24.

The closest Continental Army troops to McDougall were at Fort Montgomery, which was located on the west bank of the Hudson River six and a half miles north of Peekskill. Four and a half miles further upriver from Fort Montgomery was Fort Constitution, which was situated across the Hudson River from the future site of the fort (and later the U.S. Military Academy) that the Americans built at West Point later in the war. Part of the 3rd New York Regiment under the command of Colonel Marinus Willett arrived at McDougall's militia camp from the upriver forts on Monday (March 24) afternoon. Colonel Willett was able to bring only eighty men to reinforce McDougall. However, the British were unaware of the rebels' strength, and Willett led a flanking movement through a wooded area to get behind the British picket guard. At the same time McDougall's detachment "amused" (distracted) the pickets as if preparing to attack them. But Willett's men fired too soon and at too great a distance, and his position was discovered by the pickets who "fled with great precipitation to the main body." By now it was dusk and the British decided to "lay on their arms" during the night, not knowing that the rebels were too few in number to attack them. After a stressful night, the British boarded their ships early the next morning. An American officer described the closing scene: "no pursuit being made the enemy reimbarkqued [*sic*] without molestation and on Tuesday (March 25) made sail for New York." Admiral Lord Richard Howe sent a report to the Admiralty in London following the safe return of Colonel Bird's foray to Peekskill. The admiral wrote of the expedition's success: "This plentiful deposit of provisions, stores and other necessaries of various kinds, was totally destroyed: with no other loss than two seamen who were missing [probably deserted]."[16]

The Peekskill raid exposed the vulnerability of the Americans' feebly defended supply depots. The Patriots believed that their other principal depots were more secure because they were far inland, but that idea was proven wrong in April 1777 when the British overran the American depot at Danbury, Connecticut, which was twenty-two miles inland through rebel-held territory.

The town of Danbury became a major Continental Army supply depot because of its secluded location and proximity to good roads. Connecticut Loyalists had informed British intelligence in New York that the town was overflowing with foodstuffs, fodder, and hogsheads (casks) of rum. Additional encouraging intelligence was that the depot was guarded by a small detachment of Continentals and local militia.

William Tryon, the former royal governor of New York, is credited with recommending raiding the place. Tryon, who was fifty-two years old at the time, lost his prerogative at the start of the American War when the British colony of New York came under Patriot control. His fidelity to the Crown was rewarded with a commission as a major general of Loyalist troops. Lusting for revenge, the deposed governor was eager to command the Danbury raid. But Tryon had a reputation for cruel treatment of rebel prisoners, and Howe appointed Brigadier General William Erskine, a more judicious officer, as Tryon's second-in-command. Montford Browne, another former royal governor (West Florida and the Bahamas) was also eager for retribution. He joined the expedition in command of a Loyalist regiment called the Prince of Wales

American Volunteers. Browne's regiment was assigned to the expedition because it was composed almost entirely of men from Fairfield County, Connecticut, where Danbury was located.[17] Former Continental Congressman Joseph Galloway, the Pennsylvania official who "stabbed thy country, to support the crown" helped plan the expedition by gathering intelligence from Connecticut Loyalists.[18]

General Howe would have liked to confiscate the supplies at Danbury, but this would have required a slow-moving wagon train to transport the booty. Instead, he opted for a fast-moving punitive infantry attack with orders to destroy the rebel depot. Tryon and Erskine were given 1,500 regulars and 500 Provincial troops for the mission in addition to a detachment of twelve mounted troopers from the 17th Light Dragoons and six horse-drawn, three-pound field cannons. The small detachment of dragoons acted as scouts because the region the expedition would be marching through was heavily wooded and of a "rough and broken character, unsuited to the maneuvers of cavalry."[19] The plan was for General Tryon to transport his raiding party by ships to the Connecticut coast to avoid the long and strenuous overland march from New York. After landing at a remote section of the coast, they would swiftly march inland twenty-two miles to Danbury, destroy the stockpiled stores, and return to their ships before the rebels had time to assemble. To further introduce the story of the Danbury raid, here is the complete opening stanza from the satirical poem titled "The Expedition to Danbury":

Without wit, without wisdom, half stupid and drunk,
And rolling along arm in arm with his punk [Mrs. Loring],
The gallant Sir William, who fights all by proxy,
This spoke to his soldiers, held up by his doxy:
"My boys, I'm a going to send you with Tryon,
To a place where you'll all get as groggy as I am:
And the wounded, when well, shall receive a full gill [four ounces].
But the slain be allowed just as much as they will.
By a Tory from Danbury I've just been informed
That there's nobody there, so the place shall be storm'd."
(then spoke up the Loyalist Joseph Galloway)

Joe-Gallop-Away, refugee tory with several others,
"Good soldiers, go fight that we all may get rich."[20]

The Danbury expedition was quietly launched in twelve transports that sailed from the New York City waterfront on Monday, April 21, 1777. Only the expedition's senior officers knew the squadron's destination. With their usual meticulous planning, the Howe brothers distracted the attention of Patriot spies in New York from the ships embarking for the Danbury raid by sending a diversionary force composed of two Royal Navy frigates and a fleet of transports up the Hudson River as far as Dobbs Ferry. The transports carried just enough troops to make it look like they were embarking on a major offensive. At the same time, the transports carrying over 2,000 troops bound for Danbury sailed in the opposite direction: up the East River and into Long Island Sound. The weakly armed transports were unaccompanied by Royal Navy warships when they left New York City to further draw attention away from their movement by rebel spies and informers. But after entering Long Island Sound, the transports were met by the Royal Navy sloops HMS *Senegal* and HMS *Swan*. Captain Henry Duncan, the captain of the *Senegal*, assumed command of the squadron. After a delay due to contrary winds, the warships and transports reached their prearranged landing place at Compo Point (also called Cedar Point) on the Connecticut coast. Compo Point was a desolate beach located between the Connecticut towns of Norwalk and Fairfield. Despite rain and fog, longboats and barges began unloading the Danbury raiders onto the beach at 5:00 pm on Friday, April 25. The expedition was behind schedule, and there was concern that the American militia was alerted to their presence. In the poem "The Expedition to Danbury," Governor Tryon loses his swagger at the possibility of an enemy attack and retreats to the back of his army for his safety:

In cunning and canting [insincerity], deceit and disguise,
In cheating a friend, and inventing of lies,
I think I'm a match for the best of my species,
But in this undertaking I feel all in pieces;
So I'll fall in the rear, for I'd rather go last;—

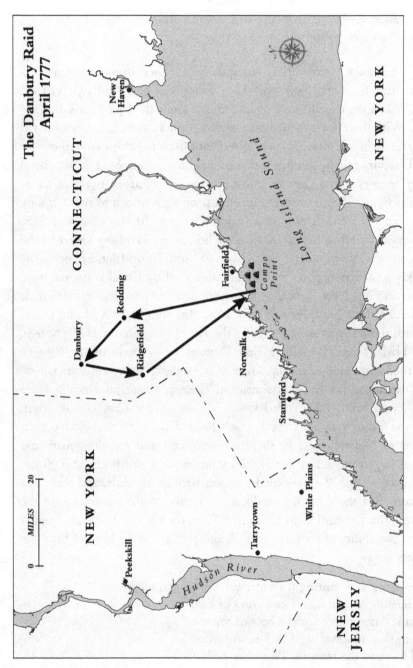

The Danbury raid, April 1777. This map shows the route of the British raid on the American supply depot in Danbury, Connecticut. The fast-moving, successful British operation took place April 25–28, 1777.

Come, march on, my boys, let me see you all past;
For his Majesty's service (so says my commission)
Requires that I bring up the whole expedition.[21]

There are various accounts of the raid, but the best one was a letter attributed to "a British officer." However, a careful reading of the letter indicates that the author was Captain Archibald Robertson, a British Army engineer who accompanied the expedition.[22] Bringing an engineer on the mission made sense; although the raiders were planning to move fast and complete their mission before the Connecticut militia could rally, an engineer could "inspect, contrive [to create in an ingenious manner] any defenses of a fortified place" or construct or repair a bridge if necessary.[23]

According to Captain Robertson, it took until 11:00 pm on the night of April 25 to get all the troops, artillery, horses, and baggage offloaded and onto the deserted beach. Tryon clearly had information about the area when he ordered some troops to occupy some well-placed high ground shortly after the first contingent came ashore. The key high ground were two hills called Compo Hill and Bennet's Rock, both of which were located a mile and a half from the beach. Once assembled, the column advanced the mile and a half to the high ground where they camped for the night, "laying on their arms [weapons]" until early on the following morning when they began their march to Danbury. Their route was north on the Redding Road (present-day Connecticut Route 58). Leading the way was Ephraim Deforest, a young officer in the Prince of Wales American Volunteers. He was a former shoemaker and tanner who "espoused the cause of the King." Deforest had lived near Danbury before fleeing to British-held New York City.[24]

When the column was about seven miles from the sea, Captain Robertson wrote, they were attacked "by a small ambuscade, from a morass [marshland], but we soon dislodged them, killed five and took a few prisoners."[25] The raiders met no further resistance during their march. They arrived at the town of Redding in the late morning where they rested for an hour and a half before marching on to Danbury, which they reached at 5:00 pm on Saturday, April 26. The town turned out to be defended by 150 Continentals and militia who fired a few shots before running off to the hills behind the town. However, "seven daring rascals" barricaded themselves into a house and began firing at the invaders. Although they were in an advantageous position, "two companies of the 15th (the East Yorkshire Regiment) attacked the defenders and put them to death by burning the house."[26] After securing the town, Captain Robertson wrote that Tryon's men set about methodically destroying the "greatest magazine the rebels had ever collected."[27] The Redcoats moved fast, working well into the night of April 26, burning whatever they could not destroy. The amount they claimed to have demolished was mind-boggling: 4,000 barrels of beef and pork; 500 barrels of flour; 100 puncheons [a cask usually holding 84 gallons] of rum; a vast quantity of rice, coffee, salt, sugar, medicine, clothing, shoes, wagons, harness, tents, ammunition, and more. The marauders discovered that supplies were stockpiled in buildings throughout the town. A barn filled with valuable animal fodder was torched. The town's meeting house was set ablaze when it was found to be filled with military stores. Private Joseph Plumb Martin passed through Danbury after the raid and found the town "had been laid in ashes" and its streets greasy with melted fat from smashed-in barrels of salted beef and pork.[28] American General John Sullivan later inspected Danbury and counted twenty-six houses that had been set on fire and reduced to a pile of ashes.[29] But the raiders spared the homes of Loyalist sympathizers which were identified by an X marked in chalk or paint on their chimneys. Having completed their work, the British camped for the night just outside of Danbury to get some rest before beginning their trek back to the safety of their ships on the following morning.

Tryon's raiders began their march back to the coast at daybreak on Sunday, April 27. To avoid militia ambushes, they took a different route than the one they used to get to Danbury. Their diversion added five miles to their march, but it was mostly across open ground.[30] Robertson reported that "the militia began to harass us early and increased every mile, galling us from their houses and fences."[31] The first random attackers were led by Connecticut militia Colonel Henry Ludington. But the British had a huge advantage in manpower, plus six cannons to combat the militia. Besides their lack of training and experience, the Connecticut militiamen had only a few Continental troops to support them. There is the story of Colonel Ludington's sixteen-year-old daughter Sybil, who rode forty miles around the countryside to rally her father's militia company. It's a great story that is even depicted on a U.S. postage stamp, but Miss Ludington's ride was the creation of a nineteenth-century writer named Martha J. Lamb.[32]

After marching nine miles, the British column approached the town of Ridgefield. It was here that the raiders met their first organized resistance led by Brigadier General Benedict Arnold, arguably the Patriot's best combat officer at the time. Arnold happened to be in New Haven, Connecticut, visiting with his sister when he was awakened at about 3:00 am on April 26 by a militiaman who told him that 2,000 British troops had landed at Compo Point. Arnold, a man of action, was soon galloping twenty-four miles along the coast over muddy, rain-soaked roads with a small escort to the town of Fairfield, close to where the British were reported to have landed. At Fairfield, Arnold learned that the British were headed toward the supply depot at Danbury. Arnold was soon joined by seventy-year-old General David Wooster, who commanded the Connecticut militia. Historian James Thomas Flexner (1908–2003) was a great storyteller, and here is his account of the action that followed from his book *The Traitor and the Spy*, first published in 1953. Flexner said Arnold and Wooster rode together toward Danbury as "farm boys joined them from lanes, with fowling pieces [a hunting gun rather than a military weapon] in trembling hands." At the town of Redding the two generals "found an excited turmoil of militia." The Patriot force numbering about 500 left Redding, according to Flexner, "down a road cut by multitudinous British feet. Arnold and Wooster led the advance towards a flickering glow which indicated that Danbury was in flames." They halted at Bethel where "more militiamen gathered, and, as dawn filtered through a heavy fog [Sunday, April 27], word came that the enemy were marching for the shore. Wooster agreed to fall on the British rear with 200 men, while Arnold blocked their path [by taking a back road to get ahead of the British] with a force that had now swelled to 500. The two old campaigners saluted each other formally, they were not to meet again in this world."[33]

Among Arnold's problems was his aggression, to the point of endangering the lives of his men. What he did following his parting with Wooster is an example of his personal courage but reckless disregard for the safety of the troops he commanded.

But first, as agreed, Wooster shadowed the rear of the British column with his 200 militiaman firing from cover or running ahead to organize surprise attacks against the enemy column. While leading his men, Wooster was mortally wounded in the belly. His son refused to leave his father, and was bayoneted to death when he refused to surrender. Wooster was later taken to the home of Nehemiah Dibble in Danbury, where he died five days later. The house (demolished in 1891) ironically was General Tryon's headquarters during his overnight occupation of Danbury.

The storybook all-night horseback ride of Sybil Ludington to alert the Connecticut and nearby New York militia to the British attack on Danbury is commemorated in this U.S. postage stamp. There is no known documentation to support the event, but historian Paula Hunt explained the acceptance of the story: "Sybil's ride embraces the mythical meanings and values expressed in the country's founding. As an individual, she represents Americans' persistent need to find and create heroes who embody prevalent attitudes and beliefs."

Meanwhile, Arnold raced ahead with his 500 militiamen to the town of Ridgefield, which was located nine miles south of Danbury. Ridgefield was on the road the British were taking to return to the coast. Just before Ridgefield, the road narrowed between a rocky ledge and the large farmhouse of Benjamin Stebbins. Here, Arnold had his men build a barricade with wagons, furniture, and whatever else they could quickly pile up. By now, Arnold had a good idea of the size of the British column and that he was outnumbered over four to one by the enemy, who also had artillery. Captain Robertson said that Arnold showed "more obstinacy than skill" at Ridgefield when he insisted that his inexperienced militiamen hold their ground. Tryon "obliged" Arnold by attacking "with his usual spirit and alacrity" by feinting a direct attack against the breastwork with part of his army while the rest moved stealthily to attack the flanks of Arnold's position. Despite a valiant defense, the rebels broke ranks and ran down Ridgefield's main street under heavy fire. Arnold, who was on horseback, is alleged to be have been the last man to retreat. As he turned his horse to flee, a platoon of Redcoats fired at him. They missed him but struck his horse nine times, which fell under him. Arnold was entangled in his dead horse's stirrups and struggling to arise when a Redcoat came charging at him with a fixed bayonet. Arnold managed to reach his pistol and shot the Redcoat dead. He then freed himself from his horse and escaped into a nearby swamp.[34]

After driving off Arnold and his men, the British broke into buildings in Ridgefield, smashing barrels of provisions and burning any building that was being used to store supplies. After trashing Ridgefield, the raiders marched three miles further south where they camped for the night (Sunday, April 27) in battle formation: "four battalions in line [in the center] and two on the wings [flanks]."[35]

Despite his defeat at Ridgefield, the tenacious Arnold made a second attempt to oppose the British as they approached the coast on the following day, Monday, April 28. This time Arnold was reinforced by his prewar friend Eleazer Oswald, who was a Continental Army artillery officer. Oswald arrived with three six-pound field cannons from New Haven. Oswald's unique place in history is that he was one of two known Continental Army officers who also fought in the French

This sign marks the site where General David Wooster was mortally wounded on April 27, 1777. Wooster was leading Connecticut militia at the time. They were harassing the rear of the British column retreating from Danbury to the waiting Royal Navy ships on Long Island Sound. *Author's photo.*

Revolution.[36] Arnold and Oswald were joined by Colonel John Lamb, who took command of the three American cannons. Arnold established a defensive position on high ground facing the only bridge across the Saugatuck River, which was located near the coast. Tryon's corps had to cross the river to reach their ships. One report of the rebels' preparations at the bridge said that "Arnold was busy throwing up works [fortifications] with 800 men."[37] Warned of the rebels' formidable position, a Loyalist named John French, who knew the area, guided the British column to a ford one mile upstream from the bridge. After fording the river, Tryon's regulars attacked the flank of Arnold's position. Short of ammunition, the British charged the rebels with their bayonets. The militiamen fled while the three American cannons were captured by Major Stuart, a volunteer on the expedition. Stuart "gained immortal honor" when he attacked the rebels' artillery with ten men and drove them out. Colonel Lamb was wounded in the action, and Arnold had a second horse shot out under him. After they scattered the militia for a second time, the exhausted Redcoats arrived at the coast where they were met by marines from the two sloops. General Erskine gave

The Keeler tavern was standing in Ridgefield, Connecticut, when the British fought Connecticut militia in the village. The British were passing through Ridgefield at the time (April 27, 1777) following their successful raid on the American supply depot in Danbury. *Author's photo.*

The retreating British column returning from the Danbury raid fought Connecticut militia in Ridgefield, Connecticut. The British fired their field artillery during the fighting. This British cannonball is a relic of the battle. It lodged in a corner post of the Keeler Tavern, where it can be seen today. *Author's photo.*

public thanks to his raiders on the beach. Robertson said "the expedition embarked on the 28th in good order though exceedingly fatigued having marched at least 35 miles [the actual distance was 27 miles]."[38] "I suppose," said Joseph Plumb Martin, that the British were "much gratified with the mischief they had done."[39] Major Charles Stuart wrote an account of the raid to his father in England in which he remarked about the countryside: "An expedition into Connecticut, of which I had the honor to make, proved to me that we had been totally unacquainted with their interior resources. I never saw a richer country or better cultivated and so well peopled."[40]

Statistics vary about the number of casualties on both sides during the four-day Danbury Raid. The most reliable information regarding British casualties is from Colonel Stephen Kemble's journal. His detailed figures read as follows: "no officers killed; twenty-three rank and file [private soldiers] killed; one drummer killed; fourteen officers wounded; 92 rank and file wounded, three sergeants wounded; one sergeant and twenty-seven rank and file missing and presumed killed, wounded and/or captured by the rebels."[41] There is no known similar record of American losses in part because there was no central command that organized the Patriot response to the British invasion. Captain Robertson speculated that the British killed 100 rebels and wounded another 200.[42] In his *Journal of Occurrences during the Late American War*, Roger Lamb estimated Patriot losses at 400 killed, wounded, or captured.[43] These two estimates are probably fairly accurate and reflect the heavy losses the Patriots sustained at Ridgefield on April 27 and the Sangatuck River the following day.

The Patriots claimed that Governor Tryon had acted cowardly throughout the raid. They spoofed his alleged behavior in the final stanza of "The Expedition to Danbury." According to the poem, Tryon was sobbing when he finally reached the coast:

So thick, so fast the balls and bullets flew,
Some hit me here, some there, some thro' and thro'
And so by thousands did the rebels muster
Under Generals Arnold and old Wooster,
That let me, let me, let me but
Get off alive—farewell Connecticut.

Meanwhile, the forage war in New Jersey continued into the spring of 1777 while according to one report, "General Howe was at New York in the lap of ease; or rather, amusing himself in the lap of a Mrs. L—— [Loring]."[44] Infuriated by the continual rebel raids and ambushes of his beleaguered troops, Lord Cornwallis decided on his own to launch a surprise attack against the American-held village of Bound Brook. Cornwallis selected the village as it was a major source of rebel attacks on his men. Also influencing Cornwallis's decision was Bound Brook's location only nine miles from New Brunswick, a distance that could be travelled in a nighttime march followed by an early morning surprise attack.

Sneaking up on Bound Brook was critical to the attack's success, as the village was located just south of the nearby American-held Watchung Mountains. If forewarned, the garrison could quickly retreat into the mountains, or be reinforced by the Patriot troops stationed at nearby Basking Ridge, Quibbletown (a section of modern Piscataway), or Samptown (present-day South Plainfield). Since Bound Brook was located on the northern shoreline of the Raritan River, another possible escape route for the American troops defending Bound Brook was to cross the river on one of the three bridges near the village and head toward American-held Hillsborough or Princeton.

Hessian Captain Johann Ewald claimed that Lord Cornwallis selected him to plan the raid on Bound Brook. Ewald was a good choice for organizing the mission, as he was in command of an outpost within four miles of Bound Brook and knew the area from his patrols and skirmishing with the enemy. For example, Ewald wrote in his journal about "paying a visit to Bound Brook" on April 4 (1777). "We drove the enemy outposts across the causeway [the Queen's Bridge across the Raritan] into the town, and returned without loss with booty of fifteen head of oxen."[45]

The plan that Ewald formulated called for a coordinated nighttime march by four British columns. Three of the units would enter the village after seizing the bridges across the Raritan. The fourth column's mission was to prevent any reinforcements reaching the hamlet from Quibbletown, which was the closest rebel outpost to Bound Brook. Cornwallis was not interested in occupying Bound Brook. His was an avenging strike: first capture the rebel garrison, then ransack the village for anything of value before returning to New Brunswick.

Lord Cornwallis personally led the raid, which began at New Brunswick on the night of April 12. Four thousand British and Hessian troops were allocated for the attack. Unknown to them at the time, their force heavily outnumbered the rebels defending Bound Brook. Commanded by Major General Benjamin Lincoln, the garrison defending Bound Brook numbered just 500 men. Lincoln had over 1,000 just a month earlier, but they were short-term militia who went home when their enlistments expired. On the day of the British attack Lincoln's command consisted of a detachment from the 8th Pennsylvania Continental Regiment, a company from the 4th Continental Artillery, and two militia companies from the Wyoming Valley of northeastern Pennsylvania. In a letter to General Washington, written just a day before the attack, Lincoln acknowledged "the weakness of our post" and that he had "carriages [wagons] kept in order ready to move on the shortest notice."[46] The village's major defense was a gun battery called the Horn Work in the center of the village facing the river. To complete the picture, General Lincoln's headquarters was about a mile west of the village in the imposing home of Philip Van Horn. General Lincoln was fast asleep in the house when the attack began at dawn on April 13.

The bulk of the Crown forces, under the command of General James Grant, approached the rebel-held village by crossing the Raritan River at Landing Lane Bridge, a mile upstream from New Brunswick. By following this route they avoided crossing the Raritan River near Bound Brook. From Landing Lane Bridge, Grant's column marched along a road with the impressive name of the Great Road Up Raritan that paralleled the eastern bank of Raritan River. The road led to the center of Bound Brook, which Grant used to his advantage to launch his attack on the village. Two of the other detachments advanced on the road along the west bank of the river. One was a corps of 400 Hessian grenadiers, fifty light dragoons, and four field pieces. They crossed the river at the Queen's Bridge, which led into the center of Bound Brook.[47] Another detachment, under Lord Cornwallis's personal command, marched further upstream where they crossed the river and attacked the village from the west. To complete their encirclement of Bound Brook, two companies of light infantry were sent further east to prevent any rebels in the village from escaping in that direction.

Ewald and thirty of his jägers were in the vanguard of Grant's column and were stealthily moving along the riverbank when they were spotted by the sentries patrolling the area. A firefight erupted with Ewald's men heavily outnumbered and pinned down behind a small stone bridge. A piece of the bridge is still standing and is one of the unique relics of the American Revolution. After about ten minutes of "murderous fire," Ewald was reinforced by the 400 grenadiers who came charging across the Queens Bridge. Meanwhile, Cornwallis's corps reached the Van Horn mansion and nearly succeeded in capturing General Lincoln. He managed to escape, but left behind his headquarters papers and personal belongings. According to one account, he escaped "profoundly undressed" (implies probably wearing only a nightshirt) minutes before the British appeared.[48] The attack would have been perfect except that the two companies sent to block the rebel garrison from fleeing eastward were late in arriving. Down in the village, General Lincoln guided his garrison through the "warm fire of

Remnants of the stone bridge that Captain Ewald took cover behind during the April 13, 1777, Battle of Bound Brook. *Author's photo.*

British musketry" before retreating into the mountains.[49] Their retreat route was north into the Watchung Mountains through Lincoln's Gap (present-day Mountain Avenue) which was located directly behind the center of colonial Bound Brook. American reinforcements arrived in the afternoon from Basking Ridge, but by then Cornwallis's men had pillaged the village and were on their way back to New Brunswick. Their booty included three brass cannons; two wagons loaded with ammunition; a number of horses; and 120 head of cattle, sheep, and hogs.[50] American losses were reported at sixty men killed, wounded or captured. The British claimed no deaths and seven men wounded.[51]

The *New York Mercury* newspaper, published in New York City by Loyalist Hugh Gaines, gave an account of the so-called Battle of Bound Brook in its April 21 issue. The report boasted that eighty-five rebels were taken prisoner. They "have been brought to town [New York City], and are the most miserable looking creatures that ever bore the name of soldiers, being covered with nothing but rags and vermin.... They are lodged in goal [jail] with their wretched brethren."[52]

While Lord Cornwallis was celebrating the success of his raid on Bound Brook in New Brunswick, twenty miles away in Morristown General Washington was witnessing the results of months of planning when he welcomed Daniel Morgan.

The last time Washington saw Morgan was in August 1775 when the Grand Army was camped in Cambridge, Massachusetts, facing British-held Boston. Morgan was the captain of one of the six companies of riflemen that was part of the Patriot army surrounding the city. Morgan was a big man: described as being over six feet tall, muscular with broad shoulders, and the visible scars of his encounters with the enemy during the French and Indian War. He was the subject of many tall tales in the old histories of the American Revolution. They are missing from present-day narratives, which are more judiciously researched and scholarly. But these good old stories were fun, and here's one about Morgan that appeared in an 1891 history of the Revolution by John Fiske. The scene is the French and Indian War during which Morgan served as a ranger protecting the Virginia frontier. According to Fiske, there was

Portrait of Daniel Morgan by artist George C. Woodbridge. *Author's collection.*

a fierce woodland fight with the Indians in which nearly all of Morgan's comrades were slain. Morgan was shot through the neck by a musket-ball. Almost fainting from the wound, which he believed to be fatal, Morgan was resolved, nevertheless, not to leave his scalp in the hands of a dirty Indian; and falling forward, with his arms tightly clasped about the neck of his stalwart horse, though mists were gathering before his eyes, he spurred away through the forest paths, until his closest Indian pursuer, unable to come up with him, hurled his tomahawk after him with a yell of baffled rage, and gave up the chase. With this unconquerable tenacity, Morgan was a man of gentle and unselfish nature; a genuine diamond, though a rough one;

uneducated, but clear and strong in intelligence and faithful in every fiber.[53]

There is some truth to this story, as Morgan was described as having a noticeable scar on his neck where he was badly wounded by a musket ball in a fight with the Indians.

Although often identified as coming from the frontier (defined as the extreme limits beyond which lies the wilderness), Morgan and many of his fellow riflemen are more accurately described as residing in the backcountry (defined as sparsely inhabited rural areas) of Virginia, Maryland, and Pennsylvania. Morgan's company was from Frederick County in western Virginia where he was a prosperous farmer whose chattels included ten slaves. Morgan lived on his farm with a common-law wife named Abigail Curry who bore him two daughters. Not much is known about Morgan's early life. He was most likely born in western New Jersey in 1735, the son of a poor Welsh immigrant farmer. Daniel ran away from home as a youth and followed a forest trace known as the Great Wagon Road, which began in Philadelphia, went southwest to Winchester, Virginia, and ended at the Yadkin River in North Carolina. Young Daniel stopped at Winchester where, according to his early biographer James Graham, "we have only occasional glimpses of Morgan's career." But Graham said that Morgan served as a Virginia Provincial soldier in the French and Indian War "and that he was frequently a member of the small parties of woodsmen [rangers] which so often went in pursuit of predatory bands of the French and Indians."[54] It was Morgan's military service and popularity in Frederick County that got him appointed as the captain of the local militia company.

The Virginia legislature authorized two volunteer rifle companies of sixty men each at the start of the Revolution to join the newly established Continental Army in Cambridge.[55] The riflemen agreed to serve for one year. The two Virginia companies selected to go were Captain Morgan's Frederick County company and Captain Hugh Stephenson's company from Berkeley County. The number of Morgan's neighbors responding to enlist for the war was overwhelming and he selected one hundred men who were marksmen with their rifles and skilled in using knives and tomahawks (a tomahawk is a weapon; a hatchet or axe are tools). Their rifles were their personal property brought from home. They were crude rifles compared to more ornate, lighter, and more graceful postwar versions known as the Pennsylvania and Kentucky rifles. As previously mentioned, the correct term for the personal rifles used by the Americans in the Revolutionary War is the American long rifle.

The arrival of the backcountry riflemen to Cambridge created great excitement in the Patriot camp, but it was soon discovered that Morgan and his fellow independent-minded riflemen refused to obey orders or to perform manual labor such as digging trenches. Instead, they spent much of their time on the front lines taking potshots at British sentries, putting on shooting demonstrations for incredulous Yankee soldiers, and provoking fistfights. Washington was infuriated with the rowdy riflemen, but other Patriot leaders had a high regard for them including John Adams, who naively praised them in a letter to his wife Abigail from Philadelphia dated June 17, 1775: "These are an excellent species of light infantry. They use a peculiar kind of gun called a rifle—it has circular grooves within the barrel and carries a ball, with great exactness to great distances. They are the most accurate marksmen in the world."[56]

What Washington perceived as troublemakers at Cambridge in 1775, he realized were the ideal troops for the partisan warfare he was fighting from Morristown in 1777. Besides wanting a corps of riflemen to harass the enemy, Washington wanted Daniel Morgan to organize and lead them. However, it took months for Washington to bring Morgan to Morristown. The problem was not Morgan's fault: he was at his Virginia home and anxious to fight. The reason for the delay is worth telling, as it gives insights into Morgan's personality and his wartime experiences prior to joining Washington at Morristown.

Morgan's Revolutionary War combat record began in August 1775, when Washington saw an opportunity to rid himself of three of the unruly rifle companies at Cambridge by sending them off with Benedict Arnold on a secret mission. Morgan's company was one of the three units selected to go with Arnold, who was a colonel at the time. When fully manned and equipped, the resolute colonel's secret mission became known as the Arnold Expedition. It consisted of 1,100 volunteers including 300 riflemen, nine Indians, and four women.

It was only after the Arnold Expedition arrived by ships at the Maine district of Massachusetts did the men learn that their objective was the walled city of Quebec, the capital of British-held Canada. The plan was for Arnold to surprise Quebec by approaching it by boats using the network of rivers and lakes in the Maine wilderness.

The Arnold Expedition was formally launched from Fort Western (present-day Augusta), Maine, on September 24, 1775. The corps advanced from Fort Western up Maine's Kennebec River with 100 tons of provisions and baggage packed into 220 bateaux (boats with pointed bows and sterns), with the men trekking alongside on the riverbank.[57] The riflemen led the way, clearing a path through the trackless wilderness and watching for any sign of ambushes by British regulars or their Indian allies. Morgan had no known schooling, read with difficulty, wrote almost illegibly, and was confused by the simplest arithmetic problem. But despite these shortcomings, he became the informal commander of the three rifle companies on the Arnold Expedition because of his military experience, dominant personality, concern for the welfare of his men, and good judgment.

Arnold had only rudimentary maps of Maine and believed the distance from Fort Western to Quebec was 120 miles. But the actual distance the expedition travelled turned out to be 270 miles, including going back and forth to portage the expedition's 220 bateaux over rapids and waterfalls. When provisions ran low and snow began to fall, some of the men turned back and others died of starvation or disease. But Arnold and a cadre of his fiercely determined officers, including Morgan, motivated the remaining men to push on. After a harrowing journey Arnold crossed the St. Lawrence River with 650 "famine proof veterans" on the night of November 13, 1775. They reached the outskirts of Quebec the following morning only to find the walled city was well defended.

Brigadier General Richard Montgomery eventually joined Arnold after arriving in Canada via Fort Ticonderoga and Lake Champlain. Together Montgomery and Arnold commenced a desperate attack to capture Quebec in the midst of a ferocious snowstorm at 2:00 am on December 31, 1775.[58] They assaulted the city from two sides.

Montgomery's attack with 300 New York troops ended in disaster when he was killed and his men retreated. On the other side of the city, Arnold advanced with 500 men, most of whom were veterans of the Arnold Expedition, including Captain Morgan. Arnold was struck early in the attack by a musket ball in his leg and was bleeding profusely. He had to be carried away to safety while his men pressed on with Captain Morgan taking the lead in a heroic but futile attempt to capture the city. The attackers were eventually trapped in Quebec's narrow streets and forced to capitulate. Eyewitnesses said that Morgan was the last man to surrender. They claimed that he stood surrounded by enemy troops with his sword in his hand and his back to a wall. Saying that he would never surrender to "scoundrels" and "cowards," he finally handed his sword to a priest and joined the others as a prisoner of war.[59]

The surviving officers of the Arnold Expedition were imprisoned separately from the enlisted men. The officers were locked up and closely guarded in two rooms on the top floor of a Jesuit seminary in the center of Quebec. They made several daring attempts to escape during the winter, but each was thwarted by their alert guards.[60] Months later, Sir Guy Carlton, the humane governor of Canada, wanted to rid Quebec of the imprisoned Americans and began releasing them on parole until they could be exchanged for British prisoners. Morgan was allowed to leave Quebec on parole with several other captives on August 11, 1776. They left aboard several transport ships bound for British-held New York City where they arrived a month later. Finally, on September 24, 1776, Morgan and his fellow parolees were loaded into longboats and rowed to American-held New Jersey near the town of Elizabeth. Once ashore, they were set free on their honor to remain as cloistered civilians until such time as they were exchanged.

Washington heard about Morgan's exploits on the Arnold Expedition including a favorable recommendation from Arnold, who was promoted to brigadier general following his failed but heroic Canadian campaign. Arnold wrote to General Washington recommending that Morgan be among the first officers to be exchanged for his "bravery and attachment to the public cause."[61] Washington agreed with Arnold and wrote Congress on Morgan's behalf on September 28, 1776. In his letter Washington said, "His conduct as an officer on the expedition with General Arnold last fall; his intrepid behavior in the assault upon Quebec when the brave Montgomery fell—the inflexible attachment he professed to our cause during his imprisonment and which he perseveres in... entitles him to the favor of Congress."[62]

In the same letter, Washington told Congress that he had learned that Colonel Hugh Stephenson had died suddenly while recruiting men for the "rifle regiment ordered lately to be raised." Washington was referring to the 11th Virginia Regiment authorized by the Virginia legislature on September 16, 1776.[63] Washington recommended Morgan as a "fit and proper person to succeed to the vacancy... that in his promotion, the States will gain a good and valuable officer." The Virginia legislature agreed, and Morgan was promoted on November 12 from a captain to the colonel and commanding officer of the 11th Virginia Regiment. He had to be secretly promoted because he was still on parole, waiting to be swapped for a captured British Army captain. Morgan was finally exchanged on January 14, 1777, and immediately began recruiting men for his new regiment. He selected his fellow Arnold Expedition veteran Christian Febiger as his second-in-command. Morgan also appointed several other Arnold Expedition veterans as officers in his new regiment, including Charles Porterfield, William Heth, and Peter Bryan Bruin. It took months for Morgan and his officers to recruit men for the regiment and send them to Philadelphia for variolation against smallpox. Morgan finally arrived at Morristown in mid-April with the first 190 men of his Virginia regiment. His unit was made up of a mixed lot of men from Virginia of differing abilities and experience. Their prerequisite was that they owned a rifle and were reasonably adept at using it. They went into action under Morgan's command immediately after arriving.

The attacks by Morgan's riflemen and other rebel partisans increased with the arrival of spring. Their relentless ambushes and raids infuriated the British officers versed in conventional warfare, among whom was William Dansey, a captain in the 33rd Regiment of Foot. Captain Dansey expressed his anger in a letter to his mother written from Piscataway, New Jersey, on April 20, 1777. He said that the weather had turned "exceedingly pleasant" which brought about an increase in rebel activity: "The rebels like other venomous animals of this continent begin to turn out of their lurking holes and harass us with small scouting parties."[64] Captain Dansey's statement is confirmed by reports of continuous American partisan attacks taking place in New Jersey in late April and all of May, some of which undoubtedly included Morgan's Virginia riflemen. They included an April 21 American attack against a British picket guard near Bonhamtown (a section of modern-day Piscataway), killing one and wounding two; a May 10 fight with the British, also near Bonhamtown, with reports of having killed or wounded 70 regulars; and a May 17 firefight near Metuchen with the Americans claiming to have inflicted "heavy casualties."[65] Some of the rebel attacks involved thousands of men, including a May 10 attack made by an estimated 1,500 to 2,000 Americans against the 42nd British regiment stationed in Piscataway. The engagement began when rebels fired at the regiment's picket guards from a nearby woods. The entire regiment turned out and heavy fighting ensued. Following the American withdrawal, the British suffered nine enlisted men killed and fifteen wounded.[66] Morgan's riflemen were particularly active during this period, especially as the number of men in his regiment increased during the month of May from 273 on May 3 to 441 on May 21.[67]

Washington was impressed with Morgan's leadership and wanted to make him even more effective by having him command an elite corps of 500 riflemen recruited from all of the Continental Army regiments.[68] Washington implemented his plan in the June 1, 1777, General Orders, which included the following:

> *The commanding officers of every corps [regiment] is to make a report early tomorrow morning, to his brigadier, of the number of rifle-men under his command—in doing which, he is to include none but such as are known to be perfectly skilled in the use of these guns, and who are known to be active and orderly in their behavior.*[69]

Washington confirmed that Morgan's new corps was recruited from the Grand Army regiments in an August 16, 1777, letter to New York governor George Clinton: "These are all chosen men, selected from the Army at large."[70] For his new corps Morgan selected men in the army who not only owned rifles but were expert marksmen, self-reliant, experienced in stalking game and fighting off marauding Indians. Such men were described as "approaching like foxes, fighting like lions and disappearing like birds." They included some of the best men from the 11th Virginia Regiment and experienced veterans from other rifle companies organized earlier in the war and disbanded. Morgan's new unit also incorporated individual men from rifle companies that had suffered heavy casualties or surrendered, such as some members of Colonel Moses Rawlings's Rifle Company who had not joined the unit when it was captured at Fort Washington in November 1776.[71]

Washington called Morgan's new unit the Provisional Rifle Corps, which he also identified as the Corps of Rangers. However, it became popularized in the literature of the American Revolution as Morgan's Rifle Corps. Morgan's new unit is sometimes incorrectly referred to as the 11th Virginia Rifle Corps. The confusion is that Morgan was listed as the commanding officer of both units. This is correct, but Christian Febiger, who was second-in-command of the 11th Virginia Regiment, became its acting commander. Febiger was well-suited for the command. He was a young Danish-born businessman residing in Boston at the outset of the war. Febiger joined the Patriot cause, fought at the Battle of Bunker Hill, and was an officer on the Arnold Expedition where, according to one account, he "behaved with all the resolution, calmness, and intrepidity... and has given many specimens of his great military abilities."[72]

Morgan's new elite rifle corps was operational by June 13 as evidenced by the fact that Washington gave him orders on that date which read in part: "The Corps of Rangers newly formed and under your command, are to be considered as light infantry.... In case of any movement of the Enemy you are instantly to fall upon their flanks and gall them as much as possible." Washington closed his orders to Morgan with a seemingly strange comment: "I have sent for spears which I expect shortly to receive and deliver to you."[73] Supplying Morgan's riflemen with spears is a clue to the shortcomings of the American rifle during the

Revolutionary War. Contemporary evidence of the dissatisfaction with rifles as an infantry weapon are highlighted by a letter that Brigadier General Peter Muhlenberg wrote to Washington in February, 1777. Muhlenberg commanded a Pennsylvania regiment of riflemen at the time: "Rifles of are little use, I would therefore request Your Excellency to convert my regiment into musketry [smoothbore muskets]."[74] The major disadvantages of the rifles was that they were slow to load and they could not mount a bayonet. The lack of a bayonet left the rifleman helpless against an enemy charge. Historians George Scheer and Hugh Rankin pointed out another drawback to the rifle in combat in their book, *Rebels and Redcoats*. They note that the lightweight and perfectly balanced American rifle "was the weapon of the professional hunter and woodsman." But "surrounded by the smoke of a battle line, the rifleman could not aim carefully enough to take advantage of their weapon's unbelievable accuracy."[75]

The British quickly understood the shortcomings of the American riflemen. British Colonel George Hanger said that he learned how to defeat them from his friend Lieutenant Colonel Robert Abercromby, a British light infantry officer. Hanger explained that when a corps of rebel riflemen appeared, Abercromby "ordered his troops to immediately charge them with the bayonet; not one man out of four [riflemen] had time to fire, and those that did had no time to load again; the light infantry not only dispersed them instantly but drove them for miles over the country."[76]

Another British officer had different advice for dealing with riflemen: "about twilight is found the best season for hunting the rebels in the woods, at which time their rifles are of very little use... and it frequently happens that they find themselves run through by body by the push of a bayonet, as a rifleman is not entitled to any quarter."[77] An additional and compelling condemnation of the American rifle was made by author Garry Wills, who wrote, "The riflemen were wielding an instrument never intended for battle."[78]

By the time Washington reached Morristown in 1777, he was aware of the problems with the rifle as a combat weapon. But he went ahead anyway and ordered Morgan to organize an elite rifle corps. The reason was that the rifle was ideally suited for the irregular warfare that Washington was fighting in New Jersey. Historian Harold Peterson made this point in his classic book, *Arms and Armor in Colonial America*. Writing about the American rifle, Peterson said, "it had accuracy and range, but it was handicapped by its slowness and lack of a bayonet. Obviously, it was useless as an arm for regular infantry, but its assets and the special skills of its users made it a fine weapon for certain troops, such as light infantry, scouts, snipers, and skirmishers."[79]

Morgan proved to be a resourceful and practical officer with a natural aptitude for encouraging his troops. He brought to the partisan war being waged in New Jersey a talent for using the rifle to its advantage. Contemporary accounts state that Morgan's men made no effort to create a military appearance. They wore what they had, and their clothing was comfortable and practical. This supposes the romantic notion that Morgan's riflemen wore clothing and moccasins made from buckskin (animal hides, usually deerskin) while stalking the British and Hessians in New Jersey. Fortunately, there are several eyewitness accounts describing their clothing, none of which mention riflemen wearing buckskin garments. One account described the riflemen wearing "a hunting shirt [a long garment resembling a jacket] and pantaloons [loose fitting trousers], their clothing fringed on every edge and in various ways."[80] Silas Deane saw a group of riflemen in Philadelphia early in the war and described their clothing in greater detail in a letter to his wife: "They take a piece of Ticklenburgh [another name for linen derived from the German town spelled Tecklenburg, famous at the time as a source for this fabric] or tan cloth [probably wool, which was the other popular fabric at the time] that is stout and put it in a tanning vat until it has the shade of a dry, or fading leaf, then they make a kind of frock of it [a hunting shirt] reaching down below the knee, open in front, with a large cape, they wrap it round them tight on a march and tie it with their belt on which hangs their tomahawk."[81]

Riflemen may have worn moccasins at times, particularly when they were hunting game over soft woody terrain in the summer. However, moccasins were impractical for long marches or extended military campaigns—they wore out quickly, and they stayed damp and clammy if they got wet or could freeze in cold weather. Riflemen, like all other soldiers of the Revolution, wore shoes whenever they could get them. Some historians insist that the riflemen carried extra leather with them and made new moccasins as their old ones wore out. Such a scenario is impractical. People in the eighteenth century, like today, used common sense. Why bother with the trouble of making moccasins when shoes were sturdier, lasted longer, and were often supplied for free by the army? A final comment about riflemen wearing moccasins is that Daniel Morgan is depicted wearing shoes in artist John Trumbull's painting, *The Surrender of General Burgoyne at Saratoga, 16 October 1777* (painting completed in 1821 for the Rotunda of the U.S. Capital Building). Trumbull was an American officer during the Revolutionary War and was a stickler for accurately showing details of uniforms and weapons. As for boots, while most people in colonial America wore shoes, heavy work boots were favored by farmers, while lighter and more expensive boots were worn for riding.

During the spring of 1777, Washington's army had increased substantially. By mid-May, recruits arrived in Morristown to give him an army of 8,188 officers and enlisted men organized into thirty-eight regiments.[82] With these new levies, Washington was able to expand his attacks on the British and Hessians stationed in New Jersey. But even as the fighting in New Jersey intensified, General Howe continued to socialize in New York City. His aide, Captain Muenchhausen, recorded the details of one event:

> *May 20, A ship's aide today gave a party on the ship Fanny for Admiral and General Howe as well as some other men and several ladies. They danced on the upper deck until three o'clock in the morning. Big and small boats had races and the best ones were given handsome presents by the Admiral.*[83]

In another reference to New York's indulgent social life, British Captain Peebles wrote in his diary on April 10, 1777, that some of his fellow officers had passed through the city on their way to New Jersey and all agreed "that there's nothing going on there but luxury and dissipation [immorality] of all kinds."[84]

Loyalist Thomas Jones was fuming that General Howe seemed to be more interested in his social life than defeating Washington's army. Jones blamed Sir William for "suffering ten thousand veterans under experienced generals to be cooped up in Brunswick and Amboy for nearly six months by about six thousand militia under the command of an inexperienced general."[85] But behind the scenes at British headquarters at the Apthorp Mansion in Manhattan, the Howe brothers were busy corresponding with their superiors in London, stockpiling provisions, expediting reinforcements, and planning their 1777 campaign to seize Philadelphia.[86] In the midst of their planning they received dispatches from London stating that the King had approved of a plan proposed by General John Burgoyne to invade New York State from Canada. The ministry had devised a new plan for ending the war, and Sir William was expected to cooperate in its execution.

6

A Great Empire and Little Minds*

Virtually every history of the American Revolution makes liberal use of "strategy." The word "strategy" is derived from the Greek word *strategia* meaning generalship. A present-day definition of strategy in military parlance is "the art of projecting and directing the larger military movements and operations of a campaign." While the word existed in the late seventeenth century, it was not well known or widely used. In his authoritative study of strategy during the American Revolution, Dave R. Palmer noted that "strategy was not a word George Washington used. It entered the language some years after his death."[1] A review of the letters and orders from the period reveal that while both the British and Americans understood and implemented strategy, they used the words "campaign," "plan," "a grand matter," or "operations" to express their ideas.[2]

The word "stratagem," however, was in common use at the time and appears to be close in meaning to strategy. But the two words have very different connotations. Stratagem is defined as "a plan or scheme for deceiving an enemy."[3] Here are two examples of sentences from the correspondence of the Revolutionary War that illustrate its meaning. The

---

* Chapter title from a speech by Edmund Burke in the House of Commons on March 22, 1775: "Magnanimity in politics is not seldom the truest wisdom; and a great empire and little minds go ill together." See William I. Crane, ed., *Edmund Burke's Speech on Conciliation with the American Colonies* (New York: D. Appleton and Company, 1900), 129.

first is a letter George Washington wrote to Brigadier General William Maxwell on December 8, 1776. In his letter, Washington told Maxwell to bring boats to the remote village of Tinicum on the Pennsylvania side of the Delaware River. Washington warned Maxwell, "The boats at other places ought, in my opinion, to be destroyed or removed to Tinicum, least [*sic*] they should be possessed by some stratagem of the enemy."⁴ In the second example, the Pennsylvania Board of War wrote Washington on April 19, 1777: "In the course of this week we have been very fortunate in detecting the stratagems of a number of secret enemies."⁵

As this narrative continues, I will use the word "strategy" with the understanding that it is a modern word. This leads to a review of the word "tactics," which is closely associated with strategy. The *Oxford English Dictionary* defines tactics as "the art of handling forces in battle or in the immediate presence of the enemy." The word not only existed during the American Revolution; it was used in its traditional sense. As mentioned in my introduction to this book, the word "tactics" appears in Captain George Smith's *Military Dictionary* published in London in 1779. Captain Smith defined tactics as "the art of disciplining armies and ranging them into forms for fighting and maneuvering."⁶

The politicians and generals who dictated strategy during the American Revolution had a significant impact on the outcome of the war. George Washington was responsible for American strategy during the entire conflict. His authority to dictate strategy was established in his June 19, 1775, commission from the Continental Congress appointing him general and commander-in-chief of army of the United Colonies. His appointment stated: "And you are hereby vested with full power and authority to act as you shall think for the good and welfare of the service."⁷ Washington flexed his control of American strategy early in the war when he sent the 1,000-man Arnold Expedition to Canada in August 1775 without Congress's knowledge. Washington continuing to determine American strategy later in the war is evinced by a letter written to him by John Jay in 1779, stating that "the sense of Congress that your Excellency consider yourself at liberty to direct the military operations of these states in such manner as you think expedient."⁸

Washington was an astute politician who carefully built and maintained relationships with influential members of Congress and state governments who defended his strategic decisions during the war. He also protected his control of strategy by keeping them informed and respectfully listened to their advice. Important visitors to army headquarters got the deluxe treatment, including discussions of strategy with Washington at carefully orchestrated dinners attended by genial members of his staff and the charming wives, daughters, or nieces of his senior officers. Visiting fact-finding committees from Congress returned from army headquarters satisfied with Washington's leadership and increasingly disinclined to watch him with a wary eye as the war went on.[9] To his credit, Washington held councils of war with his senior line commanders [combat officers] and took their opinions seriously when making strategic decisions. But any notion that Washington sought the advice of his wartime aides-de-camp, particularly Alexander Hamilton, regarding strategy is nonsense or "poppycock," according to Hamilton biographer James Thomas Flexner.[10] The general's aides assisted and advised Washington on administrative matters and were involved with intelligence gathering and analysis. If they attended councils of war, it was to take notes and draft follow-up letters, reports, and orders.

Turning to Great Britain, its strategy during the American Revolution was controlled by King George III. The ability of the King to dictate colonial policy requires clarification, as Britain was (and is) a constitutional monarchy with legislative power vested in the members of the two houses of Parliament. The lower house, called the House of Commons, is an elected body which usually institutes legislation. The upper house, called the House of Lords, is primarily an advisory body. The King maintained a majority in the House of Commons during the American Revolution in part through patronage, granting favors or making appointments to offices in return for political support. George III used his patronage to maintain a majority in the House of Commons by conferring prestigious titles to its members, appointing them to lucrative government positions, and allowing them to embezzle money in return for their support.

King George's attitude toward the growing unrest in the American colonies was to "listen to nothing from the illegal [Continental] Congress." His harsh response to the colonists' respectful petitions for a redress of their grievances was his proclamation that they were unlawful agitators: "our officers, civil and military [said the King] are obliged to exert their utmost endeavors to suppress rebellion, and to bring the traitors to justice."[11]

The King's hard-line position toward the American colonists was shared by Britain's leading government officials: the prime minister and the members of his cabinet. The prime minister is chosen by the members of the House of Commons, and he, in turn, fills the cabinet positions. The prime minister during most of the American War was Sir Frederick North, better known in history as Lord North. His cabinet included a secretary of state for the colonies, also known as the American secretary, the colonial secretary, the secretary of state for the American department or the first lord of trade, and secretary of state for North America and the West Indies. The position was responsible for the administration of Great Britain's North American Colonies including Canada. The post was created in 1768 to deal with American opposition to efforts by the British government to enforce existing laws and add new taxes. The secretary of state for the colonies during the majority of the American Revolution was Lord George Germain (1716–1785). He was the third person appointed to the position, which he held from November 1775 to February 1782. The post was eliminated following the loss of the American colonies in 1783. Lord North deferred the conduct of the war to Lord Germain, who shared the King's tough policy toward the Americans. The King and Germain worked closely together on Britain's wartime strategy. It was said that the King and Germain followed every detail of each campaign with the strongest interest. The King even had large maps of the American colonies made, showing troop dispositions according to the latest dispatches.[12]

In evaluating why Britain lost the American War, Lord George Germain stands out among the people responsible for the defeat. George Germain was his adopted name; he was born George Sackville. The name change will be explained shortly. George was described as having "an air of high birth and dignity."[13] The Earl of Shelburne (1737–1805) described him as "a tall man with a long face, rather strong features, clear blue eyes, not too corpulent, and a mixture of quickness and a spot of melancholy in his look."[14] Germain was born on January 26, 1716, with the title of Lord George Sackville. His father was Lionel Sackville, first Duke of Dorset and Lord Lieutenant of Ireland. Following an impressive college education, young George became his father's secretary and entered politics as a member of the Irish Parliament. In 1737 he decided to follow the family tradition of military service, and his father appointed him a captain in the 6th Dragoon Guards (also called the Inniskilling Guards), an Irish cavalry regiment in the British Army. It is confusing to follow his military and political career because, as a wealthy member of the British nobility, he drifted in and out of politics and military service. For example, he fought in the 1745 Battle of Fortoney during the War of the Austrian Succession while he served as a member of the House of Commons representing the district of Dover located on the English Channel. Promoted to the rank of general, his military career came to an ignominious end during the Seven Years' War when he was accused of disregarding repeated orders to attack a routed French Army during the Battle of Minden (August 1, 1759). His failure allowed the French to successfully retreat, and Sackville was court-martialed for his insubordination. Sackville was found guilty of disobedience, and King George II, the reigning monarch at the time, "ensured that every humiliation went with his conviction," including being dismissed from the army and a statement entered into all regimental books that he was unfit to serve in any military capacity. Despite this huge setback, Sackville continued as a member of the House of Commons but kept a low profile, eating at home and avoiding fashionable social life.

Sackville was able to rebuild his political career following the death of his antagonist King George II and the ascension of George's grandson to the throne in 1760 as King George III. The new King was sympathetic toward Sackville, who supported the King's "vigorous firmness" in dealing with the growing unrest in the American colonies. In 1770 Sackville had the fortuitous opportunity to legally change his name under the terms of the will of his aunt, Lady Elizabeth Germain, who left him a huge inheritance provided he adopted her surname of Germain.[15]

As Lord George Germain, he became the leading member of the House of Commons to support the King's hard-line stance toward the American colonies. For example, in a speech in the House on May 22, 1774, following the news of the Boston Tea Party, Germain said, "What is the state of Boston? Anarchy and confusion.... Have they any redress for any one grievance but what depends upon the will of the licentious multitude [mob]?"[16] The King considered Germain's political beliefs to be of more consequence than his military reputation and arranged for him to be appointed Secretary of State for the Colonies. The position included substantial wartime powers including control of the army in the American colonies.

There is a trend today to treat Germain as an able administrator operating under difficult circumstances. For example, Louis Marlow, who published a scholarly biography about Germain, said "During his American Secretaryship [sic] Lord George's [George Germain] natural sagacity [intelligence] did not desert him. Circumstances, to a large extent, imposed his errors. All government officers, from the King downwards, lived in a fog of misinformation that rarely lifted."[17] Germain may have been intelligent, but his dogged insistence on directing the fast-paced war from London was a costly mistake. He was also a poor choice as a wartime American secretary because his reputation as "the ghost of Minden" made him unpopular with the generals he commanded.

Germain came to power at a time when Britain needed brilliant leadership to deal with the rebelling colonists. Instead they got a pompous, overbearing windbag. Germain was, in the words of Francis Vinton Greene, "probably the most incompetent official that ever held an important post at a critical moment."[18] It is questionable whether any other British statesman or general could have done better when we consider the handicaps under which Germain operated. He was expected to manage a war that was 3,000 miles from London. His letters and orders took weeks, if not months, to cross the ocean by ship to reach their recipients. And, as historian Greene pointed out, "when they reached their destination the state of facts on which they were based had usually changed. Yet he [Germain] undertook to direct the operations at this distance."

Germain also suffered from underestimating the strength of the Patriots. England during the war was a refuge for exiled Loyalists who convinced Germain that the majority of the colonists were only awaiting the presence of British Redcoats to restore imperial order. Remarking on this misconception, British General Henry Clinton said that Germain was listening to the "misinformation of overzealous Loyalists induced to flatter themselves that the malcontents in America were greatly inferior in number to the friends of the old constitution [the King and the British Parliament]."[19]

Germain was also fighting a war that Britain was ill-prepared to win. At the start of the American Revolution in 1775, Britain had an army of 48,647 men stationed throughout the British Empire. The largest number of troops (15,000) were stationed in England, followed by 12,000 in Ireland and 8,000 in North America. The balance were distributed among the West Indies, Africa, India, Minorca, Gibraltar, and Scotland.[20] The largest army that Germain was able to scrape together to fight in America consisted of 31,625 officers and men fit for duty, including Hessian auxiliaries, for the 1776 New York campaign.[21] Germain should have realized that the British Army was too small to win the war when he offered Lord Jeffery Amherst (1717–1797) the command of the army in America. Amherst was commander-in-chief of the British Army during the French and Indian War, and was familiar with the region's vast size and challenging geography. Amherst said that he required a minimum of 75,000 troops to defeat the rebels.[22] Amherst's sobering request should have made the King consider negotiating an end to the war in 1775, when the colonists had limited demands. Instead, the King instructed Germain to hire Hessian auxiliaries to supplement the British Army. The Hessians proved to be courageous soldiers, but they had no stake in the outcome of the war and were plundering indiscriminately in this land of plenty, turning Loyalists into Patriots.

Germain considered several different strategies to defeat the rebels when he first came to power. One was a naval blockade of the American coast, which was quickly abandoned when it was realized that the Royal Navy did not have enough ships to blockade every port from Portsmouth,

New Hampshire to Savannah, Georgia. In addition, the navy would have to patrol over 1,000 miles of coastline with numerous inlets, bays, and rivers where the Patriots could offload military equipment and supplies.

Admiral Samuel Graves, who commanded the Royal Navy squadron in America, proposed a different strategy, which was to terrorize the civilian population into submission. His idea was implemented when a Royal Navy squadron attacked and burned the town of Falmouth (present-day Portland), Maine, on October 18, 1775. All of Falmouth's public buildings and three-fourths of its homes were destroyed in the attack, sending "a thousand unoffending men, women and children out-of-doors just as the sharp Maine winter was coming on to starve and freeze them."[23] The destruction of Falmouth only resulted in increased Patriot defiance and fueled the movement toward declaring independence from Britain. For example, after learning that the British had burned Falmouth, independence activist James Warren wrote John Adams asking, "what can we wait for now?"[24] Also contributing to abandoning the slash-and-burn policy were opposition members of Parliament, who looked upon the American colonists as fellow Englishmen.

The strategy that the King and Germain ultimately selected was called the "Line of the Hudson." It was a good strategy, based on controlling the Hudson River, which would separate New England from the rest of the warring states. The New England states were major supporters of the rebellion. They were also an important source of provisions and manpower for Washington's Grand Army which, by late 1776, was operating in New Jersey and Pennsylvania. The British did not have to control every mile of the Hudson to isolate New England—just the ferry crossings, which were the only places where wagon trains of supplies and provisions and reinforcements could cross the river. Once the British controlled the Hudson, they could advance inland from the river to defeat Washington's weakened Grand Army and systematically subjugate each state.

Washington understood the strategic importance of the Hudson and repeatedly stated that enemy occupation of the river would be fatal to the Patriot cause.[25] British General Henry Clinton agreed, and believed that General Howe should have focused on controlling the Hudson River in late 1776 instead of chasing Washington through New Jersey. Clinton said, "the river Hudson naturally presents itself as a very important object the possession of which on the first breaking out of the disturbances [start of the rebellion] might have secured to Great Britain a barrier between the southern and eastern colonies."[26]

The British seizure of New York City in 1776 gave them unopposed access to the Hudson River, which was navigable for ocean-going ships of the period for 150 miles to Albany, New York. This gave the British Army the advantage of being able to operate in the interior of the continent with the formidable support of the Royal Navy.

By late 1776, the British Army was in a strong position to implement the Line of the Hudson strategy. They had one army under General Howe in New York City, along with a fleet of Royal Navy warships and transports that could move north on the Hudson and another army under the command of General Guy Carleton in Canada that could move south. At this point, Germain should have appointed one person based in America to command the two armies and coordinate their movements. Instead, he allowed them to operate as independent commands, which he attempted to supervise from London.

Into this situation stepped British Lieutenant General John Burgoyne in early 1777. But before exploring his role in the war, it is important to mention another handicap under which Germain operated: Germain had never been to America, which contributed to his misconceptions about the region's geography. For example, although the Bronx River appears on period maps, it is hardly wider than a creek as it meanders through Westchester County, New York. Yet, Germain suggested that the Royal Navy send warships up the Bronx River to attack rebel positions.[27]

Germain's lack of knowledge of America resulted in his belief that General Guy Carleton was too passive in pursuing the war in 1776. Germain's explicit criticism was that Carleton retreated back to Canada in 1776 when he was only three miles away from Fort Ticonderoga in late October 1775. But Germain was shortsighted in his condemnation of Carleton, who was a capable and experienced officer. Carleton had boldly advanced into New York State when reinforcements led by Burgoyne arrived at Quebec in the spring of 1776. With Burgoyne as his

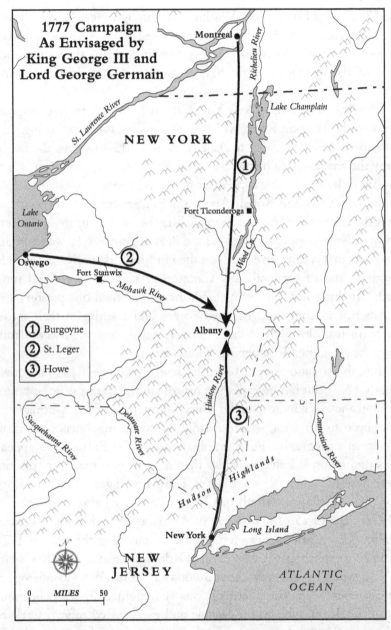

This is the 1777 campaign envisioned by King George III and Lord George Germain.

second-in-command, Carleton drove the Americans out of Canada and forced them to retreat to Fort Ticonderoga in upper New York State. After defeating an American gunboat fleet on Lake Champlain (the Battle of Valcour Island) on October 11, Carleton's flotilla continued to sail south and landed troops three miles from the American fortress. Although his men faced stiff resistance from the fort's forward redoubts, Carleton continued to probe the fort's defenses into early November. Carleton came to the conclusion that it would take a protracted siege to capture the fort and, with winter approaching, he ordered his army to return to Canada. After arriving back in Quebec, Carleton began planning to capture Fort Ticonderoga in the spring of 1777 while Burgoyne sailed to England for the winter on the last ship to navigate the St. Lawrence River before it froze.

After arriving in London, Burgoyne exploited Germain's low opinion of Carleton by promoting himself as the aggressive officer who could overrun Fort Ticonderoga and march to Albany. Burgoyne met several times with the King and Germain during the winter and presented them with his written plan, which he titled "Thoughts for Conducting the War from the Side of Canada." It described how Burgoyne would rapidly advance from Montreal to Albany where he would open communications with the commander-in-chief (General Howe) in New York who would determine Burgoyne's subsequent moves. An excerpt from Burgoyne's proposal illustrates his assertive plan: "I would not lose a day to take possession of Crown Point with Brigadier Fraser's corps [a reference to Brigadier General Simon Fraser, who was one of Burgoyne's principal officers during the 1776 campaign and was wintering in Canada]. The brigade [Fraser's brigade] would be sufficient to prevent insult during the time necessary... to proceeding in force [south] to Ticonderoga."[28] The key to the success of Burgoyne's plan was to include a large number of cannons that he would use to lay siege to Fort Ticonderoga and force it to surrender.

Burgoyne's proposal also called for a smaller expedition to move east from Fort Oswego (present-day Oswego, New York) on Lake Ontario along the Mohawk River to Albany. The expedition's purpose was to create a diversion that would draw American troops away from Burgoyne's main army.[29]

The King and Lord Germain were enthusiastic about Burgoyne's plan, and Germain gave Burgoyne a letter dated March 26, 1777, addressed to Carleton. The letter gave Burgoyne command of the troops in Canada already preparing to renew the invasion of New York State. Burgoyne carried the letter with him to Canada.

Burgoyne departed London on March 27 and travelled overland to the English seaport of Plymouth where he boarded the frigate HMS *Apollo* for the voyage to Canada. There are stories that Burgoyne's personal baggage included cases of champagne, fine claret, and brandy, which contributed to his men calling him "Gentleman Johnny." However, that nickname was the creation of later historians.[30] After an uneventful voyage, the *Apollo* arrived at Quebec City, the capital of Canada, on May 6.[31] While Burgoyne's return to Canada was anticipated by General Carleton, the letter that he brought from Lord Germain was an unexpected and degrading blow. It instructed Carleton to retain 3,000 of the troops already in Canada for the defense of the province and to turn over the balance, amounting to 7,173 officers and men, to Burgoyne, who would lead them in a renewed offensive from Canada into New York State.[32] Carleton was to remain behind in Canada. Cloaked in tactful wording, the missive was a humiliating condemnation of Carleton's generalship and revelation that Burgoyne had spent the winter in London scheming behind Carleton's back. An excerpt from Germain's letter illustrates how Carleton was reduced to a demeaning minor role in the 1777 offensive from Canada:

> *after having furnished him [Burgoyne] in the fullest and completest manner with artillery, stores, provisions, and every other article necessary for his expedition, and secured to him every assistance which it is in your power to afford and procure, you are to give him orders [technically Carleton was Burgoyne's superior] to pass Lake Champlain; and from thence, by the most vigorous exertion of the force under his command, to proceed with all expedition to Albany, and put himself under the command of Sir William Howe.*[33]

It is important to quote another excerpt from Germain's letter that was critical to subsequent events. The text reads, "I shall write to Sir William

Howe, from hence [London], by the first packet [a fast ship carrying dispatches and mail]."[34] Germain's letter was supposed to inform Howe of Burgoyne's intention to reach Albany, where he was to receive further instructions from Sir William. But Germain wrote Howe eight times between March 3 and April 19, 1777, without ever mentioning Burgoyne's mission.[35] Germain finally wrote to Howe on May 18, telling him to "cooperate with the army ordered to proceed from Canada." Howe did not receive Germain's letter until August 16.[36] But the delay in informing Howe was not important since, as historian Eric Schnitzer pointed out, "Nowhere in the plan was there a mandate for Howe to ascend the Hudson River and link with the Army from Canada at Albany, or anywhere for that matter."[37]

If you read some of the old histories of the Revolution, they explain why Howe never received a direct order from Germain to support Burgoyne. Germain's so-called lost order to Howe is one of most engaging stories from the American Revolution. However, you will not find it in any credible recent histories of the Revolution because there is no proof that the order ever existed. A typical account of the missing order appears in a book published in 1928 titled *The Turning Point of the Revolution or Burgoyne in America.* The author is Hoffman Nickerson, who began his story by explaining that Germain had accepted an invitation to spend a weekend away from London in the country. He was anxious to depart the city at a certain hour, but agreed to have his coach stop briefly at his office to sign some dispatches including a "positive order to General Howe directing him to move up the Hudson." It was discovered when Germain arrived at his office that there was no copy of the order for his records. His Lordship was anxious to leave for his weekend holiday and did not want to wait for the copy to be made, and he left, leaving the order to Howe unsigned. The order was mislaid in his absence and "Germain was fool enough to forget the whole matter." According to Nickerson, "Germain's enormous blunder robbed the British of almost certain success."[38] Another version of the story claims that the unsigned order to Howe was found in Germain's London office after Burgoyne surrendered his army.[39] In yet a different version of the story, Germain stopped at his office on his way to his weekend holiday. Upon arriving at his office his secretary reminded him that there was no letter ordering Howe to cooperate with Burgoyne. Germain said that he did not want to wait for the letter to be written; "my poor horses must stand in the street all the time, and I shan't be to my time anywhere." Germain's secretary told his boss to go and he would write the letter to Howe. However, the letter was never written.[40]

There are other, less implausible stories to explain why Germain never gave Howe a direct order to abort his Pennsylvania campaign early on and sail up the Hudson with his army to meet Burgoyne at Albany. One story that seems to have merit is that William and Richard Howe knew Germain as the "ghost of Minden," who was reluctant to give the Howe brothers a direct order. Another is that Germain's vast ignorance of America and Americans led him to believe that large numbers of New York and New England Loyalists would join Burgoyne's army, allowing him to brush aside rebel resistance and reach Albany without Howe's help.

Germain was not completely inept, and he actually took quick action to inform Howe of Burgoyne's plans and for Sir William to support the Canadian-based offensive with his army. However, the manner in which Germain did it was bizarre. The story began when General Howe gave Captain Nesbitt Balfour of the 4th Regiment of Foot the honor of carrying his official dispatch to London with the glorious news of the capture of New York City. Described as a member of Scotland's landed nobility, Balfour was selected for this honor as a reward for his courageous leadership in the Battle of Long Island, during which he was wounded. Balfour departed New York for London on September 26, 1776, with Howe's report aboard the packet ship *Halifax*.[41] It was the custom to honor the officer who brought good news, and the King rewarded Balfour by promoting him to the rank of major. Aware of Howe's esteem for Balfour, Germain appointed him as his special emissary to inform the commander-in-chief of Burgoyne's offensive upon his return to New York.[42] Germain also wanted Balfour to tell Howe that he approved of Sir William's "enterprise" (invasion of Pennsylvania and capture of Philadelphia), with the understanding that it would be concluded in time for Howe to cooperate with Burgoyne.[43] Germain also hoped that

Balfour would "convince Sir William Howe that he distresses us by not communicating his ideas more frequently and more explicitly."[44]

Balfour arrived back in New York on May 8, 1777, aboard the frigate HMS *Augusta*.[45] Upon his return, Sir William appointed him one of his aides-de-camp. There is nothing to indicate that Major Balfour risked jeopardizing his goodwill with Howe by delivering Germain's requests, based on the fact that Howe never deviated from his plans. Apparently, as far as Howe was concerned, Burgoyne would have no trouble reaching Albany with his large army and Loyalist support. As for Balfour, he was appointed a member of Parliament in 1790 and a major general in the British Army in 1793.

Howe was too busy in New York preparing for his Pennsylvania campaign to worry about Burgoyne anyway. Sir William was obsessed with invading the state and capturing Philadelphia. He believed that the fall of the rebel capital would be decisive "and that one short stroke would end the rebellion in the middle colonies."[46] Howe's other offensive operations, including invading New England from Newport, Rhode Island, were cancelled or curtailed during the winter based on Germain's failure to send him adequate reinforcements. Germain had already strained every resource to give Howe a large army for the 1776 campaign. It did not matter to Howe, who snapped back at Germain: "Restricted as I am from entering upon more extensive operations by the want of force, my hopes of terminating the war this year [1777] are vanished."[47]

Howe finalized his plans for the 1777 campaign, which he detailed in an April 2, 1777, letter to Germain. Sir William said that he would invade Pennsylvania with 11,000 men, leave 4,700 to defend New York City, and continue to station 2,400 in Newport, Rhode Island. There was no mention of any cooperation or support of Burgoyne.

Howe included a significant change in his plans in his April 2 letter to Germain. The revision was that Howe intended to withdraw all of his troops from New Brunswick and Perth Amboy and attack Philadelphia from the sea. Howe told Germain, "From the difficulties and delay that would attend the passage of the River Delaware by a march through Jersey, I propose to invade Pennsylvania by sea; and from this arrangement we must probably abandon the Jerseys."[48] The reports arriving at

Howe's New York headquarters from New Jersey throughout the winter contributed to his decision not to attempt to cross New Jersey to reach Pennsylvania. Typical comments being read at headquarters included, "our cantonments have been beaten up" and "Travelling between the posts hazardous; and in short, the troops harassed beyond measure."[49] There were other ominous reports, including one from Perth Amboy: "The rebels here spread themselves all over the country, so that we cannot go beyond our sentries with any degree of safety."[50] Howe realized that attempting to reach Pennsylvania by crossing New Jersey would result in Washington relentlessly harassing his army as it crossed the state, especially targeting Howe's supply wagons hauling the tons of necessary victuals from New York to feed his army.

On the same day (April 2, 1777) that Howe wrote Germain with his revised plans, Howe wrote to Carleton in Quebec. Howe's understanding at the time was that Carleton was planning a cautious offensive whose primary objective was seizing Fort Ticonderoga. Sir William did not know when he wrote his letter that Germain had replaced Carleton with Burgoyne. The change in command for the offensive from Canada was irrelevant; what is important is that Howe stated in his letter, "for want of sufficient strength [reinforcements] to detach a corps in the beginning of the campaign to act up Hudson's River." Howe advised Carleton to capture Fort Ticonderoga as his "first object" and then to "advance upon your frontiers after taking Ticonderoga" cautiously and perhaps delaying any further move toward Albany or into New England for his "next attention" [evaluating Carleton's options after seizing Ticonderoga].[51]

While Howe was planning his Pennsylvania campaign and Burgoyne was gathering provisions and assembling "the savages and Canadians" in Canada, Washington continued his relentless attacks on enemy foraging expeditions and outposts in New Jersey. They reached a point in May 1777 where Howe felt compelled to build a bridge across the Raritan River. Unknown to the Americans at the time, Howe wanted the bridge built to reduce the exposure of his troops to enemy attacks and to facilitate the withdrawal of New Brunswick's garrison to board the ships anchored at Staten Island and New York City for his seaborne invasion of Pennsylvania.

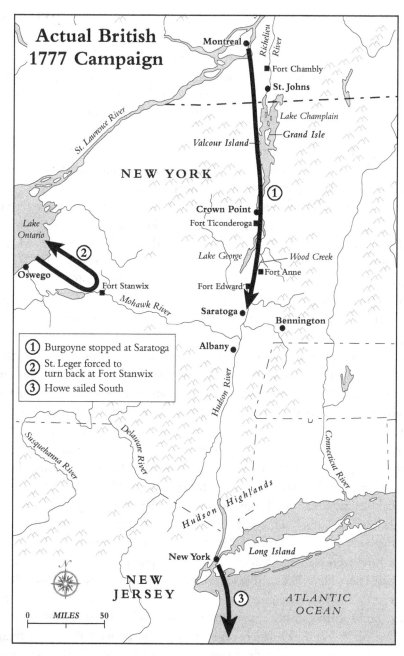

The actual 1777 British campaign.

It will be recalled that there was only a ferry (Inman Ferry) to cross the Raritan River at New Brunswick. The closest bridge was Landing Lane Bridge a mile upstream from New Brunswick. But as soon as a British or Hessian soldier left the security of New Brunswick's perimeter defenses, he became a target for marauding Americans. The danger of being attacked increased on the Piscataway side of Landing Lane Bridge and continued all the way to Perth Amboy. The only respite on the ten-mile gauntlet was the fortified village of Bonhamtown, situated halfway between New Brunswick and Perth Amboy. Travelling between the two garrison towns by boat was just as dangerous as the land route.

The bridge built across the Raritan at New Brunswick was referred to at the time as Moncrieffs [sic] Bridge in honor of Captain James Moncrief, the British Army engineer who designed and supervised the bridge's construction.[52] Work on the project began on May 10, 1777, and took one hundred men ten days to complete. A British officer described the details of its construction: "hollow piers [vertical beams] composed of green logs were placed at twenty foot distances from each other, and joined at the top with long spars, by way of sleepers [horizontal beams], which were covered with what boards we could get from barns, stables and etc. and formed a bridge in this manner of three hundred and ten yards long."[53] Captain Moncrief's bridge attracted the attention of the Patriots, who reported its construction to Washington's headquarters in Morristown. Washington was uneasy, as the bridge was a substantial structure that indicated that Sir William might be planning to quickly move large numbers of troops, wagons, and field artillery from New York for a rapid march across New Jersey to seize Philadelphia. Another possibility was that the bridge was part of the preparations for a large-scale surprise attack aimed at Morristown. At the same time that the bridge was being constructed, Washington's headquarters received reliable intelligence that a fleet of seventy transports was being made ready to sail from New York. The report mentioned that seven of the ships were modified to transport horses "and got forage on board—the rest designed for troops, stores and provisions—Philadelphia the destination talked of."[54] While Philadelphia seemed to be Howe's objective, there was speculation that the fleet being outfitted in New York was going to transport Howe's army up the Hudson River to rendezvous with Burgoyne and cut off New England from the other warring colonies. Washington's intensive intelligence gathering by spies; interrogation of deserters and prisoners; and reading captured letters, documents, and Loyalist newspapers were unable to unravel the "mystical proceedings of General Howe."[55] Unsure of Sir William's plans, Washington decided to change his strategy by "drawing together the men of the regiments [consolidating his army]." The order was issued on May 20 to assemble the Grand Army into one encampment.[56] The last time his army had operated as a single force was at the January 3, 1777, Battle of Princeton. Following the fighting at Princeton, and his arrival at Morristown, Washington's strategy was to disperse his army into detachments to harass the enemy's foraging expeditions and create the illusion that he commanded a large force. The place where he decided to reunite his army was in the Watchung Mountains above Bound Brook. His occupation of the Watchungs resulted in a response from General Howe that had a major impact on the outcome of the war. What follows in the next chapter is a detailed account of Washington's two-month-long occupation of the Watchung Mountains, one of the most interesting and overlooked episodes of the American Revolution.

7

General Howe Has Lately Made a
Very Extraordinary Movement*

The Watchung Mountain range stretches for forty-two miles from central New Jersey to the northern border of the state. Also called the Blue Hills, the range consists of two parallel ridges separated by a one-and-a-half-mile-wide level valley.[1] The easternmost ridge, looking out over the flat farmland of central New Jersey, is called the First Watchung Mountain. Behind it is a valley that gently slopes into the second ridge called the Second Watchung Mountain. Morristown lies in the hill country sixteen miles north of the second ridge of the Watchung Mountains.

Washington's Grand Army camped in the Watchung Mountains from May 28 to July 3, 1777. Called the Middlebrook encampment, it proved to be the best defensive position that Washington's army would occupy during the eight years of the American Revolution. Historian Dave Palmer declared the position "impervious to attack."[2] Other historians agreed with General Palmer's assessment, including James Kirby Martin, who called the Middlebrook encampment site "masterful."[3]

---

* Chapter title from George Washington's letter to Chevalier Anmours, dated "Head Quarters Camp at Middle Brook, June 19th 1777," in W. W. Abbot et al., eds., *The Papers of George Washington, Revolutionary War Series*, 28 vols. to date (Charlottesville: University of Virginia Press, 1985–2021), vol. 10:70. Charles-François-Adrien Le Paulmier d'Anmours (1742–1807) was a wealthy civilian with connections in the French government. He was in Philadelphia at the time as an observer for the French government to report on the war.

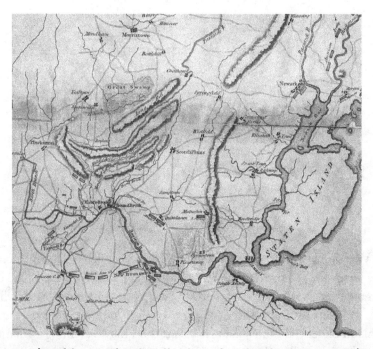

A close-up view of the map of northern New Jersey from the atlas that accompanies John Marshall's *Life of George Washington.* The map includes the movements of British and American troops during June 1777. The map is accurate, though the position of Lord Stirling's division (indicated in the center of the map as *L.Stirling*) prior to the Battle of Short Hills is questionable. I concluded that Stirling's camp was along the south branch of the Rahway River between Metuchen (spelled Matuchin on the map) and Woodbridge. The town marked on the map as *Connecticut Farms* is present-day Union, New Jersey. *Boylan* on the map (located north of Bound Brook) probably marks the site of a store operated by John Boylan. It is the present-day unincorporated community of Liberty Corner, New Jersey. The map also shows the presence of an American force near Quibbletown on June 4, 1777. This is probably a reference to a force of 700 Americans under the command of General Benjamin Lincoln that was operating in the area. *Author's collection.*

There were a number of reasons why the Watchung Mountains were an excellent defensive position for Washington's army in 1777. Among them was that the height of the First Watchung Mountain along its entire forty-two-mile-long length was only 400 to 500 feet above the surrounding countryside, but the face of the ridge was steep and densely

This is a view of the Watchung Mountains looking north from the present-day town of Greenbrook, New Jersey. Greenbrook is a few miles northeast of Bound Brook. This recent photograph shows that the Watchungs are a small but steep and heavily forested mountain range. *Author's photo.*

covered with live and fallen trees, thick underbrush, and rock formations. These obstructions prevented more than a lightly armed, agile detachment of troops to climb the mountain. In addition, there were only a few narrow passes through the First Watchung Mountain that Washington's army was able to defend with redoubts and artillery. British General James Grant recognized the formidable advantages that the Americans had by occupying the Watchung Mountains: "he can move a force from hence to any given point. We have been obliged to contract our cantonments to Brunswick, Amboy and the communications between those two places.... In short it is the most unpleasing situation I ever was in."[4]

The view from the top of the First Watchung Mountain included New Brunswick, the major British Army base in New Jersey. The town was located seven miles southeast from the Watchungs, and any large-scale daytime military movement coming from New Brunswick could be detected from the cloud of dust created by the columns of marching troops, mounted officers and light dragoons, horse-drawn wagons, cattle for butchering, and field artillery. At night, the position of an enemy force could be observed from their campfires. Sadly, an additional clue to the movement of a British army through the region was from the smoke and flames of torched Patriot farmhouses and barns.

Washington was also drawn to the Watchungs because of the mile-and-a-half-wide valley that lay between the two ridges. For easy identification I will refer to it by its present name, which is Washington Valley. The valley was flat and well-watered by several streams. It was a healthy and safe place for the commander-in-chief to move his army into tents in the spring after living in cold and crowded conditions during the winter. By late May, when the Grand Army arrived there, Washington Valley was already thickly covered with forage to feed the army's horses and cattle.

Contributing to Washington's decision to occupy the Watchung Mountains in the spring of 1777 was the advantage of interior lines. To explain, Washington Valley ran along the entire length of the Watchung range. Unsure of what direction Howe would take his army, the topography of Washington Valley gave the Americans interior lines: the ability to move troops through the valley—hidden from the enemy—southwest to defend Philadelphia or northeast to reinforce the forts guarding the Hudson River.

There is no known record of Washington personally reconnoitering the Watchungs before ordering his troops to camp there. However, a number of his senior line officers became familiar with the region during the winter forage war. The Continental Army officers who traveled through the region included Nathanael Greene, William Maxwell, John Sullivan, and Benjamin Lincoln. Nathanael Greene, for example, established his headquarters just north of the Watchungs at Basking Ridge during the winter. Greene also made several trips through the mountains during the winter to the village of Bound Brook, which was located at the base of the First Watchung Mountain.

Washington gave the job to "lay off the encampment" to General Greene. Greene began surveying the location for the encampment in the Watchungs on May 24 with the help of Clement Biddle, one of

Greene's aides-de-camp.[5] Before the war, Biddle was a wealthy merchant who served as a Continental Army quartermaster before joining Greene's military family. Biddle's experience as a quartermaster was valuable in selecting the Watchung Mountains campsite, based on a description of the duties of a quartermaster in the *Universal Military Dictionary*, published in 1779: "[He]... should be a man of great judgement and experience, and well skilled in geography: his duty is to mark the marches and encampments of an army."[6] Greene and Biddle selected a sparsely settled section of Washington Valley above Bound Brook, which they called the Middlebrook encampment. The name came from the Middlebrook Creek that flowed through the valley, down the First Watchung Mountain and into the Raritan River. There is some confusion about the location of the Middlebrook encampment as there was also a village named Middlebrook at the base of the First Watchung Mountain (eventually absorbed into present-day Bound Brook).[7] The Grand Army never bivouacked in the village of Middlebrook in 1777. They camped in Washington Valley above the village. To further confuse historians, the majority of the Grand Army spent the winter of 1778–1779 in the present-day towns of Bound Book, Bridgewater, and Somerville. They called this winter cantonment the Middlebrook encampment. To summarize: the 1777 spring Middlebrook encampment was in Washington Valley, and the 1778–1779 winter encampment was located in a wide area facing the Watchung Mountains.

The 1777 Middlebrook encampment occupied about a mile-wide section of Washington Valley. It was located in today's Warren Township, New Jersey. The present-day village of Martinsville (incorporated in 1827) lies within the boundaries of the encampment, but there was nothing on the site in 1777 except a stone farmhouse owned by Folcard Sebring (demolished in the nineteenth century). It is believed that about one hundred people lived in what is today Warren Township when Washington's army camped there. The sparse population is attributed to the isolated location of Washington Valley and the rocks lying below the surface that make the land undesirable for farming.

The first troops arrived at Middlebrook on May 28 from Morristown. Washington reached the encampment in the evening of the following day. Following Washington's orders, all the outposts established during the winter were evacuated and the army consolidated at Middlebrook. They included the Continental troops stationed at Peekskill, New York, "except the number requisite for the security of the post [Peekskill]."[8] The number of troops in the Grand Army at Middlebrook is frequently cited as being around 8,000 officers and enlisted men. This number is a good approximation based on a return (roster) of the Grand Army dated May 21, 1777. The return listed 7,363 Continental Army officers and enlisted men present and fit for duty plus an estimated 500 militia.[9] This number included 1,346 Maryland Continentals at Princeton under Sullivan's command. The sizeable force at Princeton was due to Washington's concern that the British might try to "push for Philadelphia" from New Brunswick. The plan was for New Jersey and Pennsylvania militia to join Sullivan's Continentals in blocking the attempt. Washington felt confident that the militia would turn out if called upon. His assurance was based on the fact that the militiamen turned out in large numbers and were willing to fight and remain in the field if they were operating with Continental troops. But even if heavily reinforced, Sullivan's proximity to New Brunswick was dangerous, and the commander-in-chief warned him to "use the greatest vigilance and precaution" to keep patrols out to warn him of a surprise attack.[10] Washington also instructed Sullivan not to attempt any offensive operations no matter how tempting:

> *I do not wish that you should hazard a general engagement; because, a defeat of our whole body [committing the entire Grand Army to support Sullivan] which would probably follow, from inequality of numbers would bring on a dispersion and discouragement of your troops [Continentals and militia]: whereas to harass them day and night by a number of small parties, under good officers, disputing at the same time advantageous passes [gaps into the Watchung Mountains], would do them more real injury without hazarding the bad consequences of a defeat and rout.*[11]

Unlike Princeton or Morristown, which were towns with buildings to house troops, the Middlebrook encampment was an empty field. As a result, the army lived in tents throughout the encampment, including General Washington. It was unusual for Washington to spend this much time living in tents. He usually lived in them for short periods of time when the army was on the move or until he could find a suitable building to serve as his headquarters and personal use. It is speculated that Washington occupied Folcard Sebring's farmhouse, which was on the site of the encampment.[12] However, in a letter to his brother John Augustine written in the final days of the encampment, Washington said that "I have now been in my tent about five weeks."[13] General George Weedon was with the army at Middlebrook and he wrote a description of the camp that included a reference to Washington living in a tent. Weedon said, "The whole of them [the Grand Army] are now encamped in comfortable tents on a valley covered in front and rear by ridges which affords us security. His Excellency, our good old general, has also spread his tent, and lives amongst us."[14]

A reference to Washington living in a tent warrants clarification. His field headquarters was a sequestered, heavily guarded compound, consisting of three "marques" (the word used at the time to identify a marquee or large tent). The three marques included a two-room sleeping pavilion for Washington's personal use; a large dining marquee that could hold up to fifty people and also served as a work area for his aides-de-camp, and a baggage marquee to safely store the headquarters stock of victuals, dinnerware, eating utensils, and trunks filled with carefully filed copies of correspondence. The baggage tent also held the personal belongings of Washington and his aides. There was no standard military trunk at the time, and the baggage tent would have been filled with a variety of trunks, portmanteaus (bags for carrying apparel, particularly used when travelling on horseback), packing cases, and valises that held the clothing, toilet articles, telescopes, spare bedding, and other personal gear belonging to Washington's aides-de-camp. They were all wealthy men with the exception of Hamilton, and it is interesting to speculate if Hamilton's personal belongings were equal to those of his fellow aides.

Washington learned the importance of having an impressive headquarters from the British Army as a way of upholding respect for the officer corps and maintaining discipline. As a result, Washington's headquarters was a display of class consciousness and military precision, no matter how destitute the army was.

The three tents that were at the core of Washington's headquarters compound were custom made at government expense during the winter of 1776 by the Philadelphia upholsterer Plunkett Fleeson. A passionate Patriot, Mr. Fleeson applied his expert skill at making fine furniture to supplying the Continental Army with tents, portable camp furniture, flags, and drums during the war. Each of the tents that Fleeson made for Washington had two separate layers of fabric. This design made the tents more resistant to rain and cold than the conventional (and cheaper) one-layer design. Erected near Washington's three tents were the tents of his aides-de-camp. They were probably medium-size tents (about ten feet wide, fourteen feet long, and eight feet high) in which a person could stand.[15] In comparison, the tents of the private soldiers were only six-and-a-half feet square and five feet high, and held at least five soldiers each.[16] The tents of Washington's bodyguards, called the Commander-in-Chief's Guard or Life Guard, were pitched around the headquarters compound. The guards were responsible for Washington's safety and protecting the headquarters baggage from theft. The Life Guards prevented anyone from entering the headquarters compound to disturb Washington or one of his aides. Additional sentries were posted near His Excellency's sleeping tent. To complete the picture, there would have also been an assortment of tents adjacent to the headquarters compound for the servants, cooks, washer women, grooms, and slaves who attended to the personal needs of the headquarters staff and their horses.

Washington living and working in tents during the Middlebrook encampment can be attributed to the lack of a suitable building in the area, the good springtime weather, the secure location of the encampment, and His Excellency's desire to be with his army. In fact, Washington remained with his troops throughout the American Revolution except when he traveled to Philadelphia at the request of Congress and never once went home to Mount Vernon except for a brief visit en route to Yorktown in 1781. His dedication to his army was repaid by their respect and loyalty.

Washington was concerned that the British would use the good weather beginning in the spring of 1777 to launch an offensive across New Jersey to seize Philadelphia. As a result, among Washington's first measures after arriving at Middlebrook was to order all the boats along a twenty-five-mile-long section of the Delaware River between Trenton and Coryell's Ferry (present-day New Hope, Pennsylvania) to be brought to the Pennsylvania side of the river.[17] The move was to prevent the British from commandeering the boats to cross the river. Washington also ordered Major General Thomas Mifflin to gather all the boats on the upper Delaware River and secure them on the Pennsylvania side of the river. Mifflin probably brought the boats to the upriver ferry crossing at Tinicom, Pennsylvania, where they were ready if the Grand Army had to evacuate Middlebrook and retreat across the Delaware into Pennsylvania.[18]

Washington also took action to defend the Middlebrook encampment by embedding fougasses along the crest of the First Watchung Mountain. Traces of their locations are still visible today. A fougasse is a simple explosive device made by digging a hole in the ground or constructing a crater in a pile of stone and filling it with black powder and some type of projectile such as rock. The fougasse was exploded by a fuse made of gunpowder packed into a cloth or leather tube that was waterproofed with pitch. Upon the approach of an enemy, the fuse was lit, igniting the main charge in the hole and sending a lethal shower of rock or debris into the air. Another way to explode a fougasse was with a gun lock connected to a trip wire. Constructing fougasses was well known by military engineers at the time of the American Revolution. They were used throughout the war, including in the defense of Fort Red Bank (also called Fort Mercer). A plan of Fort Red Bank drawn by the French Army engineer Thomas-Antoine, Chevalier de Mauduit du Plessis, identified the locations of the fougasses surrounding the fort.

There were three narrow passes through the First Watchung Mountain near the Middlebrook encampment. They were, from east to west, called Lincoln's Gap, Mordecai's Gap, and Steele's Gap. Lincoln's Gap (present-day Mountain Avenue in Bound Brook to King George Road in Warren) was located directly behind the colonial village

The crest of the Watchung Mountains in the vicinity of Bound Brook includes remnants of fougasses (land mines) constructed by Washington's army in 1777 to help defend their mountaintop positions. *Author's photo.*

of Bound Brook. It will be recalled that the Continentals retreated from Bound Brook into the Watchung Mountains through Lincoln's Gap when the town was surprised by the British in April 1777 (the Battle of Bound Brook). Mordecai's Gap, also called Wayne's Gap or Oliver's Gap (today's Vosseller Avenue) was located a half-mile west of Lincoln's Gap. The third pass was called Steele's Gap (today's Steele Gap Road in Bridgewater Township), located two miles west of Mordecai's Gap.

Mordecai's Gap was the most important of the three passes. An indication of the strategic importance of Mordecai's Gap is that it was heavily defended by American artillery under the command of General Knox.[19] One reason for the extra security at Mordecai's Gap was that it led to the Mount Horeb (a biblical term) Road, which ran through Washington Valley before turning north to Morristown. The name of the road changed from Mount Horeb Road to Basking Ridge Road north of the Watchung Mountains.

Standing on the crest of the First Watchung Mountain near Mordecai's Gap was the best place to view the Raritan River Valley and British-held New Brunswick. The preferred location where Washington and his officers were believed to have stood is a stone outcropping at the edge of the mountain, known today as Washington Rock. The Patriots' observations from Washington Rock toward New Brunswick were improved by using espying glasses (telescopes). While many of the older telescopes in use at the time were clumsy and up to three feet in length, advances in optics had made it possible to fabricate shorter and more powerful folding brass pocket-size telescopes. These new, small telescopes were available by the time of the American Revolution and carried by many officers during the war.[20]

Washington Rock became a tourist attraction beginning in the early nineteenth century. Historian Benson J. Lossing visited the site in the 1850s, saying that it "must ever impress the visitor with pleasant recollection of the view obtained from that lofty observatory." Lossing described how he started up Mordecai's Gap with other visitors in a wagon, which they had to abandon halfway up the mountain

and make our way up the steep declivities [a descending slope] along the remains of the old road. How loaded wagons were managed in ascending or descending this mountain road is quite inconceivable, for it is a difficult journey for a foot-passenger to make.... Having reached the summit, we made our way through a narrow and tangled path to the bold rock. It is at an elevation of nearly four hundred feet above the plain below, and commands a magnificent view of the surrounding country included in the segment of a circle of sixty miles, having its rundle [the center of a wheel or circle] southward. At our feet spread out the beautiful rolling plains like a map, through which course the winding Raritan... and little villages and neat farmhouses dotted the picture in every direction. Upon this lofty rock Washington often stood with his telescope, and reconnoitered the vicinity.[21]

Pennsylvania militia officer and artist Charles Willson Peale visited Washington Rock on June 26, 1777, and recorded the event in his diary.

Peale said that he went to the site to view "one of the most sublime prospects I have ever seen—overlooking the country as far as my eyes could see.... I had been but a short time here before General Washington came to this spot and where I spent the whole day."[22]

The positions of Washington's army at Middlebrook and Princeton were reported to British headquarters in New York by Loyalist sympathizers, spies, and British Army reconnaissance patrols. They were aware that the American entrenchments along the crest of the Watchungs were "defended by abbatis [cut-down trees with the branches facing toward the enemy] and felled timber, which rendered an immediate approach to their camp dangerous and difficult."[23] The news of the Grand Army's occupation of the Watchung Mountains arrived in New York in early June as Howe was completing his preparation for his seaborne invasion to capture Philadelphia via an amphibious landing along the Delaware River south of the rebel capital.

There was good springtime weather and green forage on the ground by early June, but Sir William's army remained in camp awaiting the arrival of reinforcements from England and accumulating provisions. Howe, for example, insisted on having six months of food stockpiled in New York before launching his attack.[24] The last of the expected reinforcements and equipment finally arrived in New York in late May. Ambrose Serle's journal entry for May 26, 1777, for example, mentioned the arrival in New York of a big convoy "with reinforcements and camp equipage [tents and other items needed to establish a camp]."[25] A few days later Serle reported that an additional seventeen transports entered New York harbor with more troops and equipment. Finally, in early June 1777, Sir William's preparations were complete, and he still had time to capture Philadelphia and turn north if he decided to cooperate with Burgoyne. What occurred next arguably ranks as General Howe's most impulsive decision during the war, one that made it impossible for him to support Burgoyne. If Burgoyne surrendering his army in upstate New York in October 1777 is often cited as the turning point of the American Revolution, then Howe wasting time chasing Washington in New Jersey contributed to Burgoyne's defeat.

General Howe decided that the news of Washington's army camped just seven miles from New Brunswick was a great opportunity to defeat the rebels in a general engagement. Crushing Washington's army would allow Sir William to trade his seaborne operation in favor of a faster overland march across New Jersey to Philadelphia. The Continentals at Princeton, even if reinforced by militia, did not pose a serious threat. With unusual speed, Sir William assembled a large army in New Brunswick in preparation for a decisive battle with Washington's Grand Army in New Jersey. Howe already had 10,000 troops stationed in New Brunswick and Perth Amboy in early June 1777. They were supposed to evacuate their posts and join the 8,000 troops in New York allocated for the seaborne invasion of Pennsylvania. Instead, on June 5 Sir William ordered the troops in New York assigned to the seaborne invasion diverted to Perth Amboy. A convoy of flat-bottomed boats on wagons left New York on June 9 for New Brunswick.[26] They joined the twenty flat-bottomed boats already in New Brunswick.[27] Their purpose was to build a pontoon bridge across the Delaware River near Trenton as part of an offensive across New Jersey to seize Philadelphia. By June 11, all the troops from New York had arrived in Perth Amboy and joined the garrison already stationed there. General Howe arrived in New Jersey on June 11 to take personal command of the campaign, and inspected the troops and fortifications at Perth Amboy that afternoon. Following his inspection tour, Howe rode to New Brunswick. Although he was travelling through territory controlled by his army, there was the constant danger of rebel ambushes, so Howe made the trip accompanied by a Hessian grenadier battalion and two British infantry regiments. In addition, twenty dragoons surrounded Howe en route. They arrived in New Brunswick in the late afternoon (June 11) without incident.[28] On June 12, the troops in Perth Amboy marched to New Brunswick, leaving a small garrison behind to guard the town. When added to the troops already in New Brunswick, Howe had assembled an army of 18,000.[29]

Washington was aware that Howe was gathering a large army in New Brunswick for a major campaign. But he was unsure if Howe's objective was to march northeast toward the Watchung Mountains or southwest to capture Philadelphia. Adding to Washington's apprehension was that he did not know the purpose of the fleet of warships and transports anchored in New York. But by June 12 Washington felt confident that at least General Howe was not planning to use the ships gathered in New York to sail up the Hudson River to cooperate with General Burgoyne. Washington wrote Major General Israel Putnam that day with an assessment of the situation:

> *From General Howe's movements within a few days past, it is clear, beyond all matter of doubt that he has dropped all thoughts of an expedition up the North River [Hudson River], having drawn the greatest part of his troops from New York and its dependencies to Amboy, and from thence to Brunswick where his main army is encamped. Great numbers of wagons are brought over [to New Jersey] and many flatboats [to build a pontoon bridge] on carriages supposed to be for the passage of the Delaware River. We have had a variety of accounts by deserters and spies all agreeing that a move will be made as soon as matters are in a proper state.[30]*

The presence of pontoon boats on carriages at New Brunswick were of particular interest to Washington. He got information about the boats from John Mercereau, a teenager from Elizabeth, New Jersey, who was an American spy. Mercereau arranged to live in New Brunswick to report on British activities in the town. He had a lame arm which kept him from military service. Young Mercereau reported the number of boats and their approximate dimensions to headquarters. Washington asked Mercereau to go to the section of the Delaware River just north of Trenton to measure the river's width to see if the British had assembled enough boats to build a pontoon bridge across the river.[31] There is no record of whether Mercereau completed his mission or how the information was transmitted to headquarters. It is speculated that he hid his reports under a rock on a small island named Shooters Island, located near the north shore of Staten Island, where they were picked up and brought to headquarters. All privileged information was probably closely guarded and eventually destroyed by Washington and his aides-de-camp.

Washington would have loved to have young Mercereau eavesdropping on a late-night dinner meeting in New Brunswick on June 11 attended by General Howe and Lord Cornwallis.[32] What transpired at that meeting is unknown but, two days later, on the night of June 13, Howe's army "set out from New Brunswick."[33] His army was travelling light, leaving behind their "camp equipage and carrying only provisions for seven days."[34] Brigadier General Edward Mathew was left behind with 2,000 men to guard New Brunswick.[35] Howe understood that it was too dangerous to try to force one of the passes leading to the Middlebrook encampment. Instead, he realized, he had to trick or force Washington into bringing his army down from his mountain stronghold and fight him in a pitched battle.

Howe's solution to pressuring Washington into a general engagement was to threaten Sullivan's garrison at Princeton. The college town was just sixteen miles southwest from New Brunswick by following the High Road. But advancing down the High Road toward Princeton would give Washington the advantage of coming off the mountains unopposed and deploying his army in Howe's rear. Such a move by Washington would trap Howe's army between two rebel forces (Sullivan's and Washington's). It would also block Howe's ability to retreat back to New Brunswick if necessary. Howe could not risk this situation, especially since he did not know the size of the American forces facing him. Typically, Howe tended to overestimate the Americans' strength.

The danger of Howe being outmaneuvered explains why he marched his army northwest from New Brunswick toward Hillsborough. It will be recalled that Washington's exhausted army marched to Hillsborough on January 3, 1777, following the Battle of Princeton. Howe's strategy was clever: He would outflank Washington by positioning his British and Hessians between the Middlebrook encampment and Sullivan's corps at Princeton. Hillsborough was less than a day's march from Princeton. Howe's objective was to force Washington to come down off the mountains and fight him on the flat plains of central New Jersey by threatening Sullivan's troops at Princeton. Sir William's troop deployment was an example of late eighteenth-century military science, which emphasized outmaneuvering an enemy, forcing them to retreat, surrender or, in this instance, fight at a disadvantage.

Howe put his plan into motion on the night of June 13, 1777. His army marched in two columns from New Brunswick, about an hour apart. Both columns would follow the same route: one mile southwest along the High Road toward Princeton, then turn northwest toward Hillsborough along the Amwell Road. The first column left New Brunswick at 10:00 pm. It was commanded by Cornwallis. His corps, estimated at 2,000 officers and enlisted men, included many of the best troops in Howe's army including light infantry, grenadiers, a detachment from the Brigade of Guards, jägers, and dragoons, plus an arsenal of field artillery. They proceeded along the Amwell Road past the village of Middlebush to Schenck's Bridge, a wooden span that crossed the Millstone River.[36] Hillsborough was just beyond the bridge. Cornwallis's column arrived at the bridge to find that the rebels had partially destroyed it and had begun firing at the British from the woods across the river. The rebel force was identified as 200 men from Morgan's Rifle Corps.[37] They skirmished with the British briefly before withdrawing, knowing that there were several fords upstream where enemy troops could wade across the narrow river and attack them. The bridge was quickly repaired, and Cornwallis's corps entered Hillsborough early on the morning of June 14.[38] They "drew up" [camped] on some high ground forming a semicircle around the village.[39] Their rear was secured by the Millstone River. The entire jäger corps of 600 men (including a newly arrived company from the principality of Anspach-Bayrouth) was with Cornwallis, and he assigned them to picket duty. They fanned out beyond the camp's perimeter. Captain Ewald said that his jäger company "covered the left towards Rocky Hill [a village on the Millstone River near Princeton]."[40] Captain John Peebles was with Cornwallis's column and reported that the rebels immediately began to skirmish with the jägers.[41] Local historians believe that Cornwallis made his headquarters at the home of Annie Van Liew (still standing and known today as the Franklin Inn).[42] The house is situated on Amwell Road on the opposite side of the Millstone River from Hillsborough. The wooden bridge across the Millstone River is nearby. However, it seems unlikely that Cornwallis would have risked

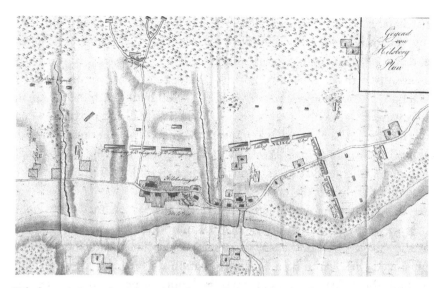

This is a photograph of the original map of the village of Hillsborough, New Jersey, that was drawn by jäger Captain Johann Ewald. It is one of the maps from Ewald's diary. The map shows the location of the British and Hessian units defending Hillsborough, including Ewald's jägers, during General Howe's 18,000-man incursion into central New Jersey that took place from June 13 to 19, 1777. *Author's photo.*

occupying an isolated building away from the protection of his army. More convincing evidence for the location of Cornwallis's headquarters is a map drawn by Captain Johann Ewald showing Cornwallis occupying an unnamed house in Hillsborough surrounded by his army.[43]

The second British column, estimated at 14,000 men, was under the command of the senior Hessian officer in America, Lieutenant General Leopold Phillip D' Heister (also spelled von Heister).[44] He was unpopular with the British because he was slow in following orders and lax in preventing his fellow Germans from indiscriminate looting. This accounts for D' Heister's column being accompanied by a number of British Army generals including Charles Gray, James Agnew, and Alexander Leslie, who were along to maintain discipline. General Howe also rode with D' Heister's corps. The van (front) of D' Heister's corps consisted of men called pioneers who wore leather aprons and carried hatchets, saws, spades, and pick-axes for "mending the ways," including repairing bridges.[45] They were escorted by troops from the 40th and 23rd British regiments. Also assigned to D' Heister's column was a recently arrived, innovative British Army rifle corps commanded by Captain Patrick Ferguson (1744–1780). Numbering a hundred men, they were armed with a new breech-loading rifle (ball and powder loaded in the rear of the gun barrel) invented by Captain Ferguson. More about Ferguson's corps follows, such as when they fought a company of Morgan's riflemen in late June on Strawberry Hill [a section of present-day Woodbridge, New Jersey].

D' Heister's column left New Brunswick as planned, one hour behind Cornwallis. They followed the same route but went only as far as the village of Middlebush, where they halted and made camp. They organized their camp in a square formation on favorable open ground around the village and built three redoubts armed with artillery to defend their position. American Colonel Timothy Pickering inspected the British camp at Middlebush after it was abandoned. He said that General Howe's headquarters was surrounded by the three redoubts.[46] Obviously, Howe was taking no chances of being kidnapped during the night by marauding rebels. The British built a fourth redoubt between Middlebush and Hillsborough to keep communications open between the two British camps. Major John André was with D' Heister's column, and wrote in his journal that the village of Middlebush was six miles from New Brunswick and Cornwallis's position at Hillsborough was two miles further down Amwell Road from Middlebush.[47] Once "hutted" (also called booths or wigwams, usually cone-shaped shelters made with tree branches and brush), André said that the Hessians began ransacking the homes of the local residents. According to André, General Howe sent a message to D' Heister "desiring him to warn the Hessians not to persist in such outrages as they would be most severely punished." It was not recorded whether Howe's warning stopped the pillaging. André also reported that "the rebel light horse [dragoons] were frequently seen hovering about Lord Cornwallis' camp, and the avenues to both camps were infested by ambuscades which fired on our patrols and sentries."[48] The major also recorded a number of casualties from rebel ambushes and raids, including two Hessians who were killed and four others wounded on June 18.

Probably unknown by the British at the time, they were being harassed by detachments from Colonel Daniel Morgan's 500-man Provincial Rifle Corps. It will be recalled that Washington instructed Morgan to recruit men who were experienced riflemen from the various regiments. Washington deployed Morgan's corps on the morning of June 13 in response to the big British build-up in New Brunswick. Washington's deployment of Morgan's corps was fortunate, as the British marched out of New Brunswick that night and headed toward Hillsborough. Washington instructed Morgan to "take post at Van Veighters [Van Veghten] Bridge," the strategic span that crossed the south branch of the Raritan River. Washington also spelled the name of the bridge in his correspondence as Vanbecters or Van Vehht's. The bridge no longer exists, but it was located between the present-day towns of Manville and Somerville. Washington instructed Morgan that "under the present appearance of things" to watch "particularly the roads leading from Brunswick towards Hillsborough and Princeton." In the same orders, Washington told Morgan, "In case of any movements of the enemy you are instantly to fall upon their flanks and gall them as much as possible."[49] Morgan had New Brunswick under observation and quickly moved his position eight miles from Van Veighters Bridge to Hillsborough once he realized that the big Crown forces column that marched out of New Brunswick on the night of June 13 was headed toward Hillsborough.

Howe believed that his nighttime march to Hillsborough had outflanked Washington. With Cornwallis at Hillsborough and less than a day's march from Princeton, Howe would force Washington to come down off the mountains to defend Sullivan's troops.

But unknown to Howe at the time, Sullivan had changed his position on June 12, one day before Howe launched his campaign. The story is that the big British build-up in New Brunswick made Washington apprehensive for the safety of Sullivan's command. Washington wrote Sullivan on June 12 saying that he feared that "you [Sullivan] are not so secure at present post as could be wished." His Excellency told Sullivan to shift his position from the level farmland surrounding Princeton to "the high ground of Rocky Hill" on the Millstone River. Rocky Hill is four miles northeast from Princeton. From his new position at Rocky Hill, Sullivan could "make a safe and secure retreat" to the Middlebrook encampment if necessary.[50]

Sullivan was given command of the Princeton garrison in mid-May. He replaced the aged Major General Israel Putnam. "Old Put," as he was called, was a Connecticut folk hero prone to fight rather than think. Putnam was left in command at Princeton when it was a small outpost during the winter whose purpose was to keep scouts out watching for any British movement toward Morristown or Philadelphia. But by May 1777, the college town had become too important to leave Old Put in command there. Sullivan was a good choice for the dangerous Princeton post. He was a competent general who understood the importance of maneuvering to gain an advantage over an enemy. Before the war he was a lawyer and successful business-man from New Hampshire with experience as a major in the colony's militia. The problem with Sullivan was that he constantly complained to Washington that he was being ill-treated and threatening to resign. Fed up with Sullivan's complaining, Washington wrote him from Morristown on March 15, 1777, "No other officer of rank, in the whole army has so often conceived himself neglected—slighted and ill-treated, as you have done—and none I am sure has had less cause than yourself to entertain such ideas."[51] But Sullivan was an intel-ligent, reliable officer who could be counted on to follow orders and take the initiative when necessary.

Washington ordered Sullivan to move again on June 14 following Cornwallis's occupation of Hillsborough. The commander-in-chief's new instructions read in part, "immediately upon the receipt of this [letter] to begin your march and reach Fleming Town [present-day Flemington, New Jersey], upon your arrival you will view the ground and post yourself on that which is most advantageous."[52] Sullivan's move to Flemington put his corps at the northern edge of a small mountain range called the Sourland Hills and within fifteen miles of the western end of Washington Valley. Sullivan's orders were to continue to "keep out small parties of militia and your own troops to reconnoiter and endeavor if possible to learn their strength.... Our move must depend entirely upon that of the enemy."[53] Sullivan's new position made sense. He was north of British-held Hillsborough and he could retreat, if necessary, along the Old York Road that ran northeast of the British position and join Washington in the Watchungs. Washington ordered General Phillippe Hubert, Chevalier de Preudhomme de Borre to reinforce the troops guarding Steele's Gap to provide support to Sullivan if necessary. As previously mentioned, Steele's Gap was the westernmost pass through the First Watchung Mountain. General Borre arrived at Steele's Gap at 3:00 am on June 18th.[54] Borre commanded a brigade at the time consisting of four Maryland regiments and the 2nd Canadian Regiment. There is no known record of how many of his troops Borre brought to Steele's Gap. It's worth mentioning again that Borre was a sixty-year-old former French Army lieutenant colonel when he arrived in America in April 1777. Congress appointed him a brigadier general and shipped him off to Washington's army in New Jersey. Washington was saddled with a number of Frenchmen at the time. He warned General William Heath about them in a July 27, 1777, letter: "I have found by experience however modest they may seem at first to be, by proposing to serve as volunteers, they very soon extend their views, and become importunate for officers they have no right to look for."[55]

Throughout this period Washington was not overly concerned that Howe's intention was to overrun Sullivan's corps at Princeton and proceed to Philadelphia. This is because Washington had reliable reports that Howe's heavy baggage and the wagons carrying the pontoon boats were left behind in New Brunswick. Besides the pontoon boats and baggage, a conspicuous bridging train apparently was still in New Brunswick. A bridging train was a horse-drawn convoy of wagons that carried the additional building materials, such as lumber, and tools to build a pontoon bridge. This intelligence coming from New Brunswick convinced Washington that Howe's sortie was meant to tempt or force the Grand Army into a general engagement. Washington shared his conclusion in a June 17, 1777, letter to Major General Benedict Arnold, who was in Philadelphia at the time:

I am clearly of opinion, that they will not move towards Philadelphia without first endeavoring to disable us and prevent our following them—The risk would be too great to attempt to cross a river [the Delaware] where they must expect to meet a formidable opposition in front [General Sullivan supported by militia], and would have such a force as ours [Washington's troops] hovering on their rear.[56]

Although Washington's army seemed to be secure in the Watchung Mountains, there was a weakness in his position that Howe failed to exploit. To explain, one of the stories about the Middlebrook encampment is that there was a secret pass leading into Washington Valley. The story is true and confirmed in a letter Washington wrote on June 17 from Middlebrook stating "our right is our only weak part."[57] What Washington was referring to was the western edge of Washington Valley just south of the village of Pluckemin. The valley ended at this point and opened through a gap onto the surrounding countryside. It was not difficult to approach this exposed end of Washington Valley through hilly but passable terrain from Cornwallis's camp in Hillsborough. Once into the gap near Pluckemin, it was six miles through Washington Valley to the Middlebrook encampment. Washington had three redoubts with artillery constructed in the valley facing Pluckemin (one of which is still there), but a large army supported by field artillery could overcome the redoubts and drive further east through the valley to the vulnerable Middlebrook encampment.

The weakness in the American defenses was described as a debouchèe [*debauchè* is French for an opening or passage] by British Army Captain William Hall in his *History of the Civil War in America*. According to Captain Hall, who participated in the New Jersey campaign, Lieutenant Colonel Charles Mawhood (who led British troops at the Battle of Princeton) offered to force his way through the gap with light infantry, but his proposal was rejected by General Howe with no explanation.[58]

Thomas Jones (the dissident Loyalist) alluded to the gap near Pluckemin when he said that a local inhabitant told Howe that he could "conduct him round the hills [Watchung Mountains] with great safety, and bring him to a place unfortified, where he might easily penetrate

These are the remnants of one of the three redoubts the Americans constructed to defend the Middlebrook Encampment from a British attack from the gap in the Watchung Mountains. The gap, still visible, is located southeast of the village of Pluckemin. *Author's photo.*

into the rebel encampment, but this information was neglected."[59] Why Howe failed to launch a flanking attack (Howe's favorite tactic) through the opening is unknown, as he tended to keep his own council. According to Thomas Jones, the reason for Howe's failure to exploit this weakness in the American defenses was Howe's incompetence: "his summers were consumed in fatiguing, expensive, and useless operations while the winters were passed away in lust and luxury."[60]

The British and American armies remained unmoved for four days, grimly eyeing each other. Howe sent out detachments and made several feints, as if to bypass the American camp and march toward Princeton and the Delaware River. But Washington was not fooled, and he remained sequestered with his army in the heights.

This is a good opportunity to explore the story that the American flag was first flown at the Middlebrook encampment. The story begins on Saturday, June 14, 1777. While the Crown forces were skirmishing with the rebels around Hillsborough and Middlebush, the Continental Congress was convening sixty miles away in Philadelphia that day. During their meeting, the delegates approved several proposals from the Marine Committee of Congress, including the design for a national flag. The so-called flag resolution read, "Resolved, that the flag of the United States be thirteen stripes, alternate red and white: that the union be thirteen stars, white in a blue field, representing a new constellation."[61] It is claimed that this flag was flown for the first time by an American Army at the Middlebrook encampment in early July, 1777. In fact, a thirteen-star American flag is flown over a twenty-acre park that was once part of the Middlebrook encampment to commemorate the purported event. There are several problems with this story, including the fact that there is no known eyewitness account of the American flag being flown at the encampment. In addition, the purpose of the flag was to identify American ships and not as a national standard for the army. Commenting on this subject, Edward W. Richardson, in his scholarly history of the flags used by the Americans during the Revolutionary War, stated, "A national standard for the Army was apparently not defined until late in the war. The thirteen-stars-and-stripes flag resolution of June 14, 1777 originated with the Marine Committee of the Continental Congress and was probably intended primarily for ships."[62] A more creditable claim for the first time the national flag was flown by an American Army was on August 3, 1777, at the siege of Fort Stanwix, New York. The fort learned about the June 14 Congressional flag resolution from the men of the 9th Massachusetts regiment who arrived to reinforce the fort.[63] The besieged Patriot garrison is believed to have cut up their shirts to make the white stripes; scarlet material to form the red was secured from red flannel petticoats of officer's wives, and the blue union was made from an officer's blue coat. In fact, there is a voucher for repayment for a coat owned by Captain Abraham Swartwout and used to make a flag. Adding to the debate, the State of Delaware claims that the American flag was first flown on September 3, 1777, at the Battle of Couch's Bridge. Like the story of the American flag being first flown at the Middlebrook encampment, the Couch's Bridge story is based on hearsay and fabrication by well-meaning local historians. But there is a ceremony that takes place on Independence Day each year at the park that was once part of the Middlebrook encampment, where a thirteen-star American flag flies twenty-four hours a day. On July 4 each year a crowd gathers around the flagpole to hear the Declaration of Independence being read. It's an inspiring experience to stand beneath the thirteen-star flag at this historic site and listen to a dramatic reading of the Declaration of Independence. The event makes even a wary historian think that maybe it's true that the American flag was first flown at the Middlebrook encampment. And now back to the war in New Jersey.

By special order of Congress, a thirteen-star American flag is flown twenty-four hours a day in the Watchung Mountains near the site of the Grand Army's Middlebrook Encampment. *Author's photo.*

Howe maintained his posts in Middlebush and Hillsborough from the morning of June 14 to the morning of June 18. During this time, Washington remained in his mountain fortress skirmishing with the enemy. The irregular warfare was constant and intense, and it became increasingly difficult for Howe to hold his positions due to unrelenting attacks on his pickets, outposts, and supply convoys by Morgan's riflemen, Continental Army troops, and New Jersey militia. Washington remained convinced during this time that Philadelphia was safe from attack. A letter that Washington's aide-de-camp Tench Tilghman wrote to General Sullivan confirmed Washington's conviction: "it was determined, upon the information received... that the most probable cause of their coming out was to attempt a Coup de Main [surprise attack] upon this army."[64]

Frustrated in his failure to lure Washington into a decisive battle, Howe began abandoning his positions at Hillsborough and Middlebush at 4:00 am on June 19. The withdrawal continued throughout the morning, and by noon the entire army was back in New Brunswick.[65] Captain Muenchhausen was there and reported that the retreat was executed without incident, "except for some shots, which the enemy fired from a distance at our rear guard and on our side patrols [troops on the flanks protecting the main column]."[66]

After arriving back at New Brunswick, the army spread out on both sides of the Raritan River near the town where they camped and spent the night. The rumor that General Howe was abandoning New Brunswick was confirmed early the next morning when several infantry regiments began marching toward Perth Amboy. The evacuation of New Brunswick continued throughout the day. The activity drew the attention of the Americans, and the area was soon swarming with rebel skirmishers. Major André reported that they began to appear at 5:00 am on June 20 when "a body of the enemy showed themselves" on the New Brunswick side of the Raritan and began firing artillery at the retreating British and Hessians. André also reported that a second rebel party suddenly appeared "and fell in with the column of march. They attacked the light infantry but were immediately driven back; they however, shifted their position from one thicket to another and hung upon the flanks and rear for some distance. They killed or wounded about twenty of our people and a woman, a grenadier's wife."[67]

Ambrose Serle heard the news in New York that Sir William was withdrawing to Perth Amboy after failing to induce Washington to come down from his mountain fortress. Writing in his private journal, Serle said that he was "mortified" that the Army was retreating from what he cynically called General Howe's "half-besieging Washington." Serle called General Howe's realization that Washington's position was too strong to be attacked "an unlucky discovery that wasted precious time and resources on a fool's errand."[68]

But there was additional criticism of Howe's unforeseen evacuation of New Brunswick, including an anonymously written satirical poem in which Sir William speaks:

I own I was staggered to see with what skill,
The rogues were entrenched on the brow of the hill;
With a view to dismay them, I showed my whole force,
But they kept their position, and cared not a curse.
There were then but two ways—to retreat or attack,
And to me it seemed wisest by far to go back;
For I thought if I rashly got into a fray,
There might both be the Devil and Piper to pay.
Then, to lose no more time by parading in vain,
I determined elsewhere to transfer the campaign.[69]

General Howe's army abandoned New Brunswick on June 22, never to return. One thousand British and Hessian soldiers had been killed or wounded since the beginning of 1777 to secure the place. Its evacuation was a sad ending to Sir William's plan to use New Brunswick as a base to launch his campaign to demoralize the rebellion by seizing Philadelphia.

8

Our Situation Is Truly
Delicate and Perplexing*

The Crown forces spent several days in New Brunswick before evacuating the place. They used the time to partially destroy the redoubts they had constructed during their seven-month occupation. They did this by leveling the glacis (sloping fronts) of the redoubts surrounding the town. Captain Montresor recorded their departure in his journal: "22nd—Sunday. At break of day the line [army] moved from Brunswick and by evening the whole encamped at [Perth] Amboy."[1] They left nothing of value behind, especially their provisions and military stores. Boats transported part of their supplies and equipment downriver to Perth Amboy, and the rest was loaded into wagons that were organized into a heavily guarded wagon train. An eyewitness to the retreat to Perth Amboy reported that "the train of artillery and wagons extends about nine miles and is upwards of 1000 in number." The same observer wrote: "All the country houses were in flames as far as we could see. The soldiers are so much enraged they will set them on fire, in spite of all the officers can do to prevent it."[2] There were also reports of widespread pillaging by the British and Hessians along their ten-mile line of march. An account

---

* Chapter title from George Washington's letter to John Rutledge, dated "Head Quarters Morris Town July 5th 1777," in W. W. Abbot et al., eds., *The Papers of George Washington, Revolutionary War Series*, 28 vols. to date (Charlottesville: University of Virginia Press, 1985–2021), vol. 10:199. Rutledge was the governor of South Carolina.

of their invectives was published in a Philadelphia newspaper, which included some gruesome details:

> *In his route he [General Howe] stole everything worth carrying off, burnt a great number of houses, wheat, &c. and hung up three women, two of them by the feet, whom he imagined were spies—in short, his whole progress through this part of the country, is marked with devastation and cruelty, more like the savages of the wilderness, than of Britons, once famed for honor and humanity.*[3]

The long, slow-moving column of troops, artillery, and wagons was a tempting target, and the retreating Crown forces were relentlessly harassed by rebel skirmishers during their retreat from New Brunswick to Perth Amboy. Morgan's riflemen were among those along their route skirmishing with the enemy.[4] Captain Montresor said that the troops he accompanied were attacked twice by rebel skulkers (cowardly sneaks) who killed one man and wounded sixteen.[5]

Lieutenant Colonel William Palfrey was one of the first Continental Army officers to enter New Brunswick after it was abandoned. Palfrey recorded his experience:

> *I was at Brunswick just after the enemy had left it. Never let the British troops upbraid the Americans with want of cleanliness, for such dog kennels as their huts were my eye never beheld. Mr. Burton's house [home of William Burton, still standing and known today as Buccleuch Mansion], where Lord Cornwallis resided [in the spring of 1777], stunk so I could not bear to enter it. The houses were torn to pieces, and the inhabitants as well as the soldiers have suffered greatly for want of provisions.*[6]

Another American officer reported that he found "numerous bodies buried in the cellars of [New] Brunswick." Apparently it was done to conceal the actual number of soldiers who had died during the British occupation.[7]

Looking back, Howe's offensive intended to draw Washington into a general engagement consumed over two weeks of good campaigning weather. The offensive began on June 6, 1777, when Howe diverted the troops ready to embark aboard ships in New York for the invasion of Pennsylvania and ended on June 22 when the Crown forces abandoned New Brunswick. In addition to wasting over two weeks, Howe lost over a hundred troops skirmishing with the rebels along with exhausting his men and horses and consuming tons of provisions.

Howe's army spent several days in Perth Amboy destroying the redoubts that protected the town and ferrying men and supplies across the Arthur Kill (*kill* is Dutch for a body of water), the narrow waterway that separated New Jersey from Staten Island. The British had no serious problems controlling Staten Island. They occupied the island in July 1776 and subsequently constructed a chain of redoubts and fortified houses facing the American-held parts of New Jersey.[8] There is a deep water inlet on the south shore of Staten Island called Princess Bay. Admiral Lord Howe moved forty-three transports there from New York to expedite the boarding of men, horses, and equipment for the seaborne invasion of Pennsylvania.[9] However, the majority of the ships assembled for the Pennsylvania campaign remained anchored in New York harbor, with boats constantly arriving at Perth Amboy to transport provisions and military stores to New York City. Admiral Howe dispatched the newly completed HMS *Vigilant* to help defend Perth Amboy during the British exodus. She was a privately owned merchant ship purchased in early 1777 by Admiral Howe, who converted her into a large seaworthy gun battery mounting fourteen large-caliber cannons.[10] The *Vigilant* was also described as a galley, which meant that she could be propelled or maneuvered with oars.[11] The *Vigilant* was anchored in the harbor of Perth Amboy with enough firepower to discourage any attempt by the rebels to attack the town during the British evacuation.[12] General Washington knew about the *Vigilant* from a British Army deserter named Thomas Bowman, who saw the ship while she was being converted in New York City.[13]

While in the process of evacuating Perth Amboy, General Howe dutifully informed Lord Germain of his failed effort to defeat Washington's army in a carefully worded report that disguised the extent of the debacle. Howe told Germain that he advanced from New Brunswick to Hillsborough and Middlebush, *with a view of drawing on an action if the enemy should remove from the mountain.... But on finding their intention to keep a position which it would not have been prudent to attack, I determined without loss of time to pursue the principal object of the campaign [capturing Philadelphia] by withdrawing the army from Jersey.*[14]

As the activity at Perth Amboy continued, a detachment of rebels described as a "flying party" [a force always in motion to keep an enemy in continual alarm] was observed on June 24 on a knoll three miles northwest of Perth Amboy called Strawberry Hill. The present-day site is a neighborhood of private homes centered on Strawberry Hill Avenue in the town of Woodbridge. The Americans occupying the knoll were 150 men from Morgan's Rifle Corps. They were surprised early the next morning (June 25th) by Ferguson's Rifle Corp. This is the first known

A modern view of Strawberry Hill where Patrick Ferguson's Rifle Corps skirmished with troops from Daniel Morgan's Rifle Corps on June 25, 1777. Strawberry Hill is present-day Strawberry Hill Avenue in Woodbridge, New Jersey. *Author's photo.*

account of Ferguson's riflemen in combat. They captured seven rebels, including a wounded officer, and chased the rest off the hill.[15]

The men in Ferguson's Rifle Corps were armed with a unique weapon—an innovative breech-loading rifle invented by Patrick Ferguson, the corps commander. His rifle could be loaded and fired up to seven times a minute, and its rifled barrel increased its range and accuracy in comparison to conventional smoothbore muskets. But the weapon saw limited action in the war, and the corps was disbanded in the autumn of 1777 after Captain Ferguson was badly wounded in the arm during the Battle of Brandywine. The prevailing nineteenth-century story was that the rifle was a success, but General Howe considered Ferguson a usurper who had gone outside the chain of command to get support for organizing his rifle corps. For example, an 1882 narrative of Ferguson's exploits noted, "Sir William Howe was jealous of the rifle corps being formed without his being previously consulted, and took advantage of Ferguson's being wounded, to reduce it and return the rifles to store [allegedly stockpiled in a barn in Pennsylvania]."[16] Praise for Ferguson's rifle prevailed into the mid-twentieth century, including an endorsement of the weapon by Harold Peterson, the nation's leading authority on military weapons at the time. In his 1956 book, *Arms and Armor in Colonial America*, Mr. Peterson said, "Despite the obvious excellence of the Ferguson rifle and its advantages over the standard British military arms, it was used by very few troops in the American Revolution."[17] More recent scholarship has shown that General Howe was actually supportive of Captain Ferguson's experimental rifle corps. In addition, he allowed the corps members to keep their rifles when the unit was disbanded and they rejoined their regiments.

The story of the failure of the British Army to adopt the Ferguson rifle begins with the fact that the gun was complicated and expensive to manufacture. It is estimated that all the expert gun makers in Britain could produce only about 1,000 Ferguson rifles a year.[18] In fact, Ferguson was authorized to raise a corps of one hundred men armed with his rifles, but he arrived in America with only sixty-seven guns. There is a record that the balance of thirty-three guns were shipped from Britain in late June 1777, but there is no evidence that they ever reached Ferguson.[19] In addition, the simple, efficient, and inexpensive British Army musket of the time (known as the Brown Bess) could be loaded and fired up to four times a minute by men with little training, and it was more lethal (fired a bigger lead ball) than any rifle. Also, contrary to folklore, British soldiers were trained to aim their muskets. Adopting the Ferguson for the British Army, assuming they could be made in large quantities, would require a complete overhaul of the tactics of the day which, in the middle of a war, was not practical. There are many stories about the Ferguson rifle, including Captain Ferguson claiming that he had George Washington in his rifle sight at Brandywine, but I wonder how many Revolutionary War enthusiasts realize that the Ferguson rifle first saw combat on present-day Strawberry Hill Avenue in Woodbridge, New Jersey.

While Captain Ferguson was chasing rebels, General Washington was at his marquee tent at the Middlebrook encampment receiving reports of the Crown forces activities in Perth Amboy. The intelligence was that Howe's army was divided between New Jersey and Staten Island. Additional information reaching headquarters reported that Billopps Ferry was busy shuttling troops across the Arthur Kill from Perth Amboy to Staten Island. Spies reported that the regiments in Perth Amboy were wrecking the fortifications that protected the town. The American officers in the field, including Greene, Maxwell, and Lord Stirling, believed that the remaining enemy troops in Perth Amboy were vulnerable and recommended attacking them. Washington agreed, and on June 23 he instructed Major General William Alexander (Lord Stirling) to "make a forcible push" against the British troops in Perth Amboy to "oblige them to go off in confusion if not with the loss of part of their stores."[20] It is advantageous to know about the troops that Lord Stirling led off the mountains toward Perth Amboy, as they would play the principal role in subsequent events.

Lord Stirling commanded one of the divisions of the Continental Army in June 1777. Washington's Grand Army at the time was divided into five divisions totaling 10,000 men.[21] Washington added additional units to Stirling's division for his mission. When fully assembled, the corps that Stirling led toward Perth Amboy consisted of 2,500 officers and enlisted men. The core of Stirling's corps was his two infantry brigades. One was identified as Conway's Brigade after its commander, Brigadier General Thomas Conway. Conway's brigade was composed of four Pennsylvania regiments and one New Jersey regiment for an estimated total of 760 men. Conway was a battle-hardened, English-speaking former French Army officer who had recently arrived in America and was appointed by Congress as a brigadier general. He was born in Ireland and raised in France, where he had risen to the rank of colonel in the French Army before joining the Patriot cause. He later proved to be a troublemaker who was barely able to conceal his contempt for Washington, whom he considered to be an amateur soldier. Stirling's other brigade was commanded by Brigadier General William Maxwell, who commanded four New Jersey regiments. In addition to his two infantry brigades, Washington assigned Morgan's Rifle Corps to Stirling's division. It consisted of an estimated 377 men. An independent unit of 150 German-speaking Americans and foreign volunteers was also added to Stirling's division. It was named Ottendorff's Corps after its founder, Major Nicholas Dietrich Baron de Ottendorff. He was a German mercenary who was commissioned by Congress in December 1776 to raise the unit. However, Washington was dissatisfied with Ottendorff and replaced him on June 11, 1777, with a capable former French Army officer named Charles Armand-Tuffin, Marquis de La Rouërie. Tuffin joined the Americans under bizarre circumstances: he departed from France in a hurry after fighting a duel with a relative of the King of France over the love of a belle of the Paris Opera. Five artillery companies were also with Stirling. Each artillery company usually had two horse-drawn field guns, giving Stirling a total of ten cannons. Each field gun normally had a crew of fifteen men. Finally, completing the composition of Stirling's division was a company of light dragoons (the 2nd Continental Light Dragoons) led by Colonel Elisha Sheldon.[22]

After leaving the Middlebrook encampment, Lord Stirling's division marched toward Perth Amboy and established a camp in "low and disadvantageous ground" between the towns of Woodbridge and the Metuchen Meeting House (present-day Metuchen). Stirling's camp was reported to be five miles northwest of Perth Amboy.[23] The location of his camp is a matter of speculation. However, we can narrow down

Lord Stirling's division was camped between the villages of Metuchen and Woodbridge on the morning of June 26, 1777. Their encampment was probably on the site of present-day Cooper Avenue Playground located along the south branch of the Rahway River. The playground is in modern Iselin, New Jersey. Stirling's division hastily abandoned their encampment when they were warned by Morgan's riflemen of the approach of Lord Cornwallis's army. *Author's photo.*

its location as we know that his camp was west of the Green Street section of Oak Tree Road in Woodbridge and east of Metuchen. He had to be near a road, as he could not march 2,500 men overland. He also needed to be near a road as he reportedly had seventy wagons with him to transport his ammunition, provisions, tents, and sundry other items.[24] In addition, Stirling needed a source of water for his 2,500 troops and numerous horses. Based on this information, Stirling probably established his camp along the northern bank of the South Branch of the Rahway River. The present-day Cooper Avenue Playground in the town of Iselin is the camp's logical location. Its position was close enough for Stirling to attack the rear guard of Howe's army in Perth Amboy at the first favorable opportunity, but far enough away to avoid a surprise attack. Colonel Morgan established a separate camp along Oak Tree

Road about a mile closer from Stirling's camp to Woodbridge. From his forward base, Morgan sent 200 of his men even closer to Perth Amboy as pickets to guard against an enemy attack. They were commanded by Captain James Dark, who was described as a "Dutchman" [A German, probably derived from the German word *Deutsch* for German. The word survives today as Pennsylvania Dutch]. Although Stirling had Sheldon's dragoons with him, Washington ordered all of his dragoons to join forces and "proceed down to Woodbridge to reconnoiter the enemy." One of the dragoon regiments was commanded by Colonel Benjamin Tallmadge, who said, "After we came in full view of them [rode close to Perth Amboy], they immediately got under arms."[25] The British sent out a large number of their own dragoons from Perth Amboy in an attempt to surround the American horsemen, who "retired" back to Stirling's camp. While the Continental Army dragoons were unable to keep Perth Amboy under observation, the Americans had their usual civilian spies and sympathizers in the town reporting on the enemy's activities.

On June 24, one day after Stirling marched off with his division, Washington led his army from the protection of the Middlebrook encampment to the plains below, where he established his headquarters in the northeast section of Quibbletown. The site of his camp is present-day Green Brook Park in Plainfield, New Jersey. His new position was well chosen. A visit to the campsite shows that it was three miles from the nearest pass into the Watchung Mountains (called Green Brook Road, it is present-day Warrenville Road in Green Brook Township), with a plentiful source of water (the Green Brook). Washington was "disencumbered of tents and baggage" at Quibbletown so he could quickly retreat to his mountain stronghold if necessary.

Washington's decision to come down from the Watchungs and advance closer to the enemy was based on his senior combat officers' recommendation to take advantage of Howe's evacuation of Perth Amboy. Washington had no specific plan in mind after establishing his camp at Quibbletown, saying afterward that he intended to "have acted as circumstances would have permitted."[26]

Colonel Timothy Pickering was with Washington's army at the time and confirmed that the troops with Washington were waiting for

This is the site of Washington's Grand Army encampment on the morning of June 26, 1777. The encampment was in present-day Green Brook Park in Plainfield, New Jersey. Washington abandoned the site and quickly retreated back into the Watchung Mountains that morning when scouts and distant cannon fire alerted him to the approach of a British army. *Author's photo.*

events to unfold. Pickering said, "June 24th—The army marched to Quibbletown, about five miles from its encampment [Middlebrook], and halted; the intelligence respecting Howe's situation not being such as to warrant our proceeding to [Perth] Amboy, where, in a plain [flat] country, he [Howe] might attack with his whole force."[27] But Washington acted aggressively by sending Stirling with a reinforced division that included Morgan's Rifle Corps, dragoons, and artillery near Perth Amboy, ready to attack Howe's rear guard.

Washington's hostile move aimed at attacking Perth Amboy was in keeping with his strategic thinking. Recall that strategy is defined as "the art of projecting and directing the larger military movements and operations of a campaign." Washington called his strategy "a war of posts," the fundamental feature of which was to avoid a battle unless it was under favorable circumstances. Washington formulated his "war

This is the view of the Watchung Mountains from Green Brook Park where Washington's Grand Army was encamped on the morning of June 26, 1777. Although Washington is reported as having come down from the Watchungs in late June, this photo shows that his Grand Army was actually camped only a short distance from the safety of the American-held mountains. *Author's photo.*

of posts" strategy following his defeat at the Battle of Long Island in August 1776. He explained his strategy in a September 8, 1776, letter to John Hancock, the president of Congress. The pertinent text in Washington's letter reads, "our side the war should be defensive, it has been even called a war of posts, that we should on all occasions avoid a general action [battle] or put anything to the risk unless compelled by necessity into which we ought never to be drawn." In the same letter, Washington expressed another aspect of his plan: "but at all events keep the Army together."[28]

Alexander Hamilton explained the commander-in-chief's strategy of keeping the army together (intact) in a June 1777 letter to Robert R. Livingston, a member of the New York State Committee of Correspondence. Hamilton wrote, "The liberties of America are an infinite [never-ending] state. We should not play a desperate game for it or put it upon the issue of a single cast of the die. The loss of one general engagement may effectually ruin us, and it would certainly be folly to hazard it."[29]

Washington's strategy is often called Fabian strategy, named after the Roman general Quintus Fabius Maximus who lived from 275 to 203 BC. General Fabius defeated the invading Carthaginians under Hannibal by avoiding battles and relying instead on irregular warfare. However, there is a difference between Washington's war of posts strategy and Fabian strategy. Washington's war of posts strategy was based on avoiding a battle to preserve his army, while General Fabius avoided a battle out of desperation: his army was too weak to fight Hannibal. He kept retreating in the hope of being provided reinforcements and recruiting men for his army.

Washington adopted Fabian warfare as a tactic and not a strategy; tactics is how strategy is implemented. As previously noted, tactics are defined as "the art of disciplining armies and ranging them into forms for fighting and maneuvering."[30] But Washington adopted irregular warfare based on his experience in fighting Indians on the Virginia frontier as opposed to studying the doctrines of General Fabius Maximus. Indian tactics are similar to Fabian tactics: ambushes, hit-and-run raids, and fighting from behind cover, with the additional Indian tactic of purposely targeting the enemy's officers. Whether Washington condoned the latter is a hotly debated subject among today's historians.

There is no known instance where Washington used the term "Fabian tactics" (or "Fabian strategy"), but there are a number of instances where others used the term during the Revolutionary War, including John Adams. Writing to his wife Abigail in September 1777, Adams said, "I am sick of Fabian systems in all quarters. The officers drink [toast to] a long and moderate war. My toast is a short and violent war."[31] Citing another example, Samuel Adams used the word Fabian in a May 1777 letter to General Nathanael Greene: "Europe and America seem to be applauding our imitation of the Fabian method of carrying on this war."[32] Washington bringing his army into action in late June 1777 is an example of his war of posts strategy. He acted to take advantage of the fact that Howe's army was divided between Perth Amboy and Staten Island.

Some historians believe that General Howe purposely delayed abandoning Perth Amboy in a last-ditch effort to lure Washington into a decisive battle. I am citing an example of this fallacious idea by a dead historian to avoid alienating a living one. The example I selected is from a history of the Revolution titled *The War for America* by Piers Mackesy (1924–2014), published in 1964. Picking up the story where Howe returned to New Brunswick after failing to bring on a general engagement with Washington, Mackesy wrote: "Washington had been tempted in vain; and he was thought too strong to be attacked. It only remained to try a ruse. On 19 June, Howe suddenly decamped and fell back rapidly on Amboy with all the appearance of a disorderly retreat."[33]

What actually happened was that Howe learned that several thousand troops from Washington's army (Stirling's reinforced division) were camped near Perth Amboy. Howe was possibly first informed of their position on the afternoon of June 25 when several rebels were captured during a "hard skirmish" near Perth Amboy. During the fighting the British suffered four killed, five wounded, and three missing (probably deserted). In the same skirmish, the British captured "several wounded Americans" who boasted that 3,000 rebels were nearby.[34] According to Captain Johann Ewald, who is acknowledged for keeping an accurate and impartial record of the Revolution: "General Howe presumed that the advance of the enemy corps [Stirling] could signal no other intention than that of falling upon our rear guard when the [majority of the] army had crossed over to Staten Island."[35] On the same day (June 25), Howe received additional intelligence that Washington had come down from the Watchungs with his army and was camped at Quibbletown.[36] The opportunity was too tempting to ignore. Howe decided to reassemble his entire army at Perth Amboy and vindicate himself by first defeating Stirling's division and then forcing Washington into a general engagement by outflanking his position at Quibbletown.

Howe had to get all the troops already aboard transports in Princess Bay back to Perth Amboy quickly. As they were mostly Hessians, he entrusted the job to his aide-de-camp Captain Friedrich von

Muenchhausen, who was fluent in German and English. Muenchhausen said that he left Perth Amboy on his mission at 4:00 pm on June 25. He carried sealed instructions to be delivered to the senior Hessian officer (Major General Johann Daniel Stirn) with the troops aboard the transports at Princess Bay. Captain Muenchhausen arrived at Princess Bay at 6:00 pm and handed the sealed envelope to General Stirn. The order read that all the transports anchored in Princess Bay were to set sail immediately and proceed to Perth Amboy. Muenchhausen said that Howe's instructions were for him to "tell the commanders [senior army officers] of each ship to have their troops ready to disembark and march against the enemy, leaving behind their tents and all their baggage." The ships arrived at Perth Amboy at midnight "despite unfavorable winds and a dark night" and the troops disembarked without mishap.[37]

Howe moved with unusual speed to reassemble his army at Perth Amboy. He later wrote Germain a report of his actions, which included a good summary of events up to the early morning of June 26, 1777. Note that Howe did not say that he purposely delayed abandoning Perth Amboy to lure Washington into a battle. Howe wrote:

> *The necessary preparations being finished for crossing the troops to Staten Island, intelligence was received that the enemy had moved down from the mountains and taken post at Quibble Town intending, as it was given out, to attack the rear of the army removing from Amboy, that two corps [a mistake, it was one corps or division] had also advanced to their left, one of 3000 men and 8 pieces of cannon [probably ten cannons is correct] under the command of Lord Stirling.*[38]

What followed was a day-long (June 26) running fight that included some of the most violent combat of the American Revolution. Unfortunately the farms, hills, forests, and swamps in which the action took place are long gone—destroyed, leveled, filled, and replaced by six-lane highways, commercial buildings, and high-density housing. The only reason to trace the route of the opposing armies is to understand the distances between locations associated with the day-long fighting. For example, although Washington is mentioned as encamped on the plains of central New Jersey, he was actually located just a short distance away from the base of the Watchung Mountains.

Returning to the story, Howe's reassembled army camped on the night of June 25 at Perth Amboy "lying on their arms" [weapons with the men and not stacked].[39] His army totaled 17,000 infantry, artillery, and dragoons. Sir William quickly devised a strategy for defeating Washington's Grand Army based on its last known position. His plan called for dividing his army into two columns.[40] One corps, called the right column, consisted of 5,000 troops under the command of Lord Cornwallis; the other corps, identified as the left column, totaled 12,000 troops led by Major General John Vaughan. Howe accompanied Vaughan's corps with overall command of the operation. The two columns would march on parallel routes within three miles of each other, with Stirling's division sandwiched between them. Once in position, Cornwallis would attack Stirling from the east (from Woodbridge) and Vaughan would attack from the west (from Metuchen). They would assault Stirling's camp at dawn and compel him to fight against overwhelming odds or surrender.

After dealing with Stirling, Howe would split his army again and move on to force Washington into a general engagement. Howe's strategy to defeat Washington called for the American commander to believe that Howe's entire army was with Vaughan, while Cornwallis's fast-moving column would secretly outflank the Grand Army by getting behind Quibbletown and blocking the Patriots' retreat into the mountains. Once Cornwallis was in position, Vaughan would advance rapidly from the opposite direction. Washington would be trapped between Vaughan and Cornwallis. It was the same strategy that Howe had successfully employed in the 1776 Battle of Long Island.

Howe's plan to defeat Washington was substantiated by several credible sources, including British Captain John André. André recorded in his journal that General Howe knew that Washington's army had come down off the mountains, then added "that the right hand column [Cornwallis] should by turning Washington's left get between his army and the mountains, whilst the left [Vaughan] marched straight to Quibbletown and attacked him."[41]

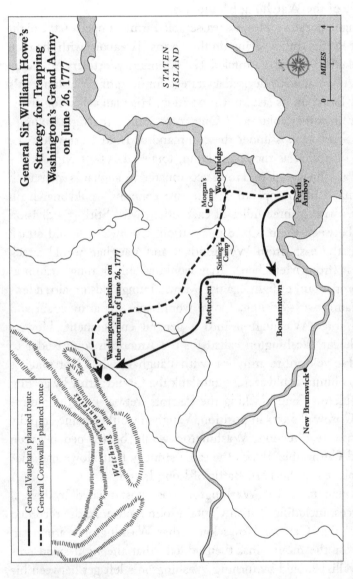

General Sir William Howe's Strategy for Trapping Washington's Grand Army on June 26, 1777

This map shows British General Sir William Howe's strategy for trapping Washington on June 26, 1777. Washington brought his Grand Army down from his Watchung Mountains stronghold based on reports that the British were abandoning Perth Amboy. Howe attempted to trap Washington's army by sending General Cornwallis with a fast-moving column to get between the Grand Army and the Watchung Mountains. At the same time General Vaughan led a larger, slower-moving diversionary force meant to distract the Americans. But Cornwallis's column was discovered by Daniel Morgan's riflemen. Warned of the enemy's approach, Washington retreated back into the mountains before Howe could execute his plan.

Note that Howe allocated only 5,000 troops to Lord Cornwallis. But what Cornwallis lacked in numbers was made up for in the quality of his corps. We are fortunate that Major Stephen Kemble, Howe's deputy-adjutant general, made a list in his journal of the units assigned to Cornwallis's column. Kemble's journal entry reads: "On 26th [of June] at four in the morning, Lord Cornwallis marched from Amboy with one battalion light infantry, one of grenadiers, some yagers [*sic*], Donop's Grenadiers, Brigade of Guards, and three brigades British [and the] 17th Light Dragoons and Rangers."[42] Kemble's list describes a potent force, trained to move fast and rout rebel skulkers, riflemen, and roving militia. To prove the point, here is a detailed review of Kemble's list. The first units listed were a battalion of British light infantry and a battalion of British grenadiers. British light infantry and grenadier battalions generally consisted of 500–600 men. These units were among the elite of the British Army fighting in America. The light infantry in particular was trained to overpower riflemen by waiting for them to discharge their weapons, then charge at them with their bayonets before the riflemen could reload. Kemble next listed "yagers": these were the German jägers armed with rifles and experienced in irregular warfare. Listed next were "Donop's Grenadiers." They were a force of 1,500 German grenadiers in three battalions commanded by Count Carl Emil Ulrich von Donop. The colonel was an ambitious young nobleman, rated among the best Hessian officers who fought in the Revolutionary War. The grenadiers were followed on Kemble's list by a unique unit called the Brigade of Guards. It consisted of officers and men from three prestigious British Army regiments: the 1st and 3rd Foot Guards and the Coldstream Regiment of Foot Guards. All three were long-established regiments with traditions and battle honors dating back as far as 1650; among their missions was to protect the King. The three Guards regiments were considered among the best regiments in the British army and had the fine uniforms, training, and equipment to justify their reputation. Their prestige enabled them to attract the top recruits and the most experienced sergeants. Volunteers from the three Guards regiments were organized in England in early 1776 into a single detachment for the war in America. Designated the Brigade of Guards, the unit consisted of 30 officers and 1,062 enlisted men. They modified their elaborate parade-ground uniforms for forest warfare in America, most notably by removing the lace from their uniforms, cutting the length of their coats, and reducing the size of the brims of their hats. The officers were ordered to look like common soldiers in the belief that the Americans were purposely aiming at them. Kemble next mentioned "three brigades British." This probably means at least eight British infantry regiments organized into three brigades; each would have been commanded by a brigadier general. The 17th Light Dragoons were mounted horsemen especially useful for reconnaissance work. Kemble's final listing was "Rangers." This is a reference to the Queens Rangers, considered the best Loyalist regiment in the war. The regiment was made up of about 300 men from New York and Connecticut. They were all highly motivated volunteers commanded at the time by Major James Wemyss. He was replaced in October 1777 by Major John Graves Simcoe.[43]

Howe gave Cornwallis a small but powerful force meant to move rapidly to cut off Washington's retreat into the mountains. Howe's strategy was put into motion when Cornwallis's column left Perth Amboy at 4:00 am on June 26. After leaving Perth Amboy, they marched through the village of Woodbridge then turned west along a good road (the present-day Green Street section of Oak Tree Road in the town of Edison) heading toward Stirling's camp. As Cornwallis advanced, he would have ordered his light infantry and rangers out in front to protect the main column from ambushes and rebel marksmen that may have been lurking on their flanks. At 6:00 am, the van (the men in the front of an army) of Cornwallis's column was fired upon by Morgan's pickets posted on Oak Tree Road, just past Woodbridge.[44] Morgan's men were outnumbered, and retreated. A Hessian account of the skirmish said that the rebel riflemen were "soon driven back after a short skirmish and the roaring voice of the grasshopper guns [a small-caliber portable cannon]."[45]

The skirmishing outside of Woodbridge was the first of several separate actions that became known as the Battle of Short Hills. It got its name from a narrow band of low, rolling hills (long gone) running northwest from Perth Amboy to the Watchung Mountains. There is a New Jersey town called Short Hills, located near Morristown, but it was founded in 1879 and has nothing to do with the 1777 Battle of Short Hills.

The presence of Morgan's pickets upset Howe's plan to surprise Stirling's division by surrounding it at dawn. The pickets fell back to Morgan's camp with the news that a strong enemy column was headed their way. Morgan in turn warned Stirling, after which both rebel camps were quickly abandoned and "retreated precipitately" down Oak Tree Road. As he retreated, Morgan was sending small detachments and individual marksmen to conceal themselves in the underbrush or behind trees to harass and slow down Cornwallis. Meanwhile, Stirling's brigades quickly retreated west on Oak Tree Road, then turned north for four miles to Raritan Road, the other important east-west road in the area. Stirling's new position put him close to the village of Scotch Plains, north of which there is a gap (New Providence Pass) into the American-held mountains. But instead of retreating into the Watchungs and leaving Morgan's men to their fate, Stirling sent reinforcements to Morgan who was continuing to harass Cornwallis's column on Oak Tree Road. Morgan's riflemen needed help as they were being assaulted and pursued by Ewald's jägers and British light infantry. The skirmishing continued for two miles west on Oak Tree Road to a pond called the Oak Tree Pond (still there and surrounded by a small park), which gave the ensuing mêlée its name: the Oak Tree Pond Engagement. It was here that Morgan's riflemen were met by the first American reinforcement to arrive on the scene. They were eighty men from Ottendorff's Corps. With Morgan's men, they concealed themselves in the woods facing Oak Tree Road. Cornwallis's column arrived at the pond at 8:00 am where they were ambushed by "a steady fire" from the bushes and behind trees.[46] Cornwallis counterattacked with his British light infantry and German jägers supported by field artillery firing grape shot. The rebels fought tenaciously, but were driven back into the woods behind them. Ottendorff's Corps were mauled in the fighting. Its commander, Colonel Charles Armand, said that thirty-two of his men were killed or captured.[47]

At 8:30 am, additional American reinforcements arrived at the pond: Conway's brigade, which went into action as Morgan and Armand's men were retreating. Conway posted his 760 men and three cannons on a hill on the opposite side of Oak Tree Road from Morgan's position and began firing into Cornwallis's column on the road.[48] Cornwallis sent his British and German grenadiers to attack Conway's brigade. According to one credible British report of the action, "they [Conway's brigade] held their position until we approached them whereupon they hurriedly withdrew into the woods behind them."[49]

Meanwhile, the sound of cannon fire coming from Oak Tree Road was heard at Washington's camp at Quibbletown, located less than four miles away.[50] Alarmed by the gunfire, Washington quickly withdrew his army from Quibbletown and retreated back to his mountain stronghold. Historian Washington Irving eloquently described the scene: "Washington had timely notice of his [Cornwallis's] movement and penetrating his design, regained his fortified camp at Middlebrook, and secured the passes of the mountains."[51] General Howe later reported to Lord Germain in London that Washington "retired to the mountains with the utmost precipitation."[52] Washington made no effort to reinforce Stirling. Washington has been censured for leaving his subordinate's division to face overwhelming odds, but Douglas Southall Freeman in his respected seven-volume biography of George Washington felt differently: "Patience, conservation of force and a courageous refusal to be goaded into battle with a superior adversary—these had been among the most powerful weapons with which Washington had kept the Army alive and had evaded or had held at bay the King's fine regiments."[53] Apparently, both Howe and Cornwallis had intelligence that Washington was gone and they turned their attention to at least defeating Stirling's division, which represented about a quarter of Washington's Grand Army.

Cornwallis knew from local Loyalists, deserters, and prisoners that Stirling had retreated north toward Scotch Plains. Cornwallis followed Stirling by turning north from Oak Tree Road. After turning, his column marched through a large uninhabited tract strewn with ponds and swamps (mostly long gone) known as the Ash Swamp. Meanwhile, Conway's brigade, along with the other Americans who fought in the Oak Tree Pond Engagement, fled north ahead of Cornwallis's column and found Stirling with Maxwell's brigade posted in a strong position on high ground in the Ash Swamp overlooking Raritan Road. They were four miles east of Scotch Plains. One explanation for Stirling deciding to fight rather than run was that he wanted to get his wagon train back into the mountains before he followed it to safety. The site that Stirling selected to deploy his division was "a bare hill" facing a wheat field. It was protected by a "thick woods" on one side and deep ravines and heavy underbrush on the other side. The Americans had only three cannons to defend their position; these were captured from the Hessians at the 1776 Battle of Trenton. Stirling placed his artillery on what is presently the 14th green of the Plainfield County Club golf course (opened in 1921). A small section of the Ash Swamp remains intact as the Ash Brook Reservation, but it is beyond the area where the fighting took place.

Cornwallis's column came down Raritan Road, saw Stirling's men, and promptly deployed into battle formation. The best description of the ensuing general engagement (General Cornwallis vs. General Stirling) was written by Captain Ewald who was there:

> *The enemy had taken his position on the steep bush-covered heights. The jägers tried to approach the enemy in the rear through the ravines, and the Hessian grenadiers ascended the slope [the wheat field facing Stirling's hilltop position] on the right supported by the [Brigade of] Guards. The enemy was attacked with the bayonet and driven back, whereby Colonel Minnigerode and his grenadier battalion (part of von Donop's command) greatly distinguished themselves, taking from the enemy three Hessian guns which had been captured at Trenton.*[54]

General Stirling's horse was shot from under him and General Maxwell "came within a hair's breadth of being captured" when the Hessian grenadiers charged the American defense line.[55] Colonel Israel Shreve also fought in the battle leading the 2nd New Jersey regiment, and he described the vicious fighting: "we stood them one hour and half most part of the time very hot [it was an extremely hot day], the musket balls flew like a shower of hail stones."[56] There are several accounts of the fighting to confirm the story that Captain John Finch, an officer in the

Brigade of Guards, rode up within pistol range of Lord Stirling. Upon seeing Stirling, Finch shouted, "come here, you damned rebel, and I will do for you." Stirling yelled something back to Finch, "but directing the fire of four marksmen [probably Morgan's men] upon him, which presently silenced the hardy fool, by killing him on the spot."[57]

The battle ended when the outnumbered Americans fled east down Raritan Road toward Scotch Plains. Captain George Ewing from Maxwell's brigade said that the American retreat was organized: "We were obliged to retreat which we did in good order."[58] According to grenadier Captain John Peebles, the Crown forces "killed a good many of the rebels, took three of their cannons and about 150 prisoners."[59] The day was oppressively hot and humid, and many of the heavily dressed Hessian and British troops were dropping out from exhaustion and could not go on. One of the Hessian regiments reported that at least one man "fell to the ground dead owing to the great heat."[60]

Vaughan's column, which was supposed to attack Washington's camp at Quibbletown, has not figured into the story because they played no part in the day-long fighting. They caught up with Cornwallis's column just after Stirling's division retreated toward Scotch Plains. Captain Muenchhausen was with Vaughan's corps and his journal confirmed that Vaughan's corps arrived after the fighting in the Ash Swamp: "A little while after the encounter [the fighting in the Ash Swamp], after nine in the morning, not far from Scotch Plains, our column joined forces with the rear of Cornwallis'."[61]

To complete the story of the day-long Battle of Short Hills, we should at least trace Vaughan's movements. His corps of 12,000 troops left Perth Amboy at 6:00 am. They followed the road alongside the Raritan River leading to New Brunswick as far as Bonhamtown (about halfway between Perth Amboy and New Brunswick) before turning north. Vaughan left a brigade consisting of two British and two Hessian regiments with six cannons at Bonhamtown, where they were ordered to take up a defensive position facing the rebel troops known to be in New Brunswick (General Greene's division). Vaughan did not want to risk allowing the rebels to attack the rear of his column. However, unknown to Vaughan, Greene's division had rejoined Washington at Quibbletown after the Crown forces abandoned New Brunswick. After turning north, Vaughan's column marched through Metuchen. They continued north toward Quibbletown but Loyalists, deserters, and reconnaissance patrols reported that Washington was gone. His mission a failure, Vaughan turned east where his corps joined up with Cornwallis's column.

According to Washington's aide Alexander Hamilton, following the fighting in Ash Swamp, Stirling's men "ascended the pass of the mountains back of the Scotch Plains."[62] The combined British forces continued for two miles northeast past Scotch Plains to the town of Westfield where they camped for the night in the open on some high ground overlooking the town. Westfield had managed to escape the forage war and was ripe for looting. Its houses and barns were filled with treasures including livestock, food, clothing, dinnerware, and bedding. The Hessians in particular soon succumbed to what Major John André called "symptoms of a disposition for plunder."[63] A patriot report prepared in 1781 estimated that enemy soldiers broke into at least ninety-two houses in Westfield, "looting and destroying a staggering list of goods."[64]

The British and Hessian troops just stayed overnight in Westfield but according to one account they managed to "drove in all the horses, cattle, sheep and hogs they could get, I saw many families who declared they had not one mouthful to eat, nor any bed or bedding left, or a stitch of wearing apparel to put on, only what they happened to have on, and [the Crown forces] would not afford crying children a mouthful of bread or water during their stay."[65]

The Crown forces began their march back to Perth Amboy on the morning of June 27. According to American Colonel Timothy Pickering, the enemy

marked their way with the most wanton devastation, burning some houses and plundering others, breaking in places and destroying what was not portable. Places of public worship seem everywhere marked as objects of their fury and bigoted rage. At Westfield the meeting-house was converted into a slaughter-house, and the entrails of the cattle thrown into the pulpit.[66]

Howe's army spent the night of June 27 in Rahway and arrived back at Perth Amboy on the morning of the 30th. Washington sent troops and dragoons to "annoy their rear and flanks," but the short distance from Rahway to Perth Amboy allowed the British to reach the port town before the Americans arrived on the scene.[67] The British immediately began crossing over to Staten Island at 10:00 am on the 27th and the rearguard under the command of Lord Cornwallis abandoned Perth Amboy at 2:00 pm "without the least appearance of an enemy."[68] According to Captain Muenchhausen, the entire operation was supported by the battery ship HMS *Vigilant* whose fourteen 24-pounders "would have given a respectable fire had the rebels tried to attack us."[69]

The British were gone, leaving the Americans in possession of New Jersey.[70] After learning that the British were boarding ships in Staten Island and New York City, Washington said, "By means of their shipping, and the easy transportation that shipping affords, they have much in their power to lead us a very disagreeable dance."[71]

And so the British occupation of New Jersey that began on November 20, 1776, when an army commanded by Cornwallis crossed the Hudson River and overran Fort Lee ended with the hasty departure of the last Crown forces troops from the state on July 30, 1777. The British army in New Jersey was larger and better trained, armed, and equipped than the American forces throughout this period. However, they were outfoxed by Washington. The humiliating retreat of the British from New Jersey is a testimonial to Washington's war of posts strategy and the stalwart officers and men of the Continental Army who fought tenaciously to keep the British huddled behind their redoubts in New Brunswick and Perth Amboy.

9

The Chesapeake Expedition, The Source of All Our Misfortunes*

General Sir William Howe seemed to have no conception of time. To explain, eighteenth-century armies tended to launch their campaigns with the arrival of warm weather in April or early May and cease operations in October or November as temperatures dropped. Favoring campaigning during these warmer months was the abundant supply of growing forage to feed their horses and fatten their herds of beef cattle. But apparently none of this mattered in 1777 to General Howe, who wasted months of good weather. His delay in campaigning began in April and continued into May. Howe spent these two warm months occupied with his usual meticulous preparations, which included the arrival of reinforcements from Britain and Germany and the stockpiling of provisions. He then squandered the month of June 1777 attempting to lure Washington into a battle in New Jersey. Next, having decided to seize Philadelphia by transporting his army in ships, he lost the first week of July organizing his troops and boarding them on hundreds of warships and transports anchored in Princess Bay and New York City. Finally, on July 7, his army of 16,498 were aboard 266 ships with three month's supply of provisions.[1] The ships were ready to sail, but they mysteriously remained at anchor in the stifling summer heat and humidity for two weeks with no

---

* Chapter title attributed to Joseph Galloway, *Letters to a Nobleman, on the Conduct of the War in the Middle Colonies* (London: J. Wilkie, 1779), 68.

explanation. One chronicler reported that "both foot [infantry] and cavalry remained pent up in the hottest season of the year, in the unhealthy holds of the vessels."[2] Apparently, the only ones who knew the reason for the delay were General Howe and his brother. Both of them were ashore at the time, adding to the bewildering situation.

We now know that General Sir Henry Clinton was the principal cause of the delay.[3] The circumstances that allowed Clinton to keep the fleet from sailing for two weeks is worth telling in its entirety. The story begins when Clinton returned to England in the winter of 1777 with the intention of resigning from the army. The cause of his action was his hostility toward General Howe. Clinton served under Howe during the 1776 campaign, during which he had made strategic recommendations to Howe that were mostly rejected or ignored. An example concerns Washington's November 1776 retreat across New Jersey. As Washington's beleaguered army was retreating across the state, Clinton was in command of an invasion fleet that included seventy transports carrying 7,000 troops. The fleet was ready to sail from New York in late November 1776 to seize Newport, Rhode Island. Admiral Lord Howe wanted Newport as a supply base and deep-water harbor for his ships.[4] Clinton recommended that Howe allow him to divert the Newport fleet to New Jersey to cut off Washington's retreat. The particulars of this proposal were for Clinton to land his 7,000 troops at Perth Amboy and trap Washington between his corps and Cornwallis's army approaching from Newark. But Sir William vetoed Clinton's plan and ordered him to proceed to Newport. Clinton took this and other rebuffs personally, writing in his narrative, "The many circumstances which occurred in the course of the last campaign [1776] to hurt my feelings made me very desirous of retiring."[5] After arriving in London on March 1, 1777, Clinton said that he had "the satisfaction to receive from His Majesty the most gracious marks of his royal approbation of my whole services and conduct."[6] The King and Lord Germain met repeatedly with Clinton during the winter, and according to Clinton, "I had the honor of being asked... my opinions of past [actions] and the intended plans of future operations."[7] The King and Germain were impressed with Clinton and wanted him to return to the American War. Their efforts to convince Clinton to continue to serve included the King knighting him. Flattered by the attention, the newly dubbed Sir Henry Clinton said, "I was consequently obligated, in compliance with my friends' wishes [the King and Lord Germain], to re-cross the Atlantic and resume my former situation in Sir William Howe's army."[8]

Clinton arrived back in New York on July 5, 1777, to find Howe making his final preparation for his seaborne invasion of Pennsylvania. Sir Henry was opposed to Howe's plan, claiming that "I lost no time... in delivering to Sir William Howe my opinions [opposition] upon the intended southern move [Pennsylvania] with the same freedom I had done in England to the Minister [Lord Germain]."[9] Clinton was in favor of supporting Burgoyne and "with all deference suggested the many great and superior advantages to be derived at the present moment from a cooperation of his [Howe's] whole force with General Burgoyne on the River Hudson."[10] Anxious to rid himself of his irritable subordinate, Howe ordered Clinton to remain in New York and take charge of the city's defenses. Howe allocated 6,000 troops to Clinton for the defense of the city and its environs. Clinton said he complained to Howe that the force was "barely adequate to garrisoning the numerous and extensive works... and posts on Long, Staten, and York [Manhattan] Islands and Paulus Hook [today's Jersey City, New Jersey] which, comprehending a circuit of considerably more than 100 miles...."[11] Clinton believed that Washington would attack the city once Howe had departed with his fleet. He even told Howe that the American attack would come from the Heights of Morrisania [the Bronx] north of the city to avoid the few Royal Navy warships left to defend the waterways surrounding Manhattan. Howe could not ignore Clinton's contention, as the British defeats that ended the 1776 campaign (Trenton and Princeton) had eroded Howe's reputation, while Clinton apparently enjoyed the confidence of the King and Lord Germain. After days of wrangling, Howe agreed to give Clinton an additional brigade consisting of four regiments, and would add 1,700 reinforcements arriving in New York from Europe to Clinton's garrison.[12]

Howe also decided that it was prudent to await confirmation that Burgoyne had captured Fort Ticonderoga before launching his seaborne expedition. The fortress was considered to be the major American obstacle blocking Burgoyne's route to Albany. The capture of the fort would demonstrate that Burgoyne could reach Albany without Howe's support. Captain Muenchhausen, one of Howe's aides, wrote in his diary on July 14 that there were rumors that Burgoyne had captured Fort Ticonderoga and guessed, "I, for my part, am sure that we will depart when we get reliable information from Burgoyne."[13]

The fact that Howe's invasion fleet remained anchored in New York waiting for confirmation that Burgoyne had taken Fort Ticonderoga was unknown to Washington at the time. He was only aware that hundreds of ships were lying motionless in and around New York. Washington was as baffled by their inactivity as the thousands of British and Hessian soldiers confined in the ships. The Virginian was pressuring his intelligence network for information about the destination of the hundreds of fully loaded ships languishing in New York. However, only rumors and conflicting intelligence were arriving at headquarters. Lacking trustworthy information, Washington decided to move his army from Middlebrook to Morristown, where he arrived on July 4, 1777. The move to Morristown positioned his Grand Army at the center of a road system that allowed him to march his army south to Philadelphia or north to the Hudson River once he was certain of the destination of the fleet anchored in New York.

Included in the information Washington received at the time was a captured letter written by Howe to Burgoyne, stating that Howe was planning to sail his fleet to Boston. Historian Washington Irving told the story of the letter, saying that a young man presented himself at an American outpost claiming that he was a Continental Army soldier who was captured and held prisoner in New York. The young soldier said that he was offered his freedom and a large reward if he would carry a letter from General Howe to Burgoyne. The young man's "feelings of patriotism" prompted him to turn over the letter to General Putnam, the American commander in the lower Hudson River Valley. "The letter was immediately transmitted by the general [Putnam] to Washington. It was in the handwriting of Howe and bore his signature." In the letter Howe informed Burgoyne that he intended to use his fleet to seize

Boston. Howe then said that after occupying Boston, "I shall, without loss of time, proceed to cooperate with you in the defeat of the rebel army opposed to you." Washington pronounced the letter a trick, saying that "the letter was evidently intended to fall into our hands."[14] False, misleading, and conflicting information about the enemy fleet "so long the object of watchful solicitude" caused Washington to write John Rutledge (the governor of South Carolina) on July 5 from Morristown with an accurate assessment of what was known at headquarters: "By the motions among their shipping, they appear to be preparing for some expedition by water."[15]

The logical direction of the enemy fleet, when it finally departed, was up the Hudson River to support Burgoyne. This move was in keeping with the long-standing British grand strategy of taking control of the Lake Champlain–Hudson River corridor to isolate New England from the rest of the rebelling colonies. The Americans realized the danger of Howe cooperating with Burgoyne, including Connecticut's governor, Jonathan Trumbull, who wrote at the time: "Nothing under heaven can save us but the enemy's [General Howe] going to the southward."[16] But Howe had long expressed a desire to seize Philadelphia despite the logic of supporting Burgoyne. In an effort to cover all possibilities, Washington had positioned his army at Morristown to move either north or south. Believing that Howe's intension was to support Burgoyne, on July 15 the Grand Army was camped in the village of Suffern on the border of northern New Jersey.

On that same day—July 15—there was a major development in New York. It was a letter from Burgoyne announcing that he had captured Fort Ticonderoga.[17] Feeling confident that Burgoyne would reach Albany, Sir William joined his brother aboard the HMS *Eagle* on July 19. The ships moored at Princess Bay had already joined the rest of the ships anchored at New York.[18] Although the fleet was ready to sail on that date, a lack of wind prevented them from departing. Finally, on the morning of July 23, General Howe's aide von Muenchhausen was able to report "a very good wind" and the *Eagle*, the flagship of the fleet, gave the long-awaited signal for all ships to set sail and put out to sea.[19] The *Eagle* led the imposing procession of ships through the Narrows, passing

Coney (Dutch for rabbit) Island to its left and into New York's Lower Bay. From there the armada turned south past Sandy Hook, New Jersey, and into the open sea, leaving General Howe's antagonist General Sir Henry Clinton behind to defend New York City.

Washington entrusted keeping the northern New Jersey coastline under observation to David Forman (1745–1797). Forman was the son of Joseph Forman, a wealthy New Jersey ship owner. Joseph gave his son David a practical education in seamanship and a formal college education at Princeton. David joined the Patriot cause early in the war, fought in the 1776 campaign, and was appointed a brigadier general in the New Jersey militia in March 1777. General Forman had reliable men posted along the coast of northern New Jersey to observe and report on any ship movements in the region. The big British armada was spotted leaving the harbor of New York on the morning of July 23 by Forman's observers stationed near Sandy Hook. Forman sent his report to Washington that same day by a fast-riding courier. The commander-in-chief received the report the following day. The pertinent portion of Forman's missive read:

This morning [July 23] at half past six the signal guns for sailing were fired [probably from the Eagle]—the wind northwest—at seven they began to get under sail and stood to sea; after they got clear of the Hook [Sandy Hook] they steered a southeast course under very easy sail in three divisions [sections]. I attended their motion until sundown, and perceived very little difference in their course.[20]

Forman's reliable report was confirmation that the British invasion fleet had left port. But Washington remained apprehensive about its destination despite it being observed sailing south along the New Jersey coast. It could be a feint to lure Washington's army south to defend Philadelphia while Howe turned his ships around, out of sight from land, and set a course up the Hudson River to support Burgoyne. There was also the possibility that Howe's objective was to seize the important southern city of Charleston, South Carolina. Although Washington remained apprehensive, indications were that Howe's objective was Philadelphia, and Washington began to move his army south to defend the rebel capital. On July 29, five days after receiving Forman's report, Washington was at Coryell's Ferry, New Jersey (today's Lambertville). General Greene and his division were with him. Two other divisions, commanded by Major Generals Stephens and Lincoln, were camped on the New Jersey side of Howell's Ferry (modern-day Stockton, New Jersey) and four miles north of Coryell's Ferry. Even as the Grand Army moved south toward Philadelphia, General Greene was apprehensive that the army might be headed in the wrong direction: "General Howe is now at sea. His destination is unknown, the balance of evidence is generally thought to be in favor of Philadelphia."[21]

As Washington was half-heartedly moving his army toward Philadelphia, the British fleet was advancing south, paralleling the New Jersey coast but sailing beyond the view of land-based observers. On July 30, the van of the fleet reached the southeastern tip of the New Jersey coast. It was here that the Delaware River flows into Delaware Bay, also called the Delaware Capes. Cape May, New Jersey, is on the north side of the bay; Cape Henlopen, Delaware, is on the south side, and Philadelphia is ninety miles up the river. The *Eagle* sailed into Delaware Bay on the morning of July 30 and anchored within sight of Cape Henlopen. She was met by three British frigates that were patrolling the Capes and gathering intelligence from local Loyalists. The flagship of the flotilla was the forty-gun frigate HMS *Roebuck* commanded by thirty-nine-year-old Captain Andrew Snape Hamond. Captain Hamond was well known by Admiral Howe, who regarded him as a capable and experienced naval officer.

There were several Patriot observers stationed around Delaware Bay explicitly watching for the British fleet. One of them was Henry Fisher, a ship's pilot, who was observing the bay from Cape Henlopen. Fisher saw the British fleet sail into the bay on July 30 and wrote out a dispatch from the village of Lewes, Delaware, at 10:00 am: "The fleet is in sight and at this time about 4 leagues [a league is 3.45 miles] from the [Cape Henlopen] light house. There are 228 sail [ships]."[22] An express rider delivered Fisher's message to Washington at Coryell's Ferry on the morning of July 31. Washington took the news seriously. The enemy fleet was too far south to be doubling back to support Burgoyne. Their entering Delaware Bay was an ominous sign that Philadelphia was their objective. Washington left his army at Coryell's Ferry on that afternoon and rode to Philadelphia to get more information and assess the situation for himself.

As Washington was riding to Philadelphia, everyone aboard the invasion fleet was excited and anxious to get off the overcrowded ships and start the campaign. The army's horses in particular were sickly from being confined for weeks aboard the ships despite the precautions taken to keep them fit. The measures taken on behalf of the army's horses included transporting them in ships especially modified to get them aboard and offloaded quickly and safely. In addition, the sides of their shipboard stalls were lined with sheepskin "with the wool on to prevent chafing."[23]

Captain Hamond was seen boarding the *Eagle* on the morning of July 30. He was followed by several men who were later identified as Loyalists familiar with the river. Several hours later, Hamond and the Loyalists were observed leaving the *Eagle*. The wind that day was favorable for sailing up the river toward Philadelphia, but the *Eagle* raised signal flags ordering the fleet to anchor off Cape Henlopen. On the following morning (July 31), the fleet was ordered out to sea bearing south toward Chesapeake Bay.[24]

There is conflicting evidence on whether Captain Hamond and his Loyalist friends were responsible for General Howe's decision to abandon attacking Philadelphia by sailing up the Delaware River. What is known is that Hamond informed the Howe brothers of the steps the Americans had taken to defend the river.[25] He was familiar with the river and explained that although it looked wide, there was only a narrow deep-water channel capable of accommodating large ships. In addition, the ship channel was changing constantly due to shifting sandbars and changes in the current. The narrow channel was obstructed by the Americans in several places with iron chains, sunken ships, and two lines across the river of large upright timbers "like the main mast of a ship" sunk into the riverbed in wooden frames loaded with rocks. Called chevaux-de-frise, the tops of the timbers lay six or seven feet under the surface with pointed iron tips facing downstream. Any ship attempting to pass through these sinister barriers risked having its bottom ripped open by the iron spikes.[26] The rebels had also constructed three forts on the river below Philadelphia to defend the city. They included Fort Red Bank and Mud Island Fort (later renamed Fort Mifflin) facing each other on both sides of the river. In addition to these fortifications, the river below Philadelphia was said to have "many fire ships [derelict ships that could be set on fire and aimed at enemy vessels], branders [German for fire ships that drifted among enemy ships], galleys etc. ready to receive us."[27] Hamond claimed that, despite the rebel defenses, he was in favor of the fleet proceeding up the Delaware to land the troops below Philadelphia, and "proceed forthwith to the rebel capital."[28] But Sir William thought otherwise, and decided to sail further south and approach Philadelphia from unguarded Chesapeake Bay. Sir William's reasons for deciding on Chesapeake Bay included an unopposed landing, whereas he expected "great opposition" on the Delaware.[29]

Joseph Galloway, the Philadelphia Loyalist, was with the fleet aboard the schooner *Alert*.[30] He was convinced that Howe could have sailed up the Delaware River, claiming "every possible circumstance favored the maneuver." According to Galloway, the Americans' river defenses were only partially completed at the time and "the passage from the Capes [Cape May and Cape Henlopen] to Philadelphia was open; [Fort] Red Bank was not fortified or occupied; in short, there was nothing to oppose the taking possession of Mud Island fort, the city of Philadelphia, and all the rebel water guard [small armed ships and galleys] in [the] Delaware [River]."[31] Loyalists familiar with the river believed that Howe could have landed his army safety at Marcus Hook, a Delaware River town on the Pennsylvania side of the river, just below the American river defenses.[32] From Marcus Hook, the army could have marched overland to attack the rebels' river defenses, supported by the navy.

Ambrose Serle, Admiral Howe's secretary, was aboard the *Eagle* at the time and described the scene in his personal journal:

Captain Hamond in the Roebuck waited upon the Admiral. The ships lay on and off all day [remained motionless]; and at length it was determined by General Howe not to land here. The Hearts of all Men were struck with this Business, everyone apprehending the worst. O quantâ de spe! [Oh how we hoped] is the universal Cry.... What will my dear country think and say too, when this News is carried home? Horreo [I dread].[33]

Howe's decision to sail further south has been interpreted by some historians that Sir William "had no intention of cooperating with Burgoyne."[34] Their reasoning is that Howe was angry with Burgoyne, who had gone directly to the King and Lord Germain to secure his independent command. Howe retaliated by purposely taking his army to Chesapeake Bay to be too far away to ever support Burgoyne. Eric Schnitzer, the National Park Service historian at Saratoga National Historical Park, disagrees with this idea. Schnitzer explains, "I don't think Howe moved to Chesapeake Bay to put himself in a position by which it would be impossible to aid Burgoyne. It was Howe's tactical sense and not any animosity he had towards Burgoyne that made him decide to take his army to Chesapeake Bay."[35]

The decision to sail further south to Chesapeake Bay made it obvious to Howe that he was not going to be able to support Burgoyne. This realization prompted him to write Clinton in New York on July 30 from Delaware Bay:

> *July 30, 1777,*
> *We are proceeding to the head of Chesapeake Bay, and I cannot possibly determine when I shall be able to send you reinforcements. But, if you can in the meantime make any diversion in favor of General Burgoyne's approaching Albany, I need not point out the utility of such a measure.*[36]

Storms and lack of wind extended the fleet's ocean voyage to Chesapeake Bay. Men sickened, and a shortage of fodder left no option but to kill starving horses by dropping them overboard to end their suffering.[37]

A packet boat found the invasion fleet at sea on August 16. Sir William was aboard the *Eagle* at the time and sailing between Cape

Henry, Virginia, and Cape Charles, Maryland, at the entrance to Chesapeake Bay. The packet boat brought a letter from Lord Germain written May 18, 1777. It had taken three months for the letter to reach General Howe. Germain's letter stated:

> *As you must from your situation and military skill be a competent judge of the propriety of your purpose, that is the march into Pennsylvania, trusting, however, that, whatever you may meditate, it will be executed in time for you to co-operate with the army ordered to proceed from Canada [Burgoyne] and put itself under your command.*[38]

Howe was resolute to capture Philadelphia. He filed Germain's letter and continued further into Chesapeake Bay.

Finally, on August 23, 1777, the first troops came ashore on the north shore of Chesapeake Bay at Head of Elk, Maryland (present day Elkton, Maryland). They had been packed aboard ships subsisting on salted provisions for forty-eight days, from July 7 when the fleet was ready to sail from New York until August 23 when they landed at Head of Elk. They were fifty-two miles from Philadelphia when they landed at Head of Elk, as opposed to two months earlier when they were in New Brunswick, sixty miles from the rebel capital. It had taken General Howe forty-eight days to get eight miles closer to Philadelphia, with his army arriving in Maryland sickly and almost all their horses dead, dying, or emaciated and unable to carry dragoons and officers or pull the wagons and field artillery brought in the ships. After landing, Howe was delayed for another week gathering fresh provisions for his army and buying or confiscating horses to replace those lost during the long ocean voyage. The lengthy ocean voyage also gave Washington the time to march his army through Philadelphia and select a location to defend the city. Sir William had finally forced Washington into the general engagement he had sought for over two months—since June 13, to be exact, when Howe marched his army from New Brunswick to the base of the Watchung Mountains.

Washington's 11,000-man army took up a strong defensive position on the north side of Brandywine Creek to defend Philadelphia.

The American commander was watchful for Howe's favorite tactic, which was to draw attention to what appeared to be his entire army attacking the Americans on one front while he stealthily undertook to outflank them and get behind their defense line with a strong corps. Effective intelligence by the British proved to be a decisive factor in the battle that followed. In this instance, the British had the advantage. Local Loyalists, recruited by Joseph Galloway, guided Howe's outflanking column on the morning of September 11 to remote Jeffries Ford on upper Brandywine Creek. They crossed the creek unopposed, and turned Washington's right flank (got behind him) because the rebels lacked enough experienced scouts and mounted dragoons to provide His Excellency with good intelligence. In particular, Washington lacked the support of Morgan's Rifle Corps, which had been sent to Gates's Northern Army at the urging of Congress to counter Indian attacks. In the ensuing Battle of Brandywine, the Grand Army fought valiantly but was forced to retreat. Continental Army Private Elisha Stevens was there and described the fighting: "Cannons roaring, muskets cracking, drums beating, bombs flying, all around men dying."[39] Despite the defeat and over 1,000 casualties, Washington was able to regroup and spent the next two weeks maneuvering and skirmishing with the British. Sarah Logan Fisher was in Philadelphia at the time and described the scene as the British drew closer: "wagons rattling, horses galloping, women running, children crying, delegates [to Congress] flying and altogether the greatest consternation, fright and terror that can be imagined."[40]

Howe's army outmaneuvered the rebels and marched unopposed into Philadelphia on September 26. Their arrival began a nine-month-long occupation of the city that accomplished little. Philadelphia was of no strategic value. Howe accomplished nothing except adding 14,000 civilians to feed. Congress was gone by the time the British entered the city; delegates ran off first to Lancaster and then to York, Pennsylvania. Adding to Howe's failure, Washington continued to field an army. Howe was also too far away by the time he captured Philadelphia to support Burgoyne.

Burgoyne moved south from Montreal, Canada, full of confidence and bluster. On June 24, 1777, while his army was camped on the

Bouquet River forty miles north of Fort Ticonderoga, he issued a flamboyant proclamation warning the Americans who opposed him that he would unleash the thousands of Indians (the actual number was 400) to anyone who "directly or indirectly endeavor to obstruct the operations of the Kings troops, or supply or assist those of the enemy." His threat was ridiculed in the Patriot press, including this passage from a poem in which Burgoyne speaks:

"I will let loose the dogs of Hell,
Ten thousand Indians, who shall yell
And foam and tear, and grin and roar,
And drench their moccasins in gore:
To these I'll give full scope and play
From Ticonderog to Florida
They'll scalp your heads, and kick your shins,
And rip your guts, and flay your skins,
And of your ears be nimble croppers,
And make your thumbs tobacco-stoppers."[41]

But Burgoyne ran into serious trouble by the time Howe occupied Philadelphia. Burgoyne's problems began following his capture of Fort Ticonderoga. The loss of the fort prompted Congress to replace Philip Schuyler, who commanded the Northern Army, with Horatio Gates. Schuyler had established the defense of Albany north of the town along the Mohawk River. Schuyler's defense line included Van Schaick Island and Peebles Island where the Mohawk emptied into the Hudson. When Gates assumed command of the Northern Army in August 1777, he was pleased to find thirty-one-year-old Colonel Thaddeus Kościuszko, a Polish national with engineering training in France, as second-in-command of the Northern Departments Corps of Engineers. The chief engineer of the department was Colonel Jeduthan Baldwin. Gates knew Kościuszko was a talented engineer from working with him on the defenses of the Delaware River earlier in the war. It is conjectured that Gates sought Kościuszko's opinion of the position of Albany's defenses and, following his advice, Gates personally reconnoitered the ground further north looking for a better location. It was Kościuszko who recommended that Gates move his army fourteen miles further up the Hudson River from the Mohawk River to a place called Bemis Heights. This was high ground facing east, parallel to the Hudson River, and extended for three-quarters of a mile to a steep, heavily wooded bluff. It was an excellent defensive position that dominated the surrounding countryside including the main road to Albany. Gates agreed, and he moved his army and artillery to Bemis Heights on September 12. Gates's new position blocked Burgoyne's only passable route to Albany. Gates's strategy was to keep his army on Bemis Heights and eventually starve Burgoyne's army into surrendering. Some of Gates's senior officers, particularly the pugnacious Benedict Arnold, disagreed with Gates. They wanted to take the offensive and attack Burgoyne's army. But Gates prevailed. He held his defensive position and waited for Burgoyne to run out of food. Aiding Gates's strategy was that Burgoyne's supply line stretched all the way back to Canada and was under constant attack from Patriot troops. Burgoyne tried twice to break through the American defenses on Bemis Heights and failed. His two attempts were the Battle of Freeman's Farm on September 19 and the Battle of Bemis Heights on October 7. The two battles were the high points of a month-long campaign by Burgoyne to defeat Gates in what is known as the Saratoga campaign.

Adding to Burgoyne's critical situation, the diversionary force that was supposed to meet him at Albany was turned back by a heroic American defense of Fort Stanwix, New York (present-day Rome, New York). The fort was commanded by twenty-eight-year-old Peter Gansevoort, who refused to surrender his post during a twenty-one-day siege by a superior enemy force led by breveted (holding temporary rank) Brigadier General Barry St. Leger, a skillful British Army officer. St. Leger was forced to end his siege on August 23, 1777, and return to Canada when the large and temperamental Indian contingent accompanying his army became discontented with Gansevoort's stubborn defense and went home.

St. Leger's unsuccessful mission, on top of Burgoyne's two failed efforts to break through Gates's defenses at Bemis Heights, left Burgoyne in desperate need of a British army to come up the Hudson River to support him. Clinton, who was authorized by Howe to assist Burgoyne, needed to clear the American forts defending the lower Hudson River Valley before he could safely sail troops and provisions up the Hudson. The main American positions along the river at the time were Fort Clinton and Fort Montgomery, both located north of Peekskill, New York. Clinton sent a spy to reconnoiter the Americans' river defenses. He was apprehended at Peekskill and brought to General Israel Putnam. The general had him tried, found guilty by a military tribunal, and sentenced to be hanged. A British warship suddenly came upriver from New York under the flag of truce with a message from Clinton saying that the spy, whose name was Edmund Palmer, was a British Army lieutenant and insisting that Palmer should be treated as a prisoner of war. Putnam's reply, dated August 7, 1777, was brief:

Edmund Palmer was taken as a spy lurking within our lines; he has been tried as a spy, condemned as a spy, and shall be executed as a spy; and the flag [British warship] is ordered to depart immediately.
Israel Putnam
P.S.—He has, accordingly, been executed.[42]

Clinton finally launched his operation from New York with 3,000 troops on October 3. After capturing Forts Clinton and Montgomery on October 6, General Clinton sent an advance party under Major General John Vaughan further up the Hudson. Vaughan's corps went on a rampage. On October 16 they torched the town of Kingston, New York, "reducing the place to ashes." Historian Eric Schnitzer described the scene: "Other homes likewise suffered British wrath, as Vaughan unleased forces on both sides of the river to destroy more property, possessions and food stores."[43] Vaughan then proceeded further north aboard a squadron of ships to Clermont, the ancestral estate of the Patriot Livingston family. After ransacking the mansion, they burned it along with twenty-four other buildings in the area. Vaughan was at the smoldering ruins of Clermont on October 23 and forty-six miles south of Albany when General Clinton ordered him to return to New York. According to historian Eric Robson, Clinton could have advanced further up the Hudson, "knowing there was nothing between his force moving up the Hudson and Gates," but Robson claimed that Clinton, "as though appalled by his energy, returned with the entire force to New York." Robson attributed Clinton's failure to advance further up the Hudson to his "morbid intro-spection, pessimism, desire to shun responsibility and indecisiveness."[44]

On October 17, with no hope of relief and his army surrounded, Burgoyne surrendered his hungry and exhausted army.

The incriminations began soon after. In a letter written to Lord Germain following the surrender of his army, Burgoyne stated that Howe had failed to carry out his portion of the campaign. Burgoyne told Germain that his mission was to "force a junction with Sir William Howe." In the same letter Burgoyne told Germain that the link-up with Howe "was the principle, the letter, and the spirit of my orders."[45] Howe countered by stating that he had informed Burgoyne months ago that he would probably be unable to support him. Howe later insisted that his Philadelphia campaign was meant to help Burgoyne:

> If I say that had I adopted the plan of going up Hudson's River, it would have been alleged, that I wasted the campaign with a consid-erable army under my command, merely to ensure the progress of the northern army [Burgoyne], which could have taken care of itself, pro-vided I made a diversion in its favor, by drawing off to the southward the main army under General Washington.[46]

Late in the campaign, when Burgoyne's surrender seemed inevitable, he sent General Clinton a letter asking for orders. Clinton promptly replied to Burgoyne's attempt to make him responsible for the imminent defeat:

> October 6, 1777
> Not having received any instruction from the Commander in Chief [General Howe] relative to the northern army [Burgoyne], and ignorant of even his intentions concerning its operations (except his wishes it may get to Albany), Sir Henry Clinton cannot presume to send orders to General Burgoyne.[47]

Meanwhile, despite his defeat at the Battle of Brandywine and losing Philadelphia, Washington was looking for a fight. He abandoned
his war of posts strategy and attacked the British troops garrisoned in
the Philadelphia suburb of Germantown on the morning of October 4.
But Washington's tactics were too complicated for his army to execute
effectively and the battle ended with the Americans retreating. However,
Germantown was an example of Washington's aggressive character. He
never preferred a war of posts strategy or partisan tactics, but nevertheless adopted them to preserve the army. Washington wanted a regular,
eighteenth-century army that could meet the enemy on a battlefield, or
retake New York by siege and assault.[48]

The Battle of Germantown marked the last major fighting of 1777.
The year ended with Howe in Philadelphia, struggling to feed his army
and 14,000 civilians; Clinton defending New York; and Washington's
Grand Army still intact and wintering at Valley Forge. The year also
ended with France about to enter the war as America's ally.[49]

Looking back, Washington had lost more battles than he won. He
proved to be more of a risk taker than a brilliant strategist. His battle
tactics were often too complicated and required precise timing for his
inexperienced army. But despite his shortcomings, as Benjamin Franklin
pointed out, "This man sent home to England, one after another, five
of your best generals baffled [Gage, Howe, Clinton, Cornwallis, and
Carleton], their heads bare of laurels, disgraced in the opinion of their
employers."[50]

What was it that made Washington successful? To appreciate
Washington's contributions to winning American independence, it is
necessary to look beyond his battlefield performance. In this regard, I
have had the unique opportunity to study Washington's character in a
number of lesser-known events of the American War through my books
that include the story of the 1775 Arnold Expedition, the submarine
American Turtle, the 1776 Long Retreat across New Jersey, and the
organization and operation of Washington's wartime headquarters.
Among the traits that I concluded about Washington was that he was
a fast learner who did not repeat his mistakes. A good example of this
was Washington experiencing how the Royal Navy contributed to the

British success during the 1776 New York campaign. He acknowledged "the great advantage they derive from their navy" and learned to keep his army inland and away from navigable rivers where the Royal Navy could be used against him.[51]

But there is another example of Washington not repeating his mistakes that I found particularly interesting. It was his arranging for boats to take his army across the Delaware River while he was retreating across New Jersey in early December 1776. He failed to make similar arrangements a month earlier to evacuate the garrison of Fort Washington across the Hudson River. His adversary, General Howe, gave the Americans time to evacuate Fort Washington: Howe gave the fort an ultimatum to surrender on November 15, but did not launch his attack until the following morning. Howe wanted the rebels to abandon the fort rather than ordering his own troops to attack it, in keeping with eighteenth-century military strategy to outmaneuver the enemy and force them to vacate a strong defensive position or surrender. But there were no boats to evacuate the fort even if Washington wanted to abandon it. Washington did not repeat this mistake later that month. When he was in New Brunswick on December 1, he ordered Colonel Richard Humpton to "proceed immediately to the two ferries near Trentown [Trenton], New Jersey on the Delaware [River] and to see all the boats there put into the best order." Humpton was a former British Army captain who enlisted the Hunterdon County, New Jersey militia and the Pennsylvania Navy to find boats from "above and below" Trenton and bring them to Trenton, ready to transport Washington's army across the Delaware to the relative safety of Pennsylvania. Washington's plan to have boats waiting at Trenton is indicative of his management of what is termed the Long Retreat across New Jersey in late 1776. The retreat is often depicted as the British Army pursuing Washington's disorganized army. But my research into the Long Retreat shows that Washington was compelled to retreat across New Jersey because of the betrayal of General Charles Lee, who failed to reinforce him. Once underway, Washington managed to stay ahead of the British. He even stopped in Newark for five days during the retreat and turned around briefly at one point, eager to take the offensive.

I also found Washington to be resourceful and innovative. Examples are his support of David Bushnell's submarine, which arrived in New York in early July 1776. Washington supplied Bushnell, who was a civilian, with precious gunpowder and allowed him to recruit an operator for his sub (Sergeant Ezra Lee) from the army. Washington was also innovative in his selection of his aides-de-camp. He selected intelligent men for his headquarters staff and used them to advise and assist him in the administration and day-to-day operation of the army.

Washington also set a conspicuous example of courage, sacrifice, and dedication for his army. His personal courage during the war was extraordinary. Despite the fact that he had a personal bodyguard (the Commander-in-Chief's Guard also called the Life Guard) that sometimes amounted to 150 men, Washington rode virtually unprotected at the Battle of Princeton to rally his troops and lead them in a counterattack against the British.

Washington was also adept at recognizing talented men and encouraging them by promoting them to high rank and giving them responsibility. Examples are Henry Knox, Nathanael Greene, and Daniel Morgan. His selection of Benedict Arnold to lead the so-called 1775 Arnold Expedition to surprise the city of Quebec is another good example of his skill in identifying capable men. Once Washington decided on organizing the Quebec operation, he selected Arnold, a controversial officer with a reputation for confrontation, to lead it. Some accounts of the Arnold Expedition claimed that Arnold gave Washington the idea for the campaign and led it. This is incorrect: Washington picked Arnold from among men who seemed more qualified for the coveted independent command. General Howe, in comparison, alienated some of his best officers. An example is Howe's relationship with Lieutenant General Hugh Percy (1742–1817). Percy was born Hugh Smithson, the eldest son of the 1st Duke of Northumberland. His father's noble rank and influence secured the title of Lord Percy for his son. Percy was an outstanding British officer. His exploits included commanding the relief column that saved the troops sent to Concord in April 1775. The quarrel between Percy and Howe began in mid-1777 when Percy was in command of the British troops occupying Newport, Rhode Island. General Howe instructed Percy to send him 1,500 troops from his garrison for the defense of New York City. Percy replied that the Americans were preparing to attack Newport and he needed every man to defend the town. According to historian Mercy Otis Warren, General Howe responded by "threatening Lord Percy with a trial for disobedience [a court-martial], and reprimanded him in language which the earl thought derogatory to an officer of his rank, character and consequence [a member of the British nobility]."[52] Percy retaliated to Howe's affront by using his family's considerable influence to arrange for him to be recalled to England. Percy left Newport in May 1777 and was replaced by Major General Richard Prescott, who was kidnapped by the rebels two months later. General Sir Henry Clinton had a similar confrontational relationship with Lord Rawdon, another excellent British general. Rawdon resigned and went home to England in 1779.

Adding to my admiration of Washington is that he controlled the army and could have used it to overthrow the weak and inept civilian government during the war and install himself as a dictator. There is an incident late in the war when Colonel Lewis Nicola, an American officer, wrote Washington complaining about the ill treatment the army was receiving from Congress. Nicola suggested that Washington lead the army to Philadelphia, overthrow the government, and appoint himself as the King of the United States.[53] Washington's response is illustrative of his high moral standards and efforts to maintain the sovereignty of Congress. Here is an excerpt from Washington's response to Nicola's letter:

> *I am much at a loss to conceive what part of my conduct could have given encouragement to an address which to me seems big with the greatest mischiefs that can befall my country.... Let me conjure you then, if you have any regard for your country, concern for yourself or posterity—or respect for me, to banish these thoughts from your mind, and never communicate, as from yourself, or anyone else, a sentiment of the like nature.*[54]

My study of the 1777 Middlebrook encampment added to my admiration of Washington. I was impressed to learn that there were comfortable homes in nearby Morristown that Washington could have occupied as his headquarters during the Middlebrook encampment. They included the homes of the (late) Colonel Jacob Ford, Peter Kemble's Mount Kemble estate, and General Lord Stirling's manor house in Basking Ridge. But Washington chose to live in a tent with his army, and he remained with his troops throughout the encampment. In fact, Washington remained with his army throughout the war except when he was summoned to meet with Congress and a brief visit to Mount Vernon in 1781 en route to Yorktown.

In comparison, while the British garrisons in Perth Amboy and New Brunswick were living in cramped quarters and subsisting on salted provisions, their commander, General Howe, was enjoying life in New York with Mrs. Loring. The couple were at the center of a vibrant social scene in the city that included attending performances at the Theater Royal where it was reputed that some of the female parts were played by the mistresses of British officers.[55] Sir William's pursuit of pleasure did not go unnoticed, as evidenced by this poem that appeared in a Philadelphia newspaper:

Howe with his legions came,
In hopes of wealth and fame,
What has he done?
All day, at Faro play'd
All night, with whores he laid,
And with his bottle made,
Excellent fun.[56]

Washington's skillful defense of New Jersey during the first half of 1777 showed resourcefulness and innovation that goes beyond battlefield tactics. With only 3,000 men and militia, he baffled an enemy force of 10,000 well equipped with artillery and dragoons.

Washington's defense of New Jersey during the winter of 1777 convinced Howe of the danger of attacking Philadelphia by crossing New Jersey. Washington's Middlebrook encampment was the key to Washington's control of the state with an army less than half the size of his adversary's. Historians James Kirby Martin and Mark Edward Lender called Washington's Middlebrook encampment "masterful."[57] Not only did Howe not dare to attack him, but with the Continental Army intact and militia units working actively in support, Sir William perceived that there would be many risks in marching overland to Philadelphia.

If Burgoyne's defeat was the turning point of the American Revolution, then Washington's defense of New Jersey during the first six months of 1777 set the stage for the American victory. General Howe lost the month of June 1777 trying to bring Washington into a general engagement in New Jersey. His failed effort persuaded him to sail south in an armada of ships to avoid crossing New Jersey. Howe's maneuvering on land and sea to capture Philadelphia resulted in his being too far away with his army to complete his conquest in time to support Burgoyne. Commenting on Washington's defense of New Jersey, nineteenth-century historian John Fiske wrote: "In point of military skill it was, perhaps, as remarkable as anything that Washington ever did, and it certainly occupies a cardinal position in the history of the overthrow of Burgoyne."[58]

I have quoted Loyalist Thomas Jones throughout this book, but I saved his explanation of why Britain lost the American Revolution as a poignant ending to my narrative. It was written while Jones was living in exile in England. Jones lost everything in the war, including his health and dignity, because of his allegiance to Britain. He died in England in 1792, a bitter relic of British rule in America:

> *Had half the pains been taken to suppress the American rebellion, as there was to drain the British Treasure of its cash, any one year of the war would have demolished rebellion and Great Britain been at this day still in full possession of 13 opulent Colonies, of which she has been dismembered by the misconduct and inattention of one General [Sir William Howe], by the stupidity of another [Sir Henry Clinton], and by an infamous Ministry who patched up an ignominious peace, to the dishonor of the nation, the discredit of their sovereign, and to the ridicule of all Europe.*[59]

Notes

Introduction

1. Quoted in Charles Francis Adams, *Studies Military and Diplomatic 1775–1865* (New York: Macmillan Company, 1911), 153.

2. Thomas J. McGuire, *The Philadelphia Campaign*, 2 vols. (Mechanicsburg, PA: Stackpole Books, 2006), vol 1:169.

3. John Marshall, *The Life of George Washington*, 5 vols. (Philadelphia: C. P. Wayne, 1804–1807), vol. 3:106.

4. Worthington C. Ford et al., eds., *Journals of the Continental Congress, 1774–1789*, 34 vols. (Washington, DC: U.S. Government Printing Office, 1904–1937), vol. 5:784.

5. W. W. Abbot et al., eds., *The Papers of George Washington, Revolutionary War Series*, 28 vols. to date (Charlottesville: University of Virginia Press, 1985–present), vol. 6:499.

6. Alex Storozynski, "The Fiasco of July 4, 1777," *Huffington Post* blog, May 25, 2011. In the example cited, Washington spelled Kościuszko's name as Cosciusko in an August 31, 1778, letter to Henry Laurens. For the spelling error, see Abbot et al., *The Papers of George Washington, Revolutionary War Series*, vol. 16:439. In the same letter Washington spelled the name of French engineer Louis Lebegue Duportail as "Portail."

My own decision to spell the name as Kościuszko is based on the Kościuszko Foundation, which is named in the Polish engineer's honor. There is also a biography about him: James S. Pula, *Thaddeus Kościuszko: The Purest Son of Liberty* (New York: Hippocrene Brooks, 1999).

7. Letter from Samuel Chase to Thomas Johnson dated September 12, 1777, in Paul H. Smith, ed., *Letters of Delegates to Congress, 1774–1789*, 26 vols. (Washington, DC: Library of Congress, 1976–2000), vol. 7:649. In his letter Samuel Chase spelled Borre as "Debore."

8. Letter from George Washington to John Hancock, dated "Head Quarters Morris town 11th Feby 1777," in Abbot et al., *The Papers of George Washington, Revolutionary War Series*, vol. 8:305.

9. Arthur Lefkowitz, *George Washington's Indispensable Men* (Mechanicsburg, PA: Stackpole Books, 2003), 303.

10. Donald F. Johnson, *Occupied America: British Military Rule and the Experience of Revolution* (Philadelphia: University of Pennsylvania Press, 2020), 192.

11. David Ramsay, *The History of the American Revolution*, 2 vols. (Dublin: William Jones, 1795), vol. 2:576.

12. Mercy Otis Warren, *History of the Rise, Progress and Termination of the American Revolution*, 3 vols. (Boston: E. Larkin, 1805), vol. 1:338–39.

13. James Thomas Flexner, quoted in "North from the Battery, Seeking Washingtoniana," *New York Times*, February 13, 1987, section C1, 1.

14. George C. Neumann, *Battle Weapons of the American Revolution* (Texarkana, TX: Scurlock Publishing Co., 1998), 211. There were also rifles at the time of the American Revolution that had smoothbore barrels. The British Army had an estimated 1,000 government-issued rifles that were used in the American War. See ibid., 227.

15. Major John A. Tokar, "Logistics and the British Defeat in the Revolutionary War," U.S. Army Logistics University, September/October 1999, www.almc.army .mil/alog/issues/SepOct99/MS409.htm.

16. Captain George Smith, *An Universal Military Dictionary* (London: J. Millan, 1779), 241.

17. Frank Gaynor, ed., *The New Military and Naval Dictionary* (New York: Philosophical Library, 1951), 250.

18. Don N. Hagist, *Noble Volunteers: The British Soldiers Who Fought the American Revolution* (Yardley, PA: Westholme Publishing, 2020), 197.

19. René Chartrand, *Raiders from New France: North American Forest Warfare Tactics, 17th–18th Centuries* (Oxford, UK: Osprey Publishing, 2019), 6.

20. Robbie MacNiven, *British Light Infantry in the American Revolution* (Oxford, UK: Osprey Publishing, 2021), 10.

21. Colin G. Calloway, *The Indian World of George Washington* (New York: Oxford University Press, 2018), 149.

22. Dave R. Palmer, *George Washington's Military Genius* (Washington, DC: Regnery Press, 2012), 22.

CHAPTER 1

1. Charles H. Lesser, ed., *The Sinews of Independence* (Chicago: University of Chicago Press, 1976), 26–27. This number is based on Returns (strength reports) from late July 1776. No mounted troops (cavalry or light dragoons) are listed.

2. General Orders, dated "Head-Quarters White Plains Tuesday July 28th 1778," in Abbot et al., *The Papers of George Washington, Revolutionary War Series*, vol. 16:189.

3. Worthington Chauncey Ford, ed., *Journals of the Continental Congress*, 34 vols. (Washington, DC: U.S. Government Printing Office, 1904–1937), vol. 1:94.

4. Letter from Lieutenant General Hugh Percy, 2nd Duke of Northumberland, to General Harvey, dated Boston, April 20, 1775, in Charles Knowles Bolton, ed., *Letters of Hugh Earl Percy from Boston and New York, 1774–1776* (Boston: Charles E. Goodspeed, 1902), 52–53.

5. Ford, *Journals of the Continental Congress*, vol. 2:78.

6. Peter Force and M. St. Clair Clarke, eds. *American Archives: Consisting of a Collection of Authentick Records, State Papers, Debates, and Letters and Other Notices of Publick Affairs, the Whole Forming a Documentary History of the Origin and Progress of the North American Colonies; of the Causes and Accomplishment of the American Revolution; and of the Constitution of Government for the United States, to the Final Ratification Thereof.* Consists of the Fourth Series, six volumes, and Fifth Series, three volumes (Washington, DC: M. St. Clair Clarke and Peter Force, 1837–1853), Fourth Series, vol. 2:840. For Arnold's report read aloud to the delegates of the Continental Congress, see Ford, *Journals of the Continental Congress*, vol. 2:73–74.

7. For example, June 14, 1775, is cited as the date of the establishment of the Continental Army by eminent Revolutionary War historians James Kirby Martin and Mark Edward Lender on page 40 in their book, *A Respectable Army: The Military Origins of the Republic, 1763–1789* (Wheeling, IL: Harlan Davidson, Inc., 1982).

8. Ford, *Journals of the Continental Congress*, vol. 2:79.

9. Charles Francis Adams, ed., *The Works of John Adams, Second President of the United States*, 10 vols. (Boston: Charles C. Little and James Brown, 1850–1856), vol. 2:417. Here is the complete text of Adams recalling his frequently quoted speech in the Continental Congress recommending Washington to command the army; Adams did not mention the date of his speech but said that "the subject was postponed to a future day." Note that Adams did not mention Washington by name:

> I have no hesitation to declare that I had but one gentleman in my mind for that important command and that was a gentleman from Virginia, who was among us and very well known to all of us; a gentleman, whose skill and experience as an officer, whose independent fortune, great talents and excellent universal character would command the approbation of all America, and unite the cordial exertions of all the colonies better than any other person in the Union.

10. Ford, *Journals of the Continental Congress*, vol. 2:91. A fine point of history is that the army recruited from the thirteen colonies and Canada and under control of Congress was called the Continental Army.

11. John Adams to Abigail Adams, letter dated June 17, 1775, in Paul H. Smith, ed., *Letters of Delegates to Congress, 1774–1789*, 26 vols. (Washington, DC: Library of Congress, 1976–2000), vol. 1:497.

12. Henry Steele Commager and Richard B. Morris, eds., *The Spirit of Seventy-Six*, 2 vols. (New York: The Bobbs-Merrill Company, 1958), vol. 1:135.

13. Stanley Weintraub, *Iron Tears: America's Battle for Freedom* (New York: Free Press, 2005), 43.

14. General William Howe was appointed to the office of commander-in-chief, America. His responsibility encompassed all the territory from West Florida to Newfoundland. At the same time, General Guy Carleton was named the commander-in-chief, Quebec, responsible for the defense of Quebec Province. This arrangement led to friction between Howe and Carleton.

15. Letter from General Charles Lee to Dr. Benjamin Rush, dated "Camp at Valley-Forge, June 4th, 1778," in (anonymous but attributed to Edward Langworthy), *Memoirs of the Life of the Late Charles Lee* (London: J. S. Jordan, 1792), 424.

16. Frank Moore, *Songs and Ballads of the American Revolution* (New York: D. Appleton and Company, 1856), 99.

17. Letter from General Thomas Gage to William Barrington, 2nd Viscount Barrington, dated June 26, 1775, in Allen French, *The First Year of the American Revolution* (Boston: Houghton Mifflin Company, 1934), 259. Barrington was a British politician and advocate of using force if necessary to raise revenue by taxing the American colonies.

18. The population of 25,000 for New York City in 1776 is an estimate, as there was no census in American until 1790. New York was believed to be the second largest city in America in 1776. Philadelphia was first with an estimated population in 1776 of 40,000. Boston ranked third with 15,000, and Charleston was fourth with 12,000. The 1790 census reported New York's population at 33,000, making it the largest city in the United States. Philadelphia, excluding its suburbs, was second with 28,000, followed by Boston with 18,000 and Charleston at 16,000.

19. Letter from John Hancock (president of the Continental Congress) to (General) William Alexander, dated "Philada. March 15th 1776," in Smith, *Letters of Delegates to Congress*, vol. 3:378.

20. Ibid.

21. Notes from a council of war, dated Roxbury, 13 March 1776, in Abbot et al., *The Papers of George Washington, Revolutionary War Series*, vol. 3:459.

22. Thomas Jones, *History of New York During the Revolutionary War*, 2 vols. (New York: New York Historical Society, 1879), vol. 2:350. Jones (1731–1792) was a Yale graduate, wealthy landowner, and member of the New York Colony Supreme Court at the outbreak of the American Revolution. At the age of thirty-one he married Anne De Lancey, the sixteen-year-old daughter of James De Lancey, the recently deceased Royal lieutenant governor of New York. Jones remained loyal to Britain during the Revolution and was arrested, paroled, imprisoned, and his house ransacked by the Patriots during the war for his pro-British sentiments. Fearing for his life and in ill health from his years of imprisonment, Jones auctioned off his remaining assets and sailed for England in 1781 with his wife and his niece, Miss Elizabeth Floyd. It was there that Jones wrote his account of the American Revolution from 1783 to 1788. His handwritten manuscript was passed down through his family until Edward Floyd De Lancey arranged for its publication by the New York Historical Society in 1879.

Jones was shocked by the American victory in the war and blamed British incompetence and corruption for losing the war. In his biography of Jones, historian Joseph S. Tiedemann summarized Jones:

> He was born into a deferential society, where social position brought privilege. He could never be at home in a more open and democratic world, where talent produced advantages and equality wore away at elitism. Jones, of course, was not the typical American of the era. However, his passage from a privileged, pampered member of the elite into an out-of-touch, marginalized, embittered relic underscores the transformation that American political society underwent during this era as it transitioned from a deferential to a republican society.

Joseph S. Tiedemann, "Embittered Long Island Loyalist," *Long Island History Journal*, vol. 21 (2009), http://lihj.cc.stonybrook.edu/2009/articles/Thomas-jones -embittered-long-island-loyalist/.

23. Jones, *History of New York During the Revolutionary War*, vol. 2:350–51.

24. Mercy Otis Warren, *History of the Rise, Progress and Termination of the American Revolution*, 3 vols. (Boston: Manning and Loring, 1805), vol. 1:291–92. There is also an alleged (undated) letter that Mrs. Warren wrote to John Adams with similar text. The letter is in Elizabeth F. Ellet, *The Women of the American Revolution*, 2 vols. (New York: Barker and Scribner, 1849), 82. Ellet claims that the contents of the letter in her book was obtained directly from Mercy Otis Warren's descendants. While frequently quoted, the authenticity of the letter in Ellet's book is questionable. Mrs. Warren's above-mentioned history of the American Revolution is frequently cited as the first nonfiction book published by an American woman. This is incorrect. The first such book is Hannah Adams's *A Summary History of New England... Comprehending a General Sketch of the American War*, published in 1799. Mrs. Warren's history of the American Revolution is also cited as the first history of the conflict. This is also incorrect; the first history of the Revolution was published in London in 1780 during the war. It is titled *An Impartial History of the War in America*. It was anonymously published but attributed to Edmund Burke, a British politician opposed to the war. Among Burke's comments about the conflict is "A great empire [Britain] and little minds [King George III and his ministers] go ill together." The first complete history of the Revolution was published in 1788 by William Gordon.

25. Letter from John Adams to James Warren, dated Philadelphia, July 24, 1775, in *Founders Online*, National Archives, https://founders.archives.gov/gov/ documents/Adams/06-03-02-0052. James Warren fought at the Battle of Bunker Hill and was later appointed the president of the Massachusetts Provincial Congress and Paymaster General of the Continental Army. His wife was Mercy Otis Warren.

26. Warren, *History of the Rise, Progress and Termination of the American Revolution*, vol. 1:292.

27. Instructions to Major General Charles Lee, dated Cambridge, 8 January 1776, in Abbot et al., *The Papers of George Washington, Revolutionary War Series*, vol. 3:53.

28. Nineteenth-century author Washington Irving popularized the translation from Dutch of the Spuyten Duyvil section of Harlem Creek to "In spite of the devil." Irving told the story in his satirical *Diedrich Knickerbocker's History of New York from the Beginning of the World to the End of the Dutch Dynasty*, published in 1809. According to Mr. Knickerbocker, when an English fleet arrived in Dutch New Amsterdam, Governor Peter Stuyvesant sent a trumpeter named Anthony Van Corlaer to warn the Dutch settlers north of Manhattan Island of the English invasion. Corlaer had to swim across a treacherous section of Harlem Creek to carry out his mission. According to Diedrich Knickerbocker, Corlaer was determined to "swim across in spite of the devil." He plunged into the water when an enormous fish, which eyewitnesses swore was the devil, grabbed Corlaer's leg and pulled him under. Corlaer blew his trumpet as loud as he could before he sank to the bottom. Besides "In spite of the devil," Spuyten Duyvil has been translated to mean "the spitting devil."

29. Captain William Smith is a footnote in the history of the American Revolution. There is no known record of his background, education, or experience as an engineer. Captain Smith was sent from Cambridge to assist Lee in New York. The evidence is a letter from General Horatio Gates to Lee, dated February 10, 1776. Gates was in Cambridge at the time and wrote, "Has Captain [Stephen] Badlam of the Artillery & Engineer Smith arrived according to Order?" Adding to the mystery is that Smith's name was apparently misspelled as William Smyth. For example, in a letter from New York on February 19, 1776, Lee wrote, "Capt. Smyth is an excellent intelligent active Officer." Smith was later assigned to plan fortifications, including Fort Montgomery, in the Hudson Highlands.

30. *The Lee Papers*, 4 vols. (New York: New York Historical Society, 1871–1874), vol. 1:309.

31. A public house served food and drink and was open to anyone. Its counterpart was a private club, where only members could be served. The term "public house" was shortened to the modern word "pub."

32. Jones, *History of New York During the Revolutionary War*, vol. 1:82.

33. William S. Baker, *Itinerary of General Washington* (Philadelphia: J. B. Lippincott Company, 1892), 36–37.

34. Washington wrote "I have never spared the spade and pickax" in a letter to John Hancock dated "New York Head Qrs September 8th 1776," in Abbot et al., *Papers of George Washington, Revolutionary War Series*, vol. 6:249.

35. George Washington to John Hancock, New York, July 10, 1776, in Abbot et al., *Papers of George Washington, Revolutionary War Series*, vol. 5:260.

36. Harry Miller Lydenberg, *Archibald Robertson, His Diaries and Sketches in America* (New York: New York Public Library, 1930), 87.

37. Admiral Richard Howe was a viscount in the British peerage system. As such, he was addressed as Lord Howe. He also held the title of Vice Admiral of the White in the Royal Navy. Under the ranking system in use at the time, Howe was the fifth highest ranking officer in the Royal Navy and commander of a flotilla of warships designated as the Squadron of the White.

38. The term "mercenary" is defined under modern international law (the Geneva Convention Protocol of 1977) as "any person who has not been sent by a state which is not party to the conflict on official duty as a member of its armed forces." This definition applies to the Hessians who fought in the American Revolution. Mercenaries, according to the Geneva Convention, are further defined as receiving compensation "substantially in excess of that promised or paid to combatants of similar rank of function in the armed force of that party." The Hessian troops who fought in the American Revolution were paid the same wages as British soldiers.

39. Peter Kemble, *Journals of Lieutenant-Colonel Stephen Kemble* (the Kemble Papers), 2 vols. (New York: Collections of the New York Historical Society for the Years 1883 and 1884, published in 1883 and 1884), vol. 1:84.

40. Bernhard A. Uhlendorf, trans. and ed., *Revolution in America: Confidential Letters and Journals 1776–1784 of Adjutant General Major Baurmeister of the Hessian Forces* (New Brunswick, NJ: Rutgers University Press, 1957), 34.

41. Eric Robson, ed., *Sir James Murray Letters from America, 1773–1780, Being the Letters of a Scots Officer... During the War of American Independence* (New York: Barnes & Noble, 1951), 40.

42. Stephen Kemble's journal entry for August 21, 1776, states that "about 120 Light Horse" were part of the British Army that invaded Long Island on August 22. See Peter Kemble, *Journals of Lieutenant-Colonel Stephen Kemble*, vol. 1:84. Two British light dragoon regiments participated in the American Revolution; they were designated the 16th and 17th Regiments of Light Dragoons. Despite their designation as regiments, they were actually company-size units. A major reason for their small number of men was that it was expensive to outfit and maintain mounted troops in the field. Finding adequate food for their horses was a serious and ongoing problem. The 17th Light Dragoons arrived in Boston in May 1775 and served in the New York campaign the following year. The 16th Dragoons arrived in New York from England in September 1776 following the Battle of Long Island. See Philip R. N. Katcher, *Encyclopedia of British, Provincial and German Army Units 1775–1783* (Harrisburg, PA: Stackpole Books, 1973), 21, 24.

43. Eric I. Manders, *The Battle of Long Island* (Monmouth Beach, NJ: Philip Freneau Press, 1978), 61.

44. Manders, *The Battle of Long Island*, 37.

45. Kemble, *Journals of Lieutenant-Colonel Stephen Kemble*, vol. 1:85–86.

46. William Heath, *Memoirs of Major-General Heath... During the American War* (Boston: I. Thomas and E.T. Andrews, 1798), 201. Heath's complete comment on the effectiveness of a flanking action is worth noting: "A few shots on the flank or rear of an enemy serves to disconcert them more than a heavy fire from the front. The point of decision here lies not in the force, but in the mind. A company of 50 men cannot fire more shots in the same given time on the flank, or in the rear, than they could in the front; but these few shots will have more effect on the minds of the enemy, than the fire of a whole regiment in their front."

47. Henry P. Johnston, *The Campaign of 1776 Around New York and Brooklyn* (Brooklyn, NY: Long Island Historical Society, 1878), documents section, 176–79.

48. Kemble, *Journals of Lieutenant-Colonel Stephen Kemble*, vol. 1:86. Joshua Loring, the British Army's Commissioner of Prisoners issued a return of Prisoners taken on Long Island during the day-long fighting. Loring listed 1,097 American officers and privates taken prisoner on August 27th, the day of the Battle of Long Island. See Force, *American Archives*, Fifth Series, vol. 1:1258.

49. Washington Irving, *Life of George Washington*, 5 vols. (New York: G. P. Putnam & Co., 1856–1859), vol. 2:325. Washington Irving was born on April 3, 1783, and christened with the name of the great general. The story is that at the age of six, Irving was introduced to then President Washington in a New York City shop by the boy's nursemaid. She told the president that the boy was named in his honor. Washington is reported to have touched the child with his hand and blessed him. Irving spoke reverently about the incident throughout his life. Irving is best known for his short stories and histories; they include *Rip Van Winkle, The Legend of Sleepy Hollow*, and *A History of New York from the Beginning of the World to the End of the Dutch Dynasty by Diedrich Knickerbocker*. However, Irving's *Life of George Washington* is considered his magnum opus. It was also his final work; he finished the fifth volume only eight months before he died.

50. General Howe to Lord George Germain, dated Camp at Newtown, Long Island, September 3, 1776, in Force, *American Archives*, Fifth Series, vol. 1:1257.

51. Christopher Ward, *The War of the Revolution*, 2 vols. (New York: Macmillan Company, 1952), vol. 1:236.

52. General Hugh Earl Percy to the Duke of Northumberland, dated "New Town Long Island Sep. 1. 1776," in Bolton, *Letters of Hugh Earl Percy from Boston and New York, 1774–1776*, 69. New Town is present-day Elmhurst in the New York City borough of Queens.

53. Johnston, *The Campaign of 1776 Around New York and Brooklyn*, 222.

54. William Gordon, *The History of the Rise, Progress, and Establishment of the Independence of the United States of America*, 4 vols. (London: Printed for the Author, 1788), vol. 2:314.

55. Dave Richard Palmer, *The Way of the Fox: American Strategy in the War for America* (Westport, CT: Greenwood Press, 1975), 119.

56. Irving, *Life of George Washington*, vol. 2:327.

57. John Stockton Littell, ed., *Memoirs of His Own Time... by Alexander Graydon* (Philadelphia: Lindsay & Blakiston, 1846), 155–56.

58. Most Revolutionary period references refer to the town as Amboy, although Perth Amboy is also correct. To explain, the town was incorporated as Amboy in 1683. Three years later, in 1686, Amboy became the capital of East Jersey and Perth was added to its name in honor of James Drummond, 1st Duke of Perth, who was one of the founders of New Jersey.

59. Joseph Plumb Martin said that he saw four ships on the morning of September 15. The text reads, "at daybreak the first thing that saluted our eyes was all the four

ships at anchor" (see George F. Scheer, ed., *Private Yankee Doodle... by Joseph Plumb Martin* [Boston: Little, Brown and Company, 1962], 33). However other, more reliable sources said that there were five ships anchored in Kips Bay on the morning of September 15. For example, Adjutant General Major Baurmeister of the Hessian forces states that "five frigates had previously anchored close to the shore in Kips Bay about Crown Point [Manhattan] and cannonaded the enemy outposts and the extensive woods for three hours" (see Uhlendorf, *Revolution in America: Confidential Letters and Journals 1776–1784 of Adjutant General Major Baurmeister*, 48). An accurate painting by Robert Cleveley of the event shows five frigates shelling Kips Bay. For information about Cleveley's painting, see Arthur Lefkowitz, *Eyewitness Images from the American Revolution* (Gretna, LA: Pelican Publishing Company, 2017), 117–19.

60. Uhlendorf, *Revolution in America: Confidential Letters and Journals of Adjutant General Major Baurmeister*, 48.

61. Scheer, *Private Yankee Doodle... by Joseph Plumb Martin*, 33. Joseph Plumb Martin (1760–1850) was born in Massachusetts and raised by his grandparents in Connecticut. He joined the Connecticut State Troops (militia) in June 1776 at the age of fifteen and served with them throughout the 1776 New York campaign. He was discharged at the end of 1776 and reenlisted in the Continental Army in April 1777. Martin was promoted to corporal and assigned to the light infantry in 1778. In 1780 he was promoted to sergeant in the newly organized Corps of Sappers and Miners. He was among the last Continental soldiers to be discharged in 1783. Martin wrote his account of his wartime experiences, which was published in 1830. His reminiscences from the war was originally published by a Howell, Maine, publisher named Franklin Glazier. It is believed that only a few hundred copies of the book were printed. George F. Scheer (1917–1996) discovered a copy of the book in the library of Morristown National Historical Park. He edited and published Martin's narrative in 1962 with the title *Private Yankee Doodle*. Martin's narrative is an often-quoted, eyewitness account of the American Revolution. It is especially important because it is one of the few narratives written by a common soldier. Martin was seventy years old when his book was published. Scholars have questioned how Martin could have so vividly and accurately remembered the details of events that happened almost fifty years prior to the publication of his book. The only plausible explanation is that he kept a record of his experiences during the war which he used to write his book. However, no such notes have ever been found.

62. Johnston, *The Campaign of 1776 Around New York and Brooklyn*, 240.

63. For the number of American troops in lower Manhattan on September 14, 1776, see Edward G. Lengel, *General George Washington: A Military Life* (New York: Random House, 2005), 152.

64. *The Campaign of 1776 Around New York and Brooklyn*, documents section, 117.

65. Lesser, *The Sinews of Independence*, 32–33.

66. Kings Bridge was built by Frederick Philipse, a wealthy New York merchant. Philipse obtained a charter from New York Governor Benjamin Fletcher in

1693 to build and operate a toll bridge across Harlem Creek. Philipse named his span the Kings Bridge. It was the first toll bridge in America.

67. George Athan Billias, *General John Glover and His Marblehead Mariners* (New York: Henry Holt and Company, 1960), 112. Washington called Throggs Neck "a kind of island" in an October 11 letter to John Hancock.

68. Abbot et al., *The Papers of George Washington, Revolutionary War Series*, vol. 6:576.

69. North Castle appears as a small unincorporated section of Westchester County, New York, on some modern maps. However, it was a substantial area of Westchester in colonial America, encompassing the modern towns of Armonk, Banksville, and North White Plains. It also included the northern section of the Philipsburg Manor, or Philipse Manor as it was also called. Philipsburg Manor was a large and extraordinarily valuable estate bordering the east side of the Hudson River extending from the Spuyten Duyvil at the northern tip of Manhattan north to the Croton River in Westchester County. It also included a section of today's Bronx, New York. The estate was established during the Dutch occupation of New York. It was owned by Frederick Philipse III at the outbreak of the American Revolution. He was a Loyalist, and his property was confiscated by the Patriots early in the war. Some of Charles Lee's correspondence during November 1776 is dated "Camp at Philipsburg" which probably was a section of Philipsburg Manor near the modern town of Ossining, New York.

70. Lessor, *The Sinews of Independence*, 36–37.

71. Kemble, *Journals of Lieutenant Colonel Stephen Kemble*, vol. 1:97–98.

72. Letter from George Washington to Major General Nathanael Greene, dated "Head Quarters, Novr 8, 1776," in Richard K. Showman et al., eds., *The Papers of General Nathanael Greene*, 13 vols. (Chapel Hill: University of North Carolina Press, 1976), vol. 1:342–43.

73. In a letter to John Hancock dated November 9, 1776, Washington mentioned that his intelligence gathering included questioning deserters. His Excellency told Hancock, "By every information I can obtain, and the accounts I had last night by two deserters, who were very intelligent and particular, Genl Howe still has in view an expedition to the Jerseys." See Abbot et al., *The Papers of George Washington, Revolutionary War Series*, vol. 7:121.

74. Ibid., 92.

75. *The Lee Papers*, vol. 2:269.

76. Baker, *Itinerary of General Washington*, 56.

77. Littell, *Memoirs of His Own Time... by Alexander Graydon*, 203.

78. Joseph P. Tustin, trans. and ed., *Diary of the American War: A Hessian Journal by Captain Johann Ewald* (New Haven, CT: Yale University Press, 1979), 15; Captain George Smith, *An Universal Military Dictionary* (London: J. Millan, 1779).

79. Email correspondence with the author. General Palmer is the retired superintendent (commanding officer) of West Point and author of several outstanding books about the American Revolution.

80. Letter from Captain William Leslie to his father, Lord Leven, dated "Kings Bridge [northern tip of Manhattan Island] Nov 22nd 1776," in Marianne M. Gilchrist, ed., *Captain Hon. William Leslie (1751–1777), His Life, Letters and Commemoration* in *Military Miscellany II* (Gloucestershire, UK: Sutton Publishing Limited for the Army Records Society, 2005), 161.

81. Ira D. Gruber, ed., *John Peebles' American War* (Mechanicsburg, PA: Stackpole Books, 1998), 63.

82. Colonel Robert Magaw remained a prisoner for four years after surrendering Fort Washington. He was on parole during this time, which gave him some freedom on his word of honor as a gentleman that he would not escape. This allowed him to court and marry Marietta Van Brunt, a belle of Brooklyn. Magaw retired from the army following his exchange. Magaw returned to Carlisle, Pennsylvania, where he died in 1790. He was an ardent patriot who put too much confidence in what turned out to be a poorly designed fort.

83. The Palisades stretch north for approximately twenty miles from modern Jersey City, New Jersey, to Nyack, New York. They soar nearly vertical along their length from 300 feet to 540 feet in height from their base close to the Hudson River. They were called the "steep rocks" at the time of the American War. However, the area where the British landed was also known as Closter Mountain. These majestic cliffs began to be called "The Palisades" about 50 years after the end of the Revolutionary War, but I am using their modern name for ease of identification.

84. Frank Moore, *Diary of the American Revolution from Newspapers and Original Documents*, 2 vols. (New York: privately printed, 1865), vol. 1:350. According to Moore, the story appeared in the December 31 issue of the *Middlesex Journal*.

85. Andrew Burnaby, *Travels Through the Middle Settlements in North America* (London: T. Payne, 1775), 97–98.

86. The wagons that carried passengers between New York City and Philadelphia were called stage wagons. They were crude, lightweight vehicles with flat tops, pulled by four or six horses and had leather or fabric slide curtains and large wheels attached to crude springs. Luggage was stowed under the seats and heavier baggage was fastened on the rear. The passengers sat on four rows of seats; twelve people including the driver were considered a full load. In 1771, Abraham Sillman advertised that his stage would travel between New York and Philadelphia in a day and a half. More typically stage wagons made the journey in two days. John Mercereau advertised that his coach, the "Flying Machine," would run between Paulus Hook Ferry and the Indian Queen Tavern in Philadelphia in two days' time. The trip was a bone-jarring, unpleasant experience no matter which stage line a traveler took.

The High Road through New Jersey can be followed today using its modern names. The section from Paulus Hook (today a section of Jersey City) to downtown Newark is Truck Route 1–9 to Ferry Street in Newark. From Newark to Princeton it is New Jersey Route 27. The name of the road changes again to Route 206 from Princeton to Trenton. The Route 27 section of the road was designated part of the Lincoln Highway in 1912. When operational in the 1920s, the Lincoln Highway was the first paved coast-to-coast road in America running between New York City and San Francisco. In 1922, New Jersey Route 27 was also incorporated as part of the Pikes Peak Ocean-to-Ocean Highway, which connected New York City with Los Angeles.

87. Irving, *Life of George Washington*, vol. 2:440.

88. Lesser, *The Sinews of Independence*, 40.

89. Kemble, *Journals of Lieutenant-Colonel Stephen Kemble*, vol. 1:102.

90. Leonard Lundin, *Cockpit of the Revolution* (Princeton, NJ: Princeton University Press, 1940), 173.

91. Captain William Bamford, 40th Regiment of Foot, "The Revolutionary Diary of a British Officer," *Maryland Historical Magazine* 28 (1933), 17–19.

92. Edwin Nott Hopson, *Captain Daniel Neil* (Paterson, NJ: Braen Heusser Company, 1927), 11–14. New Jersey's other artillery company, designated the Western Company, New Jersey State Artillery, joined Washington's army in December 1776. Its commander was Captain Samuel Hugg. His company's arrival added two additional cannons to Washington's arsenal.

93. The Inman Ferry was named for John Inman, who started the ferry in 1686.

94. Landing Lane Bridge was built in 1772. It was a covered bridge. The bridge has been replaced several times since it was constructed. The present bridge on the site is a metal truss bridge dating from 1895.

95. Abbot et al., *The Papers of George Washington, Revolutionary War Series*, vol. 7:224–25.

96. Ibid., 232–33.

97. Journal of the Hessian Grenadier Battalion von Minnigerode, entry for December 1, 1776, translated by Joseph Tustin. Manuscript note written by Tustin in the Special Collections at Bloomsbury University. Captain von Weitershausen (also spelled Wechershausen) was wounded in the spine and died three days later.

98. Order to Colonel Richard Humpton, dated "Brunswick Decemr 1, 1776," in Abbot et al., *The Papers of George Washington, Revolutionary War Series*, vol. 7:248. The original order given to Colonel Humpton is one of the most important documents in American history. It is on display at the New Jersey Washington Crossing Visitor Center Museum. A photograph of the order is in my book, *Eyewitness Images from the American Revolution*.

99. Showman et al., *The Papers of General Nathanael Greene*, vol. 1:362.

100. Lundin, *Cockpit of the Revolution*, 158.

101. For information about the participation of the Pennsylvania Navy in clearing the Delaware River of boats, see John W. Jackson, *The Pennsylvania Navy* (New Brunswick, NJ: Rutgers University Press, 1974), 74–76.

102. Benjamin Randolph was a master cabinetmaker in Philadelphia who also boarded people in his house in the city. Martha Washington lived in Randolph's Chestnut Street house for several months. She wanted to join her husband in New York City but it was too dangerous. Martha agreed to stay with the Randolph family in the hope that she could eventually travel to New York. She remained with the

Randolphs through the late summer and fall of 1776 before returning to Mount Vernon.

103. Lieutenant Charles M. Lefferts, *Uniforms of the American, British, French and German Armies in the War of the American Revolution* (New York: New York Historical Society, 1926), 148.

104. Ernst Kipping, trans., and Samuel Steele Smith, ed., *At General Howe's Side: The Diary of General William Howe's Aide-De-Camp, Captain Friedrich von Muenchhausen* (Monmouth Beach, NJ: Philip Freneau Press, 1974), 8. I had the pleasure of knowing Sam Smith, who pursued his love of history following his retirement. His financial freedom and knowledge of printing allowed him to publish fourteen impressive books about the American Revolution at an age when most people are staring at television sets in old age homes. Sam wrote some of the books himself, while others were written by outstanding historians of the time including John Elting, Peter Guthorn, and John Reed.

105. Jones, *History of New York During the Revolutionary War*, vol. 1:136.

106. Kenneth Silverman, *A Cultural History of the American Revolution* (New York: Thomas Y. Crowell Company, 1976), 327; and Charles Sellers, *Charles Willson Peale, Early Life* (Philadelphia: The American Philosophical Society, 1947), 140–41. James Peale survived the ordeal and went on to join his older brother to become an artist much admired for his still life paintings. Peale was also an eyewitness to the Battle of Princeton and painted a composite depiction of the battle. Peale showed General Washington in the painting on horseback positioned next to an American artillery company. There is a draped flag next to Washington in the painting. Some historians claim that it is Washington's headquarters flag. This supposition is speculation, as Washington was a seasoned Indian fighter and would not have identified his position on a battlefield: Indian tactics included identifying and killing the enemy leaders first. In addition, there is no eyewitness account or creditable reference to Washington having a headquarters flag, nor is there any record in Washington's detailed wartime expense account for the purchase of a headquarters flag or the fabric, or payment to a person to make such a flag. The Continental Army tended to follow the organization of the British Army, and there is no known record that any British general had a headquarters flag during the Revolution. The Valley Forge Historical Society claimed to have Washington's headquarters flag in their collection. Their claim was based on family legend. On close examination, their flag was made of inexpensive material and poorly sewn. Washington would never have used such a poorly made flag. The flag also appears to be part of a larger flag, which did not survive. The so-called Washington's headquarters flag is currently in the collection of the Museum of the American Revolution in Philadelphia. It is unfortunate that James Peale left historians guessing about the flag he included in his painting of the Battle of Princeton.

107. Henry Carrington, *Battles of the American Revolution* (New York: A. S. Barnes & Company, 1876), 257–58.

108. Samuel Steele Smith, *The Battle of Trenton* (Monmouth Beach, NJ: Philip Freneau Press, 1965), 9.

109. For the number of Crown forces at Trenton see ibid., 31 (appendix D).

110. Arthur Lefkowitz, *The Long Retreat: The Calamitous American Defense of New Jersey 1776* (Metuchen, NJ: Upland Press, 1998), 125. This book is currently available in a paperback edition from Rutgers University Press.

111. William Willcox, ed. *The American Rebellion: Sir Henry Clinton's Narrative of His Campaigns, 1775–1782* (New Haven, CT: Yale University Press, 1954), 56.

112. Thomas Paine, "The American Crisis (also called the Crisis) Number One," pamphlet (Philadelphia: Styner & Cist, 1776).

113. The tavern was named for its owner, Mary Brown White, who was the widow of Ebenezer White.

114. Lawrence H. Curry, ed., *Martin Hunter's Journal: America 1774–1778, Valley Forge Journal 4, no. 1* (Valley Forge, PA: Valley Forge Historical Society, 1988), 239. The journal was kept by Ensign Martin Hunter from the light infantry company of the 52nd British Regiment.

115. William S. Stryker, *The Battles of Trenton and Princeton* (Boston: Houghton, Mifflin and Company, 1898), 334.

116. David Hackett Fischer, *Washington's Crossing* (New York: Oxford University Press, 2004), 392. Fischer includes a detailed list of the American ordnance at Trenton.

117. Letter from George Washington to Brigadier General William Maxwell. dated "Head Qrs, December 28th 1776," in Abbot et al., *The Papers of George Washington, Revolutionary War Series*, vol. 7:473.

118. Kipping and Smith, *At General Howe's Side: The Diary of General Howe's Aide-De-Camp, Captain Friedrich von Muenchhausen*, 8. Friedrich's letter was dated December 26, 1776, but the postscript is undated.

119. There is an often-told story that, believing that he had Washington's army trapped following the January 2, 1777, Second Battle of Trenton, Cornwallis said that he would "bag the fox in the morning." An early source for the story appears in Washington Irving's *Life of George Washington*. The story appears in volume 2, published in 1856. After describing the fighting on January 2, Irving wrote,

> At length they drew off, came to a halt and lighted their camp fires.... Sir William Erskine, who was with Cornwallis, urged him, it is said to attack Washington that evening in his camp; but his lordship declined... he had at length, as he thought, got Washington into a situation from which he could not escape... and he was willing to give his wearied troops a night's repose, to prepare them for the closing struggle. He would be sure, he said, to "bag the fox in the morning."

Cornwallis is also quoted as saying that he would "bag the fox" in twentieth-century author Richard Ketchum's book, *The Winter Soldiers* (New York: Doubleday Publishing, 1973). According to Ketchum, Cornwallis broke off his attack on Washington's position at Assunpink Creek (Second Battle of Trenton) on January

2, 1777, telling his officers, "We've got the old fox safe now.... We'll go over and bag him in the morning." However, Ketchum, a noted raconteur, gave no primary source for the story.

I reviewed eyewitness accounts of the period and numerous histories of the American Revolution looking for a creditable source for the story with no results. I selected three accounts of the event that are representative of how it was described. My first example is by Archibald Robertson, a British officer with Cornwallis's army at Trenton on the night of January 2. Robertson's diary entry for January 2, 1777, reads in part, "Our troops all lay out. Hard frost and two battalions light infantry lay in Trenton without fires by way of piquets [guards] to watch the rebels on the other side [of] the creek. January 3rd. At day break reported that the rebels were all gone" (Lydenberg, *Archibald Robertson*, 120). My second example is George Washington Parke Custis, *Recollections and Private Memoirs of Washington*, published in 1860. Custis is well known for storytelling, including his claim that he was George Washington's adopted son. Custis seemly a likely source for the "bagging the fox" tale. However, his account of the Second Battle of Trenton does not include the story. Custis wrote (page 179), "On the second of January Cornwallis, with veteran British troops came from Princeton to attack him [Washington]. There was some fighting at Trenton just at evening, when the British general, feeling sure that he could capture the whole American army in the morning, took rest for the night." Custis then goes on to explain how the Patriots decamped that night and "by an infrequented [*sic*] road" went to Princeton. "In the morning Cornwallis was mortified to find his expected prey had escaped." My third example is a respected twentieth-century seven-volume Washington biography by historian Douglas Southall Freeman who describes the events of January 2–3 in detail: "all of them [Washington's troops] seemed to understand the necessity of strict compliance with orders for complete silence. Five hundred remained to guard the Assunpink Bridge at Trenton, to feed the fires temporarily and to use pick and shovel as if they were constructing earthworks; all the other troops stole quietly off." See Douglas Southall Freeman, *George Washington: A Biography*, 7 vols. (New York: Charles Scribner and Sons, 1948), vol. 4:348. In conclusion, there is no documentation to prove that Cornwallis said that he would "bag the fox in the morning."

120. For the number of American troops and estimated number of cannons, see Lengel, *General George Washington: A Military Life*, 202.

121. There are differing accounts of the number of British troops at Princeton on January 3, 1777. I have quoted the figures stated by the eminent Revolutionary War scholar Edward Lengel (ibid., 203).

122. Rick Atkinson, *The British Are Coming* (New York: Henry Holt and Company, 2019), 547.

123. George Washington to John Hancock, dated "Pluckamin [New Jersey] January 5th 1777," in Abbot et al., *The Papers of George Washington, Revolutionary War Series*, vol. 7:523.

124. Samuel Steele Smith, *The Battle of Princeton* (Monmouth Beach, NJ: Philip Freneau Press, 1967), 3.

125. Washington identified the troops he left in Princeton in the letter he wrote to Congress from Trenton on December 5. Washington listed them as "five Virginia regiments and that of Delaware, containing in the whole about 1,200 men fit for duty, under the command of Lord Stirling." See Abbot et al., *The Papers of George Washington, Revolutionary War Series*, vol. 7:262. Author Samuel Steele Smith listed the regiments left with Lord Stirling as follows:

> Virginia continental regiment commanded by Colonel Isaac Reade
> Virginia continental regiment commanded by Colonel George Weedon
> Virginia continental regiment commanded by Colonel Charles Scott
> Virginia continental regiment commanded by Colonel Mordecai Buckner
> Delaware militia regiment commanded by Colonel John Haslet
> Pennsylvania rifle regiment (its commander Colonel Samuel Miles was captured at the Battle of Long Island)

See Smith, *The Battle of Trenton*, 28.

126. Abbot et al., *The Papers of George Washington, Revolutionary War Series*, vol. 7:262.

127. Ibid.

128. Showman et al., *The Papers of Nathanael Greene*, vol. 1:366. Washington actually started back to Princeton from Trenton with 500 men.

129. Letter from General Nathanael Greene to Catharine Greene, dated "Trenton Decem 30, 1776," in Showman et al., *The Papers of Nathanael Greene*, vol. 1:377.

CHAPTER 2

1. Harry Miller Lydenberg, ed., *Archibald Robertson, His Diaries and Sketches in America* (New York: New York Public Library, 1930), 120.

2. Letter from Henry Knox to Lucy Flucker Knox, dated "Morristown, New Jersey Tuesday, 7 January 1777," in Phillip Hamilton, *The Revolutionary War Lives and Letters of Lucy and Henry Knox* (Baltimore: John Hopkins University Press, 2017), 70.

3. Letter from a gentleman of great worth in the American Army [attributed to Dr. Benjamin Rush] to the printer of the *Maryland Journal* dated near Princeton, January 7, 1777, in William S. Stryker, *The Battles of Trenton and Princeton* (Boston: Houghton, Mifflin and Company, 1898), 468.

4. William B. Willcox, ed., *The American Rebellion: Sir Henry Clinton's Narrative of His Campaigns, 1775–1782* (New Haven, CT: Yale University Press, 1954), 60, n4.

5. Abbot et al., *The Papers of George Washington, Revolution War Series*, vol. 7:523. From the wording of Washington's text it is clear that he wanted to "have pushed on to [New] Brunswick" from Princeton on January 3, 1777. Stating that his troops "having had no rest for two nights and a day" is a reference to the condition of his soldiers on the day of the Battle of Princeton.

6. John R. Elting, *The Battle of Bunker's Hill* (Monmouth Beach, NJ: Philip Freneau Press, 1975), 40.

7. Victor Leroy Johnson, "The Administration of the American Commissariat During the Revolutionary War" (doctoral dissertation in history, University of Pennsylvania, 1941), 60.

8. A carpenter in colonial America was a man skilled in the heavy framing of a building; a joiner did the finishing work. See Richard M. Lederer, Jr., *Colonial American English* (Essex, CT: Verbatim Book Co., 1985), 44. Virtually every soldier in the British, Hessian, and American armies in the Revolution has some skill that they acquired before joining the army. There were definitely carpenters among the troops. Just how they were identified is a mystery, and did they carry carpenter tools with them?

9. *The Diary of Captain Thomas Rodney* (Wilmington, DE: Historical Society of Delaware, 1888), 37.

10. Lydenberg, *Archibald Robertson, His Diaries and Sketches in America*, 121.

11. Stryker, *The Battles of Trenton and Princeton*, 303.

12. For the number of British Army soldiers captured at Princeton, see Samuel Steele Smith, *The Battle of Princeton* (Monmouth Beach, NJ: Philip Freneau Press, 1967), 37.

13. Johnson, "The Administration of the American Commissariat During the Revolutionary War," 60.

14. "Millstone History," Millstone Borough, Somerset County, New Jersey website, www.millstoneboro.org.

15. The number of British officers captured at Princeton is mentioned in Andrew D. Mellick, Jr., *The Story of an Old Farm* (Somerville, NJ: The Unionist-Gazette, 1889), 383.

16. The strength of Colonel Hand's regiment of Pennsylvania riflemen is from "Return of the Forces of the States of America" dated December 22, 1776, in Peter Force, ed., *American Archives*, Series 5, vol. 3:1402.

17. Armies at the time were dependent on their wagon trains of equipment and provisions. This accounts for the fact that the battles of the American Revolution including Brandywine, Germantown, Monmouth, and Cowpens were fought along roads.

18. Johnson, "The Administration of the American Commissariat During the Revolutionary War," 60.

19. *The Journal of Charles Willson Peale* (Philadelphia: The Pennsylvania Magazine of History and Biography, 1914), vol. 38:283.

20. *The Diary of Captain Thomas Rodney*, 38.

21. Mellick, *The Story of an Old Farm*, 383.

22. Abbot et al., *The Papers of George Washington, Revolutionary War Series*, vol 7:519–23.

23. Captain John Henry was a Maryland officer who was in the Flying Camp in 1776. I identified him as the probable dispatch rider in Francis B. Heitman, *Historical Register of Officers of the Continental Army* (Washington, DC: Rare Book Shop Publishing Company, 1914), 286.

24. The site of the original church, built in 1757, was replaced by a new building in 1851 and is currently the home of the Pluckemin Presbyterian Church.

25. George Washington Parke Custis, *Recollections and Private Memoirs of Washington by His Adopted Son* (New York: Derby & Jackson, 1860), 186. There was an earlier and rare abbreviated edition of this book with the same title published in Washington, DC, by William H. Moore Co. in 1859. George Washington Parke Custis (1781–1857), whose nickname was "Wash," was the only son of John Park Custis (1754–1781), Martha Washington's only son from her first marriage. John Park Custis died of a camp fever during the 1781 siege of Yorktown. Despite his claims of being George Washington's adopted son, the general never formally adopted Wash, although he grew up at Mount Vernon. Wash inherited his father's large fortune which included a plantation in present-day Arlington, Virginia. His daughter, Mary Anna Randolph Custis, married Robert E. Lee. They inherited the Arlington property when George Washington Parke Custis died in 1857. The federal government seized the property during the Civil War in reprisal for Robert E. Lee joining the Confederate Army. The U.S. government turned the most attractive part of the estate into a cemetery (Arlington National Cemetery) for Union soldiers killed during the war in further retaliation for Robert E. Lee's duplicity to the Union. The balance of the plantation is now Fort Meyer, Virginia.

26. McPherson's full name is identified in Steven M. Baule, *British Army Officers Who Served in the American Revolution, 1775–1783* (Westminster, MD: Heritage Books, 2003), 125.

27. Rush, *A Memorial Containing Travels Through Life or Sundry Incidents in the Life of Dr. Benjamin Rush Written by Himself*, annotated by Louis Alexander Biddle (Philadelphia: Privately published, 1905), 98.

28. James P. Snell, *History of Hunterdon and Somerset Counties, New Jersey* (Philadelphia: Everts and Peck, 1881), 59.

29. Letters from General Alexander Leslie, dated [New] Brunswick, 18 March [1777] and from Staten Island, dated 7 July [1777], in Marianne M. Gilchrist, ed., *Captain Hon. William Leslie (1751–1777), His Life, Letters and Commemoration* in *Military Miscellany II* (Gloucestershire, UK: Sutton Publishing Limited for the Army Records Society, 2005), 166–67.

30. Mellick, *The Story of an Old Farm*, 386–87.

31. *The Journal of Charles Willson Peale*, vol. 38:284.

32. *National Park Service Historical Handbook: Morristown* (National Park Service, 2002), 1.

33. James A. Huston, *Logistics of Liberty* (Newark, Delaware: University of Delaware Press, 1991), 178.

34. Email correspondence with Eric Olsen, park ranger and historian at Morristown National Historical Park. Olsen said that General Nathanael Greene referred to Ford's home as "the Great White House at the far side of town."

35. Eric Olsen, "The Last Days of Colonel Jacob Ford," undated fact sheet, Morristown National Historical Park.

36. Email correspondence with Eric Olsen.

37. Washington submitted a list of his "lawful" expenses at the end of the war for payment. He included Martha Washington's travelling expenses from Mount Vernon to his winter quarters during the war along with the costs involved in her returning home. He justified the expense claiming "the consequence of my self-denial": he remained with the army throughout the war except for a brief visit to Mount Vernon in 1781 en route to Yorktown.

38. "Martha Washington 1777," itinerary prepared by Eric Olsen, Morristown National Historical Park.

39. General Charles Lee's army traveled from Westchester County, New York, to Morristown, New Jersey, in late 1776. His correspondence is dated Haverstraw, New York (on the west side of the Hudson River) December 4, 1776. His army next marched from Haverstraw through the Clove into northern New Jersey. On December 7, Joseph Nourse, Lee's civilian secretary, addressed a letter from the northern New Jersey village of Pompton. Lee's first letter from Morristown was written on the following day (December 8) from Morristown. General Lee was not authorized to have a secretary on his headquarters staff. Joseph Nourse (1754–1841) may have been a young volunteer who prepared Lee's correspondence and orders for his signature. Lee must have known Nourse before the war because Nourse grew up on his family's farm in Berkeley County, Virginia (present-day West Virginia). It was the same county where Charles Lee lived after immigrating to America. Nourse was eventually appointed the first register of the U.S. Department of the Treasury. The position was responsible for keeping the records of the Treasury Department. He held this job until 1829, when he was discharged by President Andrew Jackson.

40. Abbot et al., *The Papers of George Washington, Revolutionary War Series*, vol. 7:385.

41. Samuel Steele Smith, *The Battle of Trenton* (Monmouth Beach, NJ: Philip Freneau Press, 1965), 29. Historian Smith listed the three Massachusetts regiments at Morristown as two Continental Army units identified by their commanding officers: Colonel John Greaton and Colonel William Bond. The third regiment was a militia unit commanded by Colonel Elisha Porter.

42. Joseph Vose (1739–1816) was a Continental Army officer and one of the stalwarts of the American Revolution. He was born on his family's farm in the town of Milton, Massachusetts. Vose was appointed a colonel in the Massachusetts militia prior to the Revolution. He joined the Continental Army early in the war and remained a committed Patriot throughout the conflict and given the honor of

leading his regiment into New York City on November 25, 1783, following the British evacuation of the city.

43. Order to Brigadier General William Maxwell, dated "Bucks County, Pa. 21 December 1776," in Abbot et al., *The Papers of George Washington, Revolutionary War Series*, vol. 7:402.

44. Diary entry for May 25, 1773. See John C. Fitzpatrick, ed., *The Diaries of George Washington*, 4 vols. (Boston: Houghton Mifflin Company, 1925), vol. 2:112. Washington left Mount Vernon with Martha Washington's son John Parke Custis (1754–1781) on May 10, 1773, for New York City. The purpose of the trip was to enroll Custis at Kings College (now Columbia University). They travelled at a leisurely pace, including a visit with Lord Stirling. Washington's visit with Stirling was probably more than a social call. Both were businessmen at a time when most business was done between people who knew each other personally or by reputation.

45. Washington Irving, *Life of George Washington*, 5 vols. (New York: Charles T. Evans, 1856–1859), vol. 2:440.

46. Dave R. Palmer, *George Washington's Military Genius* (Washington, DC: Regnery Publishing, Inc., 2012), 145.

47. Mark Puls, *Henry Knox: Visionary General of the American Revolution* (New York: Palgrave Macmillan, 2008), 84.

48. Paul David Nelson, *General James Grant* (Gainesville: University Press of Florida, 1993), 108. Grant was famous for the speech he made in the House of Commons on February 2, 1775, stating that he could march from one end of America to the other with 5,000 troops without meeting any serious opposition from the colonists.

49. For the number of troops at New Brunswick in early January 1777, see Smith, *The Battle of Princeton*, 36. Historian Smith said that the New Brunswick garrison consisted of the 1st Battalion of Guards and 46th Infantry Regiment.

50. Edward G. Lengel, *General George Washington: A Military Life* (New York: Random House, 2005), 210.

51. Horatio Rogers, ed., *Hadden's Journal and Orderly Book, A Journal Kept in Canada and Upon Burgoyne's Campaign by Lieutenant James M. Hadden* (Albany, NY: Joel Munsell's Sons, 1884), 378. This publishing firm was started by Joel Munsell (1808–1880) and continued by his sons. The Munsells were interested in the American Revolution and they published a number of important books on the subject. Their titles included *The British Invasion from the North... with the Journal of Lieut. William Digby* (1887); William L. Stone, ed., *Journal of Captain Pausch, Chief of the Hanau Artillery During the Burgoyne Campaign* (1886); Isaac Q. Leake, *Memoir of the Life and Times of General John Lamb* (1850); William B. Stone, ed., *Letters and Journals Relating to the War of the American Revolution by Mrs. General Riedesel* (1867), and J. G. Rosengarten, *The German Allied Troops in the North American War of Independence* (1893). There is an excellent published doctoral dissertation about Munsell by David Simeon Edelstein titled *Joel Munsell: Printer and Antiquarian* (Columbia University, 1950). A bibliography of the books and pamphlets published

by Joel Munsell is also available: *A Catalog of the Books and Pamphlets Issued from the Press of Joel Munsell from 1828–1870* (New York: Burt Franklin Press, 1969).

52. Allen French, *The First Year of the American Revolution* (Boston: Houghton Mifflin Company, 1934), 259. The comment is from a letter that Lee wrote to Dr. Benjamin Rush dated "Camp at Valley-Forge, June 4th, 1778." The complete letter is in (anonymous but attributed to Edward Langworthy), *Memoirs of the Life of the Late Charles Lee* (London: J. S. Jordon, 1792), 424. Edward Langworthy (1738–1802) was a member of the Continental Congress from Georgia. In 1780 he acquired the papers of General Charles Lee, who by then had been court-martialed by the Continental Army.

53. Lengel, *General George Washington*, 141.

54. Eric I. Manders, *The Battle of Long Island* (Monmouth Beach, NJ: Philip Freneau Press, 1978), 60. The Philip Freneau Press is a little-known publisher of fourteen scholarly books about the American Revolution:

The Battle of Monmouth, by Samuel Steele Smith (1964)
The Battle of Trenton, by Samuel Steele Smith (1965)
American Maps and Map Makers of the Revolution, by Peter J. Guthorn (1966)
The Battle of Princeton, by Samuel Steele Smith (1967)
Valley Forge: Crucible of Victory, by John Ford Reed (1969)
Fight for the Delaware, 1777, by Samuel Steele Smith (1970)
The Hessian View of America, 1776–1783, by Ernst Kipping (1971)
British Maps of the American Revolution, by Peter J. Guthorn (1972)
At General Howe's Side: The Diary of General William Howe's Aide-De-Camp, Captain Friedrich von Muenchhausen, translated by Ernst Kipping and edited by Samuel Steele Smith (1974)
The Battle of Bunker's Hill, by John R. Elting (1975)
The Battle of Brandywine, by Samuel Steele Smith (1976)
The Battles of Saratoga, by John R. Elting (1977)
The Battle of Long Island, by Eric I. Manders (1978)
Winter at Morristown, 1779–1780: The Darkest Hour, by Samuel Steele Smith (1979)

It was the passion of Samuel Steele Smith, who started the press when he retired and sold his printing business. Noted author David Hackett Fischer acknowledged Sam Smith's work in his book, *Washington's Crossing*. Commenting on Smith's volumes, Fischer said, "The books received little attention from academic historians... but serious students of military history hold them in high respect." See David Hackett Fischer, *Washington's Crossing* (New York: Oxford University Press, 2004), 447.

55. Israel Mauduit, *Three Letters to Lord Viscount Howe* (London: privately published, 1781), 28.

56. Thomas Jones, *History of New York During the Revolutionary War*, 2 vols. (New York: New York Historical Society, 1879). vol. 1:121–22. Perhaps the most

famous modern use of the word "nabobs" was in a speech made by Vice President Spiro Agnew in 1970. Referring to unfriendly members of the press, Agnew called them "nattering nabobs of negativism."

57.   Joseph P. Tustin, trans. and ed., *Diary of the American War: A Hessian Journal by Captain Johann Ewald* (New Haven, CT: Yale University Press, 1979), 25.

58.   Stryker, *The Battles of Trenton and Princeton*, 37.

59.   Jones, *History of New York During the Revolutionary War*, vol. 1:128.

60.   Anonymously written pamphlet attributed to Joseph Galloway, titled *Letters to a Nobleman, on the Conduct of the War* (London, 1780), 51–52.

61.   William Bell Clark et al., eds., *Naval Documents of the American Revolution*, 13 vols. to date (Washington, DC: U.S. Government Printing Office, 1964–2019), vol. 7:256. Admiral Howe's November 23 order read in part, "to proceed with a sufficient force of troops and ships of war for making a descent on the colony of Rhode Island."

62.   Willcox, *The American Rebellion: Sir Henry Clinton's Narrative*, 56 note.

63.   *Diary of Frederick Mackenzie*, 2 vol. (Cambridge, MA: Harvard University Press, 1930), vol. 1:105.

64.   Jones, *History of New York During the Revolutionary War*, vol. 1:130.

65.   Henry Lee, *Memoirs of the War*, 2 vols. (Philadelphia: Bradford and Inskeep, 1812), vol. 1:54–55. Henry Lee was a 1773 graduate of today's Princeton University. Lee is best known during the war as the lieutenant colonel commanding a mixed corps of mounted troops and infantry known as Lee's Legion. He was the father of Confederate Army General Robert E. Lee.

66.   Sir George Otto Trevelyan, *The American Revolution*, 6 vols. (New York: Longmans, Green & Company, 1899), vol. 1:338.

67.   *The Narrative of Lieut. Gen. Sir William Howe, in a Committee of the House of Commons, on the 19th of April, 1779* (London: B. Baldwin, 1870), 5.

68.   Jones, *History of New York During the Revolutionary War*, vol. 1:128.

69.   James Thacher, *Military Journal of the American Revolution* (Hartford, CT: Hurlbut, Williams & Company, 1862), 373.

70.   Jones, *History of New York During the Revolutionary War*, vol. 1:351. Calling Loring "a blood sucking harpie," Jones explained how Loring embezzled money: "Upon the close of the campaign in 1776, there were not less than 10,000 prisoners within the British lines at New York. A Commissary of Prisoners was therefore appointed and one Joshua Loring was commissioned to the office, with a guinea a day and rations of all kinds, for himself and family.... Loring was determined to make the most of his commission, and by appropriating to his own use nearly two-thirds of the rations allowed to the prisoners, he actually starved to death about 300 of the poor wretches before an exchange took place."

71.   Ibid., vol. 2:86.

72.   *The Journal of Nicholas Cresswell* (New York: Dial Press, 1924), 229.

73.   Jones, *History of New York During the Revolutionary War*, vol. 1:716.

74.   Henry L. Williams, *Songs and Ballads of the American Revolution* (New York: Hurst and Company, 1905), 161.

75. Henry Steele Commager and Richard B. Morris, eds., *The Spirit of Seventy-Six*, 2 vols. (New York: Bobbs-Merrill Company, 1958), vol. 1:532.

CHAPTER 3

1. "General Return of the Army in the Service of the United States, November 3, 1776," in Charles H. Lesser, ed., *The Sinews of Independence* (Chicago: University of Chicago Press, 1976), 37. The regiments that Washington brought with him to New Jersey from North Castle were from Virginia, New Jersey, Delaware. and Pennsylvania.

2. Peekskill was located on the east bank of the Hudson River. Heath's 3,000 troops were responsible for manning the three American forts that were built in the area to control the Hudson River. These were Fort Independence located along Peekskill's waterfront (completely obliterated today by a quarry), and two forts further north on the river: Fort Montgomery and Fort Constitution. Fort Constitution was of particular importance as it was situated on the east bank of a sharp curve of the Hudson River. Ships had to slow down to pass through the curve, making them easy targets. West Point was later built on the west side of the river facing Fort Constitution.

3. *The Papers of Charles Lee*, 4 vols. (New York: New York Historical Society, 1871–1874), vol. 2:269.

4. *Papers of Charles Lee*, vol. 2:290.

5. *Papers of Charles Lee*, vol. 2:291–292.

6. Letter from Charles Lee to William Heath, dated "Camp at Philipsburg, November 21, 1776," in William Heath, *Memoirs of Major-General William Heath* (Boston: I. Thomas and E. T. Andrews, 1798), 88–89.

7. Heath, *Memoirs of Major-General William Heath*, 7–8.

8. Heath was appointed a brigadier general in the Continental Army on June 22, 1775, and promoted to major general on August 9, 1776. Lee was appointed a major general on June 17, 1775. Heath was subordinate to Lee based on the dates of their appointments as major generals.

9. Lee became the senior major general in the Continental Army in May 1776 following the retirement of Artemas Ward. See Washington's letter to Lee, dated New York, May 9, 1776, in W. W. Abbot et al., eds., *The Papers of George Washington, Revolutionary War Series*, 28 vols. to date (Charlottesville: University of Virginia Press, 1985–2020), vol. 4:245. Ward was made the senior major general and second-in-command of the Continental Army to appease the politicians of Ward's home colony of Massachusetts. Washington treated Ward with respect, but noticed that he liked to remain close to his Shrewsbury, Massachusetts, home. This accounts for Washington's May 9 letter to Lee that includes, "General Ward, upon the [British army's] Evacuation of Boston [in March 1776], and finding that there was a probability of his removing from the smoke of his own chimney, applied to me and wrote to Congress, for leave to resign." According to the editor of the *Papers of*

George Washington, His Excellency struck out the following phrase from his letter to Lee: "for he never did a day's duty, or was out of his house from the time of his appointment."

10. Heath, *Memoirs of Major-General William Heath*, 89–90.

11. Heath, *Memoirs of Major-General William Heath*, 94–96.

12. *Papers of Charles Lee*, vol. 2:307.

13. *Papers of Charles Lee*, vol. 2:374.

14. Samuel Chase, letter to the Maryland Council of Safety dated November 21, 1776, in Paul H. Smith, ed., *Letters to Delegates of Congress, 1774–1789*, 26 vols. (Washington, DC: Library of Congress), vol. 5:525.

15. William Hooper to Joseph Hewes, letter dated November 30, 1776, in Smith, *Letters to Delegates of Congress*, vol. 5:557. Hooper and Hewes were both North Carolina delegates to the Second Continental Congress. Hewes was born and grew up near Princeton, New Jersey, and graduated from today's Princeton University. He later moved to North Carolina. Hewes was visiting with his family in New Jersey when Hooper wrote him on November 30 with the news of the surrender of Fort Washington. Both Hooper and Hewes signed the Declaration of Independence for North Carolina.

16. *Papers of Charles Lee*, vol. 2:326.

17. *Secret Journals of the Acts and Proceedings of Congress*, 4 vols (Boston: Thomas B. Wait, 1820–1821), vol. 1:51. The entry quoted mentions sending "Colonel Stewart" to find Lee. A review of officers named Stewart who held the rank of colonel in December 1776 in Francis B. Heitman, *Historical Register of Officers of the Continental Army* (Washington, DC: Rare Book Shop Publishing Company, 1914) shows that only Colonel Charles Stewart meets the criteria.

18. Abbot et al., *The Papers of George Washington, Revolutionary War Series*, vol. 7:278.

19. Ibid., vol. 7:276.

20. Jared Sparks, *The Writings of George Washington*, 12 vols. (Boston: American Stationers Company, 1833–1837), vol. 4:534. Although Lee's letter has been subsequently published elsewhere, Sparks is cited to acknowledge that he was the first to publish a multivolume book of Washington's correspondence. The problem with Sparks's work is that he changed words and spelling. However, his text of Lee's December 12 letter to Washington is accurate.

21. For Lee going directly to Basking Ridge from Morristown on the morning of December 12, see *The Papers of Charles Lee*, vol. 4:385.

22. France began rearming and preparing for another war with Britain following the French defeat in the Seven Years' War (1756–1763). The North American segment of the conflict was called the French and Indian War. France had lost important colonies, overseas markets, and prestige in Europe as a result of being defeated in the war. The French saw the American Revolution as an opportunity to weaken Britain by helping the warring colonists. However, they did not want to openly assist the Americans, especially since they were unprepared to fight the British. As a

result, the French began to secretly assist the Americans with weapons. Their initial assistance to the colonists was arranged by the French physician Jacques Barbeu-Dubourg, who had corresponded with Benjamin Franklin. Colonel Boistertrand was recruited by Dubourg to deliver information to Franklin in Philadelphia. The colonel landed in rebel-held Portsmouth, New Hampshire, and apparently was travelling with Lee's division for his safety because the location of British garrisons and patrols in New Jersey were unclear at the time.

23.   George H. Moore, *The Treason of Charles Lee* (New York: Charles Scribner, 1860), 58.

24.   James Thomas Flexner, *George Washington in the American Revolution* (New York: Little, Brown and Company, 1968), 167. Flexner's book is the second volume of his four-volume biography of George Washington. The series was awarded a special Pulitzer Prize in 1973. The four volumes were condensed into a single book titled *Washington, The Indispensable Man*. Flexner's book gave me the idea for the title of my book about George Washington's wartime aides-de-camp, which is *George Washington's Indispensable Men*. Flexner was born in 1908 and died at the age of ninety-five in 2003. His obituary in the February 16, 2003, issue of the *New York Times* notes that Flexner "brought Washington down from Olympus, if not to eye level, at least to where we can see him plain."

25.   Phillip Papas, *Renegade Revolutionary: The Life of General Charles Lee* (New York: New York University Press, 2014), 4.

26.   The tavern in Vealtown was called the Vealtown Tavern. The building is still standing in the center of modern Bernardsville.

27.   General James Wilkinson, *Memoirs of My Own Times*, 3 vols. (Philadelphia: Abraham Small, 1816), vol. 1:105.

28.   The distance from the Vealtown Tavern in the center of modern Bernardsville to the site of the Widow White's Tavern historic marker on Mount Airy Road is four miles. Mount Airy Road existed at the time of the American Revolution.

29.   Horatio Gates sold his commission as a British Army major and purchased a modest plantation he named Travellers Rest in what is now West Virginia. Several places in the United States are named in his honor, including Horatio Street in Manhattan. Charles Lee coincidentally purchased a nearby planation that he named Prato Rio (Portuguese for stream on the meadow). Lee was a linguist and had fought in Portugal, which accounts for the unusual name of his estate.

30.   Henry Steele Commager and Richard B. Morris, eds., *The Spirit of Seventy-Six*, 2 vols. (New York: Bobbs-Merrill Company, 1958), vol. 1:500.

31.   Letter from cornet Banastre Tarleton to his mother, dated Prince's Town, December 18, 1776, in ibid., vol. 1:501.

32.   A cornet is the lowest commissioned rank in the British cavalry or dragoons. The *Universal Military Dictionary* (1779) identifies a cornet as "the third commission officer in a troop of horse or dragoons, subordinate to the captain and lieutenant, equivalent to the ensign amongst the foot [infantry]." Tarleton was commissioned a cornet on April 20, 1775. He was promoted to captain on January 8, 1778, and

appointed a lieutenant colonel commanding the British Legion on August 1, 1778. See Steven M. Baule, *British Army Officers Who Served in the American Revolution* (Westminster, MD: Heritage Boosks, 2008), 174.

33. Captain Bradford's "Account of the Capture of General Lee" in Henry P. Johnston, *The Campaign of 1776 Around New York and Brooklyn* (Brooklyn, NY: Long Island Historical Society, 1878), document section, 146.

34. Wilkinson, *Memoirs of My Own Times*, vol 1: 105.

35. Captain Vernejout, one of Lee's aides-de-camp, is mentioned as the only person in the house with Lee "to have retained his presence of mind and behaved with suitable courage on the occasion." See Moore, *The Treason of Charles Lee*, 62. Vernejout survived the attack, as evidenced by a letter that Major General John Sullivan wrote to John Hancock on the captain's behalf. Sullivan's letter is dated "Wrights Town [present day Wrightstown, New Jersey], December 22d 1776." It reads in part, "I beg leave to introduce to your Excellency's notice and acquaintance the bearer Captain Verlejou [Vernejout]. He has been with us some months and has ever discovered himself to be the gentleman and soldier at the time General Lee was taken. He acted with the greatest bravery and resolution."

36. Ibid., 61.

37. Ibid., 63.

38. Letter from Tarleton in Commager and Morris, *The Spirit of Seventy-Six*, vol. 1:502; and Moore, *The Treason of Charles Lee*, 63.

39. Boisbertrand was held prisoner by the British for two years. He escaped from prison in England and managed to return to France and his career in the French Army.

40. Papas, *Renegade Revolutionary: The Life of General Charles Lee*, 217.

41. Letter from Washington to John Hancock, dated "Camp above Trenton Falls Decr 20th 1776," in Abbot et al., *The Papers of George Washington, Revolutionary War Series*, vol. 7:385.

42. Papas, *Renegade Revolutionary*, 4.

43. Letter from Charles Lee to George Washington, dated July 1, 1778 in Abbot et al., *The Papers of George Washington, Revolutionary War Series*, vol. 15:595. For more information about earwig meaning a sycophant or whispering busybody, see Richard M. Lederer, Jr., *Colonial American English* (Essex, CT: Verbatim Books, 1985), 77.

44. Abbot et al., *The Papers of George Washington, Revolutionary War Series*, vol. 7:382.

45. Ibid., vol. 6:396–97.

46. Harry Alonzo Cushing, ed., *The Writings of Samuel Adams*, 4 vols. (New York: G. P. Putnam's Sons, 1904–1908), vol. 3:250.

47. *Papers of Charles Lee*, vol. 2:323–24.

48. Worthington Chauncey Ford, ed., *Journals of the Continental Congress*, 34 vols. (Washington, DC: U.S. Government Printing Office, 1904–1937), vol. 5:762–63. John Hancock used the term "new establishment" referring to the

raising of eighty-eight regiments in a letter to Washington dated "Philada Novr 5th 1776," in Abbot et al., *The Papers of George Washington, Revolutionary War Series*, vol. 7:89.

49. Washington called the eighty-eight regiments authorized by Congress as the new army in a letter dated January 27, 1777, to Major General Philip Schuyler. Writing to Schuyler from Morristown, Washington said, "and to draw together the new army, which gains, but slowly to make its appearance." Abbot et al., *The Papers of George Washington, Revolutionary War Series*, vol. 8:165.

50. Washington used the phrase "a handful of men" in a letter to the Pennsylvania Council of Safety. See ibid., vol. 8:107; letter to John Hancock dated "Head Quarters Morris Town 19th Jany 1777" in ibid., vol. 8:102–3.

51. Letter from George Washington to Henry Laurens, President of Congress, dated "Valley Forge, Decemb. 23d 1777," in ibid., vol. 12:683.

52. Letter from George Washington to John Parke Custis, dated "Morris Town Jany 22d 1777," in ibid., vol. 8:123. Custis was Martha Washington's son from her first marriage. While Custis was technically Washington's stepson, he was more frequently referred to as Washington's ward. Custis joined Washington's headquarters staff as a civilian aide-de-camp during the siege of Yorktown, against his mother's wishes. He died at Yorktown from a "camp fever" (probably typhus) on November 5, 1781. Custis was twenty-six when he died. He purchased valuable property during his short lifetime, including the land which is now Ronald Reagan Washington National Airport.

53. Letter from General Nathanael Greene to Governor Nicholas Cooke, dated "Morristown, Jan.10, 1777," in Richard K. Showman et al., eds., *The Papers of General Nathanael Greene*, 13 vols. (Chapel Hill: University of North Carolina Press, 1976), vol. 2:5.

54. Captain George Smith, *An Universal Military Dictionary* (London: Printed for J. Millan, 1779), 202.

55. The French adopted the fighting style of their Indian allies, whose primary type of offensive action was the ambush. See René Chartrand, *Raiders from New France: North American Forest Warfare Tactics* (Oxford: Osprey Publishing 2019), 11.

56. Letter from General Nathanael Greene to Governor Nicholas Cooke of Rhode Island dated "Morristown, Jan 10, 1777" in Showman, *The Papers of General Nathanael Greene*, vol. 2:5.

57. Charles Stedman, *The History of the Origin, Progress, and Termination of the American War*, 2 vols. (London: Printed for the Author, 1794), vol. 1:241–42.

58. George Washington to Major General Philip Schuyler, dated "Head Quarters Morris Town 18th Jany 1777," in Abbot et al., *The Papers of George Washington, Revolutionary War Series*, vol. 8:99.

59. Howard H. Peckham, ed., *The Toll of Independence: Engagements and Battle Casualties of the American Revolution* (Chicago: University of Chicago Press, 1974), 29; and Fischer, *Washington's Crossing*, 418.

60. Harry M. Ward, *General William Maxwell and the New Jersey Continentals* (Westport, CT: Praeger Publishing, 1997), 54.

61.   Extract of a letter from Raritan, New Jersey, dated January 23, 1777, in the January 29 issue of the newspaper *Pennsylvania Journal and Weekly Advertiser*. See William S. Stryker, ed., *Documents Relating to the Revolutionary History of the State of New Jersey*, 5 vols. (Trenton: John L. Murphy Publishing Company, 1901–1917), vol. 1:275.

62.   Thomas Allen Glenn, *William Churchill Houston (a New Jersey Militia Officer)* (Norristown, PA: Privately printed, 1903), 26–28.

63.   David Hackett Fischer, *Washington's Crossing* (New York: Oxford University Press, 2004), 355.

64.   Colin G. Calloway, *The Indian World of George Washington* (New York: Oxford University Press, 2018), 152.

65.   Peckham, *The Toll of Independence: Engagements and Battle Casualties of the American Revolution*, 30. The origin of Quibbletown's name was a dispute by different religious denominations regarding whether the Sabbath should be observed on Saturday or Sunday.

66.   George Washington to Nicholas Cooke, dated "Morris Town January the 20th 1777," in Abbot et al., *The Papers of George Washington, Revolutionary War Series*, vol. 8:114.

67.   Smith, *An Universal Military Dictionary*, 245.

68.   Letter from George Washington to John Hancock, dated "Genl Green's Quarters [Fort Lee, New Jersey] Novr 14th 1776," in Abbot et al., *The Papers of George Washington, Revolutionary War Series*, vol. 7:155.

69.   Mark Puls, *Henry Knox, Visionary General of the American Revolution* (New York: Palgrave Macmillan, 2008), 86–87.

70.   The development of a smallpox vaccine has eradicated the disease worldwide. However, there was an outbreak of smallpox in October 1945 in a U.S. Army hospital in Nagoya, Japan. The episode showed the alarming rate that the disease could spread. A total of twenty-two American service personnel contracted smallpox during a short period of time. The doctors at the hospital noted that every soldier who contracted smallpox had visited the hospital for some other medical problem. One of the affected men was a messenger who stopped in the hospital's laboratory for a cup of coffee and returned two weeks later with smallpox. See Murray Dworetzky, MD, "Smallpox, October 1945," *New England Journal of Medicine* 346, no. 17 (April 2002), 329.

71.   Elizabeth A. Fenn, *Pox Americana: The Great Smallpox Epidemic of 1775–82* (New York: Hill and Wang, 2001), 3.

72.   Amy Lynn Filsinger, "George Washington and the First Mass Military Inoculation," Science Reference Services, Library of Congress, 2007, www.loc.gov/rr/scitech/GW&smallpoxinoculation.

73.   Cassandra Pybus, *Epic Journeys of Freedom* (Boston: Beacon Press, 2006), 41.

74.   Letter from Thomas Jefferson to John Page, dated May 25, 1766, in Julian P. Boyd et al, eds., *The Papers of Thomas Jefferson*, 45 vols. to date (Princeton, NJ: Princeton University Press, 1950–present), vol. 1:21.

75. Smith, *An Universal Military Dictionary*, 81–82.

76. A millwright in colonial America was a person who constructed wind- or water-powered machinery used, for example, to grind flour or cut wood.

77. The complete title of the book Putnam mentioned is *The Field Engineer, Translated from the French* by John Muller. It was first published in London in 1759. John Muller was hired as an instructor at the Royal Military Academy, Woolwich, when it opened in 1741. In 1754 he was named the headmaster of the Academy. A fine point of history is that author Patrick K. O'Donnell gives a different title to the engineering book that Putnam borrowed. O'Donnell identified the book as *The Attack and Defense of Fortified Places* by John Muller, published in 1747. See Patrick K. O'Donnell, *The Indispensables* (New York: Atlantic Monthly Press, 2021), 201.

78. Rowena Buell, ed., *The Memoirs of Rufus Putnam* (Boston: Houghton, Mifflin and Company, 1903), 57–59.

79. *Diary of Frederick Mackenzie*, 2 vols. (Cambridge, MA: Harvard University Press, 1930), vol. 1:109.

80. Extract of a Letter from Fort Lee, in Peter Force, ed., *American Archives*, Fifth Series, vol. 3:741.

81. Letter from George Washington to John Hancock, dated "Camp above Trenton Falls, Decr 20th 1776," in Abbot et al., *The Papers of George Washington, Revolutionary War Series*, vol. 7:384.

82. Thaddeus Kościuszko was a Polish national. Unlike many of the Europeans who joined the Patriots, Kościuszko spoke fluent English. He attended a military school in Warsaw after which he was awarded a scholarship to attend the prestigious Ecole Royal Militaire (Royal Military School) in Paris. While in Paris, Thaddeus also studied painting and architecture at the Academie Royale de Peinture et de Sculpture (Royal Academy of Painting and Sculpture). He next attended the Ecole du Corps Royal du Génie Militaire (Royal Engineering School) located in Mézières, France. Kościuszko returned to Poland in 1774 to find the country in chaos. With no prospects to pursue his military career at home, Thadddeus returned to France. It was there that he met other ambitious young officers who were talking about the war in America. Perhaps with a letter of introduction to the American General Charles Lee (who served in the Polish Army), Kościuszko arrived in Philadelphia at his own expense in August 1776. He petitioned Congress for a commission on August 4. While he was waiting for an answer, he got a job as a civilian engineer with the Pennsylvania Committee of Defense and went to work fortifying the Delaware River. Impressed with his engineering skills, Kościuszko was commissioned as a colonel in the Continental Army by Congress on October 18, 1776.

83. Letter from George Washington to Gouverneur Morris, dated "White Plains July 24th 1778," in Abbot et al., *The Papers of George Washington, Revolutionary War Series*, vol. 16:154.

84. James Thomas Flexner, *The Young Hamilton* (Boston: Little, Brown and Company, 1978), 133. Hamilton's age is based on January 11, 1755, as the date of his birth.

85. Abbot et al., *The Papers of George Washington, Revolutionary War Series*, vol. 8:468.

86. Arthur Lefkowitz, *George Washington's Indispensable Men* (Mechanicsburg, PA: Stackpole Books, 2003), 11.

87. John C. Fitzpatrick, *The Spirit of the Revolution* (Boston: Houghton Mifflin Company, 1924), 60.

88. Irving, *Life of George Washington*, vol. 3:8.

89. Lefkowitz, *George Washington's Indispensable Men*, 293.

CHAPTER 4

1. Don N. Hagist, *Noble Volunteers* (Yardley, PA: Westholme Publishing, 2020), 129.

2. Leonard Lundin, *Cockpit of the Revolution: The War for Independence in New Jersey* (Princeton: Princeton University Press, 1940), 222.

3. Edward G. Lengel, *General George Washington* (New York: Random House, 2005), 210.

4. R. Arthur Bowler, *Logistics and the Failure of the British Army in America* (Princeton, NJ: Princeton University Press, 1975), 92–93.

5. While their rations varied based on the availability of provisions, the daily allowance of food for a British solider at the time of the American Revolution typically consisted of one and a half pounds of bread, one pound of beef or a half pound of pork, one-quarter pint of peas or one ounce of rice, one ounce of butter, and one and a half gills of rum. The quality and quantity of their victuals was better than that of an average laborer in Britain at the time. Captain Johann Ewald of the Hessel-Kassel Jäger Corps gave a list of the foods his company received from the British during the winter of 1777: "The men continued to live on salted beef and pork, peas, butter, rice and flour along with the best English beer." See Joseph P. Tustin, trans. and ed., *Diary of the American War: A Hessian Journal by Captain Johann Ewald* (New Haven, CT: Yale University Press, 1979), 55.

6. Thomas J. McGuire, *The Philadelphia Campaign*, 2 vols. (Mechanicsburg, PA: Stackpole Books, 2006–2007), vol. 1:28.

7. Charles Stedman, *The History of the Origin, Progress and Termination of the American War*, 2 vols. (London: Printed for the author, 1794), vol. 1:240.

8. Thomas Jones, *History of New York During the Revolutionary War*, 2 vols. (New York: New York Historical Society, 1879), vol. 1:171.

9. Arthur Lefkowitz, *Colonel Hamilton and Colonel Burr* (Lanham, MD: Stackpole Books, 2020), 92–93.

10. Tustin, *Diary of the American War: A Hessian Journal by Captain Johann Ewald*, 52. Writing to Governor Nicholas Cooke of Rhode Island from Morristown on January 28, 1777, Greene said that "I inspected our Posts at Bound Brook yesterday." See Richard K. Showman et al., eds., *The Papers of General*

Nathanael Greene, 13 vols. (Chapel Hill: University of North Carolina Press, 1976), vol. 2:15.

11.   David B. Mattern, *Benjamin Lincoln and the American Revolution* (Columbia: University of South Carolina Press, 1995), 36.

12.   "Return of the American Forces in New Jersey," dated "15 Mar 1777," in W. W. Abbot et al., eds., *The Papers of George Washington, Revolutionary War Series*, 28 vols. to date (Charlottesville: University of Virginia Press, 1985–2021), vol. 8:576.

13.   Letter dated "Baskenridge [New Jersey] Feb 20, 1777," from General Nathanael Greene to George Washington in Showman et al., *Papers of the Nathanael Greene*, vol. 2:24 and vol. 2:25, note 5. The number of troops in the 8th Pennsylvania Regiment is based on the March 15, 1777, "Return of the American Forces in New Jersey." The report lists 342 men in the regiment. See Abbot et al., *The Papers of George Washington, Revolutionary War Series*, vol. 8:576.

14.   Abbot et. al., *The Papers of George Washington, Revolutionary War Series*, vol. 8:576 and Showman et al., *The Papers of General Nathanael Greene*, vol. 2:27 note 6. Seven hundred Massachusetts militiamen arrived in Morristown in mid-January, engaged for two months. Their two months of active duty probably began on the day that they mustered in Massachustts.

15.   Stedman, *The History of the Origin, Progress, and Termination of the American War*, vol. 1:241.

16.   Letter from General Nathanael Greene to George Washington, dated "camp [Middlebrook, New Jersey] May 31, 1779," in Showman et al., *The Papers of General Nathanael Greene*, vol. 4:108.

17.   Letter from General Nathanael Greene to his brother Jacob Greene, dated "Valley Forge, January 3, 1778," in Charles Royster, *A Revolutionary People at War* (Chapel Hill: University of North Carolina Press, 1979), 116.

18.   Showman et al., *The Papers of General Nathanael Greene*, vol. 2:25, note 1.

19.   T. Cole Jones, *Captives of Liberty* (Philadelphia: University of Pennsylvania Press, 2020), 30. The Hessian officer was Captain Johann Ewald.

20.   Tustin, *Diary of the American War: A Hessian Journal by Captain Johann Ewald*, 108.

21.   Letter from George Washington to Colonel William Woodford dated Cambridge, 10 November, 1775 in Abbot et al., *The Papers of George Washington, Revolutionary War Series*, vol. 2:346–47. Washington's letter to Colonel Woodford included his recommended books: "As to the manual exercise, the evolutions and maneuvers of a regiment, with other knowledge necessary to the soldiers, you will acquire them from those authors, who have treated upon these subjects, among whom Bland (the newest edition) [Humphrey Bland, *A Treatise of Military Discipline*, 9th edition, [London, 1762] stands foremost; also an Essay on the Art of War [Lancelot Théodore, comte du Turpin de Crissé, *An Essay on the Art of War*, translated by Captain Joseph Otway, London, 1761]; *Instructions for Officers*, lately published at Philadelphia [Roger Stevenson, *Military Instructions for Officers Detached in the Field*, Philadelphia edition, 1775]; the *Partisan* [Captain de Jeney,

The Partisan: or, the Art of Making War in Detachment Translated from the French of [*sic*] Mr. De Jeney *by an Officer in the Army*, London, 1760]; Young [Major William Young, *Manoeuvres* [*sic*], *or Practical Observations on the Art of War*, London, 1771]; and others."

22. "Aspects of Educating and Training Military Personnel," *U.S. Marine Corps Journal*, vol. 9, no. 1 (Quantico, VA: Marine Corps University Press, 2018), 87.

23. Mr. [Captain] de Jeney, *The Partisan: or, The Art of Making War in Detachment Translated from the French of Mr. De Jeney by an Officer of the Army* (London: R. Griffiths, 1760), 115.

24. Major William Young, *Manoeuvres, or Practical Observations on the Art of War* (London: J. Millan, 1771), 21–22.

25. For an account of how the French adopted Indian warfare during the colonial wars that preceded the American Revolution, see René Chartrand, *Raiders from New France* (New York: Osprey Publishing, 2019).

26. Stedman, *The History of the Origin, Progress, and Termination of the American War*, vol. 1:240.

27. Matthew H. Spring, *With Zeal and With Bayonets Only* (Norman: University of Oklahoma Press, 2008), 15.

28. The *Pennsylvania Journal and Weekly Advertiser* issue for January 29, 1777, in William S. Stryker, ed., *Documents Relating to the Revolutionary History of the State of New Jersey*, five vols. (Trenton, NJ: John L. Murphy Publishing Co., 1901–1917), vol. 1:274.

29. Letter from Major General Lord Stirling, dated "Baskenridge [Baskingridge, New Jersey] Febr. 26, 1777," in Abbot et al., *The Papers of George Washington, Revolutionary War Series*, vol. 8:448.

30. Spanktown is sometimes cited as an earlier name for Rahway, New Jersey. However, the Revolutionary War period map by William Faden shows Spanktown as a separate area two miles southwest of Rahway. The name Spanktown is said to originate from an early settler in the region publicly taking his wife across his knee and spanking her.

31. In a letter to his brother, John Augustine Washington, dated "Morris Town Feby 24th, 1777," His Excellency mentioned "a foraging party of the enemy and a party collected from our posts." See Abbot et al., *The Papers of George Washington, Revolutionary War Series*, vol. 8:440. The colonial village of Samptown was located at the present-day intersection of Sampton and Clinton Avenues in South Plainfield, New Jersey. In 1776 the village consisted of a sawmill, a gristmill, and ten houses.

32. While often referred to as Captain Peebles, he was a lieutenant during the winter of 1777. Peebles joined the British Army as a lieutenant in March 1770. He was twenty-two years old at the time. He had contemplated becoming a physician before joining the army and had some medical training. Peebles was promoted to captain in October 1777. See Steven M. Baule, *British Army Officers*

Who Served in the American Revolution (Westminster, MD: Heritage Books, Inc., 2008), 142.

33. Gruber, *John Peebles' American War*, 95–97.

34. Peter Kemble, *Journals of Lieutenant Colonel Stephen Kemble* (the Kemble Papers), 2 vols. (New York: Collections of the New York Historical Society for the Years 1883 and 1884, published in 1883 and 1884), vol. 1:110.

35. Gruber, *John Peebles' American War*, 97.

36. Harry Miller Lydenberg, ed., *Archibald Robertson, His Diaries and Sketches in America* (New York: New York Public Library, 1930), 124.

37. Letter from George Washington to John Augustine Washington, dated "Morris Town Feby 24th, 1777," in Abbot et al., *The Papers of George Washington, Revolutionary War Series*, vol. 8:440.

38. Letter from British Colonel Allan Maclean to Alexander Cummings, in Mrs. Stuart-Wortley, *A Prime Minister and His Son, from the Correspondence of the 3rd Earl of Bute and of Lt.-General The Hon. Sir Charles Stuart* (London: John Murray, 1925), 107. Alexander Cummings was a Scottish watchmaker and instrument inventor. He was also friends with his fellow Scotsman Colonel Maclean. Cummings is best known as the inventor of the modern flush toilet, for which he was granted a patent in 1775. Prior to Cummings's design, flush toilets emitted a foul smell. He solved the problem with an S-shaped bend in the waste pipe that trapped water and prevented foul orders from re-entering the toilet. His design continues to be used in modern toilets.

39. The *Pennsylvania Journal and Weekly Advertiser* issue for March 5, 1777, in Stryker, *Documents Relating to the Revolutionary History of the State of New Jersey*, vol. 1:307–8.

40. Gruber, *John Peebles' American War*, 98.

41. David Hackett Fischer, *Washington's Crossing* (New York: Oxford University Press, 2004), 357.

42. Joseph Lee Boyle, ed., *From Redcoat to Rebel: The Thomas Sullivan Journal* (Bowie, MD: Heritage Books, Inc., 1997), 114.

43. Abbot et al., *The Papers of George Washington, Revolutionary War Series*, vol. 8:280, note 7.

44. John E. Elting, ed., *Military Uniforms in America: The Era of the American Revolution* (San Rafael, CA: Presidio Press, 1974), 64.

45. Philip R. N. Katcher, *Encyclopedia of British, Provincial, and German Army Units 1775–1783* (Harrisburg, PA: Stackpole Books, 1973), 116.

46. Ernst Kipping, *The Hessian View of America 1776–1783* (Monmouth Beach, NJ: Philip Freneau Press, 1971), 6.

47. Don Higgenbotham, *The War of American Independence* (New York: Macmillan Publishing, 1971), 132.

48. J. G. Rosengarten, *The German Allied Troops in the North American War of Independence* (Albany, NY: Joel Munsell's Sons, 1893), 16.

49. Tustin, *Diary of the American War: A Hessian Journal by Captain Johann Ewald*, 51–52.

50. Ibid., 53–54.

51. Howard H. Peckham, ed., *The Toll of Independence* (Chicago: University of Chicago Press, 1974), 32.

52. Brian Connell, *The Savage Years: The Struggle for North America* (New York: Harper & Brothers Press, 1959), 163.

53. Letter from Colonel William Harcourt to his father, Earl Harcourt, dated "[New] Brunswick, March 17th, 1777," in Henry Steele Commager and Richard B. Morris, *The Spirit of Seventy-Six*, 2 vols. (New York: Bobbs-Merrill Company, 1958), vol. 1:524.

54. Fischer, *Washington's Crossing*, 382.

55. Letter from Allan Maclean to Alexander Cummings, dated New York, February 19, 1777, in Stuart-Wortley, *A Prime Minister and His Son, for the Correspondence of the 3rd Earl of Bute and of Lt.-General The Hon. Sir Charles Stuart*, 105–6.

CHAPTER 5

1. *The Journal of Nicholas Cresswell* (New York: Dial Press, 1924), 229.

2. Thomas Jones, *History of New York During the Revolutionary War*, vol. 1:139–40.

3. E. Wayne Carp, *To Starve the Army at Pleasure* (Chapel Hill: University of North Carolina Press, 1984), 19.

4. Ibid., 20.

5. A more detailed definition of "military logistics" is the planning and implementation of the production, procurement, storage, transportation, distribution, and movement of personnel, supplies, and equipment. See Frank Gaynor, ed., *New Military and Naval Dictionary* (New York: Philosophical Library, 1951), 153.

6. Joseph Lee Boyle, ed., *From Redcoat to Rebel: The Thomas Sullivan Journal* (Bowie, MD: Heritage Books, Inc., 1997), 108.

7. Ernst Kipping, trans., and Samuel Steele Smith, ed., *At General Howe's Side: The Diary of General William Howe's Aide-De-Camp, Captain Friedrich von Muenchhausen* (Monmouth Beach, NJ: Philip Freneau Press, 1974), 10.

8. Ibid.

9. John W. Jackson, *The Pennsylvania Navy* (New Brunswick, NJ: Rutgers University Press, 1974), 17.

10. Jack Coggins, *Ships and Seamen of the American Revolution* (Harrisburg, PA: Stackpole Books, 1969), 104.

11. Gardner W. Allen, *A Naval History of the American Revolution*, 2 vols. (Boston: Houghton Mifflin Company, 1913) vol. 1:167.

12. Kipping and Smith, *At General Howe's Side: The Diary of... Captain Friedrich von Muenchhausen*, 10.

13. Letter from Brigadier General Alexander McDougall to George Washington, dated "Peekskill 29th March 1777," in W. W. Abbot et al., eds., *The Papers of George Washington, Revolutionary War Series*, 28 vols. to date (Charlottesville: University of Virginia Press, 1985–2021), vol. 9:17.

14. Kipping and Smith, *At General Howe's Side: The Diary of... Captain Friedrich von Muenchhausen*, 10.

15. Letter from Colonel Ann Hawkes Hay to George Washington, dated "Haverstraw, Sunday evening 8 OClock [*sic*] March 23d 1777," in Abbot et al., *The Papers of George Washington, Revolutionary War Series*, vol. 8:621.

16. William Bell Clark, et al., eds., *Naval Documents of the American Revolution*, 13 vols. to date (Washington, DC: Department of the Navy, 1964–2019), vol. 8:234.

17. James R. Case, *An Account of Tryon's Raid on Danbury* (Danbury, CT: privately published, 1937), 13.

18. This phrase is from an anonymously written satirical poem about Joseph Galloway published during the war. See Frank Moore, *Diary of the American Revolution, from Newspapers and Original Documents*, 2 vols. (New York: Privately Published, 1865), vol. 1:369. The first stanza of the poem reads:

Gall'way has fled, and join'd the venal Howe
To prove his baseness, see him cringe and bow;
A traitor to his country, and its laws,
A friend of tyrants and their cursed cause
Unhappy wretch! Thy interest [property] must be sold,
For continental, not for polish'd gold;
To sink [lose] the money, thou thyself cried down,
And stabb'd thy country to support the crown.

19. Case, *An Account of Tryon's Raid on Danbury*, 12.

20. Moore, *Diary of the American Revolution, from Newspapers and Original Documents*, 2 vols. (New York: Privately Printed, 1865), vol. 1:428.

21. Ibid.

22. The account of the Danbury Expedition is in the form of a letter published with the title "A British Officer's Account of the Danbury Raid." It appears in William Bell Clark et al., *Naval Documents of the American Revolution*, vol. 8:455–57. In favor of Captain Archibald Robertson as the author of the letter is that he was an engineer on the expedition. As an engineer, Robertson would not have been attached to any regiment. The fact that the letter does not focus on the exploits of any specific regiment that was on the mission indicates that it was not written by a regimental officer. In addition, Robertson's diary includes a lengthy account of the expedition, which resembles the letter written by "an unknown British officer." Robertson's diary account of the Danbury Expedition is in Harry Miller Lydenberg, ed., *Archibald Robertson, His Diaries and Sketches in America* (New York: New York Public Library, 1930), 126–28. Also compelling is that the anonymous British officer's account of the raid concludes with timely information regarding the military

situation in New Jersey. Captain Robertson was stationed in New Jersey prior to the Danbury Expedition and returned to New Jersey following his participation in the raid.

23. Captain George Smith, *An Universal Military Dictionary*, 81. It is incorrect to refer to the British Army engineers as the Royal Engineers during the American Revolution. They were honored with that distinction by King George III in 1787.

24. Case, *An Account of Tryon's Raid on Danbury*, 15.

25. Clark et al., *Naval Documents of the American Revolution*, vol. 8:456.

26. Lydenberg, *Archibald Robertson, His Diaries and Sketches in America*, 127.

27. Clark et al., *Naval Documents of the American Revolution*, vol. 8:456.

28. Scheer, *Private Yankee Doodle, Being a Narrative... by Joseph Plumb Martin*, 63.

29. Letter from General John Sullivan to the New Hampshire Committee of Safety, dated May 5, 1777, in Ottis G. Hammond, ed., *Letters and Papers of Major General John Sullivan*, 3 vols. (Concord, NH: New Hampshire Historical Society, 1930–1939), vol. 1:334.

30. Kipping and Smith, *At General Howe's Side: The Diary of... Captain Friedrich von Muenchhausen*, 12.

31. Clark et al., *Naval Documents of the American Revolution*, vol. 8:456.

32. Sybil Ludington is celebrated as the "teenage girl Paul Revere." The story of her April 16, 1777, nighttime ride first appeared in Martha J. Lamb's "History of the City of New York," published in 1880. The tale, according to Ms. Lamb, is that there was no courier available to warn Sybil's father's militia regiment that British troops were in Danbury. Sybil, who was sixteen years old at the time, decided that she would ride through the countryside to call out the militia. Sybil rode for forty miles with a stick in her hand, banging on the doors of the militiamen to turn out. Ms. Lamb claimed that the story was based on her extensive research and discussions with the Ludington family. However, there is no known documentation to support the event. But despite the lack of evidence, there are Sybil Ludington statues in Carmel, New York, and Danbury, Connecticut; various historic markers; a yearly marathon race that traces part of her alleged route; and a U.S. postage stamp issued in 1975 showing Sybil riding through the night with a stick in her hand.

33. James Thomas Flexner, *The Traitor and the Spy* (New York: Harcourt, Brace & Company, 1953), 125–26.

34. Stephen Brumwell, *Turncoat: Benedict Arnold and the Crisis of American Liberty* (New Haven, CT: Yale University Press, 2018), 79; Christopher Ward, *The War of the Revolution*, 2 vols. (New York: The Macmillan Company, 1952), vol. 2:494; and Clark et al., *Naval Documents of the American Revolution*, vol. 8:456. Congress voted that a horse properly caparisoned should be presented to General Arnold, in their name, as a token of his gallant conduct on that day.

35. Lydenberg, *Archibald Robertson, His Diaries and Sketches in America*, 128.

36. The other Continental Army officer who also fought in the French Revolution was John Skey Eustace.

37. Ira D. Gruber, ed., *John Peebles' American War* (Mechanicsburg, PA: Stackpole Books, 1998), 111.

38. Clark et al., *Naval Documents of the American Revolution*, vol. 8:456.

39. Scheer, *Private Yankee Doodle, Being a Narrative... by Joseph Plumb Martin*, 62.

40. Undated letter from Lieutenant General Charles Stuart to his father, in Mrs. E. Stuart-Wortley, ed., *A Prime Minister and His Son, Letters from Lieutenant-General Charles Stuart* (London: John Murray, 1925), 94.

41. Peter Kemble, *Journals of Lieutenant-Colonel Stephen Kemble* (the Kemble Papers), 2 vols. (New York: Collections of the New York Historical Society for the Years 1883 and 1884, published in 1883–1885), vol. 1:115.

42. Lydenberg, *Archibald Robertson, His Diaries and Sketches in America*, 131.

43. R. [Roger] Lamb, *Journal of Occurrences During the Late American War* (Dublin: Wilkinson & Courtney, 1809), 216.

44. *Historical Anecdotes, Civil and Military: In a Series of Letters Written from America in the years 1777 and 1778, to different persons in England...* (London: Printed by J. Bew, 1779), 40.

45. Joseph P. Tustin, trans. and ed., *Diary of the American War: A Hessian Journal by Captain Johann Ewald* (New Haven, CT: Yale University Press, 1979), 55.

46. Letter from Major General Benjamin Lincoln to General George Washington, dated "Bound Brook, April 12th 1777," in Abbot et al., *The Papers of George Washington, Revolutionary War Series*, vol. 9:133.

47. The Queens Bridge was a substantial wooden structure completed in 1767. It was financed through a lottery.

48. Thomas J. McGuire, *The Philadelphia Campaign*, 2 vols. (Mechanicsburg, PA: Stackpole Books, 2006–2007), vol. 1:22.

49. David B. Mattern, *Benjamin Lincoln and the American Revolution* (Columbia: University of South Carolina Press, 1997), 37.

50. Boyle, *From Redcoat to Rebel: The Thomas Sullivan Journal*, 108.

51. T. E. Davis, *The Battle of Bound Brook* (Bound Brook, NJ: Chronicle Steam Printery, 1895), 9–10.

52. Moore, *Diary of the American Revolution from Newspapers and Original Documents*, vol. 1:416.

53. John Fiske, *The American Revolution*, 2 vols. (Boston: Houghton, Mifflin and Company, 1891), vol. 1:147.

54. James Graham, *The Life of General Daniel Morgan* (New York: Derby & Jackson, 1856), 28.

55. Danske Dandridge, *Historic Shepherdstown* (Charlottesville, VA: Michie Company, 1910), 79.

56. Paul H. Smith, ed., *Letters of Delegates to Congress, 1774–1789*, 26 vols. (Washington, DC: Library of Congress, 1976–2000), vol. 1:497.

57. Arthur Lefkowitz, *Benedict Arnold's Army* (New York: Savas Beatie LLC, 2008), 83–87.

58. Ibid., 247.

59. Graham, *The Life of General Daniel Morgan*, 103.

60. Arthur Lefkowitz, *Benedict Arnold in the Company of Heroes* (El Dorado Hills, California: Savas Beatie LLC, 2012), 105.

61. Letter from Brigadier General Benedict Arnold to George Washington, dated "Ticonderoga November 6th 1776," in Abbott et al., *The Papers of George Washington, Revolutionary War Series*, vol. 7:93.

62. Letter from George Washington to John Hancock, dated "Head Quarters, Heights of Harlem Septr 28th 1776," in ibid., vol. 6:421.

63. Robert K. Wright, Jr., *The Continental Army* (Washington, DC: Superintendent of Documents, 1983), 289.

64. Manuscript letter from Captain Willian Dansey dated "Piscataway in the Jerseys, April 20th, 1777," in the collection of the Delaware Historical Society.

65. Howard H. Peckham, ed., *The Toll of Independence: Engagements and Battle Casualties of the American Revolution* (Chicago: University of Chicago Press, 1974), 33–34.

66. Gruber, *John Peebles' American War*, 111.

67. The "Return of the Grand Army" dated May 3, 1777, lists 273 men in Morgan's 11th Virginia Regiment vs. the May 21 "Return," which shows 441 men in the unit. See Charles H. Lesser, ed., *The Sinews of Independence* (Chicago: University of Chicago Press, 1976), 45–46.

68. Fred Anderson Berg, *Encyclopedia of Continental Army Units* (Harrisburg, PA: Stackpole Books, 1972), 77.

69. General Orders dated "Head Quarters, Middle-Brook, June 1st 1777," in Abbot et al., *The Papers of George Washington, Revolutionary War Series*, vol. 9:578.

70. Letter from George Washington to George Clinton. dated "Head Quarters Camp at Cross Roads [Pennsylvania], August 16, 1777," in ibid., vol. 10:636.

71. Wright, *The Continental Army*, 82.

72. "Account of the Attempt on Quebeck," which appeared in the *New York Gazette* (no date given). Author is stated as "A Soldier." See Peter Force, ed., *American Archives*, Fourth Series, vol. 4:708. Christian Febiger was never an officer in the army of Denmark, but attended a military academy there. Febiger was a businessman living in Boston prior to the war. He joined the Patriot cause and fought at the Battle of Bunker Hill. He was twenty-nine years old when he was appointed the adjutant (administration officer) of the Arnold Expedition.

73. Orders from George Washington to Colonel Daniel Morgan, dated Middlebrook, New Jersey, 13 June 1777, in Abbot et al., *The Papers of George Washington, Revolutionary War Series*, vol. 10:31.

74. Letter from Brigadier General Peter Muhlenberg to George Washington, dated "Febry 23d 1777," in ibid., vol. 8:428.

75. George F. Scheer and Hugh F. Rankin, *Rebels and Redcoats* (New York: World Publishing Company, 1957), 67.

76. Colonel George Hanger, *To All Sportsmen* (London: J. J. Stockdale, 1814), 199–200.

77. Harold L. Peterson, *Arms and Armor in Colonial America* (New York: Bramhall House, 1956), 201.

78. Garry Wills, *A Necessary Evil* (New York: Simon & Schuster, 1999), 30.

79. Peterson, *Arms and Armor in Colonial America*, 202.

80. An account by Henry Bedinger in Dandridge, *Historic Shepherdstown*, 78.

81. Letter from Silas Deane to Elizabeth Deane, dated Philadelphia, June 3, 1775, in Smith, *Letters of Delegates to Congress*, vol. 1:436.

82. *National Park Service Historical Handbook: Morristown* (National Park Service, 2002), 11. www.nps.gov/parkhistory/online_books/hh/7/hh7b.htm.

83. Kipping and Smith, *At General Howe's Side: The Diary of... Captain Friedrich von Muenchhausen*, 12.

84. Gruber, *John Peebles' American War*, 108.

85. Jones, *History of New York During the Revolutionary War*, vol. 1:177.

86. The Apthorp Mansion was built by Charles Wade Apthorp in 1764. The mansion sat on thirteen acres in the northwest section of upper Manhattan. The building stood on the intersection of present-day West 91st Street and Columbus Avenue. Apthorp was a Loyalist who fled Manhattan early in the Revolutionary War. He was able to return to Manhattan at the end of the war and reclaim his property. The house was used for various purposes through the eighteenth century, including a beer hall. It was demolished in 1891. Anyone interested in visiting a "General Howe slept here" mansion should visit Stenton, a mansion occupied by Howe during the British occupation of Philadelphia.

CHAPTER 6

1. Dave Richard Palmer, *The Way of the Fox: American Strategy in the War for America 1775–1783* (Westport, CT: Greenwood Press, 1975), 3. Retired Lieutenant General Palmer's book was republished in an amended edition as *George Washington's Military Genius* (Washington, DC: Regnery Publishing, 2012).

2. Email correspondence from Katie Blizzard, research editor, Center for Digital Editing, the Papers of George Washington.

3. Noah Webster, *An American Dictionary of the English Language*, 4th edition (New York: S. Converse, 1830), 797.

4. Letter from George Washington to Brigadier General William Maxwell, dated "Falls of Delaware South Side 8th Decemr 1776," in W. W. Abbot et al., ed., *The Papers of George Washington, Revolutionary War Series*, 28 vols. to date (Charlottesville: University of Virginia Press, 1985–2021), vol. 7:278.

5. Letter from the Pennsylvania Board of War to George Washington, dated Philadelphia, April 19th 1777, in ibid., vol. 9:213.

6. Captain George Smith, *An Universal Military Dictionary* (London: J. Millan, 1779), 241.

7. Commission from the Continental Congress, dated Philadelphia, 19 June 1775, in Abbot et al., *The Papers of George Washington, Revolutionary War Series*, vol. 1:7–8.

8. Letter from John Jay to George Washington, dated "Philadelphia, 10th may 1779," in ibid., vol. 2:425–26.

9. Palmer, *George Washington's Military Genius*, 64.

10. James Thomas Flexner, *The Young Hamilton* (Boston: Little, Brown and Company, 1978), 143.

11. "A Proclamation by the King, for Suppressing Rebellion and Sedition," August 23, 1775 in Peter Force, ed., *American Archives*, Fourth Series, vol. 3:240–41.

12. Beckles Willson, *George III, As Man, Monarch and Statesman* (London: T. C. & E. C. Jack, 1907), 329.

13. Beckles Willson, *The Life and Letters of James Wolfe* (London: William Heinemann, 1909), 104.

14. Gerald Saxon Brown, *The American Secretary: The Colonial Policy of Lord George Germain, 1775–1778* (Ann Arbor: University of Michigan Press, 1963), 38.

15. Andrew Jackson O'Shaughnessy, *The Men Who Lost America* (New Haven, CT: Yale University Press, 2013), 175.

16. "Sackville (afterwards Germain), Lord George," The History of Parliament (1689–1922) website, http://www.historyofparliamentonline.org/volume/1754-1790/member/sackville-lord-george-1716-85.

17. Louis Marlow, *Sackville of Drayton; Lord George Sackville till 1770, Lord George Germain 1770–1782, Viscount Sackville from 1782* (Totowa, New Jersey: Rowman & Littlefield, 1973), 179.

18. Francis Vinton Greene, *The Revolutionary War and the Military Policy of the United States* (New York: Charles Scribner's Sons, 1911), 264.

19. William B. Willcox, *The American Rebellion: Sir Henry Clinton's Narrative of His Campaigns* (New Haven, CT: Yale University Press, 1953), 8.

20. Willson, *George III*, 318; Americanrevolution.org, chapter 2.

21. David Hackett Fischer, *Washington's Crossing* (New York: Oxford University Press, 2004), 359.

22. Christopher Hibbert, *Redcoats and Rebels* (London: The Folio Society, 2006), 217.

23. John Fiske, *The American Revolution*, 2 vols. (Boston: Houghton, Mifflin and Company, 1896), vol. 1:168.

24. Letter from James Warren to John Adams. dated "Watertown, Octr. 20th: 1775," in Robert J. Taylor, *Papers of John Adams, General Correspondence Series*, 20 vols. to date (Cambridge, MA: Harvard University Press, 2003–2020), vol. 3:218.

25. Dave R. Palmer, *The Way of the Fox*, 44.

26. Willcox, *The American Rebellion: Sir Henry Clinton's Narrative of His Campaigns*, 11.

27. Article titled "Britannia Rules the Bronx" in the Bronx River Alliance website. bronxriver.org.

28. Lieutenant General John Burgoyne, *A State of the Expedition from Canada, As Laid Before the House of Commons* (London, J. Almon, 1780), appendix 8.

29. Kevin J. Weddle, *The Compleat Victory: Saratoga and the American Revolution* (New York: Oxford University Press, 2021), 59.

30. The earliest known reference to "Gentleman Johnny" was a book titled *Gentleman Johnny Burgoyne* by F. J. Hudleston, published by the Bobbs-Merrill Company in 1927. For Burgoyne's opulent lifestyle, see Richard M. Ketchum, *Saratoga: Turning Point of America's Revolutionary War* (New York: Holt Paperbacks, 1999), 87.

31. Burgoyne, *A State of the Expedition from Canada, As Laid Before the House of Commons*, 9.

32. For a list of the troops stationed in Canada assigned to Burgoyne, see the letter from Lord Germain to Carleton dated "Whitehall, 26th March 1777," in Burgoyne, *State of the Expedition from Canada*, appendix 15.

33. Ibid., appendices 15–16.

34. Ibid., appendix 16.

35. Jeff Shaara, *The Glorious Cause* (New York: Ballantine Books, 2003), 375.

36. David G. Martin, *The Philadelphia Campaign* (New York: Combined Books, 1993), 16.

37. Eric Schnitzer and Don Troiani, *Campaign to Saratoga—1777* (Guilford, CT: Stackpole Books, 2019), 16–17.

38. Hoffman Nickerson, *The Turning Point of the Revolution or Burgoyne in America* (Boston: Houghton Mifflin Company, 1928), 97–98.

39. Edward Barrington De Fonblanque, *Political and Military Episodes... Derived from the Life and Correspondence of the Right Hon. John Burgoyne* (London: Macmillan & Company, 1876), 233.

40. Brown, *The American Secretary: The Colonial Policy of Lord George Germain, 1775–1778*, 111.

41. Edward H. Tatum, ed., *The American Journal of Ambrose Serle*, (San Marino, CA: Huntington Library, 1940), 114.

42. John S. Pancake, *1777: The Year of the Hangman* (Tuscaloosa: University of Alabama Press, 1977), 94.

43. Leonard Lundin, *Cockpit of the Revolution: The War for Independence in New Jersey* (Princeton, NJ: Princeton University Press, 1940), 309.

44. Thomas J. McGuire, *The Philadelphia Campaign, Brandywine and the Fall of Philadelphia* (Mechanicsburg, PA: Stackpole Books, 2006), 5.

45. Ernst Kipping, trans., and Samuel Steele Smith, ed., *At General Howe's Side: The Diary of General William Howe's Aide-De-Camp, Captain Friedrich von Muenchhausen* (Monmouth Beach, NJ: Philip Freneau Press, 1974), 12.

46. Piers Mackesy, *The War for America* (Cambridge, MA: Harvard University Press, 1964), 111.

47. K. G. Davies, ed., *Documents of the American Revolution 1770–1783, Colonial Office Series*, 21 vols. (Shannon: Irish University Press, 1972–1981), vol. 14:64–65.

48. Letter from General Sir William Howe to Lord George Germain, dated 2 April, New York [1777], in ibid., vol. 14:64.

49. *Historical Anecdotes, Civil and Military: In a Series of Letters* (London: J. Bew, 1779), 5.

50. Eric Robson, ed., *Letters from America 1773 to 1780* (New York: Barnes & Noble, Inc., 1951), 38, note 4.

51. Letter from General Sir William Howe to General Sir Guy Carleton, dated April 1777 and marked confidential, in Davies, *Documents of the American Revolution 1770–1783, Colonial Office Series,* vol. 16:66.

52. Ira D. Gruber, *John Peebles' American War* (Mechanicsburg, PA: Stackpole Books, 1998), 117. James Moncrief graduated in 1762 from the Royal Military Academy at Woolwich, England. Upon graduating he was appointed a captain in the Royal Engineers. Moncrief served in various campaigns during the American Revolution. Probably his best-known service during the war was as the commanding officer of the Black Pioneers, a black noncombat Loyalist unit involved in construction projects. Consisting of escaped or emancipated slaves, its members had the motto "Liberty to Slaves" embroidered on their uniforms.

53. Robert Francis Seybolt, *A Contemporary British Account of General Sir William Howe's Military Operations in 1777* (Worcester, MA: Davis Press, 1931), 6. The author of this diary is unknown but described by Mr. Seybolt as "Apparently, it is the diary of an officer attached to the British General Staff, an eye-witness of many of the events which he describes."

54. Letter from George Washington to Major General Nathanael Greene, dated "Morris Town May 27th 1777," in Abbot et al., *The Papers of George Washington, Revolutionary War Series,* vol. 9:539.

55. Major General Nathanael Greene used this term in a May 28, 1777, letter to Congressman Samuel Adams to describe General Howe's activities. See Richard K. Showman et al., ed., *The Papers of General Nathanael Greene,* 13 vols. (Chapel Hill: University of North Carolina Press, 1976), vol. 2:100.

56. Circular to the Brigade Commanders, dated "Head Quarters, Morris Town May 20th 1777," in Abbot et al., *The Papers of George Washington, Revolutionary War Series,* vol. 9:483–84, and note on p. 484.

CHAPTER 7

1. Joseph P. Tustin, trans. and ed., *Diary of the American War: A Hessian Journal by Captain Johann Ewald* (New Haven, CT: Yale University Press, 1979), 58.

2. Dave R. Palmer, *The Way of the Fox: American Strategy in the War for America 1775–1783* (Westport, Connecticut: Greenwood Press, 1975), 134.

3. James Kirby Martin and Mark Edward Lender, *A Respectable Army: The Military Origins of the Republic, 1763–1789* (Wheeling, IL: Harlan Davidson, Inc., 1982), 81.

4.   Edward G. Lengel, *General George Washington: A Military Life* (New York: Random House, 2005), 210. Also see Paul David Nelson, *General James Grant* (Gainesville: University of Florida Press, 1993), 113. Nelson's book had a more detailed account of Grant's comments, which were contained in a letter he wrote to his friend Richard Rigby, who was a member of the British House of Commons. In the same letter Grant wrote, "These shabby, contemptible people pop at every man they see upon the road—They don't assemble in large bodies, never stay two nights in a place and tis impossible to catch them."

5.   Letter from Major General Nathanael Greene to George Washington, dated "Bound Brook, My 24, 1777," in Abbot et al., *The Papers of George Washington, Revolutionary War Series*, vol. 9:516.

6.   Captain George Smith, *An Universal Military Dictionary* (London: J. Millan, 1779), 219.

7.   For example, the authoritative *Papers of George Washington* made this mistake. Their reference to the 1777 Middlebrook encampment reads, "The new encampment was laid out in the adjoining village of Middlebrook, N.J." See Abbot et al, *The Papers of George Washington, Revolutionary War Series*, vol. 9:516, note 4.

8.   Letter from George Washington to Major General Benedict Arnold, dated "Head Quarters Camp Middle Brook, June 17th 1777," in ibid., vol. 10:59.

9.   Charles H. Lesser, ed., *The Sinews of Independence* (Chicago: University of Chicago Press, 1976), 46–47.

10.   Instructions to Major General John Sullivan, dated Morristown, 15 May 1777, in Abbot et al., *The Papers of George Washington, Revolutionary War Series*, vol. 9:436–37.

11.   Ibid.

12.   A. A. Boom, "Report on the Middlebrook Encampment" (Somerset County Historical Society, 1975).

13.   Letter from George Washington to John Augustine Washington, dated "Camp at Middle brook, June 29th 1777," in Abbot et al., *The Papers of George Washington, Revolutionary War Series*, vol. 10:149.

14.   Harry M. Ward, *Duty, Honor or Country, General George Weedon and the American Revolution* (Philadelphia: American Philosophical Society, 1979), 89.

15.   Smith, *An Universal Military Dictionary*, 243.

16.   Harold L. Peterson, *The Book of the Continental Soldier* (Harrisburg, PA: Stackpole Books, 1968), 153.

17.   The order to remove all the boats along the Delaware River from Trenton to Coryell's Ferry was written on May 30, 1777 by Washington's aide-de-camp Alexander Hamilton. See H. C. Syrett, ed., *The Papers of Alexander Hamilton*, 4 vols. (New York: Columbia University Press, 1961), vol. 1:258.

18.   David G. Martin, *The Philadelphia Campaign* (New York: Combined Books, 1993), 24.

19.   A. A. Boom, "Report on the Middlebrook Encampment." A concentration of American artillery and their artillery park is identified as being near Vosseller

Avenue in the Erskine map number 55 by Captain Scull, titled "The Road from Quibbletown to Amboy; and places by bearing" in the collection of the New York Historical Society.

20. George C. Neumann and Frank J. Kravic, *Collector's Illustrated Encyclopedia of the American Revolution* (Texarkana, TX: Scurlock Publishing Company, 1975), 259.

21. B. J. Lossing, *Pictorial Field Book of the Revolution*, 2 vols. (New York: Harper Brothers, 1850–1852), vol. 1:333–34.

22. Lillian B. Miller, ed., *The Selected Papers of Charles Willson Peale*, 4 vols. (New Haven, CT: Yale University Press, 1983–1996), vol. 1:236.

23. An Officer of the Army (attributed to British Army Captain William Hall), *The History of the Civil War in America, Vol. 1* (London: T. Payne and Son and J. Sewell, 1780), 290.

24. R. Arthur Bowler, *Logistics and the Failure of the British Army in America* (Princeton, NJ: Princeton University Press, 1975), 94.

25. Edward H. Tatum, ed., *The American Journal of Ambrose Serle* (San Marino, CA: Huntington Library, 1940), 226.

26. Tatum, *The American Journal of Ambrose Serle*, 230.

27. Ira D. Gruber, ed., *John Peebles' American War* (Mechanicsburg, PA: Stackpole Books, 1998), 115.

28. Ernst Kipping, trans., and Samuel Steele Smith, ed., *At General Howe's Side: The Diary of General William Howe's Aide-De-Camp, Captain Friedrich von Muenchhausen* (Monmouth Beach, NJ: Philip Freneau Press, 1974), 14; and G. D. Scull, ed., *The Montresor Journals, the Journal of Captain John Montresor* (New York: New York Historical Society for the Year 1881, published in 1882), 421.

29. Martin, *The Philadelphia Campaign*, 23.

30. George Washington to Major General Israel Putnam, dated "Head Quarters Middle Brook 12th June 1777," in Abbot et al., *The Papers of George Washington, Revolutionary War Series*, vol. 10:16.

31. Kipping and Smith, *At General Howe's Side: The Diary of... Captain Friedrich von Muenchhausen*, 60, note 13.

32. Ibid., 16.

33. Ibid.

34. G. D. Scull, *The Montresor Journals, the Journal of Captain John Montresor*, 422. It was not unusual for the British to leave their tents behind to be able to move faster. They built "wigwams" made of tree boughs at night.

35. Letter from General Sir William Howe to Lord George Germain dated 5 July, New York in K. G. Davies, *Documents of the American Revolution, Colonial Office Series*, 21 vols. (Shannon: Irish University Press, 1972–1981), vol. 14: 127.

36. Tustin, *Diary of the American War: A Hessian Journal by Captain Johann Ewald*, 66–67; Harry Miller Lydenberg, ed., *Archibald Robertson, His Diaries and Sketches in America* (New York: New York Public Library, 1930), 136.

37. Kipping and Smith, *At General Howe's Side: The Diary of... Captain Friedrich von Muenchhausen*, 61.

38. Ibid., 16.

39. Mrs. E. Stuart-Wortley, ed., *A Prime Minister and His Son, Letters from Lieutenant-General Charles Stuart* (London: John Murray, 1925), 110.

40. Tustin, *Diary of the American War: A Hessian Journal by Captain Johann Ewald*, 64.

41. Gruber, *John Peebles' American War*, 116.

42. The Annie Van Liew House is owned by the nonprofit Meadows Foundation. The foundation's website (www.themeadowsfoundation.org/franklin -inn) states, "During the Revolutionary War, British General Charles Cornwallis took over Annie Van Liew's house using it as his headquarters for five days in 1777." An article in the New Jersey newspaper, the *Star-Ledger* (see www.nj.com/special-projects/index) goes further, claiming that "Howe and Cornwallis made the house of Annie Van Liew in the village on the east side of the Millstone [present-day East Millstone: not a village at the time of the Revolutionary War] their headquarters."

43. Tustin, *Diary of the American War: A Hessian Journal by Captain Johann Ewald*, 67.

44. Gruber, *John Peebles' American War*, 116. Also spelled as General Leopold Phillipe von Heister, he was unpopular with General Howe. Under pressure from the British government, von Heister was relieved of his command by the Landgrave of Hessen-Kassel. His order to return home arrived on June 23, 1777.

45. Smith, *An Universal Military Dictionary*, 205.

46. Octavius Pickering, *The Life of Timothy Pickering*, 4 vols. (Boston: Little, Brown and Company, 1867–1873), vol. 1:142. Timothy Pickering (1745–1829) was the adjutant general of the Continental Army in 1777. Octavius was his son.

47. Henry Cabot Lodge, ed., *André's Journal, An Authentic Record of the Movements and Engagements of the British Army in America from June 1777 to November 1778 as Recorded from Day to Day by Major John André*, 2 vols. (Boston: Bibliophile Society, 1903), vol. 1:37.

48. Ibid., 40.

49. Orders to Colonel Daniel Morgan, dated Middlebrook, N.J., 13 June 1777, in Abbot et al., *The Papers of George Washington, Revolutionary War Series*, vol. 10:31.

50. Letter from Lieutenant Colonel Robert H. Harrison [one of Washington's aides-de-camp] to General Sullivan, dated June 12, 1777, in Otis G. Hammond, ed. *Letters and Papers of Major-General John Sullivan*, 3 vols. (Concord, NH: New Hampshire Historical Society, 1930–1939), vol. 1:383.

51. Letter from George Washington to Major General John Sullivan, dated "Morris Town March 15th 1777," in Abbot et al., *The Papers of George Washington, Revolutionary War Series*, vol. 8:580.

52. Letter from General Washington to General Sullivan, dated June 14, 1777, in Hammond, *Letters and Papers of Major-General John Sullivan*, vol. 1:389.

53. Ibid.

54. Letter from Lieutenant Colonel Tench Tilghman [aide-de-camp to Washington] to General Sullivan, dated "Head Quarters Middle Brook 18 June 1777," in ibid., vol. 1:395.

55. Letter from George Washington to Major General William Heath, dated "Morris Town July 27 1777," in Abbot et al., *The Papers of George Washington, Revolutionary War Series*, vol. 10:438.

56. Letter from George Washington to Major General Benedict Arnold, dated "Head Quarters Camp Middle Brook, June 17th 1777," in ibid., vol. 10:59.

57. Ibid.

58. An Officer of the Army, *The History of the Civil War in America, Vol. 1*, 291.

59. Thomas Jones, *History of New York During the Revolutionary War*, 2 vols. (New York: New York Historical Society, 1879), vol. 1:188.

60. Ibid.

61. Washington Chauncey Ford, et al., eds., *Journals of the Continental Congress 1774–1789*, 34 vols. (Washington, DC: U.S. Government Printing Office, 1904–1937), vol. 8:464.

62. Edward W. Richardson, *Standards and Colors of the American Revolution* (Philadelphia: University of Pennsylvania Press, 1982), 2.

63. Kevin J. Weddle, *The Compleat Victory: Saratoga and the American Revolution* (New York: Oxford University Press, 2021), 193.

64. Letter from Tench Tilghman (aide-de-camp to Washington) to General Sullivan, dated June 18, 1777, in Hammond, *Letters and Papers of Major-General John Sullivan*, vol. 1:393.

65. Lodge, *John André's Journal*, 40.

66. Kipping and Smith, *At General Howe's Side: The Diary of... Captain Fredrich von Muenchhausen*, 18.

67. Lodge, *John André's Journal*, 42–43.

68. Tatum, *The American Journal of Ambrose Serle*, 233.

69. Excerpts from a poem entitled "General Howe's Letter," in Everett T. Tomlinson, *In the Camp of Cornwallis* (New York: Grosset & Dunlap, 1902), 351. The poem was published in the July 10, 1777, issue of the *Pennsylvania Post* newspaper.

CHAPTER 8

1. G. D. Scull, ed., *The Montresor Journals, the Journal of Captain John Montresor* (New York: New York Historical Society for the Year 1881, published in 1882), 423.

2. *The Journal of Nicholas Cresswell* (New York: Dial Press, 1924), 242.

3. The *Pennsylvania Journal*, June 25, 1777 issue, in William S. Stryker, ed., *Documents Relating to the Revolutionary History of the State of New Jersey*, 5 vols. (Trenton: John L. Murphy Publishing Company, 1901–1917), vol. 1:405.

4. Howard H. Peckham, ed., *The Toll of Independence: Engagements and Battle Casualties of the American Revolution* (Chicago: University of Chicago Press, 1974), 36.

5. Scull, *The Montresor Journals, the Journal of Captain John Montresor*, 423.

6. William Gordon, *The History of the Rise, Progress and Establishment of the Independence of the United States of America: Including an Account of the Late War*, 4 vols. (London: Charles Dilly, 1788), vol. 2:472–73. William Palfrey was a prewar Boston merchant and wartime aide to Washington. He was the paymaster general of the Continental Army in 1777. Palfrey was lost at sea in 1780. William Gordon (1726–1807) was a minister and probably best remembered for allegedly reporting a derogatory comment made by Alexander Hamilton during the war. Gordon claimed that Hamilton said in a Philadelphia tavern in 1779 that "it was high time for the people to rise, join General Washington and turn Congress out of doors." Young Hamilton was incensed, claiming the story was a lie. He challenged Gordon to a duel. Commenting on the incident, historian John C. Miller in his 1960 Hamilton biography (*Hamilton, Portrait in Paradox*, 39) said, "Had not the Reverend William Gordon worn the cloth, it is likely that he would have been obliged to answer Hamilton over a brace of pistols. But prone as were the young bucks of the day to settle their disputes in the manner approved by gentlemen [dueling], they felt a certain compunction about shooting down a man of God. Fortunately for Gordon, Hamilton shared this prejudice." Another fine point of history is that Thomas Jefferson owned a copy of Gordon's *History* which was included in the sale of his book collection to the Library of Congress in 1815 following the burning of Washington by the British during the War of 1812. The book is still in the Library's collection and one of its prized volumes.

7. Thomas J. McGuire, *The Philadelphia Campaign*, 2 vols. (Mechanicsburg, PA: Stackpole Books, 2006–2007), vol. 1:51.

8. The most important British stronghold on Staten Island facing the Arthur Kill was a tavern and adjacent ferry to New Jersey known collectively as the Blazing Star. The site was defended by 100 to 200 men according to a letter General Hugh Mercer wrote to Washington on July 16, 1776. The site of the Blazing Star tavern and ferry is in the present-day neighborhood of Rossville.

9. Scull, *The Montresor Journals*, 423–24.

10. Additional information about the *Vigilant* was included in an April 23, 1777, report that Admiral Richard Lord Howe sent from aboard the HMS *Eagle* anchored in New York City to Philip Stevens, secretary to the Admiralty Board, in London:

As one or more vessels of a construction to draw but little water and be at the same time capable of carrying heavy cannon, are wanted for the proposed operations of the ensuing campaign, it has been necessary to order the *Grand Duchess of Russia* transport to be taken for that purpose. The ship being one hundred and twenty feet keel and thirty-six feet beam will be reduced and fitted for carrying three six-pounders on each side upon the quarter deck, and seven twenty-four pounders in the same manner on the main deck: which she promises to be capable of supporting with facility. She will have two spare ports in addition for moving more guns over to either side occasionally. It is proposed that she should be manned with one hundred and twenty seamen and thirty Marines, officers included: And have two sea-officers in the character of lieutenants which are requisite from the nature of her intended appointment.

See William Bell Clark et al., eds., *Naval Documents of the American Revolution*, 13 vols. to date (Washington, DC: U.S. Government Printing Office, 1964–2019), vol. 8:407.

11. John W. Jackson, *The Pennsylvania Navy* (New Brunswick, NJ: Rutgers University Press, 1974), 97.

12. Letter from Admiral Lord Howe to the British Admiralty in London dated "5 June [1777] [HMS] *Eagle*, off New York," in K. G. Davies, *Documents of the American Revolution, Colonial Office Series*, 21 vols. (Shannon: Irish University Press, 1972–1981), vol. 14:103. The *Vigilant* was built in anticipation of the British seizing Philadelphia by sailing a fleet of warships and transports up the Delaware River from the seacoast. She would be used to bombard the rebel forts and gun batteries protecting the river.

13. Jackson, *The Pennsylvania Navy*, 97.

14. Letter from General Sir William Howe to Lord George Germain, dated 5 July [1777], in Davies, *Documents of the American Revolution, Colonial Office Series*, vol. 14:128.

15. Scull, *The Montresor Journals*, 424.

16. *Blackwood's Edinburgh Magazine*, vol. 132 (Edinburgh: William Blackwood and Sons, July–December 1882), 319.

17. Harold L. Peterson, *Arms and Armor in Colonial America* (New York: Bramhall House, 1956), 219. Harold Peterson (1922–1978) was widely considered in his day to be America's leading expert on military weapons. His professional career was as a curator with the National Park Service.

18. Bob Ruppert, "The First Fight of Ferguson's Rifle," *Journal of the American Revolution*, November 2014, 8, allthingsliberty.com/author/bob-ruppert.

19. Ibid., 9.

20. Letter from George Washington to Major General Stirling, dated "Head Quarters Middle Brook 23 June 1777," in Abbot et al., *The Papers of George Washington, Revolutionary War Series*, vol. 10:115.

21. "May 1777 roster of Forces under Commander-in-Chief General Washington [The Grand or Main Army]," in Charles H. Lesser, ed., *The Sinews of Independence* (Chicago: University of Chicago Press, 1976), 46.

22. A list of the Continental Army units in Lord Stirling's division is from *The Short Hills Battlefield Study* prepared by the American Battlefield Protection Program, National Park Service (Washington, DC: 2011), appendix 3.

23. Paul David Nelson, *The Life of William Alexander, Lord Stirling* (Tuscaloosa: University of Alabama Press, 1987), 106.

24. John André mentioned that Stirling's division had about seventy wagons. The two references are "Lord Stirling, who had taken post on a rising ground, in order (it was supposed) to cover the retreat of about seventy wagons," in Henry

Cabot Lodge, ed., *André's Journal, An Authentic Record of the Movements and Engagements of the British Army in America from June 1777 to November 1778 as Recorded from Day to Day by Major John André*, 2 vols. (Boston: Bibliophile Society, 1903), 46; and "We could see the wagons ascending the mountains," in ibid., 47.

25. *Memoir of Colonel Benjamin Tallmadge* (New York: Thomas Holman, 1858), 19–20.

26. Letter from George Washington to Major General Stirling, dated "Head Quarters Middle Brook 23 June 1777," in Abbot et al., *The Papers of George Washington, Revolutionary War Series*, vol. 10:115.

27. Octavius Pickering, *The Life of Timothy Pickering*, 4 vols. (Boston: Little, Brown and Company, 1867–1873), vol. 1:142.

28. Letter from George Washington to John Hancock, "dated New York Head Qrs Septr 8th 1776," in Abbot et al., *The Papers of George Washington, Revolutionary War Series*, vol. 6:249. Washington did not invent the term "war of posts." The term was used previously in a letter dated 5 July 1776 from Samuel Chase, a Maryland delegate to the Second Continental Congress, to his fellow delegate John Adams. Writing about the American defense of New York City, Chase said, "I am miserable when I reflect on the consequences of a defeat at New York. Act on the defensive, entrench, fortify and defend passes. Make it a War of Posts. Scramble thro this summer and for the next, it will be our own fault if we have not a probability for success." See "To John Adams from Samuel Chase, 5 July 1776," *Founders Online*, National Archives, https://founders.archives.gov/documents/Adams/06-04-02-0148.

29. Lieutenant Colonel Alexander Hamilton to Robert R. Livingston, letter dated 28 June 1777, in H. C. Syrett, ed., *The Papers of Alexander Hamilton*, 4 vols. (New York: Columbia University Press, 1961), vol. 1:274.

30. Captain George Smith, *An Universal Military Dictionary* (London: J. Millan, 1779), 241.

31. Charles Francis Adams, *Familiar Letters of John Adams and His Wife Abigail Adams during the Revolution* (New York: Hurd & Houghton, 1876), 305. Washington learned from experience to calmly reason with statesmen who meddled in army business but privately called them "chimney corner politicians" who sat in comfortable houses criticizing the beleaguered army.

32. Samuel Adams to Nathanael Greene, letter dated "Philad May 12 1777," in Paul H. Smith, ed., *Letters of Delegates to Congress, 1774–1789*, 26 vols. (Washington, DC: Library of Congress, 1976–2000), vol. 7:70.

33. Piers Mackesy, *The War for America 1775–1783* (Cambridge, MA: Harvard University Press, 1964), 125. Citing a more current example of this misconception, author Albert Louis Zambone stated in his book about Daniel Morgan: "The disembarkation of troops to Staten Island had been Howe's bait to draw Washington from cover; he [Howe] ferried them back to the mainland after nightfall." Albert Louis Zambone, *Daniel Morgan* (Yardley, PA: Westholme Publishing, 2018), 127.

34. Joseph P. Tustin, trans. and ed., *Diary of the American War: A Hessian Journal by Captain Johann Ewald* (New Haven, CT: Yale University Press, 1979), 68.

35. Ibid., 69.

36. Harry Miller Lydenberg, *Archibald Robertson, His Diaries and Sketches in America* (New York: New York Public Library, 1930), 138.

37. Ernst Kipping, trans., and Samuel Steele Smith, ed., *At General Howe's Side: The Diary of General William Howe's Aide-De-Camp, Captain Friedrich von Muenchhausen* (Monmouth Beach, NJ: Philip Freneau Press, 1974), 19.

38. Letter from General Sir William Howe to Lord George Germain, dated 5 July [1777] New York, in Davies, *Documents of the American Revolution, Colonial Office Series*, vol. 14:128.

39. Lydenberg, *Archibald Robertson, His Diaries and Sketches in America*, 138.

40. Tustin, *Diary of the American War: A Hessian Journal by Captain Johann Ewald*, 69.

41. Lodge, ed., *John André's Journal*, vol 1:47.

42. Peter Kemble, *Journals of Lieutenant Colonel Stephen Kemble* (the Kemble Papers), 2 vols. (New York: Collections of the New York Historical Society for the Years 1883 and 1884, published in 1883 and 1884), vol. 1:123.

43. British Lieutenant Colonel John Graves Simcoe (1752–1806) was a respected and knowledgeable military professional. He is erroneously depicted in movies and television series as ruthlessly attacking and killing American soldiers and civilians during the Revolutionary War.

44. Kipping and Smith, *At General Howe's Side: The Diary of... Captain Friedrich von Muenchhausen*, 19. The site of the skirmish between Morgan's pickets and Cornwallis's van took place at the present intersection of Route 1 and Green Street in Woodbridge.

45. "Manuscript Journal of the Grenadier Battalion Minnigerode, June 1777," William Van Vleck Lidgerwood Collection at the Morristown National Historic Park Library. Grenadiers were elite units made up of the tallest and strongest soldiers. The Grenadier Battaillon von Minnigerode was established in 1776 and commanded from 1776 to 1779 by Obristlieutenant Friedrich Ludwig Minnigerode. This unit was part of Colonel von Donop's command.

46. Kipping and Smith, *At General Howe's Side: The Diary of... Captain Friedrich von Muenchhausen*, 19.

47. Zambone, *Daniel Morgan*, 127.

48. Conway's position was a hilltop near the crossroads, presently occupied by a water tower.

49. Kipping and Smith, *At General Howe's Side: The Diary of... Captain Friedrich von Muenchhausen*, 19.

50. Revolutionary War scholar Ray Andrews pointed out that the British in Trenton could hear the cannon from Princeton on the morning of January 3, 1777. Princeton is twelve miles from Trenton. In an email to the author, Mr. Andrews commented that Washington was able to hear cannon and musket fire from four miles away.

51. Washington Irving, *Life of George Washington*, 5 vols. (New York: Charles T. Evans, 1856–1859), vol. 3:83. Historian Christopher Ward said that it was the cannon and musket fire coming from the intense fighting between the troops of Lord Stirling and Lord Cornwallis that alarmed Washington, who "retired at once to the Middlebrook passes, and regained the heights before the enemy cut him off." Christopher Ward, *The War of the Revolution*, 2 vols. (New York: Macmillan Company, 1952), vol. 1:329.

52. Letter from General Sir William Howe to Lord George Germain, dated 5 July [1777], New York, in Davies, *Documents of the American Revolution, Colonial Office Series*, vol. 14:128.

53. Douglas Southall Freeman, *George Washington, A Biography*, 7 vols. (New York: Charles Scribner and Sons, 1948), vol. 4:435.

54. Tustin, *Diary of the American War: A Hessian Journal by Captain Johann Ewald*, 69.

55. Kipping and Smith, *At General Howe's Side: The Diary of... Captain Friedrich von Muenchhausen*, 19.

56. Manuscript letter from Colonel Israel Shreve to John Stilley, dated "Turkey Gap, Sunday 29th June 1777," in *The Short Hills Battlefield Study*. The original letter is in the Israel Shreve Papers, Buxton Collection, Prescott Memorial Library, Louisiana Tech University, Transcribed by John U. Rees. Shreve was commander of the 2nd New Jersey Regiment during the Battle of Short Hills.

57. Anonymous American extract of a letter from "Camp at Middlebrook, June 28, 1777," reported in the *Pennsylvania Journal*, July 2, 1777 issue. See Stryker, *Documents Relating to the Revolutionary History of the State of New Jersey*, vol. 1:415–16.

58. T. Ewing, *Soldier of Valley Forge* (Yonkers, NY: privately printed, 1928), 18–19. George Ewing is listed as joining the 3rd New Jersey Regiment as an ensign (lowest commissioned officer, below the rank of lieutenant) on January 1, 1777. His regiment was attached to Maxwell's brigade during the Battle of Short Hills. He later served as a lieutenant in the New Jersey militia. There is no known reference to Ewing being a captain during the American Revolution.

59. Ira D. Gruber, ed., *John Peebles' American War* (Mechanicsburg, PA: Stackpole Books, 1998), 117–18.

60. Journal of the Hessian Fusilier Regiment von Lossberg, in *The Short Hills Battlefield Study*, appendix 2.

61. Kipping and Smith, *At General Howe's Side: The Diary of... Captain Friedrich von Muenchhausen*, 19.

62. Letter from Alexander Hamilton to Robert R. Livingston, dated 28 June 1777, in Syrett, ed., *The Papers of Alexander Hamilton*, vol. 1:274. Stirling's two brigades actually split up following the fighting in Ash Swamp, according to Henry Knox. In a letter to his wife, dated Camp Middlebrook, 29 June 1777, Knox wrote, "Lord Stirling retired to Westfield and Conway retired to the main body."

63. Lodge, ed., *John André's Journal*, vol 1:39.

64. Jason R. Wickersty, "A Shocking Havoc: The Plundering of Westfield, New Jersey, June 26, 1777," *Journal of the American Revolution*, July 21, 2015, 4, allthings l iberty.com/author/jason-r-wickersty.

65. Manuscript letter from Colonel Israel Shreve to Dr. Bodo Otto, dated 29 June 1777, in *The Short Hills Battlefield Study*. The original letter is in the Israel Shreve Papers, Buxton Collection, Prescott Memorial Library, Louisiana Tech University, Transcribed by John U. Rees.

66. Pickering, *The Life of Timothy Pickering*, vol. 1:145.

67. Letter from George Washington to John Langdon, dated "Head Qrs Middle Brook, June 29th 1777," in Abbot et al., *The Papers of George Washington, Revolutionary War Series*, vol. 10:147. John Langdon was a New Hampshire delegate to the Continental Congress.

68. Letter from General Sir William Howe to Lord George Germain, dated 5 July [1777], New York, in Davies, *Documents of the American Revolution, Colonial Office Series*, vol. 14:129.

69. Kipping and Smith, *At General Howe's Side: The Diary of... Captain Friedrich von Muenchhausen*, 20.

70. B. J. Lossing, *Pictorial Field Book of the Revolution*, 2 vols. (New York: Harper Brothers, 1850–1852). vol. 1:331.

71. Letter from George Washington to his brother John Augustine Washington, dated "Camp at Middle brook. June 29th 1777," in Abbot et al., *The Papers of George Washington, Revolutionary War Series*, vol. 10:150.

CHAPTER 9

1. For the number of "embarked troops," see the detailed list in Ernst Kipping, trans., and Samuel Steele Smith, ed., *At General Howe's Side: The Diary of General William Howe's Aide-De-Camp, Captain Friedrich von Muenchhausen* (Monmouth Beach, NJ: Philip Freneau Press, 1974), 22. For the number of ships in the invasion fleet, see G. D. Scull, ed., *The Montresor Journals, the Journals of Captain John Montresor* (New York: New York Historical Society for the Year 1881, published in 1882), 427.

2. Galloway, *Letters to a Nobleman, on the Conduct of the War in the Middle Colonies*, 69.

3. Kipping and Smith, *At General Howe's Side: The Diary of... Captain Friedrich von Muenchhausen*, 63, note 32.

4. Donald F. Johnson, *Occupied America: British Military Rule and the Experience of Revolution* (Philadelphia: University of Pennsylvania Press, 2020), 29.

5. William B. Willcox, ed., *The American Rebellion: Sir Henry Clinton's Narrative of His Campaigns, 1775–1782* (New Haven, CT: Yale University Press, 1954), 61.

6. Ibid., 59.

7. Ibid. Clinton said, "I thought it my duty to give them candidly though with diffidence, as far as my little experience—added by some knowledge of the theater of the war and the strength and resources of the enemy—could enable me."

8. Ibid., 61.

9. Ibid.

10. Ibid., 62.

11. Ibid., 63.

12. Kipping and Smith, *At General Howe's Side: The Diary of... Captain Friedrich von Muenchhausen*, 21.

13. Ibid.

14. Washington Irving, *Life of George Washington*, 5 vols. (New York: Charles T. Evans, 1856–1859), vol. 3:127. General Washington also used the trick of writing and signing spurious letters containing misleading information that was purposely meant to be intercepted by the British. One fraudulent letter that Washington wrote continues to trick otherwise astute historians. The letter was written by Washington to General Charles Lee from New Brunswick on November 30, 1776. On that date, only the narrow Raritan River separated Washington's beleaguered small army from 10,000 British troops just across the river. There was also no hope of the timely arrival of Patriot reinforcements. Yet Washington wrote Lee a letter on November 30 saying in part: "The advantages they have gained over us in the past have made them so proud and sure of success that they are determined to go to Philadelphia this winter.... Should they now really risk this undertaking then there is a great probability that they will pay dearly for it for I shall continue to retreat before them so as to lull them into security." This letter was intercepted (as planned) and found by nineteenth-century historian William S. Stryker "among the German records at Marburg, Germany." The letter is quoted without questioning its truthfulness in William S. Stryker, *The Battles of Trenton and Princeton* (Boston: Houghton, Mifflin and Company, 1898), 326; Henry Steele Commager and Richard C. Morris, eds., *The Spirit of Seventy-Six*, 2 vols. (New York: Bobbs-Merrill Company, 1958), vol. 1:499; and most recently in Kevin J. Weddle, *The Compleat Victory: Saratoga and the American Revolution* (New York: Oxford University Press, 2021), 11.

15. Letter from George Washington to John Rutledge, dated "Head Quarters Morris Town July 5th 1777," in W. W. Abbot et al., eds., *The Papers of George Washington, Revolutionary War Series*, 28 vols. to date (Charlottesville: University of Virginia Press, 1985–2020), vol. 10:198. Technically, John Rutledge's title when Washington wrote him was the president of South Carolina. Rutledge was elected the governor of South Carolina in 1779. For the quote "so long the object of watchful solicitude," see Irving, *Life of George Washington*, vol. 3:126.

16. Charles Francis Adams, *Studies Military and Diplomatic, 1775–1865* (New York: Macmillan Company, 1911), 153. The Trumbull quote also appears in Sydney George Fisher, *Struggle for American Independence*, 2 vols. (Philadelphia: J. B. Lippincott Company, 1908), vol. 2:71.

17. Kipping and Smith, *At General Howe's Side: The Diary of... Captain Friedrich von Muenchhausen*, 21.

18. Letter from Brigadier General David Forman to George Washington, dated "Freehold [New Jersey], July 6th 1777," in Abbot et al., *The Papers of George Washington, Revolutionary War Series*, vol. 10:207. Forman wrote: "The ships from Amboy and Prince's Bay are gone up to New York," and enclosed a list of the movements of ships in and around New York City. The list included "fifty vessels, some very large, had sailed from Princess Bay to New York." Ibid., vol. 10:208, note 1.

19. Kipping and Smith, *At General Howe's Side: The Diary of... Captain Friedrich von Muenchhausen*, 22.

20. Letter from Brigadier General David Forman to George Washington, dated "Shrewsbury [New Jersey] the 23rd of July 1777," in Abbot et al., *The Papers of George Washington, Revolutionary War Series*, vol. 1:374.

21. General Nathanael Greene to Governor Nicholas Cooke of Rhode Island, dated "Coryells Ferry [New Jersey] July 29th 1777," in Richard K. Showman et al., ed., *The Papers of General Nathanael Greene*, 13 vols. (Chapel Hill: University of North Carolina Press, 1976), vol. 2: 128.

22. Thomas J. McGuire, *The Philadelphia Campaign*, 2 vols. (Mechanicsburg, PA: Stackpole Books, 2006–2007), vol. 1:93.

23. Letter from Brigadier General David Forman to George Washington, dated "Freehold, [New Jersey], July 6th 1777," in Abbot et al., *The Papers of George Washington, Revolutionary War Series*, vol. 10:207–8.

24. Kipping and Smith, *At General Howe's Side: The Diary of... Captain Friedrich von Muenchhausen*, 23.

25. McGuire, *The Philadelphia Campaign*, vol. 1:95.

26. "An Anonymous Diary Recording Howe's Military Operations in 1777," in Commager and Morris, *The Spirit of Seventy-Six*, vol. 1:631–32.

27. Kipping and Smith, *At General Howe's Side: The Diary of... Captain Friedrich von Muenchhausen*, 23.

28. John Buchanan, *The Road to Valley Forge* (Hoboken, NJ: Wiley & Sons, Inc., 2004), 220.

29. Ibid.

30. Edward H. Tatum, ed., *The American Journal of Ambrose Serle* (San Marino, CA: Huntington Library, 1940), 239. Serle's journal entry for Friday, July 18, 1777, reads, "Expected to sail to-day, as the wind was fair. Called on Mr. Galloway on board the Alert Schooner, in which he sails with Capt. Montresor, chief engineer."

31. Galloway, *Letters to a Nobleman, on the Conduct of the War in the Middle Colonies*, 70.

32. John W. Jackson, *The Pennsylvania Navy 1775–1781: The Defense of the Delaware* (New Brunswick, NJ: Rutgers University Press, 1974), 105.

33. Tatum, ed., *The American Journal of Ambrose Serle*, 241.

34. John Buchanan, *The Road to Valley Forge*, 219.

35. July 13, 2004, letter from Eric Schnitzer to the author.
36. Willcox, *The American Rebellion: Sir Henry Clinton's Narrative of His Campaigns*, 66.
37. "The British Campaign for Philadelphia and the Occupation of Valley Forge in 1777," National Park Service, n.d., 2, https://www.nps.gov/vafo/learn/historyculture/upload/Philadelphia%20Campaign.pdf.
38. G. Grant Robertson, *England Under the Hanoverians* (New York: G. P. Putnam's Sons, 1921), 510.
39. Charles Royster, *A Revolutionary People at War* (Chapel Hill: The University of North Carolina Press, 1979), 225.
40. Aaron Sullivan, *The Disaffected: Britain's Occupation of Philadelphia during the American Revolution* (Philadelphia: University of Pennsylvania Press, 2019), 64.
41. Kenneth Silverman, *A Cultural History of the American Revolution* (New York: Thomas Y. Crowell Company, 1976), 329.
42. Irving, *Life of George Washington*, vol. 3:139–40.
43. Eric Schnitzer and Don Troiani, *Campaign to Saratoga—1777* (Guilford, CT: Stackpole Books, 2019), 263.
44. Eric Robson, *The American Revolution* (London: Batchworth Press, 1955), 136. I don't want to stand in the way of a good story, but Eric Schnitzer, the historian at Saratoga National Historical Park, was aghast when I showed him Robson's explanation for why General Vaughan returned to New York after burning Clermont. Eric Schnitzer had a different explanation for Vaughan's return to New York, in an email to the author:

Vaughan proceeded south after he heard of Burgoyne's surrender, the refusal of his pilots to proceed past Clermont, and increased sighting of militia forces on both sides of the river. Clinton's order to Vaughan to withdraw came to Vaughan's hands after he had initiated the move. Further, Clinton's orders were based upon the fact that Howe wanted reinforcements, forcing Clinton to abandon the entire expedition. Not that it mattered in the end—Burgoyne had already surrendered. How is any of that Clinton's fault? He left NY [New York City] as soon as he could, attacked as fast as he could and Vaughan went as far north as he could.

45. A letter from Lieutenant General Burgoyne to Lord George Germain, dated Albany, 20th October, 1777, in *A State of the Expedition From Canada as Laid Before the House of Commons by Lieutenant-General Burgoyne* (London, J. Almon, 1780), appendix 14.
46. "The Narrative of Lieut. Gen. Sir William Howe," in *A Committee of the House of Commons on the 19th of April, 1779, second edition* (London: S. Baldwin, 1780), 20.
47. Willcox, *The American Rebellion: Sir Henry Clinton's Narrative of His Campaigns*, 379.
48. Royster, *A Revolutionary People at War*, 116.

49. Benjamin Franklin joined Arthur Lee and Silas Deane in Paris in 1776. Designated the American commissioners, they were empowered to negotiate a treaty with France to enter the war as America's ally. Franklin drafted a proposal for a Franco-American alliance in December 1777. According to historian Robert Middlekauff, "on December 17, 1777, Vergennes [Charles Gravier, comte de Vergennes, the French foreign minister] agreed that France would recognize the United States and enter into an alliance." See Robert Middlekauff, *The Glorious Cause* (New York: Oxford University Press, 2005), 410.

50. James MacGregor Burns and Susan Dunn, *George Washington* (New York: Times Book division of Henry Holt and Company, 2004), 27.

51. Letter from George Washington to John Rutledge, dated "Morris Town July 5th 1777," in Abbot et al., *The Papers of George Washington, Revolutionary War Series*, vol. 10:199.

52. Mercy Otis Warren, *History of the Rise, Progress and Termination of the American Revolution*, 3 vols. (Boston: Manning and Loring, 1805), vol. 1:378–79. There is a different story to explain the ill will between Howe and Percy. In the alternate tale, Howe was told that there was 15,000 tons of hay in Newport, and Sir William told Percy to ship him a large quantity. Percy replied that Howe was misinformed and there was no more than 1,440 tons of hay in Newport. The dispute escalated, and Percy secured permission to return to England. For the hay story, see R. Arthur Bowler, *Logistics and the Failure of the British Army in America* (Princeton, NJ: Princeton University Press, 1975), 69–70.

53. Letter from Colonel Lewis Nicola to George Washington, dated "Fishkill [New York] 22 May 1782," *Founders Online*, National Archives, https://founders .archives.gov/documents/Washington/99-01-02-08500.

54. Letter from George Washington to Lewis Nicola, dated "Newburgh [New York] May 22d [17]82," *Founders Online*, National Archives, https://founders .archives.gov/documents/Washington/99-01-02-08501.

55. Johnson, *Occupied America: British Military Rule and the Experience of Revolution*, 98.

56. The poem cited was titled "A Tory Medley," attributed to Francis Hopkinson. See Silverman, *A Cultural History of the American Revolution*, 336.

57. James Kirby Martin and Mark Edward Lender, *A Respectable Army* (Wheeling, IL: Harlan Davidson, Inc., 1982), 81.

58. John Fiske, *The American Revolution*, 2 vols. (Boston: Houghton, Mifflin & Company, 1891), vol. 1:307.

59. Thomas Jones, *History of New York During the Revolutionary War*, 2 vols. (New York: New York Historical Society, 1879), vol. 1:121–22.

BIBLIOGRAPHY

MANUSCRIPTS AND UNPUBLISHED SOURCES
British Captain William Dansey Letters, Delaware Historical Society
The Joseph Tustin Papers, Bloomsbury University, Pennsylvania
Revolutionary War Pension and Land Bounty Records, National Archives

PRIMARY SOURCES
Adams, John. Adams, Charles Francis, ed. *The Works of John Adams, Second President of the United States*. 10 vols. Boston: Charles C. Little and James Brown, 1850–1856.

Adams, Samuel. Cushing, Harry Alonzo, ed. *The Writings of Samuel Adams*. 4 vols. New York: G.P. Putnam's Sons, 1904–1908.

Andre, John. Lodge, Henry Cabot, ed. *Andre's Journal. An Authentic Record of the Movements and Engagements of the British Army in America from June 1777 to November 1778*. 2 vols. Boston: Bibliophile Society, 1903.

Baurmeister, Adjutant General Major. Uhlendorf, Bernhard A., ed. *Revolution in America: Confidential Letters and Journals 1776–1784 of Adjutant General Major Baurmeister of the Hessian Forces*. New Brunswick, NJ: Rutgers University Press, 1957.

Burgoyne, Lieutenant-General John. *A State of the Expedition from Canada, As Laid Before the House of Commons*. London: J. Almon, 1780.

Burnaby, Andrew. *Travels Through the Middle Settlements in North America*. London: T. Payne, 1775.

Clark, William Bell, ed. *Naval Documents of the American Revolution*. 11 vols to date. Washington, DC: U.S. Government Printing Office, 1964–1996.

Clinton, Sir Henry. Willcox, William, ed. *The American Rebellion: Sir Henry Clinton's Narrative of His Campaigns, 1775–1782*. New Haven, CT: Yale University Press, 1954.

Cresswell, Nicholas. *The Journal of Nicholas Cresswell 1774–1777*. New York: The Dial Press, 1924.

Custis, George Washington Parke. *Recollections and Private Memoirs of Washington by His Adopted Son*. New York: Derby & Jackson, 1860.

Davies, K.G., ed. *Documents of the American Revolution 1770–1783*. Colonial Office Series, 21 vols. Shannon: Irish University Press, 1972–1981.

Ewald, Captain Johann. Tustin, Joseph P., ed. *Diary of the American War: A Hessian Journal by Captain Johann Ewald.* New Haven, CT: Yale University Press, 1979.

Ewing, T. *Soldier of Valley Forge.* Yonkers, NY: Privately printed, 1928.

Force, Peter and Clarke, M. St. Clair, eds. *American Archives, Consisting of a Collection of Authentick Records, State Papers, Debates and Letters and Other Notices of Publick Affairs, the Whole Forming a Documentary History of the Origin and Progress of the North American Colonies; of the Causes and Accomplishment of the American Revolution; and of the Constitution of Government for the United States, to the Final Ratification Thereof.* 4th series, 6 vols; 5th series, 3 vols. Washington, DC: M. St. Clair Clarke and Peter Force, 1837–1853.

Ford, Worthington C. et al., eds. *Journals of the Continental Congress 1774–1789.* 34 vols. Washington, DC: United States Government Printing Office, 1904–1937.

Galloway, Joseph. Attributed. *Letters to a Nobleman, on the Conduct of the War in the Middle Colonies.* London: J. Wilkie, 1779.

Graydon, Alexander. John Stockton Littell, ed. *Memoirs of His Own Time, by Alexander Graydon. With Reminiscences of the Men and Events of the Revolution.* Philadelphia: Lindsay and Blakiston, 1846.

Greene, Nathanael. Showman, Richard K. et al., eds. *The Papers of General Nathanael Greene.* 13 vols. Chapel Hill: The University of North Carolina Press, 1976–2005.

Hamilton, Alexander. Syrett, Harold C. and Cooke, Jacob E., eds. *The Papers of Alexander Hamilton.* 27 vols. New York: Columbia University Press, 1964–1981.

Heath, Major-General. *Memoirs of Major-General William Heath, Containing Anecdotes, Details of Skirmishes, Battles and Other Military Events During the American War.* Boston: I. Thomas and E.T. Andrews, 1798.

Historical Anecdotes, Civil and Military in a Series of Letters Written from America. London: Printed by J. Bew, 1779.

Jefferson, Thomas. Boyd, Julian P. et al., eds. *The Papers of Thomas Jefferson.* 45 vols. to date. Princeton, NJ: Princeton University Press, 1950–present.

Jones, Thomas. De Lancey, Edward Floyd, ed. *History of New York During the Revolutionary War.* 2 vols. New York: The New York Historical Society, 1879.

Howe, General Sir William. *The Narrative of Lieut. Gen. Sir William Howe, in a Committee of the House of Commons on the 19ᵗʰ of April, 1779.* London: S. Baldwin, 1780.

Kemble, Stephen. *Journals of Lieutenant-Colonel Stephen Kemble,* 2 vols. New York: New York Historical Society, 1883–1884.

Knox, Henry. Hamilton, Phillip, ed. *The Revolutionary War Lives and Letters of Lucy and Henry Knox.* Baltimore, MD: Johns Hopkins University Press, 2017.

Lee, General Charles. *The Lee Papers.* 4 vols. New York: The New York Historical Society, 1871–1874.

Lee, Henry. *Memoirs of the War.* 2 vols. Philadelphia: Bradford and Inskeep, 1812.

Leslie, Captain William. Gilchrist, Marianne M., ed. *Captain Hon. William Leslie (1751–1777): His Life, Letters and Commemoration.* Published in *Military Miscellany II.* Gloucestershire, UK: Sutton Publishing Limited for the Army Records Society, 2005.

Lesser, Charles H., ed. *The Sinews of Independence: Monthly Strength Reports of the Continental Army.* Chicago: University of Chicago Press, 1976.

Mackenzie, Captain Frederick. *Diary of Frederick Mackenzie.* 2 vols. Cambridge: MA: Harvard University Press, 1930.

Martin, Joseph Plumb. *A Narrative of Some of the Adventures, Dangers and Sufferings of a Revolutionary War Soldier*. Hallowell, ME: Glazier, Masters and Company, 1830. Republished: Scheer, George F., ed. *Private Yankee Doodle*. New York: Little, Brown and Company, 1962.

Mauduit, Israel. *Three Letters to Lord Viscount Howe*. London: Privately published, 1781.

Montresor, Captain John. Scull, G. D., ed. *The Montresor Journals, The Journal of Captain John Montresor*. New York: The New York Historical Society, 1882.

Moore, Frank. *Diary of the American Revolution from Newspapers and Original Documents*. 2 vols. New York: Privately printed, 1865.

Muenchhausen, Captain Levin Frederick Ernst von. Kipping, Ernst and Smith, Samuel Steele, eds. *At General Howe's Side, 1776–1778: The Diary of General William Howe's Aide de Camp, Captain Friedrich Von Muenchhausen*. Monmouth Beach, NJ: Philip Freneau Press, 1974.

Murray, Sir James. Robson, Eric, ed. *Letters from America, 1773–1780: Being the Letters of a Scots Officer, Sir James Murray, to His Home During the War of American Independence*. New York: Barnes & Noble, 1951.

Peebles, Captain John. Gruber, Ira D., ed. *John Peebles' American War: The Diary of a Scottish Grenadier, 1776–1782*. Mechanicsburg, PA: Stackpole Books, 1998.

Percy, Lieutenant General Hugh. Bolton, Charles Knowles, ed. *Letters of Hugh Earl Percy from Boston and New York, 1774–1776*. Boston: Charles E. Goodspeed, 1902.

Putnam, Rufus. Buell, Rowena, ed. *The Memoirs of Rufus Putnam*. Boston: Houghton, Mifflin and Company, 1903.

Rodney, Captain Thomas. *The Diary of Captain Thomas Rodney*. Wilmington, DE: The Historical Society of Delaware, 1888.

Robertson, Royal Engineer Archibald. Lydenberg, Harry Miller, ed. *Archibald Robertson, His Diaries and Sketches in America*. New York: New York Public Library, 1930.

Rush, Benjamin. Annotated by Biddle, Louis Alexander. *A Memorial Containing Travels Through Life or Sundry Incidents in the Life of Dr. Benjamin Rush Written by Himself*. Philadelphia: Privately published, 1905.

Secret Journals of the Acts and Proceedings of Congress. 4 vols. Boston: Thomas B. Wait, 1820. Volume one was cited.

Serle, Ambrose. Tatum, Edward H., ed. *The American Journal of Ambrose Serle*. San Marino, CA: The Huntington Library, 1940.

Smith, Paul H., ed. *Letters of Delegates to Congress 1774–1789*. 26 vols. Washington, DC: Library of Congress, 1976–2000.

Stryker, William S., ed. *Documents Relating to the Revolutionary History of the State of New Jersey*. 5 vols. Trenton, NJ: John L. Murphy Publishing Company, 1901–1917.

Stuart, Lieutenant-General the Honorable Sir Charles. Mrs. Stuart-Wortley, ed. *A Prime Minister and His Son, for the Correspondence of the 3rd Earl of Bute and of Lt.-General the Hon. Sir Charles Stuart*. London: John Burray, 1925.

Sullivan, Major-General John. Hammond, Otis G., ed. *Letters and Papers of Major-General John Sullivan, Continental Army*. 3 vols. Concord, NH: New Hampshire Historical Society, 1930–1939.

Sullivan, Thomas. Boyle, Joseph Lee, ed. *From Redcoat to Rebel: The Thomas Sullivan Journal*. Bowie, MD: Heritage Books, Inc., 1997.

Tallmadge, Benjamin. *Memoir of Colonel Benjamin Tallmadge*. New York: Thomas Holman, 1858.

Thacher, James. *Military Journal of the American Revolution*. Hartford, CT: Hurlbut, Williams & Company, 1862.

Washington, George. Abbot, W. W. et al., eds. *The Papers of George Washington, Colonial Series*. 10 vols. Charlottesville: University of Virginia Press, 1983–1995.

Washington, George. Abbot, W. W. et al., eds. *The Papers of George Washington, Revolutionary War Series*. 28 vols. to date. Charlottesville: University of Virginia Press, 1985–present.

Washington, George. Fitzpatrick, John C., ed. *The Diaries of George Washington*. 4 vols. Boston: Houghton Mifflin Company, 1925.

Washington, George. Sparks, Jared, ed. *The Writings of George Washington*. 12 vols. Boston: American Stationers Company, 1833–1837.

Wilkinson, General James. *Memoirs of My Own Times*. 3 vols. Philadelphia: Abraham Small, 1816.

SECONDARY SOURCES

Adams, Charles Francis. *Studies Military and Diplomatic 1775–1865*. New York: The Macmillan Company, 1911.

Adams, Hannah. *A Summary History of New England, from the First Settlement at Plymouth, to the Acceptance of the Federal Constitution, Comprehending a General Sketch of the American War*. Dedham, MA: Printed for the author by H. Mann and J. H. Adams, 1799.

Allen, Gardner W. *A Naval History of the American Revolution*. 2 vols. Boston: Houghton Mifflin Company, 1913.

An Officer of the Army. Attributed to British Army Captain William Hall. *The History of the Civil War in America*. London: T. Payne and Son and J. Sewell, 1780.

Atkinson, Rick. *The British Are Coming*. New York: Henry Holt and Company, 2019.

Baker, William S. *Itinerary of General Washington from June 15, 1775, to December 23, 1783*. Philadelphia: J. B. Lippincott Company, 1892.

Baule, Steven M., with Gilbert, Stephen. *British Army Officers Who Served in the American Revolution 1775–1783*. Westminster, MD: Heritage Books, Inc., 2003.

Berg, Fred Anderson. *Encyclopedia of Continental Army Units*. Harrisburg, PA: Stackpole Books, 1972.

Billias, George Athan. *General John Glover and His Marblehead Mariners*. New York: Henry Holt and Company, 1960.

Blanco, Richard L., ed. *The American Revolution, An Encyclopedia 1775–1783*. 2 vols. New York: Garland Publishing, Inc., 1993.

Bowler, Arthur R. *Logistics and the Failure of the British Army in America*. Princeton, NJ: Princeton University Press, 1975.

Brown, Gerald Saxon. *The American Secretary: The Colonial Policy of Lord George Germain, 1775–1778*. Ann Arbor: The University of Michigan Press, 1963.

Brumwell, Stephen. *Turncoat: Benedict Arnold and the Crisis of American Liberty*. New Haven, CT: Yale University Press, 2018.

Buchanan, John. *The Road to Valley Forge*. Hoboken, NJ: Wiley & Sons, Inc., 2004.

Burke, Edmund (attributed). *An Impartial History of the War in America, between Great Britain and Her Colonies: From Its Commencement to the End of the Year 1779; Exhibiting a Circumstantial, Connected and Complete Account of the Real Causes, Rise and Progress of the War, Interspersed with Anecdotes and Characters of the Different Commanders, and Accounts of Such Personages in Congress as Have Distinguished Themselves during the Contest, with an Appendix Containing a Collection of Interesting and Authentic Papers Tending to Elucidate the History.* London: R. Faulder... and J. Milliken, 1780.

Burns, James MacGregor and Dunn, Susan. *George Washington.* New York: Times Book division of Henry Holt and Company, 2004.

Calloway, Colin G. *The Indian World of George Washington.* New York: Oxford University Press, 2018.

Carp, E. Wayne. *To Starve the Army at Pleasure.* Chapel Hill: University of North Carolina Press, 1984.

Carrington, Henry. *Battles of the American Revolution.* New York: A.S. Barnes & Company, 1876.

Case, James R. *An Account of Tryon's Raid on Danbury.* Danbury, CT: Privately published, 1927.

Chartrand, René. *Raiders from New France: North American Forest Warfare Tactics, 17th–18th Centuries.* Oxford, UK: Osprey Publishing, 2019.

Coggins, Jack. *Ships and Seamen of the American Revolution.* Harrisburg, PA: Stackpole Books, 1969.

Commager, Henry Steele and Morris, Richard B., eds. *The Spirit of Seventy-Six.* 2 vols. New York: The Bobbs-Merrill Company, Inc., 1958.

Connell, Brian. *The Savage Years: The Struggle for North America.* New York: Harper & Brothers Press, 1959.

Crane, William J. *Edmund Burke's Speech on Conciliation with the American Colonies.* New York: D. Appleton and Company, 1900.

Dandridge, Danske. *Historic Shepherdstown.* Charlottesville, VA: The Michie Company, 1910.

Davis, T. E. *The Battle of Bound Brook.* Bound Brook, NJ: Chronicle Steam Printery, 1895.

De Fonblanque, Edward Barrington. *Political and Military Episodes . . . Derived from the Life and Correspondence of the Right Hon. John Burgoyne.* London: Macmillan & Company, 1876.

De Jeney, Captain. *The Partisan: Or the Art of Making War in Detachment, Translated from the French by an Officer of the Army.* London: R. Griffiths, 1760.

Ellet, Elizabeth F. *The Women of the American Revolution.* 2 vols. New York: Barker and Scribner, 1849.

Elting, John R. *The Battle of Bunker's Hill.* Monmouth Beach, NJ: Philip Freneau Press, 1975.

Elting, John R. ed. *Military Uniforms in America: The Era of the American Revolution.* San Rafael, CA: Presidio Press, 1974.

Fenn, Elizabeth A. *Pox Americana: The Great Smallpox Epidemic of 1775–1782.* New York: Hill and Wang, 2001.

Fischer, David Hackett. *Washington's Crossing.* New York: Oxford University Press, 2003.

Fiske, John. *The American Revolution.* 2 vols. Boston: Houghton Mifflin Company, 1891.

Fitzpatrick, John C. *The Spirit of the Revolution*. Boston: Houghton Mifflin Company, 1924.

Flexner, James Thomas. *George Washington in the American Revolution*. New York: Little, Brown and Company, 1968.

Flexner, James Thomas. *The Young Hamilton*. Boston: Little, Brown and Company, 1978.

Flexner, James Thomas. *The Traitor and the Spy*. New York: Harcourt, Brace & Company, 1953.

Freeman, Douglas Southall. *George Washington: A Biography*. 7 vols. New York: Charles Scribner's Sons, 1948–1957.

French, Allen. *The First Year of the American Revolution*. Boston: Houghton Mifflin Company, 1934.

Gaynor, Frank, ed. *The New Military and Naval Dictionary*. New York: The Philosophical Library, Inc., 1951.

Glenn, Thomas Allen. *William Churchill Houston*. Norristown, PA: Privately printed, 1903.

Gordon, William. *The History of the Rise, Progress, and Establishment of the Independence of the United States of America*. 4 vols. London: Printed for the author, 1788.

Graham, James. *The Life of General Daniel Morgan*. New York: Derby & Jackson, 1856.

Green, Francis Vinton. *The Revolutionary War and the Military Policy of the United States*. New York: Charles Scribner's Sons, 1911.

Hagist, Don N. *Noble Volunteers: The British Soldiers Who Fought the American Revolution*. Yardley, PA: Westholme Publishing, 2020.

Hanger, Colonel George. *To All Sportsmen*. London: J.J. Stockdale, 1814.

Heitman, Francis B. *Historical Register of Officers of the Continental Army*. Washington, DC: The Rare Book Shop Publishing Company, 1914.

Hibbert, Christopher. *Recoats and Rebels*. London: The Folio Society, 2006.

Higgenbotham, Don. *The War of American Independence*. New York: Macmillan Publishing, 1971.

Hopson, Edwin Nott. *Captain Daniel Neil*. Paterson, NJ: Braen Heusser Company, 1927.

Hudleston, F. J. *Gentleman Johnny Burgoyne: Misadventures of an English General in the Revolution*. Indianapolis: Bobbs-Merrill Company, 1927.

Huston, James A. *Logistics of Liberty*. Newark: University of Delaware Press, 1991.

Irving, Washington. *Diedrich Knickerbocker's History of New York from the Beginning of the World to the End of the Dutch Dynasty*. New York: Printed for the author, 1809.

Irving, Washington. *Life of George Washington*. 5 vols. New York: G.P. Putnam & Co., 1856–1859.

Jackson, John W. *The Pennsylvania Navy*. New Brunswick, NJ: Rutgers University Press, 1974.

Johnson, Donald F. *Occupied America: British Military Rule and the Experience of Revolution*. Philadelphia: University of Pennsylvania Press, 2020.

Johnston, Henry P. *The Campaign of 1776 Around New York and Brooklyn*. Brooklyn, NY: The Long Island Historical Society, 1878.

Jones, T. Cole. *Captives of Liberty*. Philadelphia: University of Pennsylvania Press, 2020.

Katcher, Philip R. N. *Encyclopedia of British, Provincial and German Army Units, 1775–1783*. Harrisburg, PA: Stackpole Books, 1973.

Ketchum, Richard M. *The Winter Soldiers*. New York: Doubleday Publishing, 1973.

Ketchum, Richard M. Saratoga: *Turning Point of America's Revolutionary War*. New York: Holt Paperbacks, 1999.

Kipping, Ernest. *The Hessian View of America 1776–1783*. Monmouth Beach, NJ: Philip Freneau Press, 1971.

Langworthy, Edward (attributed). *Memoirs of the Life of the Late Charles Lee*. London: J. S. Jordan, 1792.

Lamb, Roger. *Journal of Occurrences During the Late American War*. Dublin: Wilkinson & Courtney, 1809.

Lederer, Richard M. *Colonial American English*. Essex, CT: Verbatim Books, 1985.

Lefferts, Lieutenant Charles M. *Uniforms of the American, British, French and German Armies in the War of the American Revolution*. New York: The New York Historical Society, 1926.

Lefkowitz, Arthur. *The Long Retreat: The Calamitous American Defense of New Jersey 1776*. Metuchen, NJ: The Upland Press, 1998.

Lefkowitz, Arthur. *George Washington's Indispensable Men*. Mechanicsburg, PA: Stackpole Books, 2003

Lefkowitz, Arthur. *Benedict Arnold's Army*. New York: Savas Beatie LLC, 2008.

Lefkowitz, Arthur. *Benedict Arnold in the Company of Heroes*. El Dorado Hills, CA: Savas Beatie LLC, 2012.

Lefkowitz, Arthur. *Eyewitness Images from the American Revolution*. Gretna, LA: Pelican Publishing Company, 2017.

Lefkowitz, Arthur. *Colonel Hamilton and Colonel Burr*. Lanham, MD: Stackpole Books, 2020.

Lengel, Edward G. *General George Washington: A Military Life*. New York: Random House, 2005.

Lesser, Charles H. *The Sinews of Independence: Monthly Strength Reports of the Continental Army*. Chicago: The University of Chicago Press, 1976.

Londahl-Smidt, Donald M. *German Troops in the American Revolution (1) Hessen-Cassel*. Oxford, UK: Osprey Publishing, 2021.

Lossing, B. J. *Pictorial Field Book of the Revolution*. 2 vols. New York: Harper Brothers, 1850–1852.

Lundin, Leonard. *Cockpit of the Revolution: The War for Independence in New Jersey*. Princeton, NJ: Princeton University Press, 1940.

Mackesy, Piers. *The War in America 1775–1783*. Cambridge: MA: Harvard University Press, 1964.

MacNiven, Robbie. *British Light Infantry in the American Revolution*. Oxford, UK: Osprey Publishing, 2021.

Manders, Eric I. *The Battle of Long Island*. Monmouth Beach, NJ: Philip Freneau Press, 1978.

Marlow, Louis. *Sackville of Drayton: Lord George Sackville till 1770, Lord George Germain 1770–1782, Viscount Sackville from 1782*. Totowa, NJ: Rowman & Littlefield, 1973.

Marshall, John. *The Life of George Washington*. 5 vols. Philadelphia: C. P. Wayne, 1804–1807.

Martin, David G. *The Philadelphia Campaign*. Conshohocken, PA: Combined Books, Inc., 1993.

Martin, James Kirby and Lender, Mark Edward. *A Respectable Army: The Military Origins of the Republic, 1763–1789*. Wheeling, IL: Harlan Davidson, Inc., 1982.

Mattern, David B. *Benjamin Lincoln and the American Revolution*. Columbia: University of South Carolina Press, 1995.

McGuire, Thomas J. *The Philadelphia Campaign*. 2 vols. Mechanicsburg, PA: Stackpole Books, 2007.

Mellick, Andrew D. *The Story of an Old Farm*. Somerville, NJ: The Unionist-Gazette Inc., 1889.

Middlekauff, Robert. *The Glorious Cause*. New York: Oxford University Press, 2005.

Moore, Frank. *Songs and Ballads of the American Revolution*. New York: D. Appleton and Company, 1856.

Moore, George H. *The Treason of Charles Lee*. New York: Charles Scribner, 1860.

Nelson, Paul David. *The Life of William Alexander, Lord Stirling*. Tuscaloosa: The University of Alabama Press, 1987.

Nelson, Paul David. *General James Grant*. Gainesville: University of Florida Press, 1993.

Neumann, George C. *Battle Weapons of the American Revolution*. Texarkana, TX: Scurlock Publishing Company, 1998.

Neumann, George C. and Kravic, Frank J. *Collector's Illustrated Encyclopedia of the American Revolution*. Texarkana, TX: Scurlock Publishing Company, 1975.

Nickerson, Hoffman. *The Turning Point of the Revolution or Burgoyne in America*. Boston: Houghton Mifflin Company, 1928.

O'Donnell, Patrick K. *The Indispensables*. New York: Atlantic Monthly Press, 2011.

O'Shaughnessy, Andrew Jackson. *The Men Who Lost America*. New Haven, CT: Yale University Press, 2013.

Palmer, Dave R. *The Way of the Fox: American Strategy in the War for America*. Westport, CT: Greenwood Press, 1975.

Palmer, Dave R. *George Washington's Military Genius*. Washington, DC: Regnery Press, 2012.

Pancake, John S. *1777: The Year of the Hangman*. Tuscaloosa: University of Alabama Press, 1977.

Papas, Phillip. *Renegade Revolutionary: The Life of General Charles Lee*. New York: New York University Press, 2014.

Peckham, Howard H., ed. *The Toll of Independence: Engagements & Battle Casualties of the American Revolution*. Chicago: The University of Chicago Press, 1974.

Peterson, Harold L. *Arms and Armor in Colonial America 1526–1783*. New York: Bramhall House, 1956.

Pickering, Octavius. *The Life of Timothy Pickering*. 4 vols. Boston: Little, Brown and Company, 1867–1873.

Pula, James S. *Thaddeus Kościuszko: The Purest Son of Liberty*. New York: Hippocrene Brooks, 1999.

Puls, Mark. *Henry Knox: Visionary General of the American Revolution.* New York: Palgrave Macmillan, 2008.

Pybus, Cassandra. *Epic Journeys of Freedom.* Boston: Beacon Press, 2006.

Ramsay, David. *The History of the American Revolution.* 2 vols. Dublin: William Jones, 1795.

Richardson, Edward W. *Standards and Colors of the American Revolution.* Philadelphia: The University of Pennsylvania Press, 1982.

Robertson, G. Grant. *England Under the Hanoverians.* New York: G.P. Putnam's Sons, 1921.

Robson, Eric. *The American Revolution.* London: The Batchworth Press, 1955.

Rosengarten, J.G. *The German Allied Troops in the North American War of Independence.* Albany, NY: Joel Munsell's Sons, 1893.

Royster, Charles. *A Revolutionary People at War.* Chapel Hill, NC: The University of North Carolina Press, 1979.

Schnitzer, Eric and Troiani, Don. *Don Troiani's Campaign to Saratoga—1777.* Guilford, CT: Stackpole Books, 2019.

Sellers, Charles. *Charles Willson Peale, Early Life.* Philadelphia: The American Philosophical Society, 1947.

Seybolt, Robert Francis. *A Contemporary British Account of General Sir William Howe's Military Operations in 1777.* Worcester, MA: The American Antiquarian Society, 1931.

Shaara, Jeff. *The Glorious Cause.* New York: Ballantine Books, 2003.

Silverman, Kenneth. *A Cultural History of the American Revolution.* New York: Thomas Y. Crowell Company, 1976.

Smith, Captain George. *An [sic] Universal Military Dictionary.* London: Printed for J. Millan, 1779.

Smith, Samuel Steele. *The Battle of Trenton.* Monmouth Beach, NJ: Philip Freneau Press, 1965.

Smith, Samuel Steele. *The Battle of Princeton.* Monmouth Beach, NJ: Philip Freneau Press, 1967.

Snell, James P. *History of Hunterdon and Somerset Counties, New Jersey.* Philadelphia: Everts and Peck, 1881.

Spring, Matthew H. *With Zeal and With Bayonets Only.* Norman: University of Oklahoma Press, 2008.

Stedman, Charles. *The History of the Origin, Progress and Termination of the American War.* 2 vols. London: Printed for the author, 1794.

Stevenson, Roger. *Military Instructions for Officers Detached in the Field.* Philadelphia: R. Aitken, 1775.

Stryker, William S. *The Battles of Trenton and Princeton.* Boston: Houghton Mifflin Company, 1898.

Sullivan, Aaron. *The Disaffected: Britain's Occupation of Philadelphia during the American Revolution.* Philadelphia: University of Pennsylvania Press, 2019.

Trevelyan, George Otto. *The American Revolution.* 6 vols. New York: Longmans, Green & Company, 1899.

Ward, Christopher. *The War of the Revolution.* 2 vols. New York: The Macmillan Company, 1952.

Ward, Harry M. *General William Maxwell and the New Jersey Continentals*. Westport, CT: Praeger Publishing, 1997.

Warren, Mrs. Mercy Otis. *History of the Rise, Progress and Termination of the American Revolution*. 3 vols. Boston: Printed by Manning and Loring, for E. Larkin, 1805.

Webster, Noah. *An American Dictionary of the English Language*. 4th edition. New York: S. Converse, 1830.

Weddle, Kevin. *The Compleat* [sic] *Victory, Saratoga and the American Revolution*. New York: Oxford University Press, 2021.

Weintraub, Stanley. *Iron Tears: America's Battle for Freedom*. New York: Free Press, 2005.

Williams, Henry L. *Songs and Ballads of the American Revolution*. New York: Hurst and Company, 1905.

Wills, Garry. *A Necessary Evil*. New York: Simon and Schuster, 1999.

Willson, Beckles. *George III, As Man, Monarch and Statesman*. London: T.C. & E.C. Jack, 1907.

Willson, Beckles. *The Life and Letters of James Wolfe*. London: William Heinemann, 1909.

Wright, Robert K., Jr. *The Continental Army*. Washington, DC: Center for Military History, United States Army, 1980.

Young, Major William. *Manoeuvers, or Practical Observations on the Art of War*. London: J. Milan, 1771.

Zambone, Albert Louis. *Daniel Morgan*. Yardley, PA: Westholme Publishing, 2018.

PERIODICALS, MONOGRAPHS, AND WEBSITES

Bamford, Captain William. "The Revolutionary Diary of a British Officer." *Maryland Historical Magazine* 28, 1933.

Blackwood's Edinburgh Magazine 132, July–December 1882: 219.

Bronx River Alliance website. *Britannia Rules the Bronx*. https://bronxriver.org/.

Dworetzky, Murray, MD. "Smallpox, October 1945." *The New England Journal of Medicine* 346, no. 17, April 2002.

"Educating and Training Military Personnel . . . A Historical Study." *United States Marine Corps Journal* 9, no. 1, 2018. Quantico, VA: Marine Corps University Press.

Filsinger, Amy Lynn. "George Washington and the First Mass Military Inoculation." *Science Reference Services*, Library of Congress website: www.loc.gov/rr/scitech/GW &smallpoxinoculation.

Flexner, James Thomas. "North from the Battery, Seeking Washingtoniana." *New York Times*, February 13, 1987: section C1, page 1.

Founders Online, National Archives. https://founders.archives.gov/.

History of Parliament (1689–1922). www.historyofparlimentonline.org.

Hunter, Martin, British Army ensign. Curry, Lawrence H. ed. "Martin Hunter's Journal: America 1774–1778." *Valley Forge Journal* 4, no. 1, 1988.

Johnson, Victory Leroy. *The Administration of the American Commissariat During the Revolutionary War*. PhD Dissertation in History, University of Pennsylvania, 1941.

"Manuscript Journal of the Grenadier Battalion Minnigerode, June 1777." *The William Van Vieck Lidgerwood Collection*, Morristown National Historic Park Library.

Millstone New Jersey History. www.millstoneboro.org.

Paine, Thomas. *The American Crisis Number One*. Pamphlet. Philadelphia: Styner & Cist, 1776.

Peale, Charles Willson. "The Journal of Charles Willson Peale." *The Pennsylvania Magazine of History and Biography* 38, 1914: 283.

Ruppert, Bob. "The First Fight of Ferguson's Rifle." *Journal of the American Revolution* website, November 2014. https://allthingsliberty.com/author/bob-ruppert/: 8.

Short Hills Battlefield Study. American Battlefields Protection Program, National Park Service, 2011.

Storozynski, Alex. "The Fiasco of July 4, 1777: Misspelling of Kosciuszko's Name." *Huffington Post* blog, May 25, 2011.

Wickersty, Jason R. "A Shocking Havoc: The Plundering of Westfield, New Jersey, June 26, 1777." *Journal of the American Revolution* website, July 21, 2015. www.allthingsliberty.com/author/Jason-r-wickersty: 4.

Tiedemann, Joseph S. "Embittered Long Island Loyalist." *Long Island History Journal* 21, 2009. http://lihj.cc.stonybrook.edu/2009/articles/Thomas-jones-embittered-long-island-loyalist/.

Tokar, Major John A. "Logistics and the British Defeat in the Revolutionary War." U.S. Army Logistics University on-line. www.almc.army.mil/alog/issues/SepOct99/MS409.htm.

Van Liew House, Somerset County, New Jersey. www.themedowsfoundation.org.

Morristown. *National Park Service Historical Handbook: Morristown*. www.nps.gov/parkhistoryonline-books/hh/7/hh7b.htm

Index

abatis, term, 41
Abercromby, Robert, 114, 178
Adams, Hannah, 281n24
Adams, John, 20, 34, 172, 242;
  and Washington, 7, 14–15,
  279n9
Adams, Samuel, 110, 242
Agnew, James, 219
aides-de-camp, 123–24; baggage
  of, 209–10; duties of, 53; and
  strategy, 185
Albany, NY, 1, 267–68
Allen, Ethan, 13
Amboy. *See* Perth Amboy, NJ
American long rifle, 8, 41, 172
American War (Revolution): early
  phases of, 11–62; term, 7
Amherst, Jeffery, 189
amusette, 143
André, John, 220, 228–29, 245,
  253, 324n24
Andrews, Ray, 326n50

Anmours, C.-F.-D. de, 203
Anspach-Bayrouth, 218
Apollo, HMS, 194
Apthorp, Charles Wade, 315n86
Apthorp Mansion, 181, 315n86
Aquidneck Island, 89
arms: amusette, 143; fowling
  pieces, 33; rifles, 8, 41, 172,
  220, 235
Arnold, Benedict, 17, 145, 273;
  and Danbury, 159–63; and
  Saratoga campaign, 13–14,
  172–75, 268
Arnold's Tavern, 80–81
Arthur Kill, 87, 88*f*, 233, 236
artillery, 115–16; grasshopper
  guns, 248; horses and, 130
Augusta, HMS, 197

Baldwin, Jeduthan, 267
Balfour, Nesbitt, 196–97
Barbeu-Dubourg, Jacques, 301n22

About the Author

Arthur S. Lefkowitz is an independent historian whose previous books include *The Long Retreat: The Calamitous Defense of New Jersey, 1776; George Washington's Indispensable Men: Alexander Hamilton and the Other Aides-de-Camp Who Helped Win the Revolutionary War; Benedict Arnold's Army: The 1775 American Invasion of Canada during the Revolutionary War*, and *Colonel Hamilton and Colonel Burr: The Revolutionary War Lives of Alexander Hamilton and Aaron Burr* (Stackpole, 2020). Lefkowitz is a member of the Board of Governors of the American Revolution Round Table and has lectured at various National Park Service sites, the Fraunces Tavern Museum in Manhattan, and at the new Museum of the American Revolution. He lives in New Jersey.